THE INTERNATIONAL RESPONSIBILITY OF THE EUROPEAN UNION

How is the international responsibility of the European Union determined? In the context of the multilayered and ever-evolving Union legal order, the Lisbon Treaty has introduced considerable changes to the Union's participation in international affairs. These have rendered this thorny question an even more pressing concern not only for the European Union and its Member States, but also for third countries and international organisations.

Based on papers delivered at the biannual EU/International Law Forum organised by the University of Bristol in May 2011, this volume brings together EU and international law experts to address the various questions raised by the Union's international responsibility. It discusses horizontal issues, such as the concept of responsibility of international organisations in the evolving international legal order and the different techniques available for determining responsibility. It also focuses on specific policy areas (trade, investment, environment, security and defence, human rights) by approaching them from both an EU and an international law perspective.

The International Responsibility of the European Union

European and International Perspectives

Edited by

Malcolm Evans
and
Panos Koutrakos

·HART·
PUBLISHING

OXFORD AND PORTLAND, OREGON
2013

Published in the United Kingdom by Hart Publishing Ltd
16C Worcester Place, Oxford, OX1 2JW
Telephone: +44 (0)1865 517530
Fax: +44 (0)1865 510710
E-mail: mail@hartpub.co.uk
Website: http://www.hartpub.co.uk

Published in North America (US and Canada) by
Hart Publishing
c/o International Specialized Book Services
920 NE 58th Avenue, Suite 300
Portland, OR 97213-3786
USA
Tel: +1 503 287 3093 or toll-free: (1) 800 944 6190
Fax: +1 503 280 8832
E-mail: orders@isbs.com
Website: http://www.isbs.com

British Library Cataloguing in Publication Data
Data Available

ISBN: 978-1-84946-328-7

Typeset by Forewords Ltd, Oxford
Printed and bound in Great Britain by
MPG Printgroup Ltd

ACKNOWLEDGEMENT

Most of the chapters of this book are based on papers presented at a workshop which took place at the University of Bristol on 12–13 May 2011. The organisation of this workshop was possible due to the funding provided by the European Commission under the Jean Monnet Chair in European Law at the University of Bristol.

Contents

PART IV: RESPONSIBILITY OF THE EU IN SUBSTANTIVE POLICY AREA

List of Contributors

ALESSANDRA ASTERITI is part time Lecturer in Law at the University of Strathclyde.

ENZO CANNIZZARO is Professor of International Law at University of Rome 'La Sapienza'.

ANDRES DELGADO-KASTELEIRO is Lecturer in Law at Durham University.

LEONARD DEN HERTOG is EXACT Marie Curie PhD Fellow at the Universities of Cologne and Edinburgh.

EILEEN DENZA was a Professor of Law at University College London.

MALCOLM EVANS OBE is Professor of Public International Law at the University of Bristol.

JONI HELISKOSKI is a Legal Advisor at the Finnish Ministry of Foreign Affairs.

CHRIS HILSON is Professor of Environmental Law at the University of Reading.

PETER JAN KUIJPER is Professor of the Law of International Organisations at the University of Amsterdam.

JAN KLABBERS is Professor of International Organisations Law at the University of Helsinki, and Director of the Academy of Finland Centre of Excellence in Global Governance Research.

PANOS KOUTRAKOS is Professor of European Union Law at the City Law School, City University London.

JORIS LARIK is a Researcher at the European University Institute, Florence.

FREDERIK NAERT is a member of the Legal Service of the Council of the EU and an affiliated senior researcher at the KU Leuven.

PHOEBE OKOWA is Reader in International Law at Queen Mary, University of London.

ESA PAASIVIRTA is a Legal Advisor at the European Commission Legal Service and Visiting Professor, College of Europe, Bruges.

CATHERINE REDGWELL is Professor of International Law at UCL (University College London).

ALLAN ROSAS is Judge at the Court of the Justice of the European Union.

CHRISTIAN TAMS is Professor of International Law at the University of Glasgow.

CHRISTIAN TOMUSCHAT is Emeritus Professor at Humboldt University of Berlin.

RAMSES A WESSEL is Professor of the Law of the European Union and other International Organisations at the Centre for European Studies of the University of Twente, the Netherlands.

Introduction

THIS VOLUME IS the product of the Tenth EU/International Law Forum hosted by the University of Bristol Law School in May 2011. The Forum, and the ensuing series of books to which it has given rise over the years, reflect the need to ensure that scholarship in European Law and scholarship in International Law are not carried out in isolation. The Forum aims to bring these two strands closer together and ensure that they remain in contact by exploring areas and developments of common interest.

The increasingly prominent role of the Union on the international scene has rendered this work of the Forum ever more topical. It has also given it a sense of urgency, as it has been raising unique questions with which both the international legal practice and doctrine have been grappling. The Seventh Forum, held in 2005, had as its starting point the unique constitutional features of the European Union, and then placed them within the wider debate about the constitutionalisation of the international legal order.[1] It sought to ascertain the extent to which there is an osmosis between the idiosyncratic constitutional maturity of the Union, and the emerging debate about global constitutionalism which still underpins the development of the international economic order. The Ninth Forum, held in 2009, relied upon this analysis and reframed it in a policy-oriented context: it enquired about whether the debate about transnational constitutionalism is borne out by policy developments on the ground, and explored the interactions between the approach of the EU and that adopted at international level.[2]

This volume takes a step further and explores the central issue of international responsibility which underpins the interactions between the EU and third countries and international organisations. The law of international responsibility has been the subject of intense study by international lawyers.[3] However, a number of factors have rendered it of central significance for the Union. The first factor is the increasingly prominent role of the Union on the international scene. Since the adoption of the Maastricht Treaty in 1993, the Union started raising its international profile not only

[1] N Tsagourias (ed), *Transnational Constitutionalism: International and European Perspectives* (Cambridge, Cambridge University Press, 2007).

[2] M Evans and P Koutrakos (eds), *Beyond the Established Legal Orders—Policy Interconnections Between the EU and Rest of the World* (Oxford, Hart Publishing, 2011).

[3] For a recent illustration see J Crawford, A Pellet and S Olleson (eds), *The Law of International Responsibility* (Oxford, Oxford University Press, 2010).

in economic and trade matters but also in the area of foreign and security policy. This gradual process has led to the intense first decade of the twenty-first century when, positively middle aged, the Union was courageous enough to articulate its vision for a robust international posture with ambition and rigour, and to adjust its constitutional make up in a way which would purport to facilitate its objectives.

In this vein, the Laeken Declaration, the document adopted by the European Council in December 2001 which signaled the beginning of the process leading to the adoption of the Lisbon Treaty, refers to the Union as[4]

> a power wanting to change the course of world affairs in such a way as to benefit not just the rich countries but also the poorest. A power seeking to set globalisation within a moral framework, in other words to anchor it in solidarity and sustainable development.

This bold vision underpinned the process which led to the negotiation, conclusion and long and painful death of the Treaty Establishing a Constitution for Europe. It also underpins the Lisbon Treaty which entered into force on 1 December 2009.[5] This policy and legal framing of the increasingly confident and active Union has given rise to the emergence of another conception of responsibility which underpins the Union's international activities. The Laeken Declaration states that[6] 'in a globalised, yet also highly fragmented world, Europe needs to shoulder its responsibilities in the governance of globalisation', and the European Security Strategy, endorsed by the European Council in December 2003, points out that[7]

> The increasing convergence of European interests and the strengthening of mutual solidarity of the EU makes us a more credible and effective actor. Europe should be ready to share in the responsibility for global security and in building a better world.

This is a soft, almost moral, understanding of responsibility and it emerges as a central theme which shapes the Union's international role. Therefore, the reach of its international ambitions, and the deeply embedded sense of responsibility towards the world render the definition and implications of its legal responsibility a matter of priority for academic scholars, practitioners and policy-makers alike.

[4] Ibid.

[5] For an assessment of the external relations provisions of the Lisbon Treaty, see P Craig, *The Lisbon Treaty—Law, Politics, and Treaty Reform* (Oxford, Oxford University Press, 2010) ch 10; P Koutrakos, 'The European Union's Foreign and Security Policy after Lisbon' in D Ashiagbor, N Countouris and I Lianos, (eds), *The European Union after the Treaty of Lisbon* (Cambridge, Cambridge University Press, 2012) 185.

[6] Laeken Declaration, 14–15 December 2001, 2.

[7] *A Secure Europe in a Better World—European Security Strategy* (Brussels, 12 December, 2003) 1.

There is another factor which makes this exercise worthwhile, namely the work of the International Law Commission on the Draft Articles on the Responsibility of International Organisations. The long gestation of its proposals has coincided with a period of considerable development of the Union's idiosyncratic constitutional character which led to the current set of primary rules. Therefore, the question whether the proposed rules provide a legal space flexible enough to accommodate the unique features underpinning the constitutional maturity of the Union is worth-exploring. This is all the more so given the lingering ambiguity about the main tenets and legal implications of responsibility, particularly in relation to international organisations.

There is a third factor which highlights the need for this exercise, namely the methodological characteristics of the study of the law of international responsibility so far. This has been carried out mainly by international law scholars and, only relatively recently and to a limited extent, by EU law scholars.[8] However, these communities do not necessarily approach the issue in the same manner, their points of reference may be considerably varied and, in any case, they do not interact frequently enough. This volume aims to bring them together and enable them to converse about different aspects of the international responsibility of the Union.

The above legal, political and methodological factors determine the approach and structure of this collection of essays. On the one hand, it identifies areas of common interest and, on the other hand, it approaches them from both the international and EU law perspective. This becomes clear from the start, as Tomuschat and, then, Kuijper and Paasivirta provide a conceptual exploration of the notion of international responsibility from these two points of view respectively. By framing their analysis within the broader international law framework and, then, within the specific features of the Union order and the challenges these raise in terms of distinguishing the Union's responsibility from that of its Member States, the two chapters set out the canvas against which a number of horizontal themes will be examined.

A couple of common themes emerge from the various contributions to this volume. These include the concern whether the legal idiosyncrasies of the EU may be accommodated within the framework of the existing rules and proposals on international responsibility. Another theme, not unrelated to the above, has to do with the new dimensions that responsibility

[8] See, eg P Eeckhout, 'The EU and its Member States in the WTO—Issues of Responsibility' in L Bartels and F Ortino (eds), *Regional Trade Agreements and the WTO Legal System* (Oxford, Oxford University Press, 2006) 449; F Hoffmeister, 'Litigating against the European Union and Its Member States—Who Responds under the ILC's Draft Articles on International Responsibility of International Organizations?' (2010) 21 *European Journal of International Law* 723; PJ Kuijper and E Paasivirta, 'Further Exploring International Responsibility: The European Community and the ILC's Project on Responsibility of International Organisations' (2004) 1 *International Organisations Law Review* 111.

has acquired in the highly volatile and constantly evolving current international order. It is in this vein that Klabbers explores the ways in which accountability has become a central tenet of the functioning of international organisations, and Redgwell explains the difficulties of applying our traditional understanding of responsibility in one of the most important areas of environmental law, namely climate change.

These themes are examined separately in chapters adopting a horizontal and a vertical approach. The former deals with the manner in which international actors and legal mechanisms tackle responsibility and include international courts (Evans and Okowa), the Court of Justice of the European Union (Rosas) as well as three important tools for determining and engaging international responsibility, namely *erga omnes* and *ius cogens* (Tamms and Asteriti) and declarations of competence (Heliskoski).

A vertical approach to responsibility is adopted by chapters which focus on substantive policy areas. Whilst it makes no claim to comprehensiveness, this book focuses on policy areas both sufficiently diverse to reflect the scope of the Union's international role, and sufficiently topical to convey its involvement in areas where other international actors are quite active. To that effect, it explores the issues of international responsibility which the Union's activities raise in trade (Larik and Delgado Casteleiro), finance and investment (Denza), environment (Hilson, Redgwell), human rights (Cannizzaro), and security and defence (Naert, Wessel).

Consistently with the previous edited collections originating in the Bristol EU/International Law Forum, this book by no means seeks to provide a definitive account of its subject matter. Instead, it is work in progress into the enquiry about the fit between the incrementally evolving and consistently idiosyncratic EU legal order and the public international legal orthodoxy underpinning the law of international responsibility. It is a contribution to the ongoing conversation between the EU and international legal scholarship which constitutes the core objective of the Bristol Forum.

Malcolm Evans and Panos Koutrakos
Bristol, July 2012

Part I

Setting the Scene

I

Attribution of International Responsibility: Direction and Control

CHRISTIAN TOMUSCHAT

I. INTRODUCTION

HUMAN BEINGS CAN act either for themselves or on behalf of other persons. Our modern world is replete with corporate bodies, and any such organisation is made up of human beings who form its will, who shape its decisions and who eventually implement the decisions taken. Accordingly, it is one of the main tasks of every legal system to determine under what conditions human conduct can or must be attributed to the organisations which are necessarily dependent on agents who represent their corporate will.[1] Within the field of private law the relevant rules are mostly fairly similar to the rules governing the issue in public law, and not even international law is a remote outpost with totally different views on the matter. Indeed, the main questions to be answered come up in every context: who should reap the benefits of a sophisticated system of division of functions, and who should bear responsibility in case injury has been caused to third persons by an agent acting on behalf of others?

In most private law systems, rules have been evolved over centuries, partly dating back to the Roman epoch. Constitutional law, too, is faced with the necessity of determining the circumstances under which persons may act as public officials and to what extent responsibility is entailed by their actions. In international law, no high degree of sophistication has been attained to date. The ground rule of attribution, the basic pillar of state responsibility which permits identifying authorship, is almost trivial. As formulated in Article 4(1) of the International Law

[1] Aptly recalled by A Tzanakopoulos, *Disobeying the Security Council. Countermeasures against Wrongful Sanctions* (Oxford, Oxford University Press, 2011) 17.

Commission (ILC) Articles on Responsibility of States for internationally wrongful acts (ARS):[2]

> [t]he conduct of any state organ shall be considered an act of that State under international law, whether the organ exercises legislative, executive, judicial or any other functions, whatever position it holds in the organization of the State, and whatever its character as an organ of the central government or of a territorial unit of the State.

In other words, a state must assume full responsibility for all of its agents, in whatever branch of government they may have acted. This proposition reflects the classic position of a world where every piece of territory of the globe was placed under the unrestricted jurisdiction of a sovereign state. Accordingly, any governmental act emanating from a territorial source was automatically attributed to the public authorities responsible *ratione territorii*. The only major difficulty resides in determining who qualifies as a state organ. In the world of today, states progressively privatise functions which in earlier times appertained to the governmental core of sovereignty.[3] The clause of Article 4(2) ARS, according to which the internal law of the state concerned is determinative, does not resolve that riddle.[4] Moreover, no clear concepts have evolved in international jurisprudence as to the responsibility under international law of the state acting as a businessman in commercial matters.[5]

In a globalised world with its many functional inter-connections the simple model of Article 4(1) ARS does not suffice any longer to deal with the diversity of the factual instances that require solutions and answers. In fact, the ARS deal also with instances that depart from the paradigmatic model of a territorial state that, through its agents, exercises the full range of public power in its territory. Different situations are envisaged. Article 5 provides for instances where a state empowers persons or entities not forming part of the formal structure of the state machinery to exercise elements of governmental authority, Article 6 takes account of cooperation between states where one state places some of its organs at the disposal of another one, Article 8 deals with situations where actions are carried out on the instructions of, or under the direction or control of a state, and Article 9 covers the de facto exercise of governmental authority by persons or entities not authorised to do so. Lastly, Article 11 establishes a rule for cases of ex post acknowledgment of acts carried

[2] Taken note of by UN (United Nations) General Assembly, GA Resolution 56/83, 12 December 2001.

[3] On the limits of privatisation see S Chesterman, '"We Can't Spy … If We Can't Buy!": The Privatization of Intelligence and the Limits of Outsourcing Inherently Governmental Functions"' (2008) *European Journal of International Law* 19 1055, 1069–73.

[4] See ILC commentary on Art 4(2), YbILC 2001, vol II, part two, 42, para 11.

[5] See, eg C Tomuschat, 'In the Twilight Zones of the State' in I Buffard et al (eds), *International Law Between Universalism and Fragmentation. Festschrift in Honour of Gerhard Hafner* (Leiden and Boston, Martinus Nijhoff, 2008) 479, 489ff.

out by any third persons. However, these are exceptional situations, not frequently encountered in practice.

From a systemic viewpoint, it is not easy to see what the common denominator between these different situations is. All the rules framed by the ILC are offshoots of practice. Each one owes its emergence to a specific case or class of cases where it has shown its usefulness.[6] It may perhaps be a vain endeavour to look for such a red thread. In any event, the explicit words 'on the instructions of, or under the direction or control', appear only in Article 8 although they may perhaps indicate the general direction of the path to be followed. The drafters of the ARS have seen no need to condense in a dogmatic formula the concept which underlies the different particularisations of the rule of attribution enshrined in their project.

The 'normalcy' of International Organisations (IOs) is different. States have emerged as entities endowed with the totality of the public powers conceivable in a human community. By contrast, IOs are invariably given a limited mandate. They are agencies for the discharge of specific tasks which their founders are unable to perform in individual isolation. It is common knowledge that, notwithstanding some beginnings during the nineteenth century, only the twentieth century saw a general upsurge of IOs, due to the many complex challenges with which the international community became progressively confronted. Generally, states take care to maintain a clear distance between statehood—with full sovereign powers—and IOs, which are only endowed with clearly defined competences in a restricted field of international cooperation. IOs have never been endowed with full powers or complete governmental machinery in all fields of action—since such breadth of powers inevitably raises the question of whether the founding states can still be regarded as sovereign.[7] Thus, the UN (United Nations) does not enjoy legislative powers,[8] and even the EU (European Union), the best developed of all currently existing IOs, lacks generally executive competences so that its legislative acts need to be enforced by the Member States.[9] Accordingly, IOs must rely

[6] The most famous case in point is Art 11 ARS which goes back to the judgment of the International Court of Justice (ICJ) in *United States Diplomatic and Consular Staff in Tehran*, ICJ Reports 1980, 3, 35, para 74.

[7] Indeed, one of the great fears of the German Federal Constitutional Court is that through the successive measures of conferral of powers on the EU, Germany may lose genuine statehood, see especially: judgment of 30 June 2009 on the Lisbon Treaty, *Entscheidungen des Bundesverfassungsgerichts* (*BVerfGE*) 123, 267, 332; English translation: www.bverfg.de/entscheidungen/es20090630_2bve000208en.html (margin n 180).

[8] However, through some of its recent resolutions, the Security Council has affirmed its power not only to deal with specific crisis situations, but also to enact regulations for structural threats to international peace and security: Resolutions 1373 (2001), 28 September 2001 (Fight against terrorism) and 1540 (2004), 28 April 2004 (Weapons of mass destruction).

[9] The most important exception to this ground rule is provided by Art 105 TFEU (Treaty on the Functioning of the European Union) in competition matters.

largely on their members for the attainment of their purposes. Whereas states are virtually omni-capable entities, legally equipped to face up to any challenge that may arise in the course of history, IOs lead only a partial existence within the field of societal life which has been assigned to them. In other words, states are able to rely on their own forces to deal with any eventuality, whereas IOs are structurally dependent on assistance from outside by their members. Accordingly, the problem of attribution plays for them an infinitely more important role than for states. Whose responsibility will be entailed if some unforeseen events occur in the pursuit of common goals? For the UN, this is a question which arises on a daily basis with regard to the UN Security Council's function to ensure international peace and security. Since Article 43 of the UN Charter, which provides for the establishment of a permanent UN force, has remained a dead letter,[10] the UN was compelled to look for other ways and means in order to perform its core task. In each case, it is compelled anew to request the help of the Member States—which may be granted, but which may also be denied or provided solely under conditions which the troop-contributing countries will determine to a large degree on their own.

The following considerations shall attempt to clarify the appropriate criteria for the assessment of issues of attribution. As a first step, on a more abstract level, the available avenues will be scrutinised (II). After having discussed a federal state analogy, which, if feasible, would greatly facilitate the task to be addressed, the focus will be on the solutions suggested by the International Law Commission (ILC) both in the ARS as well as in its Draft articles on the responsibility of international organizations (DARIO),[11] as well as on the case law of international courts. In III, in order to gain a better overview, the different factual patterns of cooperation of international organisations with their member states in the discharge of specific tasks will be analyzed. Lastly, on the basis of that operation of stock-taking, we will define the relevant criteria of attribution, trying, in particular, to find out whether the same characteristics should apply to the issue both with regard to states and IOs (IV). Some concluding observations will provide a short summary of our reflections (V).

II. THE LEGAL RULES ON ATTRIBUTION

In the following, the main emphasis will be placed on the issue of attribution in respect of conduct of IOs and their member states. This

[10] See J Frowein and N Krisch, Comments on Art 43, in B Simma et al (eds), *The Charter of the United Nations. A Commentary*, 2nd edn, vol I (Oxford, Oxford University Press, 2002) (margin n 11) 763.

[11] Report of the ILC on the work of its 63rd session [2011], UN doc A/66/10, 52.

is the field where in recent years the most serious problems requiring concrete answers have arisen. Obviously, at the same time the relevant parallel problems concerning state responsibility will also have to be studied.

A. The Federal State Analogy

Under general international law, as embodied in the ARS, the federal state constitutes a unity. Reference was already made to Article 4 ARS where no distinction is drawn between conduct of the central organs of a federal state and conduct of its component units. Any act or omission is attributed to the state as subject of international law. According to the ARS, the secondary state level has no legal relevance whatsoever.[12] For potentially injured third parties, this is an ideal situation. They do not have to make inquiries about the internal distribution of competences within the federal architecture. The federation may from time to time feel that to burden it with responsibility for acts of its component states is unjust insofar as its constitutional framework denies it any competence to ensure conduct in conformity with the relevant international obligations. However, from the viewpoint of international law the paramount consideration is that the confidence of third states deserves primacy. In order to do justice to their international commitments, states have ample opportunities to organise their constitutional systems accordingly.[13] If they refrain from so doing, the ensuing legal disadvantages should be borne by themselves and not by extraneous third parties.

It may be tempting to draw an analogy between state responsibility and the responsibility of IOs. To the extent that a federal state can be held accountable for acts or omissions of its component states, it might be possible likewise to hold an IO accountable for the acts of its member states whenever they are involved in implementing the policies of the IO's central institutions. However, such analogy would have no firm ground. The basic fact is that an IO and its members are not recognised as an organisational unit vested with unitary international personality. Normally, the instruments in the hands of an IO are much less efficient than the mechanisms that operate within a state. It is clear that no IO may exercise full control over its members. Attribution would therefore mean that an IO could be burdened with responsibility for acts or omissions the substance of which it may disapprove and of which it may not even

[12] On the status of subordinate entities see C Tomuschat, 'Component Territorial Units of States under International Law' in Società Italiana di Diritto Internazionale (ed), *Regioni e Autonomie Territoriali nel Diritto Internazionale ed Europeo* (Napoli 2006) 31–58.

[13] For the relevant lacunae in the US Constitution see *Medellin v Texas*, 552 US 491 (2008).

have cognizance. In fact, in the legal literature normally the inverse situation of an IO emancipating itself from the will of its founding members is being debated.[14] It would run against the essential characteristics of an IO to assume that its power grip overcomes the original philosophy of the members as principals and the IO as their agent.[15] However, considerable divergences of opinion may be noticed in the legal literature. Thus, regarding NATO's air operations against the former Yugoslavia in the Kosovo conflict, Torsten Stein assigned responsibility to the Member States of the Alliance[16] while Alain Pellet, arguing that NATO is an autonomous subject of international law, argued that it was the Alliance itself and not its Member States that had to assume responsibility.[17]

B. Sources of Positive Law

(i) Rules of attribution pertain to the field of general international law which to date has seen no codification by way of treaty. International responsibility is one of the rare fields where informal sources are still dominating. Inevitably, too, the question arises whether such issues that are intimately interwoven with factual considerations are really susceptible to regulation through general and abstract rules much beyond statements of general propositions that are of no great help in a controversial case. It is for that reason that the deployment of military forces is normally regulated by way of treaties if and to the extent that the deployment occurs on the basis of mutual agreement. Such treaties on the status of forces will specify in detail where the border-line between domestic jurisdiction and the extraterritorial jurisdiction of the visiting or occupying forces runs; notably they will take care of all issues relating to delictual responsibility. NATO has concluded two agreements for that purpose.[18]

[14] See, eg DG Hawkins et al, 'Delegation under Anarchy: States, International Organisations and Principal-Agent Theory' in id (eds), *Delegation and Agency in International Organisations* (Cambridge, Cambridge University Press, 2006) 3–38.

[15] The EU, however, may be considered by third states as a unitary subject where in a specific field competences have been transferred to it; see WTO, Panel Report in *European Communities—Protection of Trademarks and Geographical Indications for Agricultural Products and Foodstuffs*, Case WT/DS174/R, 15 March 2005, para 7.98.

[16] 'Kosovo and the International Community. The Attribution of Possible Internationally Wrongful Acts: Responsibility of NATO or of its Member States?' in C Tomuschat (ed), *Kosovo and the International Community. A Legal Assessment* (The Hague, Kluwer Law International, 2002) 181, 191.

[17] 'L'imputabilité d'éventuels actes illicites. Responsabilité de l'OTAN ou des Etats membres', ibid, 193, 201.

[18] Status of Forces Agreement, 19 June 1951, www.nato.int/cps/en/natolive/official_texts_17265.htm?selectedLocale=en; Supplementary Agreement, 3 August 1959, www.mod.uk/NR/rdonlyres/A921BCF9-97C5-4716–8262–44F96196061E/0/nato_sofa_supplementary_agreement.pdf.; see also the Agreement Among the States Parties to the North Atlantic Treaty and the Other States Participating in the Partnership for Peace Regarding the Status of their Forces, http://www.nato.int/cps/en/natolive/official_texts_24742.htm?selectedLocale=en.

Within the framework of the UN, a model agreement was elaborated for the deployment of peacekeeping forces,[19] and this agreement is regularly resorted to when there is a need to define the rights and duties of military units put at the disposal of the UN by any one of its members. Likewise, the EU has established a Status of Forces Agreement[20] that governs the legal position of armed forces being deployed in another member country; in addition, the EU has begun concluding such agreements with third states to which EU troop contingents have been sent.[21]

It stands to reason that no such conventional regime can be found where the use of military force was decided unilaterally as in the case of NATO's intervention in the former Yugoslavia with a view to protecting the Kosovar Albanians against genocidal attacks. It has never been clarified to what extent the blame for any violations of international humanitarian law was to be put on NATO or on the states actively participating in the air operations.[22] Accordingly, when attempting to use the ICJ for its defence, the former Yugoslavia—under changing names—brought legal action against all NATO members involved in the hostilities.[23] No application could be brought against NATO as an IO.

(ii) As far as soft law sources are concerned, the ARS, which the ILC adopted in 2001 after decades of intensive work, enjoy a high degree of authoritativeness, reflected in the frequent recourse of the ICJ to their provisions.[24] There seems to be broad agreement that the ILC has succeeded in capturing the gist of the general rules of international law in the field of state responsibility, notwithstanding the lack of a comprehensive formula explaining the different rules as arising from a common ground. While the ARS have received the blessing of the GA though not directly, but indirectly,[25] the corresponding rules regulating the responsibility of IOs are still at an embryonic stage. When the ILC started its work on

[19] Model status-of-forces agreement for peace-keeping operations, Report of the Secretary-General, 9 October 1990, UN Doc A/45/594.

[20] Of 17 November 2003, [2003] OJ C321/6. See comments by A Sari, 'The European Union Status of Forces Agreement (EU SOFA)', *Journal of Conflict & Security Law* 13 (2008) 353–91.

[21] See, eg the Agreement between the EU and the Central African Republic on the status of the European Union-led forces in the Central African Republic, [2008] OJ L136/46.

[22] See nn 16, 17. *Cf* also UN Special Rapporteur G Gaja, Second Report on Responsibility of International Organizations, UN doc A/CN.4/541, 2 April 2004, para 7.

[23] The relevant judgments were delivered on 15 December 2004, see, eg *Legality of Use of Force (Serbia and Montenegro v Belgium), Preliminary Objections*, ICJ Reports 2004, 279.

[24] In *Application of the Convention on the Prevention and Punishment of the Crime of Genocide (Bosnia and Herzegovina v Serbia and Montenegro)*, ICJ Reports 2007, 43, 207, 217, Arts 8 and 16 ARS took centre stage. More recently, reference to the ARS was made in the judgment on *Pulpmills on the River Uruguay (Argentina v Uruguay)*, 20 April 2010, para 273. See also *Legal Consequences of the Construction of a Wall in the Occupied Palestinian Territory, Advisory Opinion*, ICJ Reports 2004, 136, 195, para 140.

[25] As already noted (above n 2), the GA confined itself to 'taking note' of the ARS. This means that the ARS were acknowledged as an excellent piece of legal craftsmanship whose authority derived essentially from its inherent qualities.

international responsibility in 1962 according to a new concept focused exclusively on secondary rules, the decision was taken at the same time to confine the rules to be drafted strictly to responsibility of the state.[26] It was felt that to include IOs in the scope *ratione materiae* might confront the Commission with many problems of an unforeseen nature that would require responses different from those appropriate for states. Accordingly, a 'without-prejudice clause' was included in Article 57 ARS. After the final adoption of the ARS in 2001, it was a matter of logical consistency to begin work on the responsibility of IOs, obviously in light of the rules that had been found to accommodate best the needs and interests of states. In 2011, under the rapporteurship of Giorgio Gaja, the ILC adopted on first reading a set of 67 articles (DARIO)[27] which will first have to be examined by the GA before they can go through a further review process by the ILC.[28] In other words, no definitive codification proposals are present for the time being. However, since the general choice of the ILC was to remain as close to the text of the ARS, one may expect that no great changes are to be expected during the continuation of the work.

The Draft Articles on the Responsibility of International Organizations (DARIO) contain one provision (Article 7) which deals specifically with instances where an IO relies on outside assistance in order to discharge its mandate. This provision is framed as follows:

> **Conduct of organs of a State or organs or agents of an international organization placed at the disposal of another international organization**
>
> The conduct of an organ of a State or an organ or agent of an international organization that is placed at the disposal of another international organization shall be considered under international law an act of the latter organization if the organization exercises effective control over that conduct.

The criterion of 'effective control' would seem to be simple and straightforward at first glance. But it involves many ambiguities since it can be extremely doubtful when, under what factual circumstances, an IO is able to exercise 'effective control' over military forces put at its disposal by another IO or, which is the most frequent case, by a state. Control over a troop contingent is never full and complete. There will always be some degree of autonomous action, even though an attempt may have been made to establish a tight system of supervision.

[26] See Special Rapporteur Ago, 1036th meeting, 5 August 1969, YbILC 1969, vol I, 241, para 25; Report of the ILC on the work of its 21st session, A/7610 Rev 1, ibid, vol II, 233, paras 79–84.

[27] Report of the ILC on the work of its 63rd session [2011], UN doc A/66/10, 52.

[28] By resolution 66/100, 9 December 2011, the GA took note of the draft articles and decided to consider at a later stage the elaboration of a convention on the basis of those articles. In any event, a future review process by the ILC will have to take place under the guidance of a new Special Rapporteur since Giorgio Gaja was elected judge of the ILC on 10 November 2011.

It is remarkable that Article 7 DARIO differs from the text of Article 6 ARS, the corresponding provision in respect of state responsibility. Article 6 ARS reads:

> The conduct of an organ placed at the disposal of a State by another State shall be considered an act of the former State under international law if the organ is acting in the exercise of elements of the governmental authority of the State at whose disposal it is placed.

In the official commentary on Article 7 DARIO, this change is explained by the observation that the characterization 'governmental authority' is unsuitable to international organizations.[29] Whatever one may think of this semantic problem, the fact remains that the shift from the exercise of governmental authority to the degree of control exercised by the IO changes the general perspective. While the exercise of governmental authority is essentially related to the prevailing legal position, effective control introduces an element that is primarily grounded in the factual situation. This difference in shade is relevant in spite of the specification in the commentary on Article 6 ARS that the relevant organ of the foreign state must act under the 'exclusive direction and control' of the receiving state, 'rather than on instructions from the sending State'.[30] While for Article 6 ARS the determinative criterion is primarily conformity with the legal order of the receiving state, Article 7 DARIO relies exclusively on the command power of the relevant IO. In fact, it may be a crucial issue how far an IO, such as the UN, must go in imposing its will on military forces that cooperate in the discharge of its mandate under the UN Charter.

It is also worth noting that the DARIO do not contain a provision reflecting the essence of Article 8 ARS ('Conduct directed or controlled by a State').[31] The official commentary on this omission states that persons acting under such circumstances would have to be regarded as agents of the relevant organisation,[32] meeting the wide definition in Draft Article 4.[33] It may well be indeed that there is little practice regarding cases where an IO has made recourse to outside forces not pertaining to its organigram in order to reach objectives that it could not obtain by regular methods. In any event, however, in the area of state responsibility the most significant instances of attribution of conduct have occurred against

[29] ILC [2011] Report, above n 11, 86, para 4.

[30] YbILC 2001, vol II, Part Two, 44, para 2.

[31] Second Report Gaja, above n 22, para 66. Art 8 ARS reads: 'The conduct of a person or group of persons shall be considered an act of a State under international law if the person or group of persons is in fact acting on the instructions of, or under the direction or control of, that State in carrying out the conduct'.

[32] ILC [2011] Report, above n 11, 86, para 11.

[33] 'There is an internationally wrongful act of an international organization when conduct consisting of an act or omission (a) is attributable to the organization under international law; and (b) constitutes a breach of an international obligation of that organization'.

the backdrop of Article 8 ARS. Consequently, Article 8 ARS belongs to those provisions the interpretation and application of which shed a bright light on the issue of attribution—and which may have to be relied upon also in connection with IOs notwithstanding their neglect by the Special Rapporteur of the ILC.

(iii) The relevant case law comprises a number of decisions that evince sharp contradictions. The most famous judgment was rendered by the ICJ in 1986 when it had to adjudicate the application brought by Nicaragua against the United States on account of the support provided by the United States to the Nicaraguan Contra rebels who had their logistical bases in Honduras. The question was to what extent the United States could be made accountable for the violent acts committed by the Contras in the territory of neighbouring Nicaragua. Although the ICJ acknowledged that the Contras depended largely on the United States, it refused to attribute their acts and activities directly to the United States. It held:

> For this conduct to give rise to legal responsibility of the United States, it would in principle have to be proved that that State had effective control of the military or paramilitary operations in the course of which the alleged violations were committed.[34]

This dictum was severely criticised by the International Criminal Tribunal for the Former Yugoslavia (ICTY) in its *Tadic* judgment of 15 July 1999.[35] The ICTY observed that the test favoured by the ICJ was 'at variance with international judicial and State practice', which it sought to prove by referring to a number of cases where likewise determinations had to be made on issues of attribution. In fact, it can hardly be denied that some domestic and international tribunals have applied a seemingly more flexible standard when the question arose whether actions by private groups could be attributed to a state in the background that provided factual and financial support. According to the ICTY, overall control represents the test which is commonly accepted and practiced in that connection.

In the genocide case of *Bosnia and Herzegovina v Serbia and Montenegro*, where an assessment of the assistance given to the Bosnian Serbs by the Serbian army had to be made, the ICJ responded to the objections raised by the ICTY by refuting the main points dwelt upon by their colleagues from the criminal law branch.[36] The ICJ observed that the issues ruled upon by the ICJ and by the ICTY were not the same: whereas the ICJ

[34] ICJ, *Case Concerning Military and Paramilitary Activities in and against Nicaragua (Nicaragua v United States of America)*, ICJ Reports 1986, 14, 65, para 115.

[35] ICTY, *Prosecutor v Tadic* (1999) 38 *International Legal Materials* 1518, 1540ff. The findings in *Tadic* were later confirmed in the *Čelebići* case (2001) 40 *International Legal Materials* 630, 634–36 margin numbers 12–26.

[36] ICJ, *Application of the Convention on the Prevention and Punishment of the Crime of Genocide (Bosnia and Herzegovina v Serbia and Montenegro)*, ICJ Reports 2007, 43, 206–11, paras 396–407.

had to examine the legal position under the auspices of state responsibility, the ICTY had to decide whether the armed conflict in the territory of the former Yugoslavia was of an international character. Second, the ICJ emphasised that the test employed by the ICTY would unduly broaden the scope of state responsibility well beyond the traditional principle, namely that a state is only responsible for its own conduct. In an article written shortly afterwards, Antonio Cassese attempted to show that the ICJ failed to appraise the legal position correctly.[37] Notwithstanding his vigorous plea for the standard preferred by the ICTY, it would appear that the arguments may rather tilt in favour of the ICJ. But more will be said about the issue in the following.

As far as the case law regarding IOs is concerned, the most important judicial pronouncement of the recent past is the decision by which the European Court of Human Rights (ECtHR), in *Behrami and Saramati v France, Norway and Germany*, rejected the claims brought by the applicants as inadmissible.[38] The facts of those cases are simple and complicated at the same time. On the basis of Security Council Resolution 1244 (1999) of 10 June 1999, two missions were sent to the Yugoslav province of Kosovo: on the one hand the United Nations Interim Administration Mission in Kosovo (UNMIK), an 'international civil presence', responsible, inter alia, for 'performing basic civilian administrative functions where and as long as required', and on the other hand NATO's Kosovo Force (KFOR), entrusted with keeping order and peaceful conditions in Kosovo (under the aegis of NATO). Several injurious occurrences entailed charges against both UNMIK and KFOR as well as the states operating through these or inside these institutions, that basic human rights obligations had been infringed. In *Behrami*, two little children suffered injuries, in one case lethal injuries, when they played with bomblets which had not been cleared from the ground. In *Saramati*, a Kosovar citizen had been arrested and detained by KFOR officers, no heed being given to the guarantees of the European Convention on Human Rights (ECHR). It was an almost logical consequence for the victims to seise the ECtHR in order to sanction the states whose officers had allegedly acted negligently in defiance of the applicable rules of the ECHR.

Both applications failed. The ECtHR took the view that the controversial conduct—an omission in *Behrami*, a positive act in *Saramati*—was neither attributable to the military contingents of the nations involved in the two operations, nor to NATO, which had the operational command, but to the UN Security Council. It proceeded to a somewhat ambiguous combination of the two competing criteria of 'effective control', on the

[37] A Cassese, 'The *Nicaragua* and *Tadic* Tests Revisited in Light of the ICJ Judgement on Genocide in Bosnia' (2007) 18 *European Journal of International Law* 649, 667.

[38] ECtHR, *Behrami and Behrami v France and Saramati v France, Germany and Norway*, Applications 41412/01 and 78166/01, Decision, 2 May 2007.

one hand, and 'overall control', on the other, by stating that the Security Council retained 'ultimate authority and control', which it saw as determinative in attributing the conduct complained of to the UN. No weighty objections can be raised against the finding that the foreign elements acting on behalf of UNMIK were not accountable as authorities of their home countries. UNMIK was a peacekeeping operation established by the Security Council under its full command, the troop-contributing countries retaining control over their contingents only with regard to disciplinary and criminal matters. Therefore, the operational activities of UNMIK were in the sense of Article 4 DARIO true UN activities. With regard to KFOR, one of whose officers had issued the controversial arrest warrant, the legal position was infinitely more complex. Security Council Resolution 1244 (1999) did not establish KFOR as a department of the world organisation but acknowledged that KFOR was to remain outside the institutional framework of the UN. The relevant provision (para 7) said that the Security Council '[a]uthorizes Member States and relevant international organizations to establish the international security presence in Kosovo'. On the other hand, paragraph 4 of Annex 2 made clear that KFOR would be strongly connected with NATO: 'The international security presence with substantial North Atlantic Treaty Organization participation must be deployed under unified command and control . . .'.

In other words, the military operation in Kosovo under the protective shield of KFOR was one of those operations to which the Security Council has had recourse many times during the last two decades when the objective of restoring peace and security in some part of the world could not be realized by peacekeeping troops under the command of the UN. The first major instance of such an authorisation given to a coalition of states occurred in 1990 when, through Resolution 678 (1990) of 29 November 1990, the Security Council allowed Member States co-operating with the Government of Kuwait 'to use all necessary means' for the liberation of Kuwait and for the restoration of international peace and security in the area. It stands to reason that the Security Council lacks direct means of supervision and control in case it confines itself to conferring a mandate on states or entities which perform those tasks under their own responsibility, in a cooperative relationship with the Security Council.

The decision of the ECtHR in *Behrami and Saramati* is drafted in very careful terms. Nonetheless, the reader is not really apprised of the grounds that motivated the Strasbourg judges to retain 'ultimate authority and control' as the relevant criterion of attribution. Operational command, 'delegated' to KFOR, was rejected as determinative. And no mention is made of 'effective control', the standard chosen, as mentioned, by the ICJ in its jurisprudence. One may well agree with the result reached by the ECtHR; yet, a fully persuasive rational line of reasoning cannot be discerned in the decision. It is no wonder, therefore, that *Behrami and Saramati* has been criticised by the majority of the commentators.[39]

III. THE DIFFERENT FACTUAL PATTERNS

A. Participation by National Authorities in Norm-Setting Activities at International Level

Since in a broader political sense IOs can be classified as common agencies of their members, all IOs have organs in which persons from those members are represented. In the last analysis, the norm-setting activities of all IOs, including the EU, can be traced back to their members. This is particularly conspicuous in the case of the permanent members of the Security Council. Without the consent—or at least the abstention[40]—of any of the permanent members no substantive resolution of the Security Council may be adopted. Hence, it would certainly not be too far-fetched to argue that at least the permanent members of the Security Council can be made accountable if a resolution under Chapter VII violates fundamental human rights.

A similar question came up before the German Federal Constitutional Court a few years ago with regard to the approval of a Directive of the European Community on coordination of the television activities of the Member States of the Community.[41] The *Land* of Bavaria argued that the Federal Government should have taken into account the interests of the German *Länder* in giving its approval to the Community instrument, since, according to the internal distribution of powers, the *Länder* hold authority over the broadcasting and television sector. For the Constitutional Court, there was no doubt that acting in Brussels was also subject

[39] A Breitegger, 'Sacrificing the Effectiveness of the European Convention on Human Rights on the Altar of the Effective Functioning of Peace Support Operations: A Critique of *Behrami* & *Saramati* and *Al Jedda*' (2009) 11 *International Community Law Review* 155, 167; M Milanović and T Papić, 'As Bad As It Gets: The European Court's *Behrami* and *Saramati* Decision and General International Law' (2009) 58 *International & Comparative Law Quarterly* 267–96; A Peters, 'Die Anwendbarkeit der EMRK in Zeiten komplexer Hoheitsgewalt und das Prinzip der Grundrechtstoleranz'(2010) 48 *Archiv des Völkerrechts* 1, 34, 41; JP Schütze, *Die Zurechenbarkeit von Völkerrechtsverstößen im Rahmen mandatierter Friedensmissionen der Vereinten Nationen* (Berlin, Duncker & Humblot, 2011) 164; LA Sicilianos, 'L'(ir)responsabilité des forces multinationales' in *International Law and the Quest for its Implementation*. Liber Amicorum *Vera Gowlland-Debbas* (Leiden and Boston, Brill, 2010) 95, 104 s.

[40] Abstention by a permanent member does not hinder the adoption of a resolution, see ICJ, *Legal Consequences for States of the Continued Presence of South Africa in Namibia (South West Africa) notwithstanding Security Council Resolution 276 (1970), Advisory Opinion*, ICJ Reports 1971, 16, 22, para 22.

[41] Council Directive 89/552/EEC, 3 October 1989 on the coordination of certain provisions laid down by Law, Regulation or Administrative Action in Member States concerning the pursuit of television broadcasting activities [1989] OJ L298/23.

to the provisions of the Basic Law and could thus be challenged if a *Land* opined that the Federation had infringed the dividing line separating federal from *Länder* powers or had failed to behave according to the standards of 'federal loyalty' ('*Bundestreue*').[42]

It is not easy to say whether the same logic should apply to the Security Council of the UN. The Security Council is an organ of the international community, or, in other words, of humankind at large. If one assumed that every delegate in the GA and in the Security Council was subject to its national constitution and additionally to any international treaty binding on his or her country, the decision-making process at the UN would find itself greatly hampered. One may argue that to accept such an extensive arsenal of checks contradicts not only Article 27 VCLT, according to which no state may invoke the provisions of its domestic law as justification for its failure to perform a treaty, but also Article 103 of the Charter, the provision claiming precedence of the Charter over any other treaty commitments. In fact, in *Behrami and Saramati* the ECtHR held:

> Since operations established by UNSC Resolutions under Chapter VII of the UN Charter are fundamental to the mission of the UN to secure international peace and security and since they rely for their effectiveness on support from member states, the Convention cannot be interpreted in a manner which would subject the acts and omissions of contracting parties which are covered by UNSC Resolutions and occur prior to or in the course of such missions, to the scrutiny of the Court. To do so would be to interfere with the fulfilment of the UN's key mission in this field including, as argued by certain parties, with the effective conduct of its operations. It would also be tantamount to imposing conditions on the implementation of a UNSC Resolution which were not provided for in the text of the Resolution itself. This reasoning equally applies to voluntary acts of the respondent States such as the vote of a permanent member of the UNSC in favour of the relevant Chapter VII Resolution and the contribution of troops to the security mission: such acts may not have amounted to obligations flowing from membership of the UN but they remained crucial to the effective fulfilment by the UNSC of its Chapter VII mandate and, consequently, by the UN of its imperative peace and security aim.[43]

In other words, the ECtHR shows great respect for the Security Council.[44] Without explicitly mentioning Article 103 of the Charter, the quoted passage is visibly influenced by that provision.[45] It is not easy to reject

[42] Judgment, 22 March 1995, *BVerfGE* 92, 203, 228.

[43] See n 38 above, para 149.

[44] T Tridimas and JA Gutierrez-Fons, 'EU Law, International Law, and Economic Sanctions against Terrorism: The Judiciary in Distress?' (2008–2009) 32 *Fordham International Law Journal* 660, 686, call it a 'deferential judgment'.

[45] In a series of subsequent decisions, the ECtHR has maintained its line of reasoning: *Kasumaj v Greece*, Application 6974/05, Decision, 5 July 2007; *Gajic v Germany*, Application 31446/02, Decision, 28 August 2007; *Berić and others v Bosnia and Herzegovina*, Application 36357/04, Decision, 16 October 2007, paras 27, 28.

the reasoning of the Strasbourg judges.[46] The UN Charter stands above the great mass of other multilateral treaties. Without characterizing it as a 'world constitution',[47] one must acknowledge that the Charter contains the great structural principles of today's world order, particularised by General Assembly Resolution 2625 (XXV).[48] In that regard, no other treaty can rival with it. In particular, the Security Council has been entrusted with the supreme authority of ensuring international peace and security, regardless of national connections and interests. Consequently, one would go against the philosophy of the Charter by contending that acts of the Security Council may at the same time be attributed to its members. In other words: piercing the veil is not admitted as a legitimate method. Resolutions of the Security Council have the quality of acts of the UN—and nothing else.

B. Implementation of International Acts by National Authorities

Increasingly, national authorities are placed at the service of international institutions. The frontrunners of this development were the different organisations of European integration, which have by now crystallised in the EU. From the very outset, normative acts with direct effect for the individuals concerned belonged to the toolbox of the integration process. Under the Treaty on the Functioning of the European Union (TFEU), the Union may enact regulations which shall be directly applicable in all Member States (Article 288). Such regulations will normally be enforced by domestic authorities. Already within the institutional structure of the European Coal and Steel Community, the first institutional configuration of the great European project, it was made clear that decisions by national authorities applying Community law were indeed national acts, attributable to the state concerned without any reservation. However, care was taken to ensure that national judges could not, at their discretion, rule on the lawfulness of the underlying Community acts. For that purpose, the procedure of preliminary rulings was introduced, according to which domestic judges were debarred from unilaterally rejecting such acts as allegedly being invalid; instead, the judges were placed under an obligation to refer such issues to the Court of Justice of the European Communities (today: Court of Justice of the European Union under Article 267 TFEU) as the sole judicial body empowered to handle matters of a 'constitutional'

[46] For a different view see I Cameron, 'Protecting Legal Rights. On the (In)security of Targeted Sanctions' in P Wallensteen and C Staibano (eds), *International Sanctions. Between Words and Wars in the Global System* (London, Routledge, 2005) 181, 187.

[47] The most prominent protagonist of this approach is Bardo Fassbender, *UN Security Council Reform and the Right of Veto* (The Hague, Kluwer Law International, 1998) 89ff.

[48] Adopted without vote on 24 October 1970.

nature.[49] The implicit rationale of the mechanism of preliminary rulings is that the international nature of the legal foundation of a domestic act of implementation does not change the parameters of attribution. States must assume full responsibility for the measures of execution through which they carry out their obligations within a hierarchically superior international system. However, they are exonerated from the burden of reviewing on their own the lawfulness of the orders imparted to them from the higher level.

The system of preliminary rulings does not resolve any questions which may arise in respect of the compatibility of such EU-based national decisions with the ECHR. Although the EU is committed to the fundamental rights protected under the ECHR, which are at the same time constitutive elements of the EU's legal order as 'general principles' (Article 6(3) TEU), discrepancies may arise from time to time. It is not an iron rule that the Luxembourg Court will invariably follow the line of the Strasbourg Court on any emerging issues. In *Bosphorus*, the ECtHR offered a solution of compromise for that kind of conflict. At stake was the impoundment of an aircraft leased by a Turkish airline from JAT, the Yugoslav airline, which figured on an embargo list issued by the Security Council. After the Security Council's decision had been implemented by a Community regulation, the Irish Government impounded the aircraft, in strict compliance with its Community obligations. The case was first brought to the Court of Justice of the European Communities[50] and thereafter to the ECtHR. The ECtHR had to rule on the issue of jurisdiction pursuant to Article 1 ECHR in order to ascertain whether it was authorized to look into the merits of the application. Jurisdiction is of course different from attribution. However, the relevant considerations run largely parallel to one another. The ECtHR found:

> In the present case it is not disputed that the act about which the applicant company complained, the detention of the aircraft leased by it for a period of time, was implemented by the authorities of the respondent State on its territory following a decision made by the Irish Minister for Transport. In such circumstances the applicant company, as the addressee of the impugned act, fell within the 'jurisdiction' of the Irish State, with the consequence that its complaint about that act is compatible *ratione loci*, *personae* and *materiae* with the provisions of the Convention . . .[51]

It thereby implicitly concluded that the actions complained of were attributable to Ireland and could not be shrugged off by arguing that the Irish authorities had done nothing else than implement a Community decision for which the European Community had to be made accountable—

[49] See judgment in Case 314/85 *Foto Frost* [1987] ECR 4199.
[50] ECJ, Case C-84/95 *Bosphorus v Ireland* [1996] ECR I-3978.
[51] Application 45036/98, judgment, 25 March 1997, para 137.

or else the Security Council as the author of the embargo list. Recognizing the difficult situation in which a state eager to comply with all of its international obligations finds itself, the ECtHR pointed out that

> State action taken in compliance with such legal obligations is justified as long as the relevant organisation is considered to protect fundamental rights, as regards both the substantive guarantees offered and the mechanisms controlling their observance, in a manner which can be considered at least equivalent to that for which the Convention provides.[52]

This presumption of lawfulness may be compared—and has been compared—to the presumption established by the German Constitutional Federal Court in its *Solange II* decision[53] where it stated that it would refrain from reviewing secondary acts of Community legislation 'as long as' the protection afforded by the Community corresponded 'generally' to the level of protection afforded by the constitutional order of Germany.

To follow the jurisprudence ushered in by *Bosphorus* is difficult in particular with regard to the UN since the UN does not grant access to justice to persons who may be adversely affected by its measures. It is well-known that the freezing orders of the Security Council have met with opposition in quite a number of countries, in particular in the Member States of the EU. The judgment of the CJEU in *Kadi*[54] may be seen as an act of rebellion against the authority of the Security Council. However, in the final analysis, this problematique does not come within the scope of attribution, the specific subject matter of this contribution. In sum, there can be no doubt that decisions taken by national authorities are and remain national decisions even though they may be based on legal foundations from an international source.[55]

C. Placing Military Contingents at the Disposal of an IO

The most difficult chapter of attribution is constituted by arrangements according to which troop contingents are put at the disposal of a regional alliance or of the UN. As already pointed out, such arrangements are made on a daily basis since the UN has no standing force of its own. By necessity, it must call on Member States if the need arises to send military units to a given trouble spot. Contrary to optimistic beliefs nurtured during the early years of the UN, troops acting on the strength of a mandate of the UN do not embody the good as such. More than once,

[52] Ibid, para 155.

[53] *Entscheidungen des Bundesverfassungsgerichts* (*BVerfGE*) 73, 339, 22 October 1986; English translation: *Decisions of the Federal Constitutional Court*, vol 1/II (Baden-Baden, Nomos, 1992) 613.

[54] Cases C-402/05 P and C-415/05 P, 3 September 2008.

[55] Same conclusion reached by Tzanakopoulos, above n 1, 34–37.

heavy charges have been brought against some units for massive wrongdoing.[56]

In connection with the case of *Behrami and Saramati* adjudicated by the ECtHR, it was already pointed out that in respect of the UN two fundamentally divergent methods must be distinguished. For an outsider, they may appear similar, but upon reflection one comes easily to the conclusion that indeed one is faced with phenomena which differ profoundly. (i) Peacekeeping operations,[57] which may be launched by the Security Council, are mostly designed to ensure peace and security in a situation where the general conditions are still fairly fragile after an armed conflict. Peacekeepers were originally conceived of as a force which should never use its arms, except for purposes of self-defence. When during the wars in the former Yugoslavia peacekeepers had to witness time and again scenes of horror and brutality without being allowed to intervene for the protection of the victims, this toothless version of peacekeeping was abandoned. Peacekeeping missions are meanwhile carried out under the most diversified mandates. It has been generally recognized that 'robust' peacekeeping may become necessary lest the idea of peacekeeping lose its good reputation. In accord with this development, the danger has increased that peacekeeping operations may result in injuries to the detriment of the populations concerned.

Peacekeeping operations are placed under the authority of the Security Council, which delegates its responsibility to the Secretary-General who will generally appoint a Special Representative in the theatre concerned as well as a military commander. National troop contingents are fully integrated into the peacekeeping structures. The relevant national commanders retain control only over disciplinary matters and matters of criminal prosecution for offences that have been committed by any of the members of their contingents.[58] As a logical consequence, the conduct of peacekeepers is attributed to the UN, and the UN is ready to assume responsibility for any injuries that may have been caused.[59] This state of affairs stands in full conformity with Article 6 DARIO. The practice indicated in that provision

[56] See, eg SC Resolution 1592 (2005), 30 March 2005, para 11, reaffirming 'concern regarding acts of sexual exploitation and abuse committed by UN personnel against the local population', and the ensuing Report of the UN Secretary-General, UN Doc S/2005/506, 2 August 2005, paras 69–77.

[57] For a recent overview see M Bothe, 'Peacekeeping Forces' in *Max Planck Encyclopedia of Public International Law* (e-publication, 2011).

[58] It is a matter of common knowledge that the UN has no criminal justice system of its own.

[59] Letter of the UN Legal Counsel of 3 February 2004, *UN Juridical Yearbook* 2004, 352, 354, paras 6, 7; M Hirsch, *The Responsibility of International Organizations Toward Third Parties. Some Basic Principles* (Dordrecht, Martinus Nijhoff, 1995) 66–71; P Klein, La responsabilité des organisations internationales dans les ordres juridiques internes et en droit des gens (Bruxelles, Bruylant, 1998) 377, 380; *Stephens v Cyprus, Turkey and the UN*, Application 45267/06, Decision, 11 December 2008.

suffers exceptions only in situations where a national contingent deliberately places itself outside the instructions imparted to it.[60] Furthermore, the UN reserves the right, but only with internal effect, to recover funds spent as compensation to victims from the troop-contributing countries in case injury was caused intentionally or by gross negligence.[61] However, to date no judicial procedures have been established for the pursuit of such reparation claims, handled exclusively by the UN bureaucracy, which fortunately seems to work quite effectively. Nonetheless, the lack of judicial machinery amounts to an inroad into the guarantees laid down in Article 14 of the International Covenant on Civil and Political Rights. (ii) To grant an authorization to use of 'all necessary means', ie including armed force, is one of the most far-reaching decisions the Security Council can make under Chapter VII of the Charter. There is no explicit provision empowering the Security Council to take such a shortcut to enforcement action, except for regional arrangements which the Security Council is even expected to use for that purpose (Article 53(1)). It is this privileged position of regional arrangements which initially triggered a heated debate on the notion of 'regional arrangement'.[62] However, this debate has dried up in light of the recent practice of the Security Council that had its point of departure, after some cursory first experiences, in Resolution 678 (1990) of 29 November 1990 for the liberation of Kuwait. At that time, no other remedy could be envisaged for the purpose of providing assistance to Kuwait. Since the UN is devoid of a standing military force, the alliance supporting Kuwait could have relied on a regional arrangement but no such arrangement existed in the area concerned. It was thus necessity which dictated the solution: only the United States with its paramount military power was capable of resisting and defeating the Iraqi armed forces. Accordingly, 'Member States co-operating with the Government of Kuwait' were authorized to commence military operations against Iraq.[63]

The principle of non-use of force is the backbone of the contemporary

[60] See examples given in the commentary to Art 7 DARIO, ILC [2011] Report, above n 11, 88, para 8.

[61] Model Memorandum of Understanding between the UN and contributing states, Annex to the note of the Secretary-General on Reform of the process for determining reimbursement to Member States for contingent-owned equipment, UN doc A/51/967, 27 August 1997, Art 9: "The United Nations will be responsible for dealing with any claims by third parties where the loss of or damage to their property, or death or personal injury, was caused by the personnel or equipment provided by the Government in the performance of services or any other activity or operation under this Memorandum. However, if the loss, damage, death or injury arose from gross negligence or wilful misconduct of the personnel provided by the Government, the Government will be liable for such claims."

[62] See, eg R Kolb, Comments on Art 53, in JP Cot et al, *La Charte des Nations Unies. Commentaire article par article*, vol II (Paris, Economica, 2005) 1409–13; G Ress and J Bröhmer, Comments on Art 53, in B Simma et al, *The Charter of the United Nations. A Commentary,* vol I (Oxford, Oxford University Press) 861ff margin nn 8 and 9.

[63] It is true, however, that the military operations against Iraq could also be justified on the basis of Art 51 of the Charter as collective self-defence.

international legal order. Sovereign equality of states in a true sense is only guaranteed if international relations are placed under the leitmotiv of peace. Likewise, human rights and the rule of law cannot flourish amidst the turmoil caused by armed hostilities. After the horrors of World War II, the drafters of the UN Charter were fully aware of this simple truth. Accordingly, they restricted the legitimate use of armed force to two situations: every state was granted the right to defend itself if attacked by armed force, and the Security Council was given wide discretion as to determinations on the use of collective force for the maintenance and restoration of international peace and security (Article 39). Within the Security Council, such decisions cannot be taken lightly. On the one hand, any substantive decision of the Security Council requires a majority of nine members; on the other hand, the five permanent members must be included in that majority or must at least opt for abstention on the issue to be decided (Article 27(3)).[64] It stands to reason that these procedural limitations serve the interests of the international community at large. The power to decide on peace and war is not a personal entitlement of the members of the Security Council, but a responsibility to be discharged in the interest of all members of the world organization. Accordingly, the Security Council is debarred from handling its powers under Chapter VII in an arbitrary fashion. In particular, it may not divest itself of those powers by delegating them freely to other entities, since they are vested in the Council as an institution of the UN. As shown above, the argument of necessity militates in favour of permitting third parties—states and IOs, perhaps even private entities—to assist the Council in its actions against threats to international peace and security. But the Security Council must remain at the centre of any such operation. It must impart the general direction, and it must also be able to issue instructions on any essential choices in the course of an operation. Otherwise, the confidence of the Member States will be frustrated; Chapter VII does not permit such freewheeling use of the powers of which the Security Council is the trustee but not the owner.

It is in light of those considerations that answers must be sought as to whether conduct of an operation mandated by the Security Council may be attributed to the UN. Scrutinising the relevant practice,[65] the observer finds that the resolutions of the Security Council authorizing the use of force by 'coalitions of the willing' may be framed in different ways. Resolution 678 (1990) is the model of a resolution setting out a broad mandate but spending little thought on how to control the actions of the military

[64] The ICJ, *Legal Consequences for States of the Continued Presence of South Africa in Namibia (South West Africa) notwithstanding Security Council Resolution 276 (1970), Advisory Opinion*, ICJ Reports 1971, 16, 22, confirmed many decades ago that the abstention of a permanent member does not impede the adoption of a Security Council Resolution.

[65] For an exhaustive overview see Schütze, above n 39, 48–75.

force thus authorized. Quite a number of other resolutions follow this path of light-handedness. After the United States and the United Kingdom had invaded Iraq in 2003, the Security Council, apparently seeking to provide a slight coating of lawfulness on the legal situation obtaining de facto in the country, issued Resolution 1483 (2003) of 22 May 1983 in which it called upon the occupying powers to 'promote the welfare of the Iraqi people through the effective administration of the territory' (para 4), apparently in the knowledge that its real impact on the situation on the ground was minimal. A few months later, through Resolution 1511 (2003), it recognised half-heartedly the Authority established by the occupying powers with its 'specific responsibilities, authorities, and obligations under applicable international law', authorising 'a multinational force under unified command to take all necessary measures to contribute to the maintenance of security and stability in Iraq.[66] The only mechanism of supervision was a reporting obligation established under para 25 of that Resolution. In parallel to the Coalition Provisional Authority, the Secretary-General appointed a Special Representative, who had no powers of command nor any other kind of authority over the invasion force. It was very clear that the invasion had come first, without any authorisation by the Security Council, and that the subsequent resolutions had no other function than to recapture the unlawful operation by introducing some modest elements of a new legality pursuant to the dictum: *ex iniuria novum ius oritur*.

A more recent example is provided by Resolution 1973 (2011) of 17 March 2011 under which states and/or regional organisations or arrangements willing to protect the Libyan people were authorised again to take 'all necessary measures', the discrete formula which includes armed force.[67] Here a reporting obligation was inserted directly into the authorising paragraph, but it appears that otherwise the Security Council abstained from keeping to itself the direction of the operations that were to be expected. In the latest resolution of the Security Council on Libya that dealt with the ongoing conflict, Resolution 2009 (2011) of 16 September 2011,[68] no

[66] Security Council Resolution 1511 (2003), 16 October 2003, paras 1, 13. Resolution 1483 (2003), 22 May 2003, had given recognition to the Coalition Authority only in the Preamble (para 13).

[67] 4. *Authorizes* Member States that have notified the Secretary-General, acting nationally or through regional organizations or arrangements, and acting in cooperation with the Secretary-General, to take all necessary measures, notwithstanding paragraph 9 of resolution 1970 (2011), to protect civilians and civilian populated areas under threat of attack in the Libyan Arab Jamahiriya, including Benghazi, while excluding a foreign occupation force of any form on any part of Libyan territory, and *requests* the Member States concerned to inform the Secretary-General immediately of the measures they take pursuant to the authorization conferred by this paragraph which shall be immediately reported to the Security Council.

[68] Immediately after Gaddafi's death, attention shifted to preventing the dangers resulting from the proliferation of weapons of all types, see Security Council Resolution 2017 (2011), 31 October 2011.

mention was made of any report submitted by the nations that availed themselves of the authorisation to protect the civilian population by armed force, a finding which tends to underline the low degree of control the UN could in fact exercise with regard to Libya.

Under such conditions, when the Security Council stays deliberately in the background, leaving a wide margin of discretion to the relevant coalition of the willing, it would be difficult to ascribe the ensuing conduct to the UN—except if one would argue that to confer such broad powers on individual states or other collective entities is per se a breach of the Charter, an unlawful derogation from Chapter VII.

Dan Sarooshi has attempted to introduce into the debate a distinction between authorisation and delegation. According to his view, authorisation has a limited scope whereas delegation means transfer of discretionary decision-making.[69] Since to conduct armed operations involves by necessity many choices, 'authorisations' to use force inevitably amount to true delegations of power.[70] However, because of the far-reaching nature of such delegations, the Security Council needs to reserve to itself 'overall authority and control'.[71] In that latter regard, broad agreement exists in the relevant legal literature.[72]

In *Behrami and Saramati*, the ECtHR followed exactly the path indicated by Sarooshi. Also the words 'overall authority and control' are the words used by Sarooshi. However, the ECtHR did not succeed in making its approach plausible. A comparison between the different cases of authorisation found in the practice of the Security Council would have been necessary but was not carried out by Sarooshi either. In the case of Kosovo, Resolution 1244 (1999) was not a resolution born out of the constraints of daily politics, but a coherent ensemble of objectives and measures of implementation. The actions to be performed by KFOR were not authorised in isolation. UNMIK and KFOR were tied together. The Security Council had devised a comprehensive plan concerning the future development of Kosovo for an interim period during which 'substantial autonomy and meaningful self-administration for Kosovo' were to be attained. In fact, the UN assumed full responsibility for Kosovo through the two institutions created on the basis of the resolution, namely

[69] D Sarooshi, *The United Nations and the Development of Collective Security. The Delegation by the UN Security Council of its Chapter VII Powers* (Oxford: Clarendon Press, 1999) 4–15. By contrast, E de Wet, *The Chapter VII Powers of the United Nations Security Council* (Oxford, Hart Publishing, 2004) 258–60, uses the two concepts of authorisation and delegation as synonyms.

[70] Ibid, 13.

[71] Ibid, 34, 155.

[72] See, eg N Blokker, 'Is the Autorization Authorized? Powers and Practice of the UN Security Council to Authorize the Use of Force by "Coalitions of the Able and Willing"' (2000) *European Journal of International Law* 11 541, 554; V Gowlland-Debbas, 'The Limits of Unilateral Enforcement of Community Objectives in the Framework of UN Peace Maintenance' (2000) *European Journal of International Law* 11 361, 369f.

UNMIK and KFOR. Both operations were intimately interconnected, KFOR was assigned the task of establishing a secure environment in which the international civil presence can operate (para 9 c), and the UN Secretary-General was requested to appoint a Special Representative 'to control the implementation of the international civil presence', who was also instructed to 'coordinate closely with the international security presence to ensure that both presences operate towards the same goals in a mutually supportive manner' (para 6). Given this framework, KFOR had little room for autonomous decisions. The crucial political decisions remained fully in the hands of the Security Council, and for matters of daily implementation UNMIK together with the Special Representative had the decisive word. It was evident, furthermore, that COMKFOR, the Norwegian Commander of KFOR, acted exclusively for the fulfilment of KFOR's tasks under Security Council Resolution 1244 (1999) when issuing the controversial warrant for the arrest of Saramati. Not the slightest connection with the Norwegian Government could be established in that regard. Under these circumstances, the distancing of the UN Secretary-General from the holding in *Behrami and Saramati*[73] carries little weight.

It was an open misunderstanding of *Behrami and Saramati* when the British House of Lords in *Al-Jedda*[74] and *Al-Skeini*,[75] two cases where Iraqi citizens had died at the hands of British occupation forces in Iraq, believed to be able to rely on the European precedent to fend off British responsibility by attributing the relevant actions to the UN. No reasonable account was taken of the factual circumstances. The Authority established in Iraq by the occupying forces was at no time under any kind of control of the Security Council, and it was also true that in *Al-Jedda* the victim had died in a prison that was under the sole authority of the British forces, the same fate that had befallen one of the applicants in *Al-Skeini*. Accordingly, the conclusion reached by the ECtHR that the relevant facts were to be attributed to the United Kingdom and not to the UN was inescapable.[76]

[73] Report of the Secretary-General on the United Nations Interim Administrative Mission in Kosovo, UN doc S/2008/354, 12 June 2008, para 16: 'It is understood that the international responsibility of the United Nations will be limited to the extent of its effective operational control'.

[74] *R (on the application of Al-Jedda) v Secretary of State for Defence* [2007] UKHL 58, 12 December 2007.

[75] *Al-Skeini and others v Secretary of State for Defence* [2007] UKHL 26, 13 June 2007.

[76] *Al-Jedda*, Application 27021/08, Judgment, 7 July 2011; *Al-Skeini*, Application 55721/07, Judgment, 7 July 2011.

IV. THE APPROPRIATE CRITERIA OF ATTRIBUTION

At the end of the discussion on the different criteria of attribution, the question should be clarified whether the ECtHR acted judiciously in choosing the formula 'ultimate authority and control' rather than the criterion of 'effective control' as preferred by the ILC in its draft on the responsibility of IOs (Article 7). Undoubtedly, the ILC followed the gist of the corresponding provision of the ARS (Article 6), although in different terminology, by opting for 'effective control'; at the same time, it drew on Article 8 ARS which found no specific place in DARIO. The difference lies in the required intensity of control or supervision. The choice adopted by the ILC might provide the correct answer if the responsibility of states and the responsibility of IOs were to be assessed from the same viewpoint. However, serious doubts emerge as to that assumed parallelism.

(i) From the very outset, it should be observed that the issue is not susceptible of being resolved by semantic quibbles over the different words used in the discussion. There can be no magic formula. Sarooshi's distinction between authorisation and delegation may point in the right direction but the question remains where the borderline should be drawn. Ultimate control and overall control are so close to one another that their application to actual occurrences can hardly yield any definite results. It seems more promising to inquire whether emphasis is to be placed on normative criteria or rather on factual elements. Recently, Antonios Tzanakopoulos has advocated the concept of normative control—which seems to open up new perspectives which have not been sufficiently explored hitherto.[77]

(ii) For states, to carry out operations targeting third states by relying on outside forces, persons or groups outside their institutional machinery but which act on their instructions or under their direction is a rare phenomenon. More often than not, in such instances illegitimate aims are being pursued. In fact, the provision of Article 8 ARS is specifically intended to make states accountable in cases where they hide behind private groups of whose actions they deny having knowledge. The support given to the Contras by the United States Government is the most prominent case in point. Generally, in resorting to the services of such groups a state breaches its obligations under the ground rules of the international legal order as they have been codified in GA Resolution 2625 (XXV) of 1970. However, there can be no presumption of unlawful conduct. In their mutual relations, states seek to influence one another through the most diverse means and methods. It should not be assumed lightly that a state, as a consequence of contacts with private entities that later commit criminal acts to the detriment of other states, must be considered

[77] Tzanakopoulos, above n 1, 40–45. See also the explanations by K Schmalenbach, *Die Haftung Internationaler Organisationen* (Frankfurt et al, Peter Lang, 2004) 107–11 on the terms 'command' and 'control'.

liable for those acts on the basis of the applicable rules of attribution. Rightly, therefore, the ICJ pointed out in the *Bosnian Genocide* case that the standard applied by the ICTY would excessively enlarge the scope of international responsibility.[78]

The general situation of IOs is entirely different. As already pointed out, IOs are never established as completely self-sufficient entities. Structurally, they have to rely on their members in many respects. Regarding military operations, in particular, it is evident that the UN can never control national contingents put at its disposal to the same full extent as a national government controls its own forces. Regarding peacekeeping forces, this simple truth has put its hallmark on the relevant practice in that the UN assumes full responsibility for all the units integrated into any such operation. Where, on the other hand, the Security Council confines itself to authorising the use of force by coalitions of the willing, there is no escaping the conclusion that the members of such coalitions enjoy a greater degree of discretionary decision-making. However, the relevant practice evinces patterns with different features. Some of the operations authorised by the Security Council can be equated with the conferral of blanket powers without any real directive authority retained by the Security Council. The resolutions regarding Iraq subsequent to the invasion of the country by the forces of the United States and the United Kingdom provide an illustrative example in point. On the other hand, in respect of Kosovo, Security Council Resolution 1244 (1999) brought into being an operation providing for institutional machinery that ensured a strong influence of the UN. In such instances, the situation is not essentially different from patterns where the UN puts into operation its own machinery. It would be awkward, therefore, to focus on effective control of each and every individual action. Where a network of loyal cooperation has been built, albeit through the instrument of an authorisation, the UN may trust that its orders and directions will be faithfully complied with. The general structure ensures then effectiveness and reliability, which can be perfectly expressed through the concept of 'ultimate authority and control'.[79]

An additional argument may be derived from a different dimension of appropriateness. Where a 'true' UN operation is launched which pursues specific UN objectives, as opposed to other situations where the authorisation constitutes but a fig leaf for an operation dominated and controlled by third parties, it would be utterly unjust to let the coalition of the willing bear also the cost of any fatalities and injuries. In a strict sense,

[78] See Cassese, above n 37; ICJ Reports 2007, 43, 210, para 406.

[79] We do not agree with the blunt statement of the official ILC commentary, ICJ [2011] Report, above n 11, 83, para 5, that no attribution to the UN is conceivable when the Security Council authorises the military forces of states or international organisation to take necessary measures outside 'a chain of command linking those forces to the United Nations'.

this argument lies outside the scope of attribution. But it corresponds to sound logic to require that the principal, the IO, should bear the costs for the damage caused by its agents.

(iii) There are instances where, apart from the general considerations set out above, the basic arrangements for the operation to be conducted make clear from the very outset that the units working in cooperation with the UN will be acting under their sole and exclusive responsibility. When, in the absence of the Soviet Union from the Security Council in June 1950, the Council recommended to the members of the World Organisation to 'furnish such assistance to the Republic of Korea as may be necessary to repel the armed attack and to restore international peace and security in the area',[80] it specified at the same time that the operation was to be conducted under the command of the United States; the only link between the operation and the UN was the authorisation to use the UN flag and the request to provide the Security Council with reports 'as appropriate' on the course of action taken under the unified command.[81] These stipulations made it clear that the operation of defence against the North Korean attack was not a UN operation proper although it enjoyed the political backing of the World Organisation. A similar assessment is required by the work of EULEX, the Rule of Law Mission of the European Union in Kosovo. Formally, EULEX operates under the cover of Security Council Resolution 1244 (1999). But the Security Council has never fully endorsed the initiative of the EU which, originally, introduced itself almost like a stowaway passenger on the boat launched by the UN.[82]

(iv) Societal phenomena may have many faces. The quest for a correct answer to the question of attribution should not blind our eyes to the eventuality of dual attribution, both to the troop-contributing country and the IO concerned. In each and every case, a careful examination of the relevant facts is necessary. The ILC has openly acknowledged that indeed in the situation covered by Article 7 DARIO such dual attribution may eventually be the ineluctable outcome.[83] The recent judgment of the Court of Appeal of The Hague concerning the Srebrenica massacre provides a good case in point.[84] Although the Court did not exclude responsibility of the UN, an issue not under its jurisdiction, it con-

[80] SC Resolution 83 (1950) concerning Korea, 27 June 1950.

[81] Ibid. There is broad agreement in the legal literature that the UN operation in Korea did not constitute a genuine UN operation to be attributed to the World Organization, see Klein, above n 59, 378; Schmalenbach, above n 77, 202ff.

[82] It is significant that the reports of the EULEX Mission form an independent part of the Report of the UN Secretary-General on UNMIK, see latest report S/2011/675, 31 October 2011, Annex I.

[83] ILC [2011] Report, above n 11, Comments on Art 3, 81, para 6; Comments on Chapter II, 83, para 4.

[84] Court of Appeal of The Hague, *Nuhanovic v Netherlands*, Case No 200.020.174/01, para 5.9, www.zoeken.rechtspraak.nl/ResultPage.aspx (English translation).

cluded that the Netherlands could not exonerate itself from any blame, proceeding from the assumption that more than one party could have effective control. Looking into the events preceding the massacre, the Court could clarify that instructions given to the Dutchbat from governmental sources had largely determined the conduct of the contingent, its absolute passiveness vis-à-vis the worst human tragedy Europe had witnessed since World War II.

(v) Questions of attribution, a chapter of international responsibility, are logically distinct from issues of jurisdiction. However, it has appeared that access to justice determines largely the debate on the relevant issues of substantive law. In fact, attribution of conduct to the UN is tantamount to saying that for individuals no judicial remedy exists—apart from some particular areas like staff disputes that may be carried before the administrative tribunals which almost all IOs have established.[85] The UN enjoys 'immunity from every form of legal process' before domestic courts,[86] and the same rule applies to the Specialised Agencies.[87] States find themselves in the same situation. They can use all political means at their disposal to voice their grievances against the UN, but on the legal level they are defenceless. The UN has no standing before the ICJ, neither as applicant nor as respondent, and hence cannot be sued before the World Court. If, by contrast, specific conduct can be attributed to a state or a regional organisation, many remedies may become available. In some countries, any governmental act susceptible of infringing private rights may be submitted for review;[88] additionally, if domestic remedies remain of no avail, an application to the ECtHR may provide a last opportunity of vindicating a right allegedly encroached upon. Quite visibly, many authors tend to examine issues of attribution in light of this context. There is a clear tendency to favour attribution to states or else even to regional organisations, denying attribution to the UN, since it is felt that attribution to the UN would lead to unjust results, namely a lack of enforceability of legal entitlements through judicial means. It is in this sense that the outcry by Marko Milanovic and Tajana Papic in their comments on the Behrami and Saramati case: 'It is staggering that

[85] The former UN Administrative Tribunal, established by GA Resolution 351 A (IV), 24 November 1949, was replaced as of 31 December by the UN Dispute Tribunal and, as appellate instance, the UN Appeals Tribunal.

[86] Convention on the Privileges and Immunities of the United Nations, 13 February 1946, 1 UNTS 15, Art II, s 2.

[87] Convention on the Privileges and Immunities of the Specialized Agencies, 21 November 1947, 33 UNTS 261, Art II, s 4.

[88] The main example is Germany where the Basic Law stipulates in Art 19(4), first clause: 'Should any person's rights be violated by public authority, he may have recourse to the courts'.

such a message of unaccountability could have been sent by a court of human rights' must be understood.[89]

(vi) Lastly, a word of caution closely related to the preceding observations should be said. In the legal debate on the responsibility of IOs, states and IOs have mostly been treated as subjects of equal quality. But from a factual viewpoint, this is not the case. The recognition of IOs as subjects of international law[90] should not divert attention from the fact that IOs have normally only poor substantive resources. Financially, they are generally totally dependent on their members. Thus, as debtors, they are endowed with only modest assets that could serve as guarantee in case responsibility should be implemented through judicial remedies and measures of constraint. In practice, it may happen that a specific IO cannot even be found by ordinary mail services—an eventuality which of course lies far beyond any experiences a claimant will make with the UN, the EU or the Council of Europe. In any event, however, an IO is not automatically the same stable entity as a state which, by definition, has a territory and a population. Drastically spoken, an IO may sometimes consist of no more than an office building together with the related equipment.[91] This observation militates against mechanically drawing up general rules that do not take account of the degree of solidity of an IO.

V. CONCLUSION

Our main conclusion is that Article 6 ARS and Article 7 DARIO do not ideally fit together. Article 6 ARS contemplates situations that from the very outset smack of unlawful manipulation while Article 7 DARIO regulates a standard situation of IOs which is not marred by any degree of suspicion. In order not to expose states to unfounded charges of wrongdoing the criterion of 'effective control' is appropriate, while the relationship of trust and loyal cooperation between IOs and their supporters justifies opting for the looser criterion of 'ultimate authority and control' if an authorisation to use force is surrounded by a tight network of supervision and control. In such instances, it is not necessary that the IO concerned be in effective control of each and every single act carried out by the military contingents placed at its disposal.

[89] See n 39, 289. See also the comments by L Doswald-Beck, *Human Rights in Times of Conflict and Terrorism* (Oxford, Oxford University Press, 2011) 23ff.

[90] ICJ, *Reparation for injuries suffered in the service of the United Nations, Advisory Opinion*, ICJ Reports 1949 174, 179.

[91] With a fair degree of scepticism, P Reuter (the former special rapporteur of the ILC on the treaties of IOs), 'Sur quelques limites du droit des organisations internationales' in E Diez et al (eds), *Festschrift für Rudolf Bindschedler* (Bern, Stämpfli, 1980) 491, 505, observed that 'dès l'origine le crédit des organisations internationales semblait mince'.

2

EU International Responsibility and its Attribution: From the Inside Looking Out

PIETER JAN KUIJPER* AND ESA PAASIVIRTA**

I. INTRODUCTION

THIS CONTRIBUTION VENTURES to set out some introductory remarks about EU (European Union) responsibility under international law from an EU perspective. It is only natural that the draft rules on the responsibility of international organisations prepared by the International Law Commission[1] over the last decade under the unflagging stewardship of its rapporteur Professor Giorgio Gaja will be referred to, as well as the contribution that the European Commission, together with the Member States, has tried to make to the discussion leading up to these draft rules.[2] Moreover, wherever appropriate, reference will be

* Professor in the Law of International Organizations, University of Amsterdam

** Legal Service of the European Commission; Adjunct Professor, University of Helsinki. The views are personal.

[1] UNGA, 'Annotated preliminary list of items to be included in the provisional agenda of the 66th regular session of the General Assembly 66/100' (20 June 2011) UN Doc A/66/100, 137 taking note of the report and ILC, 'Report of the International Law Commission on the Work of its 63rd Session' (26 April-3 June and 4 July-12 August 2011) UN Doc A/66/10 for the relevant ILC report and for the draft rules and commentaries thereto.

[2] The European Commission throughout the work of the ILC on the topic has commented extensively and sometimes forcefully on the various drafts. These comments are to be found in the documents prepared by the UN Secretariat that collect the remarks of different international organisations. They were normally prepared in a dialogue with the Member States in the so-called COJUR committee of the Council of Ministers, composed of the legal advisors of the Ministries of Foreign Affairs of the Member States. See UNGA, 'Responsibility of International Organisations: Comments and Observations Received from International Organisations' (2004) UN doc A/CN 4/545 (2005) UN Doc A/CN 4/556 (2007) UN Doc A/CN 4/582 (2008) UN Doc A/CN 4/593, and (2011) UN Doc A/CN 4/637. It is obvious from the outset that the Commission is most concerned with the problem of attribution or

made to the practice of international organisations and in particular of the EU institutions and instrumentalities in order to elucidate our views.

First of all, it is important to recall that the Treaty of Lisbon has brought clarity to the issue of the (international) personality of the Union. There is now only one EU and no longer the EU and the European Community, which were able to conclude international agreements independently from one another. Secondly, it is still true that most of the international responsibility of the Union is likely to be responsibility *ex contractu*; the accession of the EU to the European Convention of Human Rights (ECHR) will also contribute to that.

In this connection it is useful parenthetically to point out once more that in some cases, given the bearer(s) of the contractual obligations, the question of who is responsible is immediately clear. In the case of international agreements concluded by the EU alone, the responsibility arises for the organisation alone, even if the Member States are actually the vehicles for carrying out certain obligations under the agreement, as is normal and inherent in the structure of the EU.[3] The same is true for Member State-only agreements: without doubt responsibility will fall on the Member States alone, even though the Member States may have contributed to treaty conflict situations coming about between their treaties and the EU Treaty.[4] On the other hand there are contractual situations with a more open texture of obligations, such as the so-called mixed agreements and obligations of customary international law, where responsibility is likely to have to be apportioned as between Member States and the Union.

Returning to the question of contractual and non-contractual responsibility, there is little doubt that the trend in the development of the Common Foreign and Security Policy towards more and more operational actions, will also confront the Union with a greater risk of non-contractual responsibility. In both instances action of the Member States or their police or troop contingents will be at issue, which are carried out, however, within a Union framework and (sometimes) under EU command and control.

Therefore, inevitably pride of place will be given to the relationship between the EU and its Member States, especially where it concerns the question of attribution of wrongful acts or of responsibility itself. This relationship between the organisation and its Member States is more complicated in the EU than in any other international organisation, both in

apportionment of responsibility between the Union and Member States and with the role played by the rules of the organisation.

[3] See nn 17, 18 and accompanying main text.

[4] An example is provided by the continuance of Bilateral Investment Treaties of the Member States, whereas in the meantime the power on foreign direct investment has been passed to the EU in the new Art 207 of the Treaty on the Functioning of the European Union (TFEU).

respect of treaty and non-treaty obligations incumbent on the EU alone, and in respect of the obligations flowing from the by now well-known mixed agreements concluded between the EU and its Member States on the one side with one or more third states on the other side. Moreover, the 'rules of the organisation' that, according to the draft rules of the International Law Commission (ILC), may have a bearing on the responsibility of the organisation, are more extensive and complicated in the EU than in any other international organisation, especially insofar as the terms 'rules of the organisation' refer to the internal (constitutional) law of the organisation[5] and not merely to the idea that an international organisation may enable its Member States to contract out of general international law and create a *lex specialis* in a specific domain.[6] The invocation of 'rules of the organisation' in order to help determine the responsibility of the organisation, in particular in relation to that of its Member States, implies a tearing at the veil that an international organisation throws over its Member States and, in the case of the EU, often an interference in the internal division of powers between the Union and its Member States, of which the European Court of Justice (ECJ) is the guardian.[7] Thus delicate 'constitutional' issues are linked in the EU to the issue of 'rules of the organisation'.

Accordingly, this contribution will start with highlighting some paradoxes inherent in the structure and the action of the EU (and its Member States) on the international scene. These paradoxes are closely related, as we will see, to the 'rules of the organisation', ie of the EU, which may have consequences for the international responsibility of the Union, at least from the internal vantage point.

After a brief discussion of the attitude of the ILC to issues related to the 'rules of the organisation' and the 'corporate veil' in the law of international organisations, a further analysis will be undertaken of the different points where the 'rules of the organisation' may influence the responsibility under international law of the EU. In this respect the rules of attribution of wrongful acts and of responsibility, as laid down in the ILC rules, create particular dilemmas for the EU in the light of the fundamental structure of its foreign relations law and therefore deserve special

[5] Note that in the corresponding Art 2 (b) of the ILC's Articles on State Responsibility such rules are indeed called 'internal rules'.

[6] See generally, C Ahlborn, 'The Rules of International Organisations and the Law of International Responsibility' (2011) *International Organisations Law Review* (Forthcoming), Amsterdam Law School Legal Studies Research Paper no 2011–04, www.ssrn.com/abstract=1825182 (accessed 12 December 2011). On the point of 'rules of the organisation' referring to two different aspects of the law of the organisation, ibid fn 23ff and accompanying text.

[7] See on these issues, but in relation to the 1986 Convention on the Law of Treaties between International Organisations and between States and International Organisations, CM Brolmann, *The Institutional Veil in Public International Law: International Organisations and the Law of Treaties* (Oxford, Hart Publishing, 2007) 226–28.

attention. Hence different models of attribution will be distinguished and applied to the responsibility of the EU in relation to that of its Member States. These models and their possible application in different circumstances will be analyzed respectively from the perspective of the EU and from that of the ILC.

Finally some conclusions will be drawn and some policy advice that may flow from these conclusions may be advanced.

II. SOME PARADOXES

Of all the international organisations in the world, the EU at first sight seems to be the one that on the international scene is the most powerful and the most independent from its Member States. It has a High Representative for Foreign Affairs, who is in charge of the foreign policy of the Union and comparable to a Foreign Minister.[8] It has about as many so-called delegations as big powers have embassies.[9] These are manned by members of its own diplomatic service[10] and by civil servants of the European Commission. The Commission is charged with the EU's external representation outside the domain of the Common Foreign and Security Policy.[11] The EU is the organisation that by far concludes the most international agreements compared to other international organisations.[12] Many of these agreements are of a highly substantial character and very broad in their coverage. The EU has even become a Member of other international organisations as if it were some kind of state.[13]

Nevertheless the EU is also the international organisation that in many ways is the one most closely linked to its Member States and, according to its own internal rules, very difficult to distinguish from them. Thus the Member States are bound by the international agreements concluded by

[8] Arts 26(3) and 27 TEU (Treaty on European Union).

[9] Art 221 TFEU. In total the EU has 130 delegations accredited to third states and seven to international organisations, such as the UN and its specialized agencies in New York, Geneva, Vienna, Rome and Nairobi, the WTO, the Council of Europe, the OECD and the African Union. (EU External Service Directory www.eeas.europa.eu/delegations/web_en.htm, accessed 16 March 2012).

[10] This service is handicapped by its unhelpful name 'European External Action Service' (EEAS), but this cannot hide the fact that it is a diplomatic service nevertheless.

[11] Art 17(1) TEU.

[12] According to information obtained from the Council registry of international agreements, the EU is party to hundreds of international agreements that are presently in force, of which approximately 109 are so-called mixed agreements. See also www.consilium.europa.eu/policies/agreements.

[13] The EU is a Member of the WTO, the FAO, the Codex Alimentarius Commission, the Hague Conference of Private International Law and many international fisheries organisations. In several international organisations the necessary provisions for enabling the EU to become a member have been completed, but have not yet been ratified by the necessary number of Member States; this is the case for CITES and the World Customs Organisation.

the EU, according to Article 216(2) TFEU—which at first sight is hard to reconcile with the separate international personality from their Member States, which all international organisations are supposed to have. As the ECJ has stated already early in the life of the Union, this treaty provision lays down an obligation that Member States have to the Union, not to third states.[14] It follows that this obligation of the Member States can be enforced by the European Commission through the so-called infringement procedure.[15] This constitutes an enforcement mechanism of international agreements that most federal authorities cannot brandish against their federated states.[16] As a matter of fact, this obligation of the Member States to the Union guaranteeing a proper implementation of international agreements concluded by the Union is the expression of a broader principle governing the way the Union works.

According to Article 4(3) TEU and Article 291(1) TFEU Member States are bound to carry out the obligations flowing from the EU Treaties and from the acts of its Institutions; this entails that they shall adopt the measures of national law necessary to implement the legally binding acts of the Union, and this includes the international agreements concluded by the Union. The EU is accordingly not equipped with a fully-fledged layer of 'federal' government, in spite of EU 'agencies' sprouting left, right and centre.[17] The basic principle is that the Members States' authorities implement, carry out and execute EU law, including the international obligations of the Union, and their implementing legislation adopted at Union level.[18]

Finally the EU and its Member States in their mutual relations are tied together by a duty of sincere co-operation, earlier and perhaps more cor-

[14] Case 104/81 *Kupferberg* [1982] ECR 2641, para 31.

[15] It must be said that infringement procedures with a view to enforcing EU treaty obligations against a Member State are relatively rare. See Case C-61/94 *Commission v Germany (International Dairy Agreement)* [1996] ECR I-3989, para 15; Case C-13/00 *Commission v Ireland* [2002] ECR I-2934 and Case C-239/03 *Commission v France (Etang de Berre)* [2004] ECR I-9325. The number of such infringement procedures that have not been brought to litigation because the Member State in question complied, is unknown. See further in greater detail below pp 59–60.

[16] *Cf* the well-known tribulations of the US Government before the Supreme Court in the aftermath of the Avena case, see *Sanchez-Llamas v Oregon* 548 US 331 (2006) and *Jose Ernesto Medellin v Texas* 552 US 491 (2008). Also M Lišková, 'European Exceptionalism in International Law' (2008) 19 *European Journal of International Law* 463, 463–66 and E Samson, 'Revisiting Miranda after Avena: The Implications of Mexico v United States of America for the Implementation of the Vienna Convention on Consular Relations in the United States' (2005) 29 *Fordham International Law Journal* 1068.

[17] On the agencies phenomenon, see inter alia EIL Vos, 'Reforming the European Commission: What Role to Play for EU Agencies?' (2000) 37 *Common Market Law Review* 1113, 1116–20 and EIL Vos, 'Agencies and the European Union' in T Zwart and L Verhey (eds), *Ius Commune Europaeum, 42. Agencies in European and Comparative Law* (Antwerpen, Intersentia Publishing, 2003) 113–47.

[18] On this so-called 'executive federalism', see R Schütze, From Rome to Lisbon: 'Executive Federalism in the (New) European Union' (2010) 47 *Common Market Law Review* 1385.

rectly called the principle of Union loyalty. This principle, presently laid down in Article 4 TEU, has always played an important role in ensuring the solidarity and the single representation of the Union and Member States in international relations. The ECJ has called upon this principle in the early days of what was then still the European Community to found the notion of implied powers and the necessary parallelism between the exercise of the internal powers of the Union and the concomitant exclusivity of the external powers of the Union.[19] Recently the Court has turned to this principle in order to make Member States refrain from certain unilateral action on the international scene and from creating faits accomplis that would make it harder for the Union to act internationally in the fields of its competence.[20]

The principle of sincere co-operation is of particular importance in policy areas, where the Union and its Member States have shared powers[21] and where, on the basis of these shared powers, they conclude so-called mixed agreements with third states or have to act in international relations in concert with the Member States in some other way. Since the constant development thus far has been in the direction of more and more Union action and legislation in the fields of shared powers—in the field of international relations one can think of such areas as environment, transport, energy and security and justice—the need for respecting this duty of sincere co-operation from both sides, from the Union side and from the Member States' side, in relations with third states has become ever more pressing. There is little doubt that it is even seen as oppressive by some Member States.[22]

In the relatively new fields of the Common Foreign and Security Policy (CFSP), and in particular of the Common Security and Defence Policy (CSDP) as developed in the Lisbon Treaty, the EU is even more dependent on its Member States. The Union and the Member States are bound together also in these domains by a comparable vow of loyalty and soli-

[19] Case 22/70 *Commission v Council* (AETR) [1971] ECR 263.

[20] Cases 466–69, 471–72 and 475–76/98 *Commission v different MS* (Open Skies) [2002] ECR I-9427ff; Case C-266/03 *Commission v Luxemburg* (Danube case) [2005] ECR I-4805; Case C-45/07 *Commission v Greece* (IMO case) [2009] ECR I-00701; and Case C-246/07 *Commission v Sweden* (POPs case) [2010] ECR I-3317. This case law has been subjected to criticism from the Member States and from academic circles. See, eg PJ Slot and J Dutheil de la Rochère, 'Case C-466/98, *Commission v United Kingdom*; C-467/98, *Commission v Denmark*; C-468/98, *Commission v Sweden*; C-469/98, *Commission v Finland*; C-471, *Commission v Belgium*;, C-472/98, *Commission v Luxemburg*; C-475/98, *Commision v Austria*; C-476/98, *Commision v Germany*. (Open skies judgments) Judgments of the Full Court of 5 November 2002' (2003) 40 *Common Market Law Review* 697; M Cremona 'Extending the Reach of the AETR Principle: *Commission v Greece* (C-45/07)' (2009) 34 *European Law Review* 754; M Cremona 'Case C-246/07, *Commission v Sweden* (POPs)' (2011) 48 *Common Market Law Review* 1639.

[21] For a list of shared powers, see Art 4(2) TEU.

[22] See especially Case 246/07 *Commission v Sweden* (POPs case) [2010] ECR I-3317 and the reaction from Member States and commentators (see n 20).

darity as in the other domains of Union activity.[23] This is very important, since all the operational activities in this domain are carried out by the military or police contingents of the Member States. Maintaining this loyalty is also important, since Member States have greater possibilities for 'constructive abstention', than in other areas of Union law, when decisions are taken.[24] Such abstention does not break the necessary unanimity for a valid CFSP or CSDP decision, at least as long as the number of Member States abstaining in this way does not rise above one third of the membership. The accompanying declaration should make clear that the Member State concerned is not opposing the Union from going ahead; it also entails the consequence that the Member State concerned does not contribute financially or operationally, for instance by making troops available, to the implementation of the decision so taken.[25]

The Union loyalty in the framework of the CFSP may also take on great importance, when in international relations matters of high politics (CFSP and CSDP) are mixed up with matters of low politics (the technical and trade related issues, where the Union has important internal and external competences). This is often the case in international organisations, such as the UN and many of its specialized agencies, where, moreover, the EU often is, at the present juncture, in the impossibility of obtaining membership. In such situations the EU may be to a large extent dependent on the loyalty of its Member States in order to defend its interests and its positions based on its internal and external policies in the fields of low politics at issue.

However, Union loyalty in the CFSP and CSDP domains is of an entirely political nature, since the ECJ has no jurisdiction over this field, except for the protection of the dividing line between the application of the intergovernmental method and the 'Community method'.[26]

The EU, therefore, is the victim of a paradox in international relations. It seeks to act as a strong and unified actor towards the outside world in international relations and that is what it is supposed to do according to its latest charter, the Treaty of Lisbon.[27] However, because of its basic

[23] See Art 24(3) TEU. Note also that the provision of loyal cooperation in Art 4 TEU is relevant also for the CFSP aspects since that provision is placed under Title I 'common provisions'.

[24] See Art 31(1) TEU.

[25] See Art 41(2) and Art 44 TEU.

[26] See Art 40 TEU. For the single case on this issue (and based on Art 47 TEU, the non-identical predecessor of the actual Art 40), see Case C-91/05 *Commission v Council (Ecowas)* [2008] ECR I-3651.

[27] One of the main objectives of the Treaty on the European Constitution and later of the Treaty of Lisbon was to enhance and unify the external action of the EU to a greater extent than hitherto. See, eg The European Convention, The Secretariat, 'Final Report of Working Group VII: External Action', CONV 459/02, Brussels, 16 December 2002; Laeken Declaration on the Future of the European Union (2001) *Bulletin of the European Union* No 12; P Koutrakos (ed), 'The European Union's External Relations a Year after Lisbon', CLEER Working Paper 2011/3 (The Hague, TMC Asser Institute, 2011).

structure, it is highly dependent on its Member States for carrying out its policies and implementing its laws, including in the field of international relations. This is all the more true in areas that are of shared competence, where the duty of sincere cooperation plays an important role. The more power the EU wields in areas of exclusive power and in areas of shared powers, the greater this dependency becomes and the more it becomes visible to its partners in international relations as well. The Treaty of Lisbon, which articulates these features of the Union's basic structure better and in more detail than the earlier versions of the EU founding treaties, also has enhanced this visibility and thus contributed to the deepening of the paradox. To resort once more to the language of the corporate (or rather institutional) veil that the EU as an international organisation casts over its Member States, this veil at the same time has to become stronger and more transparent.[28]

It is at this juncture in its development that the EU is now increasingly exposed to the question of its responsibility under international law, both from the inside and the outside. From the inside there are the Member States that want to bear what they regard as their own responsibility, when they implement and execute Union law, in particular in the domain of human rights.[29] From the outside third states, such as the US, want to have the division of powers—and the concomitant responsibility—between Union and Member States clearly spelled out to them.[30] Another important element in the outside challenges has been the ILC's draft rules on the international responsibility of international organisations.

These developments put the rules of the organisation to the test, which, as we have seen above, are closely linked to the strength and the transparency of the EU institutional veil. In this connection, it may be noted that transparency of the veil is one thing and may be helpful to the veil's strength, if the underlying 'rules of the organisation' can be shown to be rational and effective for the functioning of the organisation, of its Member States and of the international system. Quite another thing is a tearing or a lifting of the veil that leads to a weakening of the veil and has negative effects on the EU, its Member States and the international system.

[28] At least that seems to have been the ambition of the Lisbon Treaty-makers. Whether they have found the right quality fibre in order to achieve this result is still an open question.

[29] See the discussions concerning the question of the representation of the EU before the ECHR below at pp 64–65.

[30] See, eg the result of the EU-US negotiations with respect to the Galileo system. (Agreement as adopted by Council Decision 2011/901/EU of 12 December 2011 on the conclusion of the Agreement on the promotion, provision and use of Galileo and GPS satellite-based navigation systems and related applications between the European Community and its Member States, of the one part, and the United States of America, of the other part [2011] OJ L348/1) See also PM Olson, 'Mixity from the Outside: the Perspective of a Treaty Partner' in C Hillion and P Koutrakos (eds), *Mixed Agreements Revisited* (Oxford, Hart Publishing, 2010) 331–48.

III. THE EU INSTITUTIONAL VEIL, THE RULES OF THE ORGANISATION AND THE ILC'S RULES ON RESPONSIBILITY

In the light of the preceding section it should be clear that the challenge inter alia posed to the EU, in respect of its responsibility under international law, consists of finding on the one hand a balance between the upholding of 'rules of the organisation' that are inherent in the EU system and determine to what extent the EU will draw down its institutional veil over its Member States. As such they have an influence on the responsibility of the EU and/or its Member States under international law and as such there is some need that they are accepted, or at least tolerated by third parties. This means that an internal mechanism should be devised for apportioning the respective responsibility of the Union and the Member States properly and transparently between them, so that they will be considered clear and fair by Member States and third states alike. It may not be possible to create such a combination for all domains and situations of Union activity; the balance found may have to be different in, and adaptable to, different situations.

In order to show the full scope of the challenge that the EU is facing, this section first will still devote a few lines to the internal challenges to the rules of the organisation underpinning external action of the EU and thus also its international responsibility. Next it will set out in greater detail how and where the rules of the organisation, which are of special importance for the external functioning and structure of the EU, play a role in respect of responsibility of the EU. Subsequently these rules of the organisation will be confronted to the instances where the ILC has accepted (or not) that the rules of the organisation are relevant in determining attribution of allegedly internationally wrongful acts to the organisation and/or its Member States or in directly imposing responsibility on the organisation and/or its Member States. After that the next section will consider how different attribution models may help us to think clearer about the issues and bring us closer to a balanced solution.

A. Internal Challenges and Their Consequences

First a brief return to the internal challenges to certain 'rules of the organisation' as an element in the present situation confronting the EU is in order. Brief mention has already been made of the modalities of the defence of cases brought by individuals against the EU under the ECHR, once the EU will have acceded to the Convention. The accession to the Convention is supposed to cover the respect of Human Rights and Fundamental Freedoms by the Union's institutions and by the Member

States in their application of Union law. The draft agreement between the EU and the Council of Europe creates a system of co-defendants before the European Court of Human Rights (ECtHR), in which the European Commission and a Member State can both appear the one next to the other. This can raise issues about the questions to which of the two the alleged wrongful act can be attributed and which of the two de facto and/or de jure can put right what has gone wrong in the light of the European Convention.[31] Or does the proposed system point to acceptance of shared responsibility in all cases of (alleged) breach of the ECHR? A lot will depend on how the system of co-defendants, once it is up and running, will actually work.

Another important challenge arises regularly in the conclusion of so-called mixed agreements, to which Member States and the EU are together becoming parties, since the issue areas covered by the treaty supposedly fall under the competences of the Union and under competences that have remained with the Member States. However, as Alan Rosas has pointed out, the Union and the Member States regularly conclude so-called 'false mixed agreements', that is to say agreements where it is actually not necessary (but merely possible, and sometimes not even that) to have resort to 'mixity'. Examples of 'false mixity' are nearly all association agreements for which there is a sufficient legal basis in Article 217 TFEU and its predecessors, but which in large majority, except for the former association agreements with Cyprus and Malta, have been concluded as mixed agreements.[32] Other well-known techniques to make agreements with third states needlessly mixed are the inclusion of clauses on 'political consultations' (pre-Lisbon) and 'forgetting' that certain clauses containing remaining vestiges of Member State competence can in certain circumstances be regarded as 'ancillary' or included in broad Union powers, such as development cooperation, according to standing case law of the Court.[33] Member States in this way express their need to remain visible

[31] See Council of Europe 8th Working Meeting of the CDDH Informal Working Group on Accession of the EU to the ECHR (CDDH-UE) 'Draft legal instruments on the accession of the European Union to the European Convention on Human Rights' (19 July 2011) CDDH-UE(2011)16. At present the discussion of this draft agreement is being blocked in the Council by certain Member States. For further detailed discussion of this draft in the light of different attribution models, see pp 64–65 below.

[32] See A Rosas, 'The European Union and Mixed Agreements' in: Alan Dashwood and Christophe Hillion (eds), *The General Law of EC External Relations* (London, Sweet & Maxwell, 2000) 203–07; and A Rosas, 'Mixed Union–Mixed Agreements' in M Koskenniemi (ed), *International Law Aspects of the European Union* (The Hague, Kluwer Law International, 1998) 128–32. In the first article Rosas extensively discusses the sorry history of the Member States resisting the new Association Agreement with South Africa in the late 1990s becoming a pure EC agreement, followed by extortionist antics by Italy and Greece over the protection of grappa and ouzo respectively with their ratification as a bargaining chip.

[33] See Case C-268/94 *Portugal v Council (Agreement with India)* [1996] ECR I-6207, paras 30ff, in which the Court regarded provisions on many different specific forms of cooperation, such as in the areas of energy, tourism and combating drugs, as being included in

on the international scene, even when that is strictly not justified by their remaining powers in certain domains under Union law. They are very sensitive to losing the outside signs of sovereignty in their relations to other States. On the other hand, it may create the impression that there is still a possibility of Member state responsibility for breach of certain of the treaty obligations vis-à-vis third states, where this is actually not the case. It is fairly easy to arrive at the conclusion that this is a loss-loss-loss situation for the Union, the Member States and the functioning of the international system.But how to distinguish such cases of 'false mixity' from those where Member States have important remaining powers covered by some of the treaty obligations and hence actually should discharge the responsibility for the breach of such obligations? In case of 'real mixity' the ECJ is willing to go to great lengths and look in great detail, in order to make clear where in respect of the international obligations contained in an international agreement concluded by the EU and/or the Member States the obligations of the one or the other lie.[34] However, 'false mixity' could only be detected by the ECJ in cases where the European Commission would seek an Opinion on an international agreement about to be concluded, or the annulment of a just concluded treaty, to the effect that its co-conclusion by the Member States was against the Treaty. Such cases are very rare for all kinds of legal and political reasons and concentrated mainly in the field of trade policy.[35] Insofar as 'false mixity' was created by the Member States insisting in the European Council on including political consultation clauses in international agreement, whereas the rest of the agreement was beyond doubt within the European Community's powers, this is a manifestation of 'mixity' that should disappear after the Lisbon Treaty.[36]

Another challenge results from the fast increasing internal EU legislation that has considerable international repercussions, more particularly in areas where there are many international agreements or organisations to which the EU cannot become a party, for the simple reason that belonging to such agreements or organisations is not foreseen for the EU or other international organisations in the agreement or founding treaty in question. This leads to all kinds of anomalies in international relations, including problems with respect to international responsibility. The ECJ

the broad power of development cooperation. This case seems to have been quickly forgotten in the later practice of the Council on concluding international agreements.

[34] See for a recent example Case C-366/10 *ATAA et al v Secretary of State for Energy and Climate Change* ECR I (21 December 2011), paras 57–72.

[35] See such cases as Opinion 1/94 [1994] ECR I-5267 and Opinion 1/2008 [2009] ECR I-11129.

[36] Due to the single international personality of the Union (Art 47 TEU) and to the integrated character of the Union's external action, where elements of CFSP and CSDP and former European Community external relations powers are supposed to go together (Art 21 TEU). In reality, however, Member States are insisting in the Council on continuing mixity.

has fashioned a succession theory for such treaties and organisations, that is to say that the European Community/Union can be considered to have succeeded to the rights and the obligations of its Member States under an international agreement. However, it applies only in case the entire scope of the agreement is covered either by an exclusive power of the Union, such as the common commercial policy, or by a cumulation of EU legislation in the field of shared powers of the Union.[37] If there is no succession, even though there is extensive legislation on many aspects of the matters covered by the international agreement/organisation, as was the case with respect to the Chicago Convention on Air Transport, the big question is whether nevertheless there can be Union responsibility in the areas of aviation policy covered by Union law.

The answer to that question, as given by the ECJ from the internal perspective, has been variable in the case of mixed agreements. In one case the ECJ has clearly decided that an obligation in a mixed agreement, where there is no specification whether the obligations fall upon on the Union or on the Member States, has to be fulfilled by both the Union and the Member States as a matter of joint responsibility.[38] In another case, however, the Court came to the conclusion that a Member State could be responsible under Union law for breaching a mixed agreement in area that was 'largely covered' by Union law (even if the actual breach was on a point that was not covered by Union law).[39] This would seem to indicate that the external responsibility vis-à-vis the other parties to the agreement for such a breach would be the Union's. These judgments of the ECJ, however, only determine where responsibility lies under international law to the extent that the rules of the organisation are allowed to play a role in that question.

B. Union Structure and 'Rules of the Organisation' of the ILC

As appears from Section II above on the paradoxes inherent in the structure and foreign affairs law of the EU and from Subsection A above on the internal challenges to this structure, the kind of rules of the organisation that are of great importance to the EU, where it concerns matters of international responsibility, are the rules on the structure of the EU as such and its implications for the relations between the EU and its Member States.

The ILC draft rules on the responsibility of international organisations

[37] See Joined Cases 21–24/72 *International Fruit Company v Produktschap voor Groenten en Fruit* [1972] ECR 1219, paras 14–18 and Case C-366/10 *AAA et al v Secretary of Sate for Energy and Climate Change* ECR I (21 December 2011), para 71.

[38] Case C-316/91 *Parliament v Council (EDF)* [1994] ECR I-625, paras 29–33.

[39] Case C-239/03 *Commission v France (Etang de Berre)* [2004] ECR I-9325.

refer to, and take account of, the 'rules of the organisation' in various provisions. In Article 6 the rules of the organisation are allowed to play a role in who or what are organs and agents of the organisation and thus the rules of the organisation are directly linked to the question of attribution. As has been explained elsewhere, for the Union it is particularly important whether or not its Member States can be regarded as organs or agents of the organisation when implementing Union law.[40] In Articles 22 and 52 the rules of the organisation play a limiting role in relation to countermeasures. Countermeasures by the organisation against its Members and by its Members against the organisation are possible only insofar as the rules of the organisation allow this. This is indeed important for the EU because from very early on the Court of Justice has made it plain that there is no place in the jurisdictional system of the Union for the countermeasures of general international law.[41] Similarly Article 45, without an explicit reference to the rules of the organisation, helps safeguard the jurisdictional system of the Union by accepting that exhaustion of 'local remedies' may have to take place within the organisation. Finally, for the sake of completeness, we refer to the rule that the internal law of the organisation may not be advanced as a justification for failure to comply with its obligations (Article 32), a rule that is parallel to a similar provision in the rules on state responsibility.[42]

From this brief overview it results that, apart from Article 6 and the question what is an organ or an agent whose actions can trigger the attribution of unlawful acts to the organisation, most of the articles on the rules of the organisation in the draft articles, though important for the Union, in particular for the integrity of it jurisdictional system, do not really deal with the big structural questions which are important if the Union is going to be able to fit somehow into the rules on responsibility of the ILC. It is for that reason that we now turn in greater detail to the question of attribution and the rules possibly applicable to the relationship between the Union and its Member States in the ILC rules.

[40] See E Paasivirta and PJ Kuijper, 'Does one size fit all?: The European Community and the Responsibility of International Organisations' (2005) 36 *Netherlands Yearbook of International Law* 169, 188–92. In the ILC's comments to Art 6 of the draft articles, no opening is left to regard the Member States under certain circumstances as agents of the EU and the comments to Art 64 even seem to reject it, see ILC, 'Report of the International Law Commission on the Work of its 63rd Session' (26 April-3 June and 4 July-12 August 2011) UN Doc A/66/10 and Add 1, 84–85 and 168–70, www.un.org/law/ilc/ (accessed 12 February 2012).

[41] Cases 90 and 91/63 *Commission v Luxembourg and Belgium* [1964] ECR 625, English Special Edition, 631.

[42] On the question of the relation (or confusion?) between the rules of the organisation and the internal law of the organisation, see Ahlborn, fn 6, 25–27.

IV. RESPONSIBILITY OF THE ORGANISATION: DIFFERENT ATTRIBUTION MODELS

One of the two main conditions for international responsibility consists of attribution of the acts concerned to the organisation. This is a central issue in international law for obvious reasons: the main actors are states and international organisations, both corporate bodies that necessarily act via organs and officials.

This section reviews different EU external relations configurations a bit more closely as far as relevant to issues of attribution. The EU has different operational modes and that is relevant for the external relations field including for issues of responsibility. Sometimes its mode of behaviour via its own organs can be assimilated to 'traditional' international organisations, in other instances not.

The question of attribution is a classic question of customary international law and the rules are well settled for most purposes. However, the emergence of the EU as a global actor has raised new issues in this context. These issues have also been exposed to the ILC when working on its draft articles on the responsibility of international organisations (2011).[43] While the EU's specific concerns have not been taken into account to any appreciable degree in the final articles,[44] Article 64 of the draft articles lays down a *lex specialis* rule, which indicates that there may be special rules of international law relating to the responsibility of organisations, which reflects the diversity of international organisations.

This review summarizes different models of attribution that are relevant in the case of the EU's international responsibility. These are called the 'organic model', the 'competence model' and the 'consensus model'. The aim is to capture the essential features of EU action in different fields of operation and consider the implications for purposes of responsibility and attribution.

[43] See the sources mentioned in fn 2. On attribution in particular UNGA 'Responsibility of International Organisations: Comments and Observations Received from International Organisations' (2004) UN Doc A/CN 4/545 18–25.

[44] In this the EU is not alone. For instance the IMF has insistently criticised specific aspects of the draft, notably the provisions on direction and control and aid and assistance, and the UN Office of Legal Affairs has expressed, although in a late stage of the work, very serious concerns about the little attention paid to the UN's long-standing practice in the field of peace-keeping in relation to the effective control test. See in particular UNGA 'Responsibility of International Organisations: Comments and Observations Received from International Organisations' (2011) UN Doc A/CN 4/637/Add 1. Little of this was taken into account by the ILC, whose natural constituency consists of states. Hence international organisations, as with the Vienna Convention of 1986, have been primarily the object of this exercise of codification and development of international law.

A. 'Organic Model'

By 'organic model' it is meant simply that the organisation can be shown to have been acting by its organs. In other words, the acts giving rise to claims of responsibility can be attributed to the organs of the organisation or its personnel. If this condition can be satisfied, it points in the direction of the responsibility of the organisation under international law provided other conditions for responsibility are fulfilled.

Given that corporate bodies act through organs they have created and through individuals that act for them, the question of attribution is inevitably in the forefront of issues in the context of responsibility. The practical legal needs require that rules are in place to determine how and under which conditions certain acts performed by such organs and individuals can be attributed to the body corporate. In the ILC's draft articles on the responsibility of states (2001) and the responsibility of international organisations (2011) the rules of attribution thus occupy a prominent place.

The organic approach is reflected in Article 4 of the ILC draft rules on state responsibility to identify the actors and their association with the state for determining an act of the state for purposes of state responsibility. This is a natural starting point, and it is complemented with other rules in the absence of a formal organic link with the organisation of the state. In this latter case, the actions can nevertheless be associated with the state in certain circumstances as in the case of an act of empowerment, conduct by organs placed at the disposal of a state by another state or conduct factually controlled by the state.[45]

The same approach is followed in the ILC Draft articles on the responsibility of international organisations. Thus, Article 6 of the ILC draft articles provides that the conduct of an 'organ or agent' of an international organisation shall be considered an act of the organisation and the 'rules of the organisation' apply in the determination of the functions of its organs and agents. Again, the organic approach is complemented by other rules concerning organs such as those concerning conduct by an organ which is not formally an organ of the organisation but 'placed at its disposal' and situations where conduct, while not attributable to the organisation is nevertheless 'acknowledged and adopted' as its own.[46]

Hence, the organic approach for determining the 'act of the state' or 'act of an organisation' is central in international law. That approach

[45] Arts 5–10 of the Draft Articles on Responsibility of States for Internationally Wrongful Acts, contained in the UNGA Res 56/83 (12 December 2011) UN Doc A/Res/56/83, adopted without vote.

[46] Arts 7–9 of the Draft Articles on the Responsibility of International Organisations, contained in the ILC, 'Report of the International Law Commission on the Work of its 63rd Session' (26 April–3 June and 4 July–12 August 2011) UN Doc A/66/10, 55 www.un.org/law/ilc/ (accessed 12 February 2012).

probably corresponds in large measure to the experience of lawyers anywhere in finding corresponding rules in relation to any corporate body, national or international. It also meets the practical needs for simplicity, predictability and transparency.

(i) EU Organs and Personnel

The organic model is valid for the EU when the organisation acts via its very own organs. When the relevant conduct consists of direct practical management at EU level, the organic model covers the situation. For instance, decisions on authorisation of state aid or management of competition by the EU institutions can at least in certain circumstances be attributed to the EU along organic lines. The organic model assumes that the organ concerned has a position in the organisation and can take decisions on its behalf, or that the individuals whose acts are concerned are officials of the organisation or are otherwise authorized to act on its behalf.

A variety of organs can act on behalf of the EU, including the seven main 'institutions' of the EU established by the Treaty of the European Union.[47] The list includes the European Commission, Council, Parliament and Court. The issue is reflected through the text of the Charter of Fundamental Rights, which is made a part of the EU Treaties. In specifying its field of application, Article 51 of the Charter provides that its rules are addressed to the 'institutions, bodies, offices and agencies of the Union' as well as to the Member States, but only when they are implementing Union law. In addition to the 'institutions', the Charter is addressed to other 'bodies, offices and agencies'. This phrase is used in certain provisions of the Treaties. Such bodies, offices and agencies are normally established by acts of EU secondary legislation.[48] Thus, the internal EU rules show that there exist 'institutions' and a variety of other 'bodies, offices and agencies', all of which can be considered organs of the EU for international law purposes.[49] Hence, to the extent the EU is a bearer of international

[47] Art 13 TEU.

[48] Eg Arts 15 and 16 TFEU. See Explanations relating to the Charter of Fundamental Rights [2007] OJ C303/17, 32.

[49] Ultimately this depends on the interpretation of the term 'organ' in international law. The starting point in Art 2(c) of the ILC Draft Articles is the status that any person or entity has in accordance with the rules of the organisation. In its commentary on Art 6, the ILC makes the point that the rules of the organisation are not the only criterion in this regard. See draft Arts on the responsibility of international organisations, with commentaries: ILC, 'Report of the International Law Commission on the Work of its 63rd Session' (26 April–3 June and 4 July–12 August 2011) UN Doc A/66/10, *Yearbook of the International Law Commission* (2011), paras 1–11. In the EU treaties, the phrase 'bodies, offices and agencies', appears in some contexts, eg in Art 263 TFEU (annulment proceedings), but not for instance in Art 340 (non-contractual liability). However, jurisprudence regarding the latter has extended the Union's liability to actions attributable to its 'institution or body'. See, eg Case C-234/02P *European Ombudsman v Frank Lamberts* [2004] ECR I-2803, para 59;

obligations, the acts performed by these organs can be considered as acts of the organisation for purposes of responsibility. Similarly the acts of its officials and other servants can cause the EU's international responsibility.

In this context, one may also note the High Representative for Foreign and Security Policy and the new European External Action Service (EEAS), which are novelties established by the Lisbon Treaty.[50] The High Representative can without doubt be considered as an official of the Union under international law. As regards the EEAS, this is a functionally autonomous body supporting the High Representative and consists of permanent officials as well as temporary officials seconded by the diplomatic services of the EU member states. Again, there is no doubt that the latter act as officials for international law purposes.[51]

The EEAS consists of the central administration and the EU Delegations. The latter represent the EU in third countries and international organisations.[52] In terms of internal organisation, these diplomatic missions act under the authority of the High Representative[53] and they form part of the EEAS.[54] Thus any acts performed by EU Delegations can be considered as 'EU acts' in a similar fashion as acts of diplomatic missions of states.

(ii) The EU's CSDP Missions

The Lisbon Treaty has created a single legal personality for EU activities in their entirety, and replacing the former 'three pillar' structure of the Union. This new legal personality of the Union covers inter alia the Union's activities in the framework of the common foreign and security policy, including CSDP (the Common Security Defence Policy) crisis management missions. A legal personality implies a capacity for responsibility, including for activities that in the past remained the responsibility of the Member States.[55]

see also P Aalto, *Public Liability in EU Law* (Oxford, Hart Publishing, 2011) 105, who states: 'From an organic point of view, the liability of the Union covers all Union institutions and bodies'.

[50] Arts 18 and 27 TEU.

[51] A number of adjustments had to be introduced to the Staff Regulations following the establishment of the EEAS. They provide inter alia that the EEAS is treated as an institution of the Union for the purposes of the Staff Regulations and that the officials of the Union and the temporary agents have the same rights and obligations. See Regulation (EU, EURATOM) No 1080/2010 of the European Parliament and of the European Council of 24 November 2010 amending the Staff Regulations of Officials of the European Communities and the Conditions of Employment of Other Servants of those Communities [2010] OJ L311/1, 1.

[52] Art 221(1) TFEU. See also fn 9.

[53] Art 221(2) TFEU.

[54] Art 1(4) of the Council Decision 2010/427/EU of 26 July 2010 establishing the organisation and functioning of the European External Action Service [2010] OJ L201/30, 30.

[55] *Cf* a pre-Lisbon description by the ECtHR in *SEGI and Gestoras Pro-Amnistia v 15 states of the European Union* App no 6422/02 and 9916/02 admissibility decision (EctHR, 23 May 2002), B.1: 'CFSP decisions are therefore intergovernmental in nature. By taking

At the same time, the number of CSDP missions has grown. There have been over 20 CSDP missions in third countries, covering both military and civilian crisis management aspects.[56] Such missions in the world's crisis areas inevitably imply a heightened risk for casualty, loss and damage. This can raise issues of the Union's international responsibility.

Some of the CSDP missions have been military missions, such as those conducted in FYROM ('CONCORDIA'), Democratic Republic of Congo ('ARTEMIS' and 'EUFOR RD Congo'), Bosnia and Herzegovina ('ALTHEA'), Tchad and Central African Republic ('EUFOR Tchad/RCA') and Somalia ('EU NAVCO', 'EUNAVFOR Somalia/ATALANTA'). There has also been one mixed military/civilian mission in Sudan ('AMIS II Support Mission'). Such missions pose similar issues as in the case of UN peacekeeping operations. In neither case does the organisation have standing military forces at its disposal. Instead, both the UN and the EU depends on states contributing forces to their operations.

In the case of the UN the central question has been whether the acts of the military forces should be attributed to the UN or to the states contributing troops to the operations. These are issues that will be determined on a case-by-case basis depending on who exercises 'effective control' over the operations of the troops.[57] In practice the dividing line for determining responsibility has been who maintains operational command and control, the organisation or the troops contributing states.

The EU military operations raise similar issues. Following from the establishment of the single EU legal personality, the acts of such CSDP missions can under certain conditions be attributed to the EU. The EU does not have a standing military command structure and headquarters in place.[58] The Political and Security Committee (PSC), acting under the responsibility of the European Council and the High Representative, exercises political control and strategic direction in crisis management

part in their preparation and adoption each State engages its responsibility. That responsibility is assumed jointly by the States when they adopt a CFSP decision'.

[56] For a comprehensive review of 22 such missions (as of August 2009), see F Naert, *International Law Aspects of the EU's Security and Defence Policy* (Antwerp, Intersentia, 2010) 97–191. For latest information, see www.consilium.europa.eu/eeas/security-defence/eu-operations?lang=en.

[57] KC Wellens, *Remedies against International Organisations* (Cambridge, Cambridge University Press, 2002) 52.

[58] The EU Military Committee (EUMC) is a permanent body, but it is not in the chain of command of CSDP military operations. It monitors the execution of such operations and receives reports from the Operation Commander. The Chairman of the EUMC is the primary point of contact for the Operation Commander. See Council Decision 2001/79/CFSP of 22 January 2001 setting up the Military Committee of the European Union [2001] OJ L27/4. The EU Military Staff (EUMS) provides military expertise to EU bodies as directed by the EUMS. See Council Decision 2008/298/CFSP of 7 April 2008 amending Decision 2001/80/CFSP on the establishment of the Military Staff of the European Union [2008] OJ L102/25.

operations (Article 38 TEU). The arrangements for the military command of the operations are done on an ad hoc basis.[59]

The CSDP operations generally have a status independent of the participating states, acting under the command and control of EU bodies. And yet it is not always clear under what circumstances they engage the Union and/or the Member States. It has been considered that, since a significant degree of authority over the national contingents is transferred to the EU operation, as established in the operation plan and the rules of engagement, it exercises effective control through the Council and the PSC and, in particular, through the Operation and Force Commanders.[60]

The effective control test is generally accepted in international law in the context of military operations, while it has been given different interpretations in recent judicial practice.[61] In particular, the ECtHR's decision in *Behrami and Saramati,* concerning troops in Kosovo placed at the disposal of the UN, has been subject to much debate.[62] In that case, the ECtHR used a rather different notion of effective control test than is normal as it attributed the actions of the NATO led forces in Kosovo to the UN, apparently relying in fact on political rather than effective operational control ('ultimate authority and control') as the relevant test. However, the ECtHR seems to have returned to a more traditional effective control test in the *Al Jedda* case.[63]

The effective control test is also reflected Article 7 of the ILC draft articles on the responsibility of international organisations. Phrased in general terms, it refers to states placing their organs or agents 'at the disposal of an international organisation'. It is clear from the commentary that it is inspired by issues relating to military operations and approves the effective control test as the criterion for determining attribution in the

[59] Naert (fn 56) 61–62. For command and control arrangements in military CSDP operations, see Council Doc 11096/03 EXT 1 (26 July 2006, a partially declassified version), 6–7 and 15–16: www.register.consilium.europa.eu. In this document, Operational Control (OPCON) is defined as 'The authority granted to a commander to direct forces assigned, so that the commander may accomplish specific missions or tasks which are usually limited by function, time or location; to deploy units concerned and to retain or assign tactical control of those units. It does not include authority to assign separate employment of components of the units concerned. Neither does it of itself, include administrative or logistic responsibility'.

[60] Naert (fn 56) 515–16.

[61] Nevertheless the Office of Legal Affairs of the UN complained that the effective control test, as drafted by the ILC, did not take into account the standing practice of the UN, which in its view the UN had never applied, since Member State troops placed at the disposal of the UN were normally 'transformed' into a UN subsidiary organ and in that quality automatically triggered the responsibility of the UN by their actions. See UN doc. A/CN.4/637/Add 1, Comments to Article 6 (the later Art 7). It is likely that the UN peacekeeping operations will continue to function on this basis. Obviously the situation in respect of Security Council 'authorized' peace-keeping actions is different.

[62] In Joined Cases *Behrami and Behrami v France and Saramati v France, Germany and Norway* App no 71412/01 and 78166/01 (ECtHR, 2 May 2007).

[63] *Al-Jedda v UK* App no 27021/08 (7 July 2011), paras 84–86.

absence of agreements to the contrary. This test, however, is unlikely to be applicable to UN peace-keeping operations in future.[64]

There would seem to be no reason why the EU in the context of military operations would necessarily require a radically different approach from the UN peace-keeping as both operate on the basis of troops that states have made available to them. However, the EU does not, like the UN, so far turn its police or military operations into subsidiary organs and may feel more comfortable with the 'effective control' test.

The 'organic model' applies to acts consisting of decisions or acts of the organs of the organisation or its agents or servants. It is probably a satisfactory approach to the EU to the extent that the practical management of the operation takes place at the level of the organisation.

However, the 'organic model' of attribution is unsatisfactory insofar as the EU's acts in a 'vertical mode', ie the case where the EU acts are carried out via the authorities of its Member States, instead of the EU itself having its own administrative presence in its Member States. This is in fact the EU's normal practice, which falls basically in the TFEU context rather than in the CFSP context. In that situation the 'organic model' does not capture the core features of the EU action, since the Member States are seen as remaining sovereign and not constituting organs of the organisation in a formal sense. Consequently, the Member States would always be responsible, as the immediate actors, should acts be attributed on purely organic lines. The fact that normative decisions are taken at the EU level (Council, Parliament) and on the basis of a proposal by an independent institution (Commission) is basically ignored. This is not a satisfactory outcome. It is also out of tune with the fact that the EU is a recognized global actor, alongside states, all across the 'civil' areas falling under the TFEU.

B. 'Competence Model'

The 'competence model' tries to satisfy the central operational features of EU legal system based on 'executive federalism'. This approach responds to the core of EU activities in the internal market, where the operational acts of the EU, regulations and directives, are implemented by the Member States.

According to the 'competence model' the responsibility should basically lie where the competence is. The act constituting a violation should be attributed, accordingly, either to the organisation or to the Member States.

It is assumed here that the substantive obligations are 'open textured':

[64] ILC, 'Seventh Report on Responsibility of International Organisations by Georgio Gaja, Special Rapporteur' (4 May-5 June and 6 July-7 August 2009) UN Doc A/CN.4/610, paras 25–30. On the UN's likely recourse to this provision, see n 59.

they can in principle apply to both the Union and the Member States. The most usual case is that of mixed agreements, to which both the organisation and the Member States are parties.

There are good legal reasons speaking in favour of the competence model. Under the TFEU the Member States cannot choose whether or not to apply EU law instruments as they are legally bound by them. The competence for such decisions is at the EU level. Furthermore, if decisions are taken at the EU level, a EU Member State cannot provide for restitution, ie to re-establish the situation that existed before the wrongful act was committed.[65] This is especially so when it is a question of 'juridical restitution' which would require annulment of the provisions concerned.[66] In such circumstances, only the EU institutions as competent decision-makers would be in a position to provide for the necessary restitution.

In the competence model the responsible 'organ' or 'agent' can be verified by different means. Basically, it is the duty of the EU to make clear who is responsible for its acts. This may be done by way of declarations of competence, sometimes attached to international agreements, or it can also be done by other means of communication.

In practice, the competence can also be derived from EU legislation or other acts of the organisation. They are implemented by the Member States and they define the scope of Member State action. The EU legislation sets out the basis for the assessment of the legality of the Member States' action and that it is ultimately controlled by the EU judiciary. Therefore, in such situations the Member States act under the 'normative control' of the EU.[67]

The normative control includes the idea that it is the EU rather than the Member State concerned which can remedy the alleged wrongs. In case of restitution, the primary remedy of international law, this may require legislative action by way of withdrawal of acts or their amendment, and this may lie within the EU competence.

(i) The International Practice of Making Declarations of Competence

Chronologically speaking, the so-called declarations of competence which the EU often makes in the context of multilateral treaties is the first

[65] *Cf* Art 35 Draft Articles on Responsibility of States for Internationally Wrongful Acts.

[66] *Cf* the respective commentary on Art 35 Draft Articles on Responsibility of States for Internationally Wrongful Acts: ILC, 'Report of the International Law Commission on the Work of its 53rd Session (23 April-1 June and 2 July-10 August 2010) UN Doc A/56/10 *Yearbook of the International Law Commission* 2001 vol II Part Two, 96–97.

[67] F Hoffmeister, 'Litigating against the European Union and Its Member States—Who Responds under the ILC's Draft Articles on International Responsibility of International Organisations?' (2010) 21 *European Journal of International Law* 723, 741; A Delgado-Casteleiro, 'The International Responsibility of the European Union: From Competence to Normative Control' (PhD thesis, European University Institute, 2011).

practical indication of a need to focus on normative competences of the organisation in the context of determining international responsibility.

The UN Convention on the Law of the Sea (UNCLOS) is the best known example in this context as it was the first multilateral agreement where the EU made a declaration of competence.[68] It is specified that also in case of new transfers of competence such communications should be made to the others.[69] Moreover, UNCLOS provides that as regards competences which have not been specifically declared it is presumed that the members of the organisation have retained their competence to act.[70]

Since first made in the UNCLOS framework, the EU has made specific declarations of competence several times when adhering to multilateral agreements. Most recently this was made in the context of the Agreement on Port State measures to Prevent, Deter and Eliminate Illegal, Unreported and Unregulated Fishing (2009).[71]

It may be noted that declarations of competence in the context of multilateral agreements may serve different purposes, and are not only made in consideration of possible future breaches and their consequences for international responsibility. Simply, it is relevant to know and to understand during normal international cooperation how and by whom the obligations are to be carried out. The drafting of these declarations may vary and indeed over time they may lose some of their technical accuracy because of the evolutionary development of the exclusive external powers of the EU, which follow the expansion or contraction of internal EU legislation.[72]

An essential point to be made here is that a declaration of competence constitutes a communication from the EU side to other treaty partners and it is made in order to clarify the respective competences of the organisation and its Member States. It remains, of course, for the EU to provide further clarification and information as necessary. Thus, while the obligation to make such a declaration is normally based on a

[68] Council Decision 98/392/EC of 23 March 1998 concerning the conclusion by the European Community of the United Nations Convention of 10 December 1982 on the Law of the Sea and the Agreement of 28 July 1994 relating to the implementation of Part XI thereof [1998] OJ L179/1, 1. The declaration of competence is published in [1997] OJ C155/1, 126–31 (Annex 3 to Commission (EC), 'Proposal for a Council Decision concerning the conclusion by the European Community of the United Nations Convention of 10 December 1982 on the Law of the Sea and the Agreement of 28 July 1994 on the application of Part XI thereof' COM(97) 37 final, 27 February 1997).

[69] Art 5(4) of Annex IX.

[70] Art 5(3) of Annex IX.

[71] Interestingly, in this case it was question of an 'EU only' agreement where its Member States are not parties. The Declaration concerning the competence of the European Union with regard to matters governed by the Agreement on Port State Measures to Prevent, Deter and Eliminate Illegal, Unreported and Unregulated Fishing [2011] OJ L191/3, 18 states simply, in point 4(i), that the Union 'has competence over all the matters governed by the Agreement'. For earlier practice, see Paasivirta and Kuijper, above n 40, 169, 209–10.

[72] See Art 3(2) TFEU.

treaty, the declarations as such should not be assimilated to treaty provisions. They are unilateral communications, which no doubt have legal effects, but which, as UNCLOS makes clear, may develop over time and be revised over time.[73]

On the other hand, there is a large number of international agreements where the EU is a contracting party alongside its Member States, but which do not contain any specific declaration of competence. For instance no such declaration of competence has been made in the case of the WTO, while for the EU it is a mixed agreement with participation of both the EU and the Member States. This depends largely on whether the other contracting parties request for it. It may or may not be important and, if it is, it usually forms part of negotiations.

It is clear that once a declaration of competence exists, it is relevant for determination of the proper respondent party in case of alleged breaches of obligations. However, this does not exclude supplementary information, given the dynamic nature of the EU competences.

It is not obvious that the situation where a declaration of competence has been made is unique as compared to the situation where no such declaration has been made. If such declarations are understood in terms of communication, it is arguable that a duty to inform of the competences flows from the moment the organisation enters into international cooperation with third states. In other words, one could postulate a good faith 'duty of cooperation', a rule that has its analogies in EU law.[74]

Clearly there is scope for different views in cases where such declarations of competences do not exist.[75] However, it depends ultimately whether there is a special rule of international law, which makes the competence a relevant criterion for purposes of responsibility. There are indications that point to that direction. Some authority for this proposition can be drawn from international treaty practice (Section V) taken as a whole as well as from the WTO dispute settlement practice (Subsection iii) discussed further below.

[73] See Art 5(4) of Annex IX of UNCLOS.

[74] It is well-known that the basic rule of good faith covers the negotiation, the conclusion, the performance and the interpretation of treaties, see inter alia Arts 18, 26 and 31 VCLT. For the enhanced good faith obligation, see the duty of sincere cooperation now laid down in Art 4(3) TEU and developed in numerous judgments of the ECJ. See also JT Lang, 'The Development by the Court of Justice of the Duties of Cooperation of National Authorities and Community Institutions under Article 10 EC' (2008) 31 *Fordham International Law Journal* 1483.

[75] See, eg P Eeckhout, *EU External Relations Law*, 2nd edn (Oxford, Oxford University Press, 2011) at 264, who suggests that other contracting parties appear to have the right to focus on the question of attribution of conduct under international law, rather than the internal division of competences between the EU and its Member States.

(ii) Internal EU Law Viewpoint

The basic rule of the EU—Article 13(2) of TEU—is that it acts on public powers conferred from its member states and that these public powers (competences) are limited.

The picture given by the Court of Justice in 1964 in *Costa v Enel*[76] still holds currency:

> By contrast with ordinary international treaties, the EEC treaty has created its own legal system which, on the entry into force of the treaty, became an integral part of the legal systems of the member states and which their courts are bound to apply. By creating a community of unlimited duration, having its own institutions, its own personality, its own legal capacity and capacity of representation on the international plane and, more particularly, real powers stemming from a limitation of sovereignty or a transfer of powers from the states to the community, the member states have limited their sovereign rights, albeit within limited fields, and have thus created a body of law which binds both their nationals and themselves.

Following the Lisbon Treaty, the nature of public powers is defined in Articles 2–6 TFEU. They consist of exclusive, shared and parallel competences.

The Union has explicit exclusive powers in areas of the customs union, competition, monetary policy for the Member States whose currency is the euro, the conservation of marine biological resources and common commercial policy.[77] In addition, the EU has exclusive competence for the conclusion of an international agreement when its conclusion is provided for in a legislative act of the Union or is necessary to enable the Union to exercise its internal competence or in so far as its conclusion may affect common rules or alter their scope.[78] In these cases it is only for the Union to legislate and adopt legally binding acts such as international agreements.[79]

The Union shares its competences with the Member States in a large number of areas, including areas such as internal market, agriculture, transport and environment policy. In the areas of shared competences both the Union and the member states may legislate and adopt legally binding acts. It is important to note, however, that the Member States shall exercise their competence only to the extent that the Union has not exercised its competence.[80]

The Union and the Member States have parallel competences in areas such as research, development cooperation and humanitarian aid. In these

[76] Case 6/64 *Costa v ENEL* [1964] ECR English special edition 585.

[77] Art 3(1) TFEU.

[78] Art 3(2) TFEU.

[79] Art 2(1) TFEU.

[80] Art 2(2) TFEU.

areas the exercise of the Union competence shall not result in Member States being prevented from exercising theirs.[81]

From the EU law viewpoint, responsibility should correspond to competence; these are two sides of the same thing. It is clear that in areas of exclusive competence the Union should be responsible even if the implementing acts are carried out by the Member States. It is also clear that in the area of parallel competences such as development cooperation, both the Union and the Member States may be responsible, unless an international agreement indicates otherwise.[82]

The area of shared competences is more complex. The area of shared competences is dynamic in the sense that it requires verification whether the EU has exercised its competence. If so, the Member States are to the same extent excluded from exercising their competence. Thus, developing legislation may turn shared competence areas into areas of exclusive Union competence.

Moreover, even if the Union has not fully exercised its competence in an area of shared competences the Union may have a legal interest in the matter. In practice, this can arise in the context of a mixed agreement, since the Union's international commitments are 'binding on the institutions of the Union and its Member States'.[83] This gives for instance the Commission the basis to initiate infringement proceedings if necessary to deter any violations of the Union's international commitments by Member States action or inaction.

Commission v Ireland[84] involved a commitment taken under the EEA Agreement to accede to the Bern Convention for the Protection of Literary and Artistic Works, which Ireland had failed to do. After noting that the protection of literary and artistic works is to a great extent governed by EU legislation, the Court of Justice stated:

> The Berne Convention thus creates rights and obligations in areas covered by Community law. That being so, there is a Community interest in ensuring that all contracting parties to the EEA Agreement adhere to that Convention.
>
> It follows that the requirement of adherence to the Berne Convention which Article 5 of Protocol 28 to the EEA Agreement imposes on the contracting parties comes within the Community framework, given that it features in a mixed agreement concluded by the Community and its Member States and relates to an area covered in large measure by the Treaty. The Commission is thus competence to assess compliance with that requirement, subject to review by the Court.

[81] Arts 4(3) and (4) TFEU.

[82] Case C-316/91 *Parliament v Council (EDF)* [1994] ECR I-625. Opinion of AG Jacobs, paras 67–69.

[83] Art 216(2) TFEU.

[84] Case C-13/00 *Commission v Ireland* [2002] ECR I-2955, paras 19–20.

In *Commission v France (Etang de Berre)* similar considerations are reflected. This case concerned environmental pollution of a marsh resulting from the operation of an electric power plant in France. Such pollution from land was covered by the Barcelona Convention and the related Protocol for the Protection of the Mediterranean Sea against pollution from land-based sources. It is a mixed agreement where both Member States and the Union are parties. In establishing its jurisdiction the Court made the link between internal compliance and external compliance by stating as follows:

> Since the Convention and the Protocol thus created rights and obligations in a field covered in large measure by Community legislation, there is a Community interest in compliance by both the Community and its Member States with the commitments entered into under those instruments.[85]

The above cases illustrate that a recognized legal interest can be attached to the Union even if Union legislation has not fully covered the field. Furthermore, the Union law does not distinguish the acts of the Member States from the Union interest itself. This reflects a 'vertical' view of the Union's actions, making it quite different from international law structured on more organically based lines.

(iii) WTO Dispute Settlement Practice

The competence related ideas described above are reflected in the WTO practice, though not in an entirely consistent manner.

The *Local Area Network* (*LAN*) case gave the first signs in going some way in the direction of giving effect to the 'vertical' structure of the EU system in the context of the implementation of the EU acts by the national customs authorities.[86] The case was first brought by the US against the EU and Ireland and the UK, but the claims were later merged. In this case, relating to tariff treatments of computer equipment, the EU took the position that the acts should be attributed to the organisation itself and emphasized its readiness to assume responsibility for the measures.[87] These views are reflected in the panel report inter alia recognizing the EU customs union. The EU was held solely responsible, but it is not entirely clear whether the EU responsibility was adopted on the basis that the Member States were acting as the agents of the organisation in a field of its exclusive competence (referring to 'customs authorities in the EC,

[85] Case C-239/03 *Commission v France (Etang de Berre)* [2004] ECR I-9325, para 29.

[86] WTO, 'European Communities: Customs Classification of Certain Computer Equipment. Report of the Panel' (22 June 1998), WT/DS62/R, WT/DS67/R, WT/DS68/R.

[87] Ibid, para 4.14.

including those located in Ireland and the UK')[88] or on the basis that the EU had adopted the acts as its own.

The *Selected Customs Matters* case gives further effect to an approach based on executive federalism.[89] It was brought by the US against the EU alone, complaining that the EU Customs Tariff, Customs Code and related implementing regulation were applied in a non-uniform manner (GATT Article X:3(a)). Furthermore, the US argued that the EU did not provide for a prompt review mechanism in customs matters as required (GATT Article X:3(b)). The claims were mostly rejected. This case raised central issues concerning the design and structure of the EU legal order, including the customs administration within the EU. In this regard, the EU Commission explained to the Panel that Union law is implemented by the authorities of the Member States. The EU law principles of primacy and direct effect bind on the administrations of the EU Member States. Moreover, when implementing the EU law the Member States acted under the duty of loyal cooperation. Moreover, the EU judicial system normally functions to ensure legal uniformity. It is the function of the Commission to act as the 'guardian of the Treaty' which permits it to initiate infringements procedures.[90]

The WTO panel accepted the view that the Member States acted as 'agents' of the EU when implementing EU customs measures:

> [T]he panel concludes that the authorities in the Member States—including customs authorities designated for that purpose by the Member States and independent bodies, such as a judicial authority or an equivalent specialized body –act as organs of the European Communities when they review and correct administrative actions taken pursuant to EC customs law.[91]

This case shows the readiness of the WTO panels to accept EU responsibility in situations where the Member States act in a vertical relationship to the EU in a core EU law area where it has exclusive competence. In the *EC-Geographic Indications* case[92] a similar approach was followed with regard to the treatment of geographic indications under the TRIPS Agreement. In this case, the US complaint for a violation of MFN treatment was rejected in relation to an EU-wide system of protection of geographic indications that the Member States were implementing. The panel accepted that the authorities of the Member States were acting de

88 Ibid, para 8.16.

89 WTO, 'European Communities: Selected Customs Matters. Report of the Panel' (16 June 2006), WT/DS315/R. Modified by the Appellate Body: WTO, 'European Communities: Selected Customs Matters. Report of the Appellate Body' (13 November 2006), WT/DS315/AB/R.

90 Ibid, paras 4.73–4.79.

91 Ibid, para 7.553.

92 WTO, 'European Communities: Protection of Trademarks and Geographical Indications for Agricultural Products and Foodstuffs. Report of the Panel' (15 March 2005), WT/DS 174R.

facto as organs of the Union and considered this as part of the Union's constitutional arrangements.[93]

The Union responsibility for the acts of its Member States in situations where the Member States act functionally as EU organs is by now widely accepted in the WTO practice.

In addition, the Union's responsibility has extended to situations where Member States use national measures, but this takes place in the framework of Union law. The *Biotech* dispute illustrates this situation.[94] It was a case brought against the EU alone while involving use of national safeguard measures permitted under the relevant EU directive concerning imports of genetically modified products. The Panel did not enter into further discussion on this point, but went on stating that, since the EU did not contest the case brought against it despite the measures of national origin, 'the measures are attributable to it under international law and hence can be considered EU measures'.[95] Similar approach had earlier been followed in the *Asbestos* case, involving a French decree banning asbestos, but where the EU legislation had envisaged the possibility of such measures.[96] Thus, in both cases EU responsibility was confirmed as the national measures fell within an area where EU had already legislated.

On the other hand, the *Airbus* case[97] seems to draw a line to the Union's responsibility for acts of the Member States. This case was brought by the US against the EU and four Member States (Germany, France, Spain, UK) which had all granted, separately and in parallel, subsidies to the European aerospace industry. For the Union itself this was considered a project of common European interest and was thus benefitting from support from its framework programmes and via the European Investment Bank. Some of these subsidies were found to be inconsistent with the Subsidies and Countervailing Measures Agreement, but the Appellate Body reduced their scale significantly. The EU acted throughout the dispute both for itself and its Member States, and it was ready to assume responsibility alone. However, the panel ruled on the question of the proper respondent that the fact that the four Members were EU Member States did not affect their status as WTO Members. It stated that whatever the responsibility the EU bears for the actions of its Member States, it does not diminish the rights and obligations of the Member States as WTO Members,

[93] Ibid, paras 7.97–7.98.

[94] WTO, 'European Communities: Measures Affecting the Approval and marketing of Biotech Products. Report of the Panel' (29 September 2006), WT/DS291/R, WT/DS292/R, WT, DS293/R.29.

[95] Ibid, para 7.101.

[96] Ibid, paras 3.33–3.34.

[97] WTO, 'European Communities and certain Member States: Measures Affecting Trade in Large Civil Aircraft. Report of the Panel' (30 June 2010), WT/DS316/R.

but the relationship between the EU and its Member States is rather an internal matter.[98]

The Panel takes a somewhat different approach from the WTO precedents mentioned above, which by the way were not discussed in this context either by the Panel or the parties. One explanation may be that in the earlier cases it was clearly a question of the Member States implementing an EU act or the national act involved otherwise fell within the scope of EU law. The fact that the matter concerned separate and parallel subsidies granted both by the Union and the Member States probably goes some way to explain the approach. It also seems that the subsidies granted by the Member States were not subject to a specific EU authorisation.[99]

From the viewpoint of the WTO Members, one may also say that the fact that two subsidies were granted in parallel highlights that there are two origins of the problem and thus it calls for two parallel remedies. On the other hand, when it is clear that the remedy is best offered by the organisation rather than the Member State concerned, it alone is the likely target and indeed the most suited target by all.

In general, the WTO practice has gone a long way in the direction of attributing the acts of the Member States to the EU, in particular when the Member States implement the EU law or when their acts fall within the scope of EU legislation. In those situations the EU is also in the best position to remedy the situation.

The WTO practice demonstrates that the competence based responsibility is not only about specific declarations made at the time of adhering to an international agreement. The competence goes beyond and extends to issues of remedies. The practical legal question is who, the organisation or the Member States, is in the best position to provide a remedy.[100] This applies with particular force to restitution as the primary remedy in international law. This aspect should inevitably influence the development of law in this area.

C. 'Consensus Model'

Joint responsibility can be established in international agreements in which both the EU and its Member States participate, and it can come in different forms and contexts.

Article 6 of UNCLOS provides that if the organisation or its Member

[98] Ibid, paras 7.174–7.175.

[99] Delgado Casteleiro (fn 67) 220. Due to the differences between EU state aid rules and the WTO rules on subsidies, EU Member States can escape EU control under the state aid rules while the measures may raise issue of conformity under the WTO rules. G Luengo Hernández de Madrid, 'Conflicts Between the disciplines of EC State Aids and WTO Subsidies: Of Books, Ships and Aircraft' (2008) 13 *European Foreign Affairs Review* 1, 19.

[100] Hoffmeister, above n 67, 745.

States fail to provide information in reasonable time as to who is responsible in respect of any specific matter, such failure will result in joint and several liability. Thus, joint responsibility follows the failure to inform as a secondary form of responsibility.

Joint responsibility may be the intended option, especially in bilateral association agreements, where the EU side acts as a group vis-à-vis a single third state or a regional group of states. Association agreements involve close political cooperation. Such agreements may also contain terms which relate different obligations to different forms of responsibility. Typically, this is then reflected in the definition of the term 'party' in the agreement. Many of these agreements define it in the following terms:[101] 'the "party" means country X and either the Union or its Member States or the Union and its Member States, in accordance with their respective competences'. Such clauses indicate that certain obligations of the agreement are subject to joint responsibility of the EU and its Member States.

The intent of the parties is reflected in *Parliament v Council*,[102] an inter-institutional dispute within the EU dealing with the correct budgetary procedures. In this case, it was question of the funding of the Cotonou Convention, concluded between the Union and the Member States, of the one part, and the ACP States, 'of the other part'. The ECJ held that in such cases the Union and the Member States are jointly responsible vis-à-vis the other side for the implementation of all obligations resulting from agreement, 'in the absence of derogations expressly laid down by the Convention'.[103] The Court concluded that 'in accordance with the essentially bilateral character of the cooperation' the obligation to grant the Union financial assistance fell on the Union and the Member States considered together.[104] This coincides with the parallel competences like that of development cooperation (Article 4(4) TFEU).

One may also point to the still on-going negotiations of the EU accession to the European Human Rights Convention, which seek to establish a 'co-respondent mechanism' under certain conditions.[105] Thus, the draft accession agreement provides that when an application is notified against

[101] See, eg Art 131 of the EU-Albania Agreement, Council and Commission Decision 2009/332/EC of 26 February 2009 concerning the conclusion of the Stabilisation and Association Agreement between the European Communities and their Member States, of the one part, and the Republic of Albania, of the other part [2009] OJ L107/165, 197; Art 92 of the EU-Morocco Agreement. Council and Commission Decision 2000/204/EC of 24 January 2000 on the conclusion of the Euro-Mediterranean Agreement establishing an association between the European Communities and their Member States, of the one part, and the Kingdom of Morocco, of the other part [2000] OJ L70/1.

[102] Case C-316/91 *Parliament v Council (EDF)* [1994] ECR I-625.

[103] Ibid, para 29.

[104] Ibid, para 33.

[105] Council of Europe 8th Working Meeting of the CDDH Informal Working Group on Accession of the EU to the ECHR (CDDH-UE) 'Draft legal instruments on the accession of the European Union to the European Convention on Human Rights' (19 July 2011) CDDH-UE (2011) 16.

one or more member states, the Union may become a co-respondent if it appears that the alleged violation of the Convention calls into question a 'provision of European Union law' (new Article 36(2)). This meets the situation where the Member States are implementing Union legislation. The draft accession agreement also envisages the situation where an application is notified against the Union, while the Member States become a co-respondent where the alleged violation of the Convention calls into question provisions of the founding treaties, or other provisions of primary law.

The co-respondent mechanism would be triggered by the contracting party itself at its own request. Following such request the Court would assess whether in the light of the given reasons, it is plausible that the conditions are fulfilled. In that case the co-respondent also becomes a 'party to the case' and thus normally jointly responsible, unless the respondent and co-respondent jointly ask the Court to attribute the violation only to one of them.

The draft accession agreement of the EU to the ECHR would thus allow applications against the EU Member States when implementing EU Acts, but leaves it open for the EU to become a co-respondent at its own request. This would leave room for certain adaptations as to how responsibility is put into effect while maintaining joint responsibility towards the applicant.

It remains to be seen whether the mechanism of co-respondents will reflect a more general trend. So far this is not the case, as the declarations of competence would limit joint responsibility to at most a default option.

Perhaps the reason for a co-respondent system in the case of the ECHR is the outcome, first, of the fact that the human rights are a 'qualitative' yardstick relevant to all areas of law and, second, of the need to have a simple solution which avoids ECtHR making determinations on the internal EU competence divisions.

D. Responsibility of an EU Member State as the 'Immediate Actor'

An alternative approach to attribution would focus on the 'immediate actor'. This approach has its obvious appeal, at least at first sight, in particular as it falls within traditional contours of international law. That leaves only two options open. Either the international obligations are carried out by 'institutions' or by 'organs' of an international organisation or they are carried out by states. The state-centred structures of international law make it difficult to capture the EU realities of implementation, not by its own organs but by the authorities of the Member States.

This approach is reflected in the practice of the ECtHR, but not in a wholly convincing manner. The ECtHR judgement in *Bosphorus* can be mentioned in this context.[106] This case involved an EU Regulation implementing the UNSC sanctions against Iraq, which led to impoundment of an airplane in Ireland. This corresponds to the standard practice how UNSC sanctions are implemented in the EU. The EU acts on behalf of the Member States, and it is the EU legislator which adopts a regulation, which is then directly applicable in the Member States without transforming national legislation. However, in *Bosphorus* a case was brought against Ireland under the European Convention of Human Rights, to which it is a contracting party, while the Union is not. The ECtHR attributed the acts concerned to Ireland, an EU member state, but this did not lead to its responsibility under the Convention, and indeed any concrete examination of potential violation.[107] The Court took a rather limited approach to the substance, basing itself on the assumption that there exist 'equivalent' standards of human rights protection within the EU and the framework of the Convention and concluded that that presumption had not been rebutted.

While the *Bosphorus* case is often mentioned in drawing the lines between the responsibility of the EU and its Member States, it is not a particularly illustrative example of attribution issues. It did not address an 'open textured' situation: there was no option for considering whether the substantive obligations at stake could apply either to the EU or its Member States. The Convention applied only to the Member States as only they were the contracting parties, and not the Union. Thus the attribution to a Member State was the only practical alternative, otherwise the case would have been inadmissible, a questionable choice of legal policy in a purely European context.[108] Such jurisprudence is therefore somewhat inconclusive for international law purposes and, given the limited Convention participation at the time, it has been inclined towards pragmatic rather than authoritative solutions in issues of responsibility

In any event, the ILC commentary to draft articles on the responsibility gives more importance to the ECtHR jurisprudence, and much less

[106] *Bosphorus Hava Yollari Turizm v Ireland* App no 45036/98 (ECtHR, 30 June 2005).

[107] This attribution to Ireland was all the more remarkable in the light of the ECJ Judgment in the same case, from which it transpired that there was no Irish implementation legislation and that the relevant Community Regulation on sanctions against (former) Yugoslavia gave the Irish authorities no room for manoeuvre as far as its execution was concerned. The only question was one of interpretation and that was solved by the ECJ, while relying on the text of the Security Council resolution that was being implemented by the Union, see Case C-84/95 *Bosphorus v Ministry of Transport, Energy and Communications* [1996] ECR I-3978, paras 13–18.

[108] Hoffmeister, above n 67. The assertion in the text is also corroborated by the discussion of the *Bosphorus* cases (see n 105). By comparison, the *Behrami and Saramati* case (see n 62) was different in that the acts concerned were attributed to the UN rather than the states parties to the Convention.

to the WTO jurisprudence.[109] On what basis the ILC does so, however, remains rather mysterious.

V. THIRD PARTY RECOGNITION: COMPETING PERSPECTIVES

The international law rules concerning attribution are part of customary international law and as such they require a measure of third-party recognition. They are not tailor-made for the EU, which has entered the international scene late and thus it inevitably encounters pre-existing rules and practices. Yet custom is slow to change.

The different models of attribution have different degrees of third-party recognition. The 'organic' model is well established in customary law. The same is true with what has been called the 'consensus' model. Both are well rooted in international law and do not require further discussion in this context.

The 'competence' model is more of a novelty and, from the ILC viewpoint, points to a transitional state of international law. The ILC articles on the responsibility of international organisation do not go as far as adopting special rules of attribution in the case of the EU, but the ILC work contains two interesting elements in this regard.

Firstly, the ILC articles contain a *lex specialis* that indicates that there may be special rules in the area of responsibility of organisations. Article 64 provides that the draft articles do not apply when the different aspects of responsibility are 'governed by a special rule' and that such special rules may be contained in 'the rules of the organisation applicable to the relations between an international organisation and its members'. As the commentary indicates, the *lex specialis* is made in consideration of organisations such as the EU.

Secondly, the ILC draft articles are preceded by a comprehensive 'general commentary', which outlines some significant elements related to its codification work in the area of international organisations. Thus, while ILC draft articles on the responsibility of international organisations address all international organisations, it is admitted that there is a great diversity amongst them. The general commentary also states that the draft rules are based on limited practice and that therefore they 'do not necessarily yet have the same authority as the corresponding provisions of state responsibility'. In this regard, it is noted in the commentary that the *lex specialis* is therefore of particular importance. The ILC notes furthermore that, while the rules of the organisation do not per se bind non-members, some rules of the organisation may be relevant also for non-members.[110]

[109] *Yearbook of the International Law Commission* 2011 vol II, part two, 101.
[110] Draft Articles on the responsibility of international organisations, with commentaries:

Thus, one view of the responsibility of international organisations is contained in the ILC articles. The ILC approaches international organisations 'outside in', in harmonized terms leveling out special features of the organisations. The ILC does not admit to any significant degree to the EU's operational realities based on executive federalism, but turns it into an example of the traditional model of international organisations acting through their own organs. The ILC articles take only limited steps towards meeting the needs of organisations such as the EU, providing that an organisation may 'acknowledge and adopt' the conduct of its Member States as it own (Article 9 of the ILC rules). Moreover, the acts of the Member States are seen 'in connection' with the acts of the organisation itself, pointing in the direction of joint responsibility as a standard outcome (Articles 19 of the ILC rules). It has already been noted that ILC commentary favours the 'Strasbourg jurisprudence' as compared to 'Geneva jurisprudence'.

Another view on the responsibility of international organisations is more inclined to approach them 'inside out', giving effect to their special features. The special case of the EU has been given better reception in the WTO jurisprudence than in the ILC articles.

In respect of the latter view, one could also refer more generally to the multilateral treaty practice with the EU acting as treaty partner with third states. The authors of this paper have argued elsewhere that such large-scale practice has significant implications beyond treaty-making.[111] This is also an aspect that has been entirely ignored in the ILC work. Significantly, the multilateral treaty practice has given rise to the concept of 'regional economic integration organisation' (REIO), which reflects a wide recognition of the special role and features of such an organisation as compared to other international organisations. The treaty practice plainly suggests that there is broad third-party recognition of the special public powers (competence) conferred to the organisation by its members. It also appears to recognise that such an integration organisation operates via close links between the organisation and the authorities of the Member States in implementing its international obligations. It can be argued that such large-scale treaty practice supports the existence of special rules of customary international law or at least of emerging special rules related to such organisations. All its says in fact is that the rules for 'treaty-making' and the consequences of 'treaty-breaking' should be coherent in international law.

ILC, 'Report of the International Law Commission on the Work of its 63rd Session' (26 April–3 June and 4 July–12 August 2011) UN Doc A/66/10, *Yearbook of the International Law Commission* (2011), paras 5–8.

[111] Paasivirta and Kuijper, above n 40, 169, 211.

VI. WHITHER THE EU ON INTERNATIONAL RESPONSIBILITY?

There should be no doubt, as in the past, that the EU will discharge its international responsibility if and when it arises. The EU has shown in word and deed that it can do so and this line should be kept in future. This contribution has shown, at least prima facie, that the ILC draft articles do not sufficiently take into account the specific traits of the EU structure and its functioning. If applied to the EU such as they are, the ILC articles may well become a threat to the internal law and the basic structure of the EU. Nothing can be gained by keeping this fundamental truth under wraps and trying to smother it in diplomatic niceties. The EU should simply make it clear that it will follow its own course in this matter and that it will at best be inspired by certain aspects of the ILC rules, but will never accept them as such. In fact, it seems quite possible and even likely that future treaty practice will influence the development of law in this area.

The EU legal policy in respect of its international responsibility should strike a careful balance. On the one hand third states obviously have a right to engage the responsibility of the EU and/or its Member States under international law; on the other hand that does not give them a right and should not give them an opportunity to interfere in the division of responsibility and thus (as is often the case) in the internal division of powers between the EU and its Member States. Third states certainly have a right to be informed about the division of responsibility and to be told clearly and within a decent period who will discharge the international responsibility, the Union (and through which organ) or one or more Member States or which combination of both. That, however, is as far as it goes.

The EU should continue fostering case law that accepts its position on attribution in areas of exclusive competence, even inside mixed agreements, such as the WTO, where the EU operates in 'vertical mode'. In short, the 'competence model', as presented above, should be decisive. If possible, it should be bolstered by judiciously selected, anticipatory infringement cases that suppress breaches of EU international agreements by faulty implementation or execution of EU treaty obligations by Member States even before the responsibility of the EU and/or its Member States can be invoked by third states. As has been remarked earlier the actual practice of the EU, Member States and third states may have great influence on which turn is given to the ILC draft articles. If necessary, Article 64 of the ILC draft articles should be invoked to defend this approach, since the ILC itself seems to have opened this possibility.[112]

In the field of mixed agreements, the EU should bring its house in order.

[112] See above the discussion in Section V.

Insofar as it is still necessary on the basis of old agreements, declarations of competence should be brought up to date. This should not be seen as another opportunity to start a divisive internal discussion on external relations powers, but as an exercise in good relations with the third states that are the Union's and Member States' treaty partners and in the interest of all concerned.[113] On the other hand, for new mixed agreements (if there are still any after the Lisbon Treaty[114]) no formal declarations of competence should be made any longer. These declarations have two legitimate functions: to make clear that the EU can co-conclude the agreement next to the Member States and to give some idea about who might be responsible, if something goes wrong. For the rest, they have just brought sorrow. The first function can be fulfilled by simply showing during the negotiation that the Union has important powers, exclusive or not, within the scope of the international agreement in question; there is no need to formalize that in detail. The second function can be fulfilled better by a simple clause that obliges the Union, if and when a case of potential responsibility arises, to make clear within a specific deadline, whether and how responsibility will be divided between the Union and Member States, subject to the sanction that, if not done in time, the responsibility will be joint and several.[115] No detailed declaration of competence, which needs to be updated regularly, is necessary for this function.

In respect of international agreements to which all or nearly all Member States are parties, but the Union is not, while in the meantime extensive Union legislation in the domain covered by the 'collective agreement' of the Member States with third states has been enacted, even to the point of arriving at exclusive competences within the meaning of Article 3(2) TFEU (ex ERTA), a systematic step-by-step campaign should be started to make the EU a party to these agreements.[116] This is necessary, if only for the protection of the EU citizens who now ipso facto lack the chance

[113] This could be seen as bad policy advice in this post-Lisbon era, where Member States, contrary to the spirit of the Lisbon Treaty, enthusiastically try to claw back any powers they can in the field of external relations. Indeed everything is in the timing here, but it is inevitable that sooner or later a 'cleaning-up' be done.

[114] The Lisbon Treaty was clearly intended to restrain, if not to eliminate, the practice of mixed agreements, in view of the problems of the Member States' ratifications. This was done by opening up the possibility of concluding Union agreements covering both foreign policy and economic subjects. See also Section 3(a) above.

[115] Such a provision was already included in Art 6.2 of Annex IX to the UN Convention on the Law of the Seas and, with the benefit of hindsight, one wonders why next to that a detailed declaration of competence was still considered necessary at the time. Insofar as that was believed necessary for speaking and voting rights, again a simple provision that states that such rights will be forfeited, if there is no timely declaration on who will speak and vote (the Union or the Member States), also has the merit of concentrating the minds of Union and Member State sharply without the necessity to have detailed declarations of competence.

[116] There are indications that the Commission is at present working on an inventory of major international regulatory conventions to which the Union should accede in the light of the existence of important internal EU regulation in the fields covered by these conventions.

to invoke the possible direct effect of provisions of these treaties. Again this may not be easy; resistance both from the inside and the outside may be expected.

As far as that resistance is concerned, if it is successful, the consequence will only be that the Union's adherence to agreements in whose domain it has exercised competence, sometimes even exclusive competence, remains impossible. The Union's legislative capacity in the field of the subject matter of the international agreement will remain unfettered and the Member States will remain responsible for that.[117] That is a situation that in the long run will be tolerable neither for third states nor for Member States. Something has got to give.

[117] Obviously Art 61 of the draft articles is applicable to this situation. Art 61 reads: '1. Without prejudice to articles 57 to 60, a State Member of an international organisation is responsible for an internationally wrongful act of that organisation if: (a) It has accepted responsibility for that act; or (b) It has led the injured party to rely on its responsibility. 2. The international responsibility of a State which is entailed in accordance with paragraph 1 is presumed to be subsidiary.'

Part II

Current Approaches to International Responsibility

3

Self-Control: International Organisations and the Quest for Accountability

JAN KLABBERS

I. INTRODUCTION

FOR THE LAST two decades, international lawyers and laymen alike have been discussing the possible responsibility of international organisations with vim and vigour. Academics have devoted more than a handful of PhDs to the topic, in one way or another;[1] professional organisations such as the Institut de Droit International[2] and the International Law Association[3] have devoted many sessions to the control of transnational public power; the International Law Commission (ILC) has picked up the topic and in 2011 adopted a carefully calibrated set of draft articles based on the work of its special rapporteur Giorgio Gaja;[4] the pages of academic journals and the brochures of book publishers have been filled with learned analyses and equally learned proposals;[5] entirely

[1] See, eg M Hartwig, *Die Haftung der Mitgliedstaaten für Internationale Organisationen* (Heidelberg, Springer, 1993); M Hirsch, *The Responsibility of International Organisations toward Third Parties: Some Basic Principles* (Dordrecht, Martinus Nijhoff, 1995); P Klein, *La responsabilité des organisations internationales dans les orders juridiques internes et en droit des gens* (Brussels, Bruylant, 1998); K Schmalenbach, *Die Haftung internationaler Organisationen* (Frankfurt am Main, Peter Lang, 2004). Among the more recent examples is A Tzanakopoulos, *Disobeying the Security Council: Countermeasures against Wrongful Sanctions* (Oxford, Oxford University Press, 2011).

[2] See Institut de Droit International, 'The Legal Consequences for Member States of the Non-fulfillment by International Organisations of their Obligations towards Third Parties', resolution of 1 September 1995.

[3] See International Law Association, 'Accountability of International Organisations: Final Report' in International Law Association, *Report of the Seventy-First Conference* (London, International Law Association, 2004) 164.

[4] See www.untreaty.un.org/ilc/texts/instruments/english/draft%20articles/9_11_2011.pdf (accessed on 3 November 2011).

[5] See, eg the hefty tome by J Wouters et al (eds), *Accountability for Human Rights Violations by International Organisations* (Antwerp, Intersentia, 2010).

new approaches have come up, such as the Global Administrative Law approach,[6] while the resurrection of the debate on the possible constitutionalisation of international law and international organisations owes much to the responsibility discussion.[7] And even domestic courts, including the Court of Justice of the European Union (CJEU), have started to meddle.[8]

All this activity is taking place, surprisingly perhaps, in the midst of disinterest or even fierce resistance by international organisations themselves. The bones of contention include the circumstance that international organisations have little to gain from a responsibility regime and as Ralph Wilde suggested some years ago, neither do their Member States (and most, perhaps all, states are also member states of one organisation or another).[9] Also causing difficulties is the circumstance that the ILC has been determined to follow the earlier adopted articles on state responsibility. After all, two different sets of responsibility regimes would be very awkward indeed: if states can only be held responsible for attributable wrongful acts, then a system of strict liability for international organisations would fail to convince. There is also the fear that a responsibility regime will not be able to do justice to the wide diversity of existing institutional arrangements: surely, it will not do to have an identical regime for entities as disparate as the World Bank, the EU, and, say, the European Forest Institute; hence, to the extent that organisations welcome a general responsibility regime, they nonetheless feel that their situation is different.[10]

More pointedly perhaps, a regime modeled on the articles on state responsibility[11] (as is the case with the ILC's current efforts) will be founded on two basic principles, both of which are problematic with respect to international organisations. First, responsibility can only result

[6] See B Kingsbury, N Krisch and RB Stewart, 'The Emergence of Global Administrative Law' (2005) 68 *Law and Contemporary Problems* 15; see also A von Bogdandy et al (eds), *The Exercise of Public Authority by International Institutions: Advancing International Institutional Law* (Heidelberg, Springer, 2010).

[7] See generally J Dunoff and J Trachtman (eds), *Ruling the World: Constitutionalism, International Law, and Global Governance* (Cambridge, Cambridge University Press, 2009); J Klabbers, A Peters and G Ulfstein, *The Constitutionalization of International Law* (Oxford, Oxford University Press, 2009).

[8] See in particular Case C-402/05 P *Kadi v Council and Commission* [2008] ECR I-6351.

[9] See R Wilde, 'Enhancing Accountability at the International Level: The Tension between International Organisation and Member State Responsibility and the Underlying Issues at Stake' (2006) 12 *ILSA Journal of International and Comparative Law* 395.

[10] See, eg PJ Kuijper and E Paasivirta, 'Further Exploring International Responsibility: The European Community and the ILC's Project on Responsibility of International Organisations' (2004) 1 *International Organisations Law Review* 111; E Baimu and A Panou, 'Responsibility of International Organisations and the World Bank Inspection Panel: Parallel Tracks Unlikely to Converge?' (2011) 3 *World Bank Legal Review* 147.

[11] These are conveniently reproduced in J Crawford, *The International Law Commission's Articles on State Responsibility: Introduction, Text and Commentaries* (Cambridge, Cambridge University Press, 2002).

from a wrongful act (ie a violation of international law), but it is unclear what international legal obligations rest upon international organisations beyond the treaties to which they are parties. The ICJ held, in 1980, that international organisations are also bound by 'general international law', but that is a disputed notion in its own right—it may cover secondary rules related to the making and enforcement of international law, but is unlikely to cover many primary rules of international law.[12]

Second, organisations can only be held responsible for acts that are attributable to them, but this too is problematic. Typically, organisations act via Member States and the officials of Member States; they may act in concert with one another, and they may act (increasingly perhaps) in tandem with the private sector. In those circumstances, it is by no means clear when exactly behaviour is attributable to an international organisation.[13] As the European Court of Human Rights (ECtHR) has found out, issues of attribution can lead to controversial decisions.[14] This results not so much from bad law, but rather from fundamental uncertainties arising naturally in complex situations.

Proposals concerning the possible accountability of international organisations try to avoid these problems, but only can do so for so long: eventually, it remains unclear to what extent the Recommended Rules and Practices on accountability advocated by the International Law Association (ILA) are binding upon international organisations; if so, why they are binding, and whence they spring.[15] Much the same applies, mutatis mutandis, to the rules said to make up the corpus of Global Administrative Law: here too, the sources question props up unavoidably,[16] and at least some scholars working in this mould take the question seriously enough to commit to further study.[17]

Interestingly then, some international organisations (quite a few, actually) have started to take matters into their own hands, and have devised something of an internal mechanism (or mechanisms) to stimulate accountability or, perhaps, to be seen to be concerned about accountability. This

[12] See *Interpretation of the Agreement of 25 March 1951 between the WHO and Egypt (advisory opinion)*, ICJ Reports 1980, 73, para 37.

[13] See also ch 1 by C Tomuschat in this volume.

[14] See Joined Cases *Behrami and Behrami v France* and *Saramati v France and others*, decision of 2 May 2007, reproduced in 133 *International Law Reports* 1.

[15] See International Law Association, Accountability. See also IF Dekker, 'Making Sense of Accountability in International Institutional Law' (2005) 36 *Netherlands Yearbook of International Law* 83.

[16] See, eg C Harlow, 'Global Administrative Law: The Quest for Principles and Values' (2006) 17 *European Journal of International Law* 187; BS Chimni, 'Co-optation and Resistance: Two Faces of Global Administrative Law' (2005) 37 *New York University Journal of International Law and Politics* 799.

[17] See B Kingsbury, 'The Concept of 'Law' in Global Administrative Law' (2009) 20 *European Journal of International Law* 23; the volume by von Bogdandy et al, The Exercise, is best considered an attempt to provide global administrative law (although they do not use the term) with solid international law foundations.

chapter will aim to provide something of an overview and taxonomy of such attempts at self-regulation, and will aim to place the ensuing results in a broader theoretical framework on accountability. What is the underlying conception of accountability when organisations start to regulate themselves, and is this kind of self-regulation a good thing or a bad thing?

As a matter of terminology, I will use terms such as accountability, audit, evaluation, and control more or less interchangeably, as generic terms denoting the idea that international organisations are under some form of control. One could say that the ILA appropriated a technical meaning of the term accountability, but if so, I do not intend to follow it. What should be clear though is that all these terms are treated as different from responsibility, as I will reserve that term to depict the classic legal approach based on wrongful act and attribution.

II. SELF-REGULATION: A VERY BRIEF HISTORY AND TAXONOMY

It has always been clear that the behaviour of international organisations needs to be scrutinised, and the (often unarticulated) premise underlying the dominant theory of functionalism in relation to international institutional law is that control should take place by and for the Member States. They create organisations to fulfill certain functions—it is up to them, therefore, to make sure that their creatures do not take on Frankensteinian dimensions.[18] And where the organisation did wrong, it followed that the Member States could be held responsible.[19]

The current discussion is different, though: upon realizing that often states and organisations may be on the same side, or even be indistinguishable from one another (after all, organisations often need to act through their Member States), the current discussion has given up on the idea that organisations can be sufficiently controlled by their Member States,[20] and instead places considerable hope in objective forms of control, be it by impartial bodies or by the court of public opinion, based on objective standards.[21]

Hypothetically, it is possible to distinguish various kinds of activities that might require scrutiny. The one type of activity that has given rise to

[18] See generally J Klabbers, *An Introduction to International Institutional Law*, 2nd edn (Cambridge, Cambridge University Press, 2009).

[19] See C Eagleton, 'International Organisation and the Law of Responsibility' (1959/I) 76 *Recueil des Cours* 319.

[20] More pragmatically, moreover, states often abuse their controlling powers for partisan reasons, as is once again indicated by the US threat to withhold its compulsory fee to UNESCO, since UNESCO admitted Palestine as a Member State in late October 2011.

[21] Whether such a deontological approach can work at all remains an open question. For a very brief answer expressing some doubt, see J Klabbers, 'Controlling International Organisations: A Virtue Ethics Approach'(2011) 2 *Helsinki Review of Global Governance* 49.

the recent flurry may be termed 'operational activities', an awkward term to be sure, but useful to distinguish it from other activities. Thus, for the UN, peacekeeping is an operational activity, whereas for UNHCR among its operational activities which require scrutiny are its handling of refugee applications and the way refugee camps or settlements are run.[22] A different type of activity is legislating, and while admittedly few organisations engage in law-making strictly speaking, where they do, their behaviour may well invite scrutiny, for instance on whether the legislation thus ordained is acceptable in light of the constitution of the organisation involved. A third type of activity consists of the administrative work of the organisation as classically defined (ie before the possible applicability of Global Administrative Law rose to prominence): how does the organisation treat its employees? Yet another type of activity is formed by an organisation's financial activities: is the budget solid? Are expenses properly incurred and accounted for? It is these two latter forms (staff treatment, and financial activities) that have historically been subjected to scrutiny. The former two (operational and legislative activities) have only recently been discovered as possible sites for accountability. With the exception of controlling legislative activities, I will discuss these issues of control below; the former is arguably (outside the EU context) too embryonic to warrant much discussion here, and has been extensively discussed elsewhere at any rate.[23]

A. Financial Control

The financial activities of international organisations have habitually and traditionally been subjected to scrutiny. Or rather: international organisations began to follow their incomes and expenses only when they actually started having some. The late nineteenth century public unions were often either not having a budget of their own, or costs were apportioned as the need and circumstance arose, typically with delegates paying their own way to conferences. The often very small secretariats were likely to be housed within a ministry of the host state, and thus generated no specific costs. Hence, there was no budget to speak of, and therefore no budgetary control either. Indeed, some of the early writers used this to extol the virtues of international unions: they represented international cooperation—and the promise of world peace—at virtually no cost.[24]

[22] See M Pallis, 'The Operation of UNHCR's Accountability Mechanisms' (2005) 37 *New York University Journal of International Law and Politics* 869.

[23] See GR Watson, 'Constitutionalism, Judicial Review, and the World Court' (1993) 34 *Harvard International Law Journal* 1; J Klabbers, 'Straddling Law and Politics: Judicial Review in International Law' in RStJ MacDonald and DM Johnston (eds), *Towards World Constitutionalism* (Leiden, Martinus Nijhoff, 2005) 809.

[24] See, eg repeatedly, PS Reinsch, *Public International Unions, Their Work and Organisation: A Study in International Administrative Law* (Boston, Ginn and Co, 1911).

When international organisations grew in size and became more independent, and started to have their own budgets, the call for control emerged. The International Labour Organization (ILO), created by the Versailles Peace Treaty, was linked to the League of Nations: so too in financial matters. While the Member States were to pay their own way to meetings of the ILO, the 'other expenses' of the ILO were to be carried by the League, and the Director of the ILO was responsible to the League for the 'proper expenditure', as article 399 of the Versailles Treaty had it. Nonetheless, a contemporary commentator notes that the books were initially controlled by experts, Swiss Government controllers in fact, who would report on the financial management of the ILO, both to the ILO and to the League.[25]

This reliance on Swiss Government controllers quickly proved difficult to justify, and already in 1921 the system changed. The Assembly of the League of Nations adopted a detailed Règlement concernant la gestion des Finances de la Société des Nations, and amended it repeatedly.[26] The Règlement established a Commission de Contrôle (Article 1) and a Commissaire aux Comptes (Article 4), and provided for internal control (Articles 39–42) as well as external control (Articles 43–49). The important point to note though was that the control envisaged was purely financial: what mattered was 'l'application de la plus stricte économie', as Article 41 put it.

When organisations started to grow in number, size and density, roughly following the Second World War, automatically the need for independent financial means arose, which then resulted in a call for budgetary independence, which in turn was met with a call for budgetary control. It is no coincidence that the leading studies on the financing of international organisations date back to the early 1960s, for it was only in those days that the financial independence of international organisations was well and truly established.[27] To make a long story short: international organisations have for quite some time recognised a need to have their financial records audited. They receive and spend public money, and therefore it stands to reason that independent accountants or auditing boards follow what goes on.

The UN Board of Auditors, for example, dates back to 1946 when it was created by the General Assembly during its first year, and was given the mandate of supervising the UN's accounts.[28] The Board of Auditors

[25] See M Guerreau, *L'Organisation Permanente du Travail: Une nouvelle Institution du Droit des Gens* (Paris, Rousseau et Cie, 1923) 418–19.

[26] The text of the 1931 version was reproduced in W Schücking and H Wehberg, *Die Satzung des Völkerbundes, erster Band* (Berlin, Verlag von Franz Vahlen, 1931) 525–39.

[27] See, eg JD Singer, *Financing International Organisation: The United Nations Budget Process* (The Hague, Martinus Nijhoff, 1961); JG Stoessinger et al, *Financing the United Nations System* (Washington DC, Brookings Institution, 1964).

[28] GA Res 74 (I)

supervises not just the UN itself, but the entire UN family, and advises the Advisory Committee on Administrative and Budgetary Questions of the General Assembly. It consists of three individuals, who hold the position of auditor-general in their states of residence.

Interestingly, while this Board of Auditors has been in existence since 1946, it has subsequently been followed by the creation of several other boards. In 1959 the General Assembly created the UN Panel of External Auditors,[29] consisting of the auditors of the international organisations that are part of the UN family plus the IAEA, with the task of coordinating the auditing efforts. More recently, the Office of Internal Oversight Services of the UN, itself established in 1994, has come to house an Internal Audit Division, in addition to an Investigations Division and an Inspection and Evaluation Division.[30]

B. Towards Operational Control

Financial control is one thing, but does not say much about how well the organisation in question performs, and a US report on Strengthening the United Nations from 1957, written by what may well be referred to as the foreign policy establishment of the US, already noted the connection between budgetary control and control more broadly.[31] While the final synthesis report did not say much on this, one of the preparatory reports advocated that 'All international organisations should work towards clarification, through a performance analysis, of how the revenues now received are spent by function'.[32] This signaled that budgetary control could not be seen in isolation from performance control or, as referred to above, control over legislative and in particular operational activities.

The same insight underpinned the creation of a Joint Inspection Unit (JIU) in the UN in 1966,[33] with the task of monitoring the performance of the UN in terms other than purely financial. The JIU was made into a permanent unit in 1976 as a subsidiary organ on the General Assembly,

[29] GA Res 1438 (XIV).

[30] See www.un.org/depts/oios/ (last accessed on 31 October 2011).

[31] See *Strengthening the United Nations: Report of the Commission to Study the Organisation of Peace* (New York, Harper & Brothers, 1957). The Commission was chaired by Arthur N Holcombe, and counted among its members such luminaries as Clyde Eagleton, Charles G Fenwick, Leland M Goodrich, Philip C Jessup, Eleanor Roosevelt, Stephen M Schwebel and Louis B Sohn. The main rapporteur was Inis L Claude, jr while Quincy Wright chaired the drafting committee.

[32] Ibid, 261–62 (emphasis deleted). This preparatory report was drafted under chairmanship of Gerard J Mangone, who three years earlier had published his *A Short History of International Organisations* (New York, McGraw-Hill, 1954).

[33] See GA Res 2150 (XXI). The JIU was created upon recommendation of an ad hoc committee, established in the aftermath of the financial crises of the UN following the financing of peace-keeping forces in Suez and the Congo. See generally K Hüfner, 'Joint Inspection Unit' in R Wolfrum (ed), *United Nations: Law, Policies and Practice* (Munich, Beck, 1995) 827.

and it reports both on administrative issues and on what is sometimes referred to as program management.[34] Inevitably perhaps, the work of the JIU has itself been subjected to inspection, both from inside the UN (eg by the group of High-Level Intergovernmental Experts to Review the Efficiency of the Administrative and Financial Functioning of the United Nations) and from the outside (eg by the US General Accounting Office).[35] Moreover, JIU has been in serious conflict during the mid-1980s with a different subsidiary organ of the GA: the International Civil Service Commission (ICSC), whose task is limited to personnel management and administration.[36]

A somewhat similar broadening of the control function has taken place in the EU. The old EEC and Euratom shared an Audit Board, whereas the ECSC had its own Auditor as well. These were replaced in 1977 by a Court of Auditors (based on a 1975 Treaty),[37] whose position would be upgraded to that of one of the formal institutions of the EU by means of the Maastricht Treaty. Its task was traditionally the control of legality and regularity of the accounts, but this too has been broadened to control the EU's financial management. As Lasok and Bridge summarised it two decades ago, the Court of Auditors 'not only assesses the financial soundness of operations actually carried out, but also judges whether the means employed are the most economic and efficient'.[38]

C. Staff Control

Audit boards and departments of internal oversight generally see to it that the financial side of things is well done, and as noted, have increasingly tended to work on a broad notion of what 'financial side' stands for. But in addition to being entities that aim to arrange things, international organisations are employers as well: they hire staff, and should make sure that their staff is treated decently, all the more so as their mission is, often enough, related to justice in one way or another. Indeed, the ICJ made an explicit reference to the UN's mandate when justifying the creation of the UN Administrative Tribunal (UNAT) in 1949.[39]

The UNAT is but one of a number of administrative tribunals. The

[34] See www.unjiu.org (accessed on 31 October 2011).

[35] See Hüfner, above n 33, for the details.

[36] On the dispute, see Y Beigbeder, *Management Problems in United Nations Organisations: Reform or Decline?* (London, Frances Pinter, 1987) 70–72. The same work provides further details on the ICSC at 79–94.

[37] Known as the Financial Provisions Treaty, [1977] OJ L359.

[38] See D Lasok and JW Bridge, *Law and Institutions of the European Communities*, 5th edn (London, Butterworths, 1991) 280.

[39] See *Effect of Awards of Compensation made by the United Nations Administrative Tribunal*, advisory opinion, [1954] ICJ47, 57.

oldest of these is the ILOAT, which is also the most general one in that some 50 other organisations have delegated their administrative justice to ILOAT.[40] The ILOAT started life in 1927 as the League of Nations tribunal; the ILO took it over in 1946.[41] The creation of administrative tribunals seems to have increased during the last three decades or so, and it is sometimes thought that this owes much to an Argentinean lady named Susana Mendaro. Mendaro started to work for the World Bank in 1977, encountered harassment and gender discrimination, and tried to sue the World Bank in the United States. This did not work, the Bank being immune from prosecution. Her unsuccessful suit suggested a legal vacuum, visible not only when the international organisation violates its own staff regulations or staff rules but also, and perhaps more poignantly, when the organisation in question is accused of violating general legal standards.[42] Perhaps in response to the *Mendaro* suit, the World Bank established its administrative tribunal (WBAT) in 1980. The President of the Bank at the time was Robert McNamara, who apparently stated that

> the Bank was *voluntarily* creating the Administrative Tribunal in order to bring the rule of law to the Bank's internal operations, to regulate the behaviour of management so as to assure fair treatment of staff members, and as a result to enhance the morale of the staff and to make the Bank a desirable and efficient place to work.[43]

In 1999, the ECtHR held that the immunity of organisations under domestic law may create a problem with respect to notions of access to justice and fair trial; still, as long as organisations provide for their own administrative tribunal or, alternatively, grant existing tribunals with jurisdiction over their staff disputes, things will be acceptable.[44] This then crowns a remarkable development: administrative tribunals have gone from something of a luxury product to being seen as essential elements of international organisations, without which the organisation has a serious legitimacy deficit.

[40] Indeed, its probably most well-known decision related to the OPCW: see ILO Administrative Tribunal, *in re Bustani*, judgment no 2232, 16 July 2003.

[41] See RA Gorman, 'The Development of International Employment Law: My Experience on International Administrative Tribunals at the World Bank and the Asian Development Bank' in NG Ziadé (ed), *Problems of International Administrative Law* (Leiden, Martinus Nijhoff, 2008) 201, 209.

[42] For an in-depth discussion, see M Singer, Jurisdictional Immunity of International Organisations: Human Rights and Functional Necessity Concerns' (1995) 36 *Virginia Journal of International Law* 53.

[43] This is what Gorman recalls being told by McNamara in 1980. See Gorman, above n 41, 210 (emphasis in original).

[44] See *Waite and Kennedy v Germany*, judgment of 18 February 1999, reported in 118 *International Law Reports* 121.

D. Ad Hoc Scrutiny

So far, I have discussed the emergence of audit boards and the broadening of their tasks, as well as, briefly, the creation of administrative tribunals, therewith essentially covering the policy-making task of international organisations and their activities as employers. There is another kind of scrutiny, however, which sometimes makes an appearance: the establishment of an ad hoc inquiry into some huge political scandal. For these purposes, the regular mechanisms are seen as insufficient. The leading example from the recent past is, no doubt, the Oil-for-Food investigation: an investigation into the complexities of the scheme devised by the UN to soften the impact of economic sanctions on Iraq, allowing Iraq to sell some of its oil in order to purchase food.[45] This created some potential for corruption, and the Volcker Committee, set up to investigate this particular incident, indeed found some corruption to have taken place.[46] While numbers are hard to get by, it would seem that this kind of accountability too has been on the rise in recent years: the same Paul Volcker, for example, conducted an investigation into allegations that the head of the World Bank, Paul Wolfowitz, had been treating his girlfriend, employed in the same organisation, rather more generously in terms of salary and pension rights than other employees.[47]

Related yet distinct, sometimes ad hoc commissions are set up to study the effects of the policies of international organisations. Thus, for example, the Pearson Commission was set up in 1967 at the behest of the World Bank to study the effectiveness of the Bank's development policies. These commissions typically present policy recommendations to enhance effectiveness, and they shade into the more familiar ones which come up with policy recommendations without first making an in-depth study of the effectiveness of policy (the Brandt Report, the Brundtland Report, the Brahimi Report).[48] The latter typically are established once a problem has been observed, without first verifying whether the problem does, indeed, exist. The creation of such commissions and high-level panel suggests a thin line between efficiency accountability, which is supposedly a matter of neutral observation, and effectiveness, which is accepted as being more overtly political.As a preliminary conclusion, then, the following observa-

[45] For useful discussion, see J Traub, *The Best Intentions: Kofi Annan and the UN in the Era of American World Power* (London, Bloomsbury, 2006) 323–37.

[46] See Independent Inquiry Committee into the UN Oil-for-Food Programme, 'The Management of the United Nations Oil-for-Food Programme', reproduced in J Müller (ed), *Reforming the United Nations: The Struggle for Legitimacy and Effectiveness* (Leiden, Martinus Nijhoff, 2006) 350.

[47] For details and references, see J Klabbers, 'Autonomy, Constitutionalism and Virtue in International Institutional Law' in R Collins and ND White (eds), *International Organisations and the Idea of Autonomy* (London, Routledge, 2011) 120.

[48] As mentioned in KD Wolf, 'Independent Commissions' in Wolfrum (ed), above n 43, 743.

tions can be made. First, it would seem that ordinary audit boards have been on the rise and have seen their mandates broadened. Second, there seems to be an increase in the number of administrative tribunals or at least in the number of organisations submitting to the jurisdiction of some administrative tribunal. And third, while allowing for caveats, even ad hoc investigations seem to be increasing. This alone would be reason to claim that the society of international organisations is rapidly becoming an 'audit society', in Michael Power's felicitous phrase: a society characterised by the increasing presence of auditing boards and tribunals, all keeping an eye out to make sure nothing untoward happens.[49] That said though, while this may signify a trend, it does not yet signify a revolution. It does not yet establish that the possible responsibility of international organisations is a topic of great and immediate concern to them for, even if the tasks of auditing boards have broadened and the number of administrative tribunals may have risen, one could still claim that this simply results from the increased complexity of modern life. After all, the membership of the UN has almost quadrupled since 1945; that of the EU has even more than quadrupled since 1951, and the activities undertaken by both have increased manifold—small wonder then that there is more work for auditing boards and administrative tribunals. Still, it is my contention that something more is going on; I will now turn to this qualitative change.

III. COMPLIANCE OFFICERS, INTERNAL OVERSIGHT DEPARTMENTS, AND THE LIKE

When classic texts in the law of international institutions address compliance, they usually refer to compliance by Member States with the standards or rules set by the organisation. For many years, this was considered to be the main compliance issue: organisations would set standards, but not all Member States would adhere to them.[50]

Nowadays, however, the situation is almost the reverse: when there is talk of compliance, it signifies compliance by the organisation with its own rules and standards. This is an important point: typically, compliance is conceptualised as relating to internally set standards, procedures and mechanisms. In what follows, I aim to present something of an overview as to the mechanisms that have been created, realizing all too well that given the sheer numbers of international organisations, the overview

[49] See M Power, *The Audit Society: Rituals of Verification* (Oxford, Oxford University Press, 1997). Sociologist Ulrich Beck coins the wonderfully graphic phrase 'McKinsey-Stalinism' to describe much the same. See U Beck, *Nachrichten aus der Weltinnenpolitik* (Berlin, Suhrkamp, 2010) 67.

[50] See, eg M Virally, 'La notion de fonction dans la théorie de l'organisation internationale' in S Bastid et al (eds), *Mélanges offerts à Charles Rousseau: La communauté internationale* (Paris, Pédone, 1974) 277.

is hopelessly incomplete. The mechanisms also vary rather much in their tasks, and in what they are responses to. Nonetheless, they all seem to relate, in one way or another, to control over the operational activities of international organisations; for that reason, it seems justified to treat them together. Nonetheless, it will be convenient to deal with these mechanisms in various groups.

A. Financial Institutions

Self-regulation is probably most pronounced within the financial institutions. Arguably the trend-setter here has been the World Bank, which created its Inspection Panel as early as 1993, allowing groups who feel that their (or 'others') rights have been affected by a violation by the Bank of its operational policies and procedures to file a request for inspection.[51] While this is not a judicial procedure strictly speaking and while the result is not binding on the Bank, nonetheless this signified a strong response by an international organisation to complaints about its lack of accountability.

But the World Bank does more.[52] One of its vice presidents is charged with ensuring integrity, and as of September 2010 the Bank employs an Integrity Compliance Officer. Moreover, it has enacted Integrity Compliance Guidelines. An Independent Evaluation Group, part of the Bank's set up, is charged with evaluating the work of the Bank, the IFC, the IDA and MIGA, and drawing lessons for improvement. It boasts an Office of Ethics and Business Conduct, which has even established an Ethics Helpline.[53]All this is in addition to the regular offices: legal affairs, auditing board, and controller.

Likewise, the IMF set up an Ethics Office in 2000, followed by an Independent Evaluation Office in 2001.[54] The Ethics Office set up an Ethics Hotline in 2008. A Code of Conduct for IMF Staff has been in force since 1998, and there is a separate Code of Conduct for the Members of its Executive Board, going back to 2000. Disgruntled staff members can take their grievances, since 2007, to an independent Ombudsperson.

Not to be outdone, the European Bank for Reconstruction and Development (EBRD) has established a Project Complaint Mechanism in 2009,

[51] See, eg E Hey, 'The World Bank Inspection Panel: Towards the Recognition of a New Legally Relevant Relationship in International Law' (1997) 2 *Hofstra Law and Policy Symposium* 61; Baimu and Panou, Responsibility.

[52] What follows is culled from the Bank's website: www.worldbank.org/ (accessed on 31 October 2011).

[53] See www.ieg.worldbankgroup.org/content/ieg/en/home.html (accessed on 31 October 2011).

[54] This is taken from the website of the IMF: www.imf.org/external/index.htm (accessed on 31 October 2011).

to allow complaints about its project to be made.[55] This replaces an earlier Independent Recourse Mechanism, which itself was only established in 2004. The Mechanism is directed by a Chief Compliance Officer, and the Office of the Chief Compliance Officer 'is responsible for procedures governing the ethical behaviour of Bank officials, employees and consultants, and it conducts investigations on alleged staff misconduct'.[56]

As the example of the EBRD suggests, compliance control is a big issue not just with the global financial institutions, but with the regional ones as well. The Council of Europe Development Bank has a compliance policy (dated 2007), to be overseen by a compliance officer.[57] The mission of the compliance function, as the Council of Europe Development Bank puts it, is to ensure that the bank operates in compliance with its own rules, with legislation, with its own Code of Conduct, and with 'good practices'. The compliance function itself is, intriguingly, subjected to control by the Bank's internal auditor.

The Inter-American Development Bank set up an Office of Institutional Integrity in 2004, which looks into fraud, corruption and violations of the Code of Ethics as well as related regulations and the Staff Rules.[58] The African Development Bank has an Independent Review Mechanism since 2004.[59] In addition, it has Operations Evaluation Department, aimed at promoting learning and accountability.[60] The Asian Development Bank has an Independent Evaluation Department[61] as well as Compliance Review Panel.[62] The Nordic Investment Bank (NIB), headquartered in Helsinki, seems relatively underdeveloped here: it has a Control Committee, largely consisting of parliamentarians of the participating Member States, in addition to external auditors. The Control Committee itself needs to be controlled too: there is in place a Code of Conduct to organise its tasks and responsibilities. The NIB also appears to have a small Compliance section, but its website provides no further information.[63] The European Investment Bank has an Operations Evaluation section, in addition to several auditing bodies,[64] whereas its offspring, the European Investment

[55] All this can be found on the EBRD's website: www.ebrd.com/pages/homepage.shtml (accessed on 31 October 2011).

[56] Ibid.

[57] Again, see the relevant website: www.coebank.org/ (accessed on 31 October 2011).

[58] See www.iadb.org/en/about-us/departments/about,1342.html?dept_id=OII (accessed on 31 October 2011).

[59] See www.afdb.org/en/about-us/structure/independent-review-mechanism/ (accessed on 31 October 2011).

[60] See www.afdb.org/en/about-us/structure/operations-evaluation/ (accessed on 31 October 2011).

[61] See www.adb.org/Evaluation/ (accessed on 31 October 2011, when the message appearing on screen pointed to an internal service error).

[62] See www.compliance.adb.org/ (accessed on 31 October 2011).

[63] See generally www.nib.int/ (accessed on 31 October 2011).

[64] See www.eib.org/projects/evaluation/index.htm (accessed on 31 October 2011).

Fund, has a Compliance and Operational Risk section, again in addition to several auditing bodies.[65]

Interestingly, several of the Europe-based entities came together for the First European Multilateral Development Banks Compliance Forum in July 2009. According to the press release that was issued, they did so 'in order to coordinate their efforts and to establish an enhanced cooperation in the field of fighting against corruption, money laundering, terrorist financing and financial crimes'.[66]

Now what does all this signify? Several observations can be made. First, much of the compliance offices and officers have been created during the last decade. Second, the trend is near-universal, and applies to all the financial institutions discussed above. Third, and this is something to return to below, while much of the compliance effort is directed against the organisation itself, there is a degree of overlap: some of the compliance seems directed, in part, also to those with whom the institutions do their business. Perhaps this is inherent in the activities of financial institutions: fraud and corruption can interfere anywhere in this work, and all participants, whether the organisation itself, governments, private business partners, or other entities, may be held accountable when things go wrong.

B. Security Organisations

In other sectors, auditing and compliance control seem to be less of an issue, although in the security sector some special initiatives can be found. Thus, NATO, set up in 1949 as a defensive alliance, but transformed in the 1990s into a more general security organisation, has an Office of the Financial Controller, and an International Auditing Board for NATO (IBAN), whose function is mainly to ensure that common funds are used responsibly. Noteworthy is also that NATO had started, as of 2010, to use the International Public Sector Accountancy Standards (IPSAS), a set of standards developed for use in the public sector. This too reflects an increased sense that accountability is of relevance: auditing need not just take place, but need itself be transparent and predictable; this is where IPSAS comes in.[67]

The International Atomic Energy Agency (IAEA) has an Office of Internal Oversight Services, and its website contains a whistle-blower policy stating that the IAEA has 'zero tolerance for fraud, corruption or related

[65] See www.eif.org/who_we_are/governance/cor/index.htm (accessed on 31 October 2011).

[66] Available at www.coebank.org (accessed on 2 May 2011).

[67] See www.nato.int/cps/en/SID-BAF5846B-4FA4BAE9/natolive/structure.htm#CS (accessed on 31 October 2011). For IPSAS, see www.ipsas.org/ (accessed on 31 October 2011).

forms of misconduct'.[68] The Organization for Security and Cooperation in Europe (OSCE) has an Office of Internal Oversight as well, tasked with ensuring the effective management of resources and the effective performance of the OSCE's functions.[69] Like some other organisations, it has established a hotline for reporting complaints about fraud, waste or mismanagement. In a way this befits an organisation partly dedicated to sponsoring the rule of law and good governance; there is some irony, however, involved in trying to square all this with the OSCE's ostensible extra-legal nature. The Organisation for the Prohibition of Chemical Weapons (OPCW) has not only a verification division to verify Member States' compliance, but also has an Office of Internal Oversight.[70]

C. The UN Family

In other areas, however, compliance ranks considerably lower on the political agenda. That said, the UN's Food and Agricultural Office (FAO) has an Office of Evaluation and conducted an Independent External Evaluation in 2007, on the basis of which there are currently reform discussions going on.[71] FAO also has an Office of the Inspector General, which is involved in financial auditing and performance evaluations. The UN High Commissioner for Refugees (UNHCR) too has an Inspector General's Office whose mandate is however, a bit different from that of its (almost) namesake in FAO: partly it covers the evaluation of management practices and individual staff member performance.[72]

Within the UN's World Health Organization (WHO), a body with a limited mandate operates: the Commission on Information and Accountability for Women's and Children's Health, whose task is to investigate whether donations for women's and children's health are made on time, whether resources are spent properly, and whether activities are effective, in that the envisaged results are indeed achieved. The idea is to hold donors to their pledges, and states to their commitments. This seems to be the result of a high-level political initiative: the Commission is co-chaired by the President of Tanzania and the Prime-Minister of Canada,

[68] ee www.iaea.org/About/whistleblower1109.pdf (visited on May 2, 2011, when still in good shape; accessed on 31 October 2011, when scrambled)

[69] See www.osce.org/secretariat/oio (accessed on 31 October 2011).

[70] See www.opcw.org/about-opcw/technical-secretariat/director-internal-oversight/ (accessed on 2 November 2011).

[71] For the report, see ftp://ftp.fao.org/docrep/fao/meeting/012/k0827e02.pdf (accessed on 2 May 2011).

[72] See www.unhcr.org/pages/49f0619f6.html (accessed on 1 November 2011).

and counts many leading politicians among its members. Since this is a new initiative, a first report was published in 2011.[73]

Some of the other members of the UN family have also started to incorporate accountability mechanisms. UNICEF, for example, has an Evaluation Office;[74] United Nations Industrial Development Organization (UNIDO) has a Focal Point for Ethics and Accountability, located within an Office for Internal Oversight Services;[75] United Nations Development Programme (UNDP) has an Evaluation Office, with a Focal Point and as of January 2011 a new Evaluation Policy;[76] United Nations Conference on Trade and Development (UNCTAD) has its own Evaluation and Planning Unit;[77] United Nations Environment Programme (UNEP) has an Evaluation Unit;[78] United Nations Human Settlements Programme (UN-HABITAT) has a Monitoring and Evaluation Unit,[79] and even UNESCO, infamous during the late 1970s and early 1980s, has established an Internal Oversight Service in 2001.[80] These bodies come together, moreover, in the UN Evaluation Group. The latter has adopted Principles of Working Together, the most recent version of which goes back to 2011.[81]

International Fund for Agricultural Development (IFAD), a specialised agency of the UN, has an Independent Office of Evaluation, independent since 2003, and geared towards accountability and learning and towards improving the performance of IFAD. This Independent Office of Evaluation is itself subject to scrutiny by an Evaluation Committee consisting of member state representatives.[82] The UN's World Intellectual Property Organization (WIPO) has an Independent Advisory Oversight Committee, whose tasks seems to be, predominantly, to monitor the regular auditing processes.[83] This is in addition to WIPO's Internal Audit and Oversight Division.[84]

73 See www.who.int/topics/millennium_development_goals/accountability_commission/en/ (accessed on 1 November 2011).

74 See www.unicef.org/evaluation/index_13486.html (accessed on 1 November 2011).

75 See www.unido.org/index.php?id=7850 (accessed on 1 November 2011).

76 See www.undp.org/evaluation/policy.htm (accessed on 1 November 2011). Note that with UNDP, evaluation of the organisation and of its clientele are sometimes particularly difficult to disentangle.

77 See www.unctad.org/Templates/StartPage.asp?intItemID=4420&lang=1 (accessed on 1 November 2011).

78 See www.unep.org/eou/ (accessed on 1 November 2011).

79 See www.unhabitat.org/categories.asp?catid=516 (accessed on 1 November 2011).

80 See www.unesco.org/new/en/unesco/about-us/how-we-work/internal-oversight-service/ (accessed on 1 November 2011).

81 See www.unevaluation.org/papersandpubs/documentdetail.jsp?doc_id=946 (accessed on 1 November 2011).

82 See www.ifad.org/governance/ifad/ec.htm (accessed on 1 November 2011).

83 See www.wipo.int/about-wipo/en/oversight/audit_committee.html (accessed on 1 November 2011).

84 See www.wipo.int/about-wipo/en/oversight/iaod.html (accessed on 1 November 2011).

D. Other Entities

Within commodity organisations such as the International Cocoa Organisation, the International Coffee Organisation, or the International Olive Oil Council, accountability or compliance does not seem to be much of an issue, although the International Network for Bamboo and Rattan's Networking and Partnerships Unit does seem to have some monitoring and evaluation tasks.[85] Likewise, with the classic unions, such as the International Telecommunication Union and the Universal Postal Union, there is not much attention for compliance, at least not in the sense of the creation of separate evaluation boards, compliance officers, or the like.

Similarly, with the bigger regional organisations, such as the Organization of American States (OAS), the Organisation of the Islamic Conference (OIC), and the African Union (AU), there is little or no special attention for compliance or accountability beyond the regular financial auditing. Even the OECD (Organisation for Economic Co-operation and Development), whose work covers, in part, such activities as bribery and fraud in the private sector, does not seem to go beyond normal financial auditing in regard to its own work.

E. Special Activities

Accountability mechanisms are also present where missions take over governmental task, such as UNTAET (East Timor) and UNMIK (Kosovo). The latter instituted an Ombudsperson, and currently still has a Human Rights Advisory Panel, where people can complain about possible human rights violations committed by or attributable to UNMIK.[86] The European Union Rule of Law Mission in Kosovo (EULEX) has accountability written prominently in its banner, and has for example established an Internal Investigations Unit and has set up a Human Rights Review Panel.[87] Still, post-conflict governance exercises have generally been criticised for paying relatively little attention to issues of accountability—relative to the intrusiveness of such institutions in the daily lives of people and in light of their sometimes far-reaching powers.[88]

Finally, perhaps the most notorious accountability issue of recent years relates to the workings of the Security Council sanctions mechanisms. These have been criticised for not taking accountability seriously, both in

[85] See www.inbar.int/Board.asp?Boardid=53 (accessed on 1 November 2011).

[86] See www.unmikonline.org/hrap/Eng/Pages/default.aspx (accessed on 1 November 2011).

[87] See www.eulex-kosovo.eu/en/front/ (accessed on 1 November 2011).

[88] See, eg O Korhonen, J Gras and K Creutz, *International Post-Conflict Situations: new Challenges for Co-operative Governance* (Helsinki, Erik Castrén Institute, 2006) 254–56. For a more structural analysis, see A Orford, *International Authority and the Responsibility to Protect* (Cambridge, Cambridge University Press, 2011).

the literature[89] and by courts, with the ECJ's *Kadi* decision often seen as the wake up signal. In response the Security Council introduced a focal point for De-listing in 2006[90] and, with respect to sanctions against Al Qaeda and the Taliban, established an Office of the Ombudsperson: Canada's Kimberly Prost was appointed in June 2010.[91]

IV. BRINGING SOME STRANDS TOGETHER

What patterns are revealed by the raw data provided above? First, and perhaps foremost, it would seem that accountability and compliance issues have come to be taken seriously during the last decade or so, in particular in the financial institutions and, to a (considerably) lesser extent, in the field of security and post-conflict governance.

The relevance of the timing seems to be explicable by the rise of a general auditing climate: auditing has been popular with Western Governments since the 1970s and 1980s in the wake of theories about New Public Management which, often associated with Thatcherite Britain, typically posit that public services need to be re-modeled along the lines of private businesses. The latter have the market as a correctional mechanism, but since the market is not very-well suited for public services, it follows that public services need to be supervised otherwise, in particular by means of all sorts of accountability mechanisms. It was only a matter of time perhaps for the ethos of accountability to spread to international organisations as well; after all, they too engage in public services and exercise public power. The irony, perhaps, is that many feel that New Public Management has been, by and large, unsuccessful: it has seen the creation of oversight and audit mechanisms and spawned a veritable cottage industry in the making of performance indicators, but has not done much to render public services more efficient or effective.[92]

The reason why auditing is so visible in the financial institutions would seem to reside first and foremost in the consideration that precisely here there is a lot that can go wrong, with a lot of money being at stake. Such an abundance of money creates large incentives for dubious practices (bribery, fraud, corruption). Moreover, among international organisations, these are arguably the ones that deliver direct and tangible results and, moreover, results that affect a single Member State or even a limited community or piece of territory within such a Member State: a decision

[89] Seminal is JM Farrall, *United Nations Sanctions and the Rule of Law* (Cambridge, Cambridge University Press, 2007).

[90] Security Council Res 1730 (2006).

[91] Ibid 1904 (2009).

[92] See, eg Power, Audit Society; P du Gay (ed), *The Values of Bureaucracy* (Oxford, Oxford University Press, 2005); to some extent also Ch Hood et al (eds), *Controlling Modern Government: Variety, Commonality and Change* (Cheltenham, Edward Elgar, 2004).

by the World Bank to help finance the building of a dam in India brings with it huge financial investments, and will come to affect the lives of many people rather directly; still the effects are by and large limited to India. Other states (Germany, or Brazil, say), will hardly notice. Put differently, the financial institutions are fine examples of organisations where concrete material results are of overriding importance—by contrast, they function less obviously as sites for public debate.[93]

Moreover, whenever other institutions adopt measures, these will typically exist largely on paper, and will need to be implemented by domestic governments, through domestic legislation. This has the result of putting a controlling filter in place: national parliaments can tinker with the measure and exercise some control over its implementation; national constitutional courts may have a say on the issue of how exactly the measure is to be given effect, as may national advisory bodies, and national courts might be in a position to test the legality or legitimacy of the implementing measures ex post facto. This filter is missing when it comes to decisions by the financial institutions; hence, it stands to reason that some other control mechanism is considered desirable. Much the same applies to security organisations and territorial administration missions: here too, the effect of organisational acts can be immediately felt, without there being much of a filter in place.

A second general observation to make is that evaluation, monitoring, oversight, and accountability mechanisms have become general phenomena. They appear not only in the financial institutions and with respect to security issues or territorial administration, but are present across the board: they are largely present in the UN system, but also (albeit to a lesser extent) in regional organisations and regardless of what sort of activities the organisation in question is engaged in. Nonetheless, they are not entirely ubiquitous: the classic technical or functional organisations display less of the accountability tendency, and much the same applies to the commodity organisations. It remains speculation, but a possible explanation may reside in the circumstance that with the former, Member State control is still deemed sufficient, while with the latter, the market may be deemed to exercise some control.[94]

Third, these mechanisms go far beyond the traditional idea of keeping the financial accounts in order. Admittedly, financial auditing is typically still a part of the mandate, but there is often much more at issue. Much of it has to do with effectiveness of the organisation's work, with

[93] For the distinction, see J Klabbers, 'Two Concepts of International Organisation' (2005) 2 *International Organisations Law Review* 277.

[94] Whether this is plausible is a different matter, and it is perhaps useful to remember that it was precisely the collapse of one of the commodity agreements (the International Tin Council) that indicated that international organisations should not be beyond accountability. For further discussion, see Klabbers, above n 18, 276–79.

accountability mechanisms having been put in place to help combat waste, mismanagement, fraud and corruption, and other assorted activities. Generally, they serve to enhance the effectiveness of the organisation, and therewith its legitimacy: an organisation that can deliver a good final product will in doing so enhance its 'output legitimacy', which is all the more relevant as 'input legitimacy' (the legitimacy stemming from being a veritable political community) is difficult to attain for organisations.[95]

Fourth, these accountability mechanisms seem to generate, and to some extent have already generated, a second layer: the accountability mechanisms themselves must account for their work. The old question 'Who Guards the Guardians?' takes on a new meaning: who Audits the Auditors? Who Evaluates the Evaluators? This is not surprising, of course: the creation of courts will typically, sooner or later, invite the creation of an Appellate court or some kind of review process. Accountability, in a word, begets accountability.

Fifth, there are no very clear lines separating control over the organisation's activities from control over the actions of Member States. This stems, most likely, from the common sentiment that projects are joint ventures between the organisation and the Member State where the project takes place, and this, in turn, stems from considerations of legitimacy. Put differently, it would look bad for the World Bank to be seen to order Benin or Belize to do things. Hence, the work of the Bank in Benin or Belize is presented as the result of agreement with the local authorities, and as a joint venture.[96] As a result, there is no clear division of responsibilities: when both parties 'own' a project, both are involved and incur accountability.[97]

Sixth, and perhaps a churlish but nonetheless necessary point to make, while accountability mechanisms are created left, right, and centre, they are never abolished. I have found no example of an organisation that claims that it has been evaluated to such an extent that now it knows what to do, that it has internalised those lessons, and is thus in a position to disband its accountability mechanism. In some cases, accountability mechanisms may be replaced by new and improved versions, but they are never laid to rest with gratitude for a job well done. This may either signify that the job is never well done or, more likely, that the task is

[95] See further FW Scharpf, *Governing in Europe: Effective and Democratic?* (Oxford, Oxford University Press, 1999) 7–13.

[96] See generally N Woods, *The Globalizers: The IMF, the World Bank, and Their Borrowers* (Ithaca, NY, Cornell University Press, 2006). See also R Harper, 'The Social Organisation of the IMF's Mission Work: An Examination of International Auditing' in M Strathern (ed), *Audit Cultures: Anthropological Studies in Accountability, Ethics and the Academy* (London, Routledge, 2000) 21.

[97] Public administration scholars refer to this as the problem of the 'many hands': where many hands are engaged in a task, it is difficult to disentangle the responsibilities of individual participants. See, eg M Bovens, *The Quest for Responsibility: Accountability and Citizenship in Complex Organisations* (Cambridge, Cambridge University Press, 1998).

considered to be a permanent task, involving constant scrutiny of policy-making and execution.

V. An Assessment

The cynic may argue, and quite probably not without some justification, that self-regulation by international organisations is much like self-regulation by companies, corporate social responsibility, or similar schemes: it deflects attention away from an external, intrusive accountability approach. Self-regulation provides organisations with a fig leaf of legitimacy in a world where legitimacy is a scarce commodity: an organisation without accountability mechanism can hardly call itself legitimate anymore these days.[98]

This impression may even gain in strength upon the realisation that many of the accountability mechanisms remain, to the lawyer's eye, strangely inconsequential, and curiously set up. The opinions of the World Bank Inspection Panel, the EULEX Human Rights Panel, and many similar institutions are not legally binding: for example the Security Council's Focal Point for De-listing is not much more than a focal point, quite literally, and while the various hotlines may help provide people with an outlet for their frustrations, they may not be terribly instrumental in actually getting matters investigated, let alone in seeing heads roll. Many of the mechanisms, moreover, are established within organisations; while nominally independent, their members are appointed by the very people they are supposed to evaluate, the result being that they may be too scared to bite the hand that feeds them.

The way self-regulation enacts accountability may also be seen as a device to deflect political attention. When much organisational energy is spent on audit and evaluation, and much of the focus of the stakeholders rests upon audit and evaluation, then it stands to reason to conclude that political projects are evaluated not so much on their merits, but on their effectiveness. Thus, a focus on audit allows for possibly controversial projects to slip through almost unnoticed. To put it starkly, no one discusses anymore whether the UN actually should be imposing sanctions on individuals, as long as the imposition of those sanctions follows a decent procedure. No one questions the wisdom of building dams in densely populated areas as long as the procedure has been transparent and the World Bank can be seen to have followed its own policy standards. In short, the encapsulation of evaluation allows organisations, starkly put, to engage in all sorts of activities.

[98] Indeed, for some legitimacy has become the main yardstick for behaviour, replacing legality. See A Buchanan and RO Keohane, 'The Legitimacy of Global Governance Institutions' (2006) 20 *Ethics and International Affairs* 405.

There is another side to this. Much of the call for greater accountability, in general, is in fact a call for a different politics. Much of the call for human rights accountability of the World Bank, are effectively calls upon the World Bank to pay more attention to social and economic rights. Since these are notoriously open-ended, this boils down, in effect, to advocating a change in policy, away from the neo-liberal agenda and the Washington Consensus, and towards a more social-democratic agenda. One may sympathise with this, of course, but should recognise it for what it is: a plea for a different politics, dressed up in legal language. Those who advocate the accountability of the World Bank usually do not advocate that the Bank's lending policies should take into account existing investment protection treaties, or commitments concerning market access. The language of accountability thus plays on politics in two ways: in one of its guises (the human rights guise) it endorses some kind of politics over others, whereas in the guise of effectiveness audit, it endorses de-politicisation which, de facto, amounts to a continuation of the status quo. The interesting thing therewith is that accountability has become the vocabulary in which political battles are fought, on both sides of the divide, and if that is the case, it usually pays to wonder who benefits.

Our cynic then, has sufficient reasons to be cynical, in that the accountability discourse tends to allow the organisation to do whatever it was already doing, no matter how nefarious, and even helps to legitimise it. There can be little doubt, for example, that the main reason for the Security Council to appoint a sanctions ombudsperson and to open a focal point resides in the desire to increase the legitimacy of its anti-terrorism activities, rather than in the sentiment that indeed, its sanctions could be taken with greater regard for the plight of the human beings involved or because of deeply-felt principles and convictions.

There is, however, another take on this as well, and this alternative take is not necessarily in conflict with the cynical view. The legal view on responsibility (and, by extension, on accountability as proposed by the ILA) tends to be rather limited in scope: the idea, typically, is retrospective: it is to hold that an organisation can be held responsible for its past behaviour.[99] The notion of responsibility is, therewith, predominantly reactive, and only comes into play once a wrongful act has been committed which, moreover, can be attributed to the organisation. This is fine as far as things go but, so one may conclude, it does not go very far. Indeed, in extremis, it would be possible for the organisation to commit the exact same wrong the very next day, and be held responsible again. To some extent, this is mitigated, in theory, by the idea that responsibility

[99] The same point is made in the context of the EU by C Harlow, *Accountability in the European Union* (Oxford, Oxford University Press, 2002).

may engender something of a deterrent effect (either on its own or by the poor reputation it generates for the perpetrator), but this is not an inherent element of the concept of responsibility.

Recent theoretical or conceptual work on accountability has come to recognise as much, and has come to re-think accountability as a social relationship, with an effect over time, and this effect over time consists predominantly of learning and socialisation.[100] The underlying idea is that there is little point in holding entities responsible if they would engage in the same behaviour again and again; instead, they ought to realise that their behaviour is generally undesirable, and try to ensure it will not happen again. Perhaps the most advanced (or extreme, or far-fetched) example is the Global Compact, which appeals to companies to respect certain basic standards, and does so well-nigh exclusively by insisting on learning and socialisation. In this scheme there is little room for either carrots or sticks; instead, the Global Compact bypasses carrots and sticks altogether.[101]

There are three important considerations here, which render such a socialised conception of accountability perhaps more proper for international organisations at any rate. The first is that the behaviour is better seen as undesirable than as wrongful. As noted, in strict law there is not all that much that organisations can do that would actually be unlawful—at least not without a further theory of obligation to explain why international law (other than conventional law) would bind international organisations. In those circumstances, where the concept of wrongful act does not get much mileage, the idea of accountability as a remedy for generally undesirable behaviour rather than strictly unlawful behaviour might be quite useful: while the former may, admittedly, be open-ended, the latter is clearly under-inclusive.

The second consideration is that attribution too is rather complex when it comes to the activities of international organisations. Organisations themselves are complex actors, consisting of member states and often acting through those member states who, in turn, act through individuals—this alone creates three possible layers of responsibility. What further adds to the complexity is that organisations rarely act on their own these days: they act in conjunction with other organisations (for example, think UNMIK and NATO), and increasingly with private actors as well. Hence, the three possible layers of responsibility are further complicated by the problem of the 'many hands'. As a result, even in

[100] See the excellent volume by A Ebrahim and E Weisband (eds), *Global Accountabilities: Participation, Pluralism, and Public Ethics* (Cambridge, Cambridge University Press, 2007). The Global Accountability Project of UK-based NGO One World Trust goes into the same direction: see M Blagescu, L de Las Casas and R Lloyd, *Pathways to Accountability: The GAP Framework* (London, One World Trust, 2005).

[101] For a useful discussion, see V Engström, *Realizing the Global Compact* (Helsinki, Erik Castrén Institute, 2002).

those rare cases where most would agree that some wrongful act has taken place, it is by no means self-evident to whom the wrongfulness can be attributed.

A third problem follows from this and complicates all accountability mechanisms involving delegated authority: in any principal/agent relationship, the 'principal' can only be held responsible in a meaningful way for behaviour of his or her subordinates if that was completely within his or her control. As soon as the agent is left some discretion, the responsibility of the principal changes: should the agent do something wrong, then the principal may be held responsible for lack of oversight or control but not, it would seem, for involvement in the wrongful activity itself.[102]

With this in mind, a model of accountability as creative of a social relationship may be more appropriate to the work of international organisations than a model of strict responsibility, and it would seem that, in part, the accountability mechanisms set up by international organisations, in particular the financial institutions, tap into this idea.

V. TWO IRONIES TO CONCLUDE

This chapter has suggested that in quite a few international organisations, self-regulation has become de rigueur, and that this may well contribute to (and be a manifestation of) a more sophisticated concept of accountability, insisting on learning and socialisation, than the more traditional and straightforward accountability idea that insists on the ex post facto attribution of blame and shame.

Nonetheless, amidst all this, there are two rather formidable ironies. First, any attempt to increase the efficiency of the original activity is itself creative of a considerable amount of inefficiency, as the resources put into monitoring and auditing are resources taken away from the organisation's main activity itself, as everyone who has ever worked in any bureaucracy can testify. Accountability begets not only accountability, but also begets inefficiency, in the sense that every dollar the World Food Program spends on accountability is a dollar less for the hungry and the needy.

Second, accountability mechanisms are typically put in place because actors themselves are not trusted, or cannot be trusted. Yet, all this means eventually, is that the public at large is asked to shift its trust: away from the policy-maker, and to the auditor or accountability

[102] This is to be distinguished from ultra vires acts, or from acts that have been ordained or authorised as such. At issue here is the existence of discretion. For an in-depth discussion, see M Harmon, *Responsibility as Paradox: A Critique of Rational Discourse on Government* (Thousand Oaks CA, Sage, 1995).

mechanism, and then perhaps from the first-level auditor to the second-level auditor, and so on. At some point, in other words, the public needs to trust someone, otherwise accountability becomes an infinite regression (or progression, as some would have it). It is unlikely that this cycle can be broken by accountability mechanisms themselves, no matter how sophisticated.

4

Approaches to Responsibility in International Courts

MALCOLM EVANS AND PHOEBE OKOWA

I. INTRODUCTION

DESPITE THE CENTRALITY of state responsibility to the fabric of international law, it is a paradox that many of its rules remain deeply contested. The International Law Commission (ILC) spent nearly five decades trying to codify its rules without arriving at a universally accepted text.[1] Although issues of responsibility have been central to most of the cases that have come before international tribunals, very little has been written directly on judicial contributions to the law in this area. The purpose of this chapter is therefore to provide an assessment of the approaches taken to issues of responsibility by two international judicial bodies—the International Court of Justice (ICJ) and the International Tribunal for the Law of the Sea (ITLOS)—which are germane to the principle object of this volume's enquiry. That enquiry, in essence, involves exploring the 'eternal conundrum' of who is to be held accountable for activities which give rise to legal liability when multiple actors are involved. It is possible to make these questions seem far more complex than need be the case.

Whilst the application of the relevant principles to the facts of a situation is often a difficult business, knowing what those relevant principles are should not to be difficult. And yet—as the various contributions to this volume amply illustrate—this does not appear so as regards the respective responsibilities of the EU and of its Member States when it comes to international law. It is worth emphasising this at the outset of this chapter, as it is often overlooked. For all the focus on the relationship between the EU and its Member States, in cases such as *Bosphorus*[2]

[1] For a history of the topic before the International Law Commission, See J Crawford, *The International Law Commission's Articles on State Responsibility* (Cambridge, Cambridge University Press, 2002) 1.

[2] *Bosphorus Hava Yollari Turizm v Ireland [GC]*, no 45036/98, ECHR, 2005-VI.

and *Kadi*[3] the question, at the end of the day, is one of compliance by actors within the EU legal order with their broader international law obligations. To that extent this chapter offers a complement to that of Kuijper and Passivirta in this volume and which is entitled 'EU International Responsibility and its Attribution: From the Inside Looking Out', since it might be thought of as 'the outside looking in'.[4]

Part of the problem lies in the nature of the legal orders which are being called into play in this particular debate. At the risk of making a hugely crude generalisation, it seems that to the EU lawyer, the answer to the question 'whose was the act' (which at the end of the day, is the question which needs to be answered) ultimately comes down to one of competence, understood in the lawyerly sense of under whose legal powers was the act undertaken. Responsibility (in the sense of liability) rests with those on whom authority has been vested in relation to the matter in hand. Thus from the perspective of EU law, if a Member State has transferred competence to the EU and acts in breach of EU law, then this is sufficient to ground its liability as a matter of EU law. It does not matter in the slightest whether that act may have been otherwise lawful under the domestic law of the state concerned or under the international legal order to which it is subject. The transfer of competence coupled with the exercise of that competence by the EU is sufficient to ground that responsibility.

From an international lawyer's perspective, there is nothing particularly troublesome about this. Indeed, it is precisely what occurs under every treaty regime establishing an international organisation, in which the transfers may be clearly (or relatively clearly) delineated by the constituting instrument. Although it is not so obvious at first sight, it is also what happens within any multilateral treaty regime, where the states parties assume the function of determining the scope of the obligations entered into inter se. What troubles the international lawyer is the manner in which within the EU legal order states may have the content of their obligations affected by the assertion of competence in a manner which does not map onto their international obligations outside of that legal order. And who is to be responsible then?

Once again, there would be nothing generically problematic about this, if international law has its own worked out principles for addressing this issue. It is of course in the process of doing so; with the ILC having developed its Draft Articles on the Responsibility of International Organisations (DARIO).[5] Understandably, these have attracted a great deal of attention

[3] Joined Cases 402/05 and 415/05 *Kadi and Al Barakaat International Foundation v Council and Commission* [2008] ECR I-6351.

[4] See ch 2 by Kuijper and Passivirta in this volume.

[5] Work on this topic began in 2002 following the conclusion of its work on the Articles on State Responsibility. In August 2011 the Commission adopted the Articles and

from both states and, of course, from international organisations who are rightly concerned about the potential impact which these articles will have on the respective spheres of competence that exist between them and their members.[6] The EU has been particularly exercised about the need to preserve its own spheres of competence—which is not a problem—as well as to ensure that it does not find itself internationally responsible for the conduct of its member states.[7] This latter concern may well be a problem if Member States consider such conduct to be the product of constraints imposed upon them by virtue of EU law itself and the DARIO leaves much to be desired in this crucial area—perhaps the most crucial area which it is called on to address.

Reduced to its most simple form, the problems seems to flow from the basic approach taken, which has been to carry over into the DARIO the basic approaches found in the ILC's Articles on the Responsibility of States for Unlawful Acts (ARSIWA),[8] but which are based on a rather different conceptual premise. This is that states are to be held responsible for those things which have been done on the basis of their sovereign authority, this being understood in terms of the exercise of their power and control. In essence, the DARIO takes a power-oriented approach to responsibility and transplants it into the more delicately constructed world of competences—and it is unsurprising that there is no easy fit.[9]

Commentaries (see ILC Report, 63rd Session, UN Doc A/66/10 52–53, with the text of the Articles and Commentaries 54ff). The UN General Assembly took note of the Articles and 'commended' them to the attention of Governments and international organizations 'without prejudice to the question of their future adoption or other appropriate action'. See UNGA Res. A/66/100 (9 December 2011).

[6] The extensive comments submitted by international organisations on the various drafts have been collated by the UN Secretariat and are available on the ILC website.

[7] As Kuipjer and Passivirta comment in this volume, 'It is obvious from the outset that the Commission is most concerned with the problem of attribution or apportionment of responsibility between the Union and Member States and with the role played by the rules of the organisation' (ch 2, n 2).

[8] This is made clear in the Commentary to the DARIO itself: 'In addressing the issue of responsibility of international organizations, the present draft articles follow the same approach adopted with regard to state responsibility' (General Commentary, para 3). It does, however, also claim that 'While the present draft articles are in many respects similar to the articles on state responsibility, they represent an autonomous text. Each issue has been considered from the specific perspective of the responsibility of international organizations. Some provisions address questions that are peculiar to international organizations. When in the study of the responsibility of international organizations the conclusion is reached that an identical or similar solution to the one expressed in the articles on state responsibility should apply with respect to international organizations, this is based on appropriate reasons and not on a general presumption that the same principles apply' (ibid, para 4).

[9] This is, in fact, recognised by the Articles themselves, which, having set out in Arts 58–63 (Part Five: 'Responsibility of a State in connection with the conduct of an international organisation' adds in Art 64 (Part Six: General Provisions) a general provision on *Lex Specialis*, which provides that: 'These articles do not apply where and to the extent that the conditions for the existence of an internationally wrongful act or the content or implementation of the international responsibility of an international organization, or a State in connection with the conduct of an international organization, are governed by special rules

The purpose of this chapter is to lend some substance to these generalised observations by setting aside, for the moment, the debate surrounding this issue in the context of the direct interface between International and EU law. Rather, it looks to the work of two judicial bodies engaged in the interpretation and application of international law, both of which are restrained by the limits of their own jurisdictional competence. What will be seen is that whilst both the ICJ and ITLOS, when working within a treaty-based context, carefully consider questions of responsibility from a 'competence' perspective, this does not prevent them from drawing on the 'authority' paradigm when approaching responsibility as a matter of customary international law. Hence both bodies have a tendency to draw on the ILC's Articles on State Responsibility as applicable as a matter of customary international law, and to assert the applicability of that framework in parallel with any applicable treaty regime. This can permit them to hold states responsible on the basis of customary law when this might not be possible on the basis of treaty obligations themselves. There are lessons here to be learnt for those who seek to use a competence based approach to determine the extent of an international organisation's international responsibility. It also suggests either that the debates over the impact or interpretation of the DARIO have some way to go before they meet the concerns of the EU, or that the EU may find itself potentially liable for acts of Member States—or Member States for conduct of the EU[10]—in situations where it—or they—would not think it appropriate.

II. STATE RESPONSIBILITY IN THE JUDICIAL WORK OF THE INTERNATIONAL COURT OF JUSTICE[11]

A. Introduction

The central difficulty in writing about state responsibility and the International Court is that it lacks a specific identifiable content in

of international law. Such special rules of international law may be contained in the rules of the organization applicable to the relations between an international organization and its members'. Their Commentary on this Article uses the EU as a paradigm example of the situations which might arise, but gives little indication of what this might mean in practice.

[10] For some, the debate is about ensuring the EU is not rendered liable for the actions of its members. There are others who take a less benign approach and consider it more to do with the desire of the EU to evade international responsibility by placing it on the Member States. See, for example, J Klabbers, 'Volkerrechtsfreunderlichkeit: International Law and the Union Legal Order' in P Koutrakos (ed), *European Foreign Policy: Legal and Political Perspectives* (Cheltenham: Edward Elgar Publishing, 2011), ch 3.

[11] See J Crawford, A Pellet and S Olleson, *The Law of International Responsibility* (Cambridge, Cambridge University Press, 2010) for a detailed consideration of the many aspects of state responsibility.

the court's jurisprudence as all cases before the court invariably raise questions of responsibility. Every claim that a state is in breach of a treaty obligation or an applicable rule of customary law is implicitly an indirect assertion that the responsibility of a state is engaged. Seen in this way, to ask about state responsibility is to bring the Court's entire work into contemplation. However, it is also possible to identify those instances when the circumstances giving rise to responsibility in light of the applicable rules of international law has been the central focus of the court's work, and it is with these cases that this section is concerned. It is an attempt to tease out those occasions when the Court has directly confronted the question of the conditions that give rise to responsibility of states or international organisations and the pre-requisites for their exercise.

The task is somewhat complicated because none of the cases before the International Court have directly raised the question of the responsibility of international organisations, including that of the European Union.[12] Much has been written, including in this volume, about the ILC's seminal study on state responsibility and the related project on the responsibility of international organisations. However, very little has been written about the International Court's direct contribution in this field. Yet as the court's docket reveals, there has been a substantial consideration of state responsibility issues in a number of recent cases. It is proposed in this section to examine the court's treatment of questions of responsibility in its jurisprudence and to evaluate its contribution to the wider debate on responsibility, including that of international organisations such as the European Union (EU).

As far back as 1949, in the *Reparation for Injuries* case,[13] the International Court had to confront the issue of the legal personality of the UN, in particular the question of its capacity to bring an action on the international plane, and in the process of doing so, also indirectly considered the question of whether the organisation itself could incur responsibility for violations of its obligations under international law. This it answered in the affirmative as a matter of principle, since the question of responsibility did not arise for direct consideration in the case before it. The

[12] The closest the Court came to considering questions of EU responsibility was in the 1998 fisheries dispute between Canada and Spain. In its counter-memorial, Canada argued that dispute before the International court was in substance the same dispute that existed between Canada and the EU in so far as competence in fisheries conservation and management had been transferred to the European Community. And that as a result of the agreements between Canada and the EU the dispute had become without object. The Court having reached the conclusion that it had no jurisdiction to adjudicate on the dispute submitted to it decided that it was no longer called upon to decide on whether the settlement between the EEC and Canada was dispositive. See *Fisheries Jurisdiction (Spain v Canada), Jurisdiction of the Court, Judgment*, ICJ Reports 1998, 432, para 88.

[13] *Reparation for Injuries Suffered in the Service of the United Nations, Advisory Opinion*, ICJ Reports 1949, 174.

question of responsibility of an international organisation, in this case the EEC, also lurked in the background of the *Fisheries Jurisdiction* case between Spain and Canada. One of the Canadian arguments was that the proper plaintiff to the case brought by Spain was the EEC, in so far as competence in fisheries conservation and management had been transferred to it by members of the EU. That as a result of the conclusion of an agreement between Canada and the EEC in 1995, a few months after the filing of the Spanish application, the dispute had become moot, since the 1995 agreement addressed the substantive issues at the centre of the very dispute between the two states. The Court did not pronounce on this issue. It concluded that it manifestly lacked jurisdiction to hear the merits of the dispute as a result of a Canadian reservation, the terms of which excluded disputes involving the enforcement of Canada's fisheries and conservation legislation.[14] Nevertheless the dispute highlights the possibility of EU responsibility arising by way of indirect pleading in an interstate dispute where one of the parties alleges that the proper plaintiff or defendant should be the EU, if the dispute arises in respect of a matter in which competence has been transferred to the organisation. It is, however, not clear how the Court would respond to such a counterclaim. The Court has long held that as its jurisdiction is based on state consent, it will not adjudicate on a dispute involving the rights of a third party that has not accepted its jurisdiction and is not a party to the case before it.[15] This limitation is further complicated by the fact that only states can be parties to disputes before the International Court, effectively ruling out any form of intervention by the EU at any stage in the proceedings.

The question of responsibility of an international organisation was also central to the cases brought by the Federal Republic of Yugoslavia against 10 Member States of NATO for the use of force and the violation of its sovereignty during NATO's Kosovo campaign. Yugoslavia claimed that NATO was responsible for civilian deaths, damage to its communications infrastructure including bridges on the Danube and damage to the environment. Although the military operation had been undertaken by NATO, the proceedings took the form of a classical inter-state claim since the constraints created by article 34 of the Court's statute, effectively excluded any direct claims against NATO itself. Here too the Court did not give a judgment on the merits having found that it lacked jurisdiction to proceed.[16] As a result the question whether responsibility rested with NATO or its Member States was not addressed. Nor did the Court address the question of modalities of apportioning responsibility in claims involving

[14] See n 12, para 88.

[15] *Monetary Gold Removed from Rome in 1943, Judgment*, ICJ Reports 1954, 19, 32.

[16] *Legality of Use of Force (Serbia and Montenegro v Belgium), Preliminary Objections*, ICJ Reports 2004, 279 and *Legality of Use of Force (Yugoslavia v United Kingdom), Provisional Measures, Order of 2 June 1999*, ICJ Reports 1999, 916.

multiple actors. In the *Nauru* case[17] the Court had accepted the possibility of divisible responsibility in situations where states may be jointly and severally liable for international wrongdoing. On the facts, the practical application of this principle was never worked out as the dispute was settled out of court by the parties. NATO's alleged humanitarian intervention in Libya has also raised similar questions of responsibility for consequential damage, in this instance further complicated by the fact that the intervention was undertaken under Chapter VII of the UN Charter. Should the dispute find its way before the International Court, it may be called upon to determine whether responsibility rests with NATO, its members or the UN. On this matter, even the recently concluded draft articles on state responsibility offer no easy answers.[18] Yet it is indefensible that national governments increasingly accountable for the exercise of power in domestic forums should escape such accountability if they act under the auspices of the UN or a regional organisation.

The decisions of the International Court in the *Nicaragua* case,[19] *Armed Activities in the Territory of the Congo (DRC v Uganda)*,[20] the case brought by Georgia against Russia in relation to the use of force in Georgia's breakaway Republics[21] and the *Bosnia Genocide* cases[22] have all provided the Court with the opportunity to consider questions of responsibility for acts of insurgents acting on behalf of states or on whose conduct the state was in some form implicated. These key decisions have been the occasion for consideration of some of the most controversial and uncertain areas of international law and therefore deserve extended treatment.

The Court has been equally concerned with questions of procedural capacity to bring claims. As noted in the previous paragraphs, it has addressed the question of capacity of international organisations to sue in certain circumstances; it has been concerned with situations when a state may be entitled to bring claims on behalf of those it regards as his

[17] *Certain Phosphate Lands in Nauru (Nauru v Australia), Preliminary Objections, Judgment*, ICJ Reports 1992, 240.

[18] See K Boon, 'New Directions in Responsibility: Assessing the Draft Articles on the Responsibility of International Organizations' (2011) 37 *Yale Journal of International Law* (online).

[19] *Military and Paramilitary Activities in and against Nicaragua (Nicaragua v United States of America)*, ICJ Reports 1986, 14.

[20] *Armed Activities on the Territory of the Congo (Democratic Republic of the Congo v Uganda), Judgment*, ICJ Reports 2005, 168.

[21] *Application of the International Convention on the Elimination of All Forms of Racial Discrimination (Georgia v Russian Federation), Preliminary Objections*, judgment of 1 April 2011.

[22] *Application of the Convention on the Prevention and Punishment of the Crime of Genocide, Preliminary Objections, Judgment*, ICJ Reports 1996, 595 and *Application of the Convention on the Prevention and Punishment of the Crime of Genocide (Bosnia and Herzegovina v Serbia and Montenegro), Judgment*, ICJ Reports 2007, 43; See also *Application of the Convention on the Prevention and Punishment of the Crime of Genocide (Croatia v Serbia) Preliminary Objections, Judgement*, ICJ Reports 2008, 412.

nationals.[23] It has also addressed the question of standing to bring claims for injury done to a natural person, in circumstances where there were no substantive bonds between the national in question and the state purporting to act on its behalf.[24] It has considered the question of nationality of companies and the circumstances when a state may claim on behalf of a company incorporated in its territory. A number of cases before the Court have raised the question of standing to bring an action in the public interest (*actio popularis*) and in situations where the direct interests of the litigant state are not implicated.[25]All these issues have largely arisen within the bilateral framework of inter-state litigation, and the Court has on the whole not been concerned with expansive claims of standing, and whether in principle these should extend not just to third states but also international organisations. The *de lege ferenda* rules on standing in the public interest are also largely state centred and do not concern themselves at all with the question whether international organisations may be entitled to bring claims in the public interest.

The method employed here in assessing the court's work is thematic and reflects those issues that have featured prominently in the Court's jurisprudence or are of particular interest to the EU. Four broad substantive categories will be examined in some detail. This include the Court and the question of responsibility of international organisations; the responsibility of states for conduct of non-state groups; standing to bring claims in the public interest (*actio popularis*) and state responsibility for international crimes.

B. Responsibility of International Organisations

As noted previously, questions of responsibility of international organisations have on the whole been peripheral to the Court's work. Since procedural capacity to bring claims is limited to states, it comes as no surprise that the International Court has had few opportunities to address this issue.[26] The much criticised provision in Article 34 of the Court's statute, limits capacity to bring claims to states and in general the Court will only decide

[23] *Barcelona Traction Case Light and Power Company Limited, Second Phase, Judgment*, ICJ Reports 1970, 3, paras 78–79 and *Ahmadou Sadio Diallo (Republic of Guinea v Democratic Republic of Congo, Preliminary Objections*, ICJ Reports 2007, 582.

[24] *Nottebohm, Second Phase, Judgment*, ICJ Reports 1955, 4.

[25] See, eg *East Timor (Portugal v Australia), Judgment*, ICJ Reports, 90, para 29.

[26] Art 34 of the Statute of the ICJ boldly proclaims that only states may be parties in cases before the Court. For the suggestion that the Statute ought to be amended to allow claims by individuals and other Public International Law bodies, see Hersch Lauterpacht, International Law and Human Rights, London 1950, 48ff. See also the recommendation of a study Group of the British Institute of International and Comparative Law, DW Bowett, J Crawford, I Sinclair and AD Watts, 'The International Court of Justice. Efficiency of Procedures and Working Methods' (1996) 4 *International & Comparative Law Quarterly Supp* 24.

on disputes between states on particular questions of international law and in relation to the specific dispute that it is required to adjudicate. In this sense, it is a provision that is increasingly at odds with practice given the marked proliferation of public international bodies playing an important role on the international stage.[27]

On the subject of EU responsibility, it can be stated with some confidence that the jurisdictional barrier created by article 34 prevents the International Court from pronouncing on its responsibility even in situations where a breach attributable to the EU has arisen under the terms of an applicable treaty, and even if the treaty in question confers on the Court jurisdiction to settle disputes between the parties

In one of the first cases before the International Court, discussed in the previous paragraph, the Court was asked to give an advisory opinion on the question whether the UN was entitled to bring a claim in respect of an injury done to one of its personnel, and the relationship between such a claim, and a putative one that could be brought by the state of nationality. In the *Reparations for Injuries* case a majority of the International Court confirmed that the UN had capacity to bring a claim and defend injuries suffered by one of its personnel.[28] However, it did not discuss the forum to which such a claim could be brought, but it does seem an anomaly that an organisation with capacity to bring and defend international claims, is denied the right to appear as a litigant before the ICJ. The anomaly is compounded in the case of the EU which has been granted competence to become a party to inter-state treaties, including those which confer competence on the ICJ in dispute settlement matters such as the 1982 Convention on the Law of the Sea.

Moreover, the constitutional relationship between the Court and other political organs of the UN has also acted as an impediment to any broad assumption of a jurisdictional mandate to pronounce on questions of responsibility. The Court's pronouncements are consistent with the view that it cannot review or act as an appeal court on decisions taken by political organs. In its Advisory Opinion in *Certain Expenses* case, the Court, although not called upon to decide on the issue, nevertheless declared that Member States did not have a direct right to challenge the validity of UN decisions taken by the organisation's political organs.[29] The general

[27] See H Lauterpacht, *International Law and Human Rights* (London, Stevens & Sons, 1950); W Jenks, 'The Status of International Organizations in Relation to the International Court of Justice' (1946) 32 *Transactions of the Grotius Society* 1; P-M Dupuy, 'Competence of the Court, Article 34' in A Zimmermann, C Tomuschat and K Oellers-Frahm (eds), *The Statute of the International Court of Justice: A Commentary* (Oxford, Oxford University Press, 2006) 544.

[28] See n 13. A number of dissenting judges took the view that the state of nationality should have priority when it came to claims for personal injury.

[29] The question of legality of the expenses incurred by the UN General Assembly came to the Court by way of a request for Advisory Opinion, and it is implicit in the opinion that the Court could not countenance a declaration of ultra vires or certiorari at the behest

theme of non-reviewability of the decisions of political organs was continued in the Court's decision in the *Lockerbie* case.[30] The majority of the Court refused Libya's request for provisional measures. Libya's application was a thinly disguised request for a declaration that the Security Council resolutions which had resulted in the imposition of sanctions on Libya were ultra vires, and contradicted the obligations of the parties under the 1973 Montreal Convention on the hijacking of international aircraft[31] and that as a result the Court should make a finding to that effect. In effect, Libya was arguing that the applicable provisions of the Montreal Convention on the hijacking of aircraft were dispositive, and Libya should be allowed to try the suspects herself as required under the terms of that treaty.[32] In any case concerns about due process permeated the entire dispute—the very states in dispute with Libya also controlled decision making processes in the Security Council making the need for external scrutiny even more pertinent. In its order of 14th April 1992, the Court, without much elaboration, refused to issue the interim orders sought by Libya. It affirmed the overriding character of the Security Council Resolution 748. As subsequent commentators have noted, the Court was wary of acting as a review or an appeal Court in respect of the decisions of political organs.[33] Thus, although the Court did not directly address the question of the responsibility of the Security Council, the dictum is consistent with the idea that as a judicial body, it will not pronounce on questions of responsibility arising from the decisions of the Security Council. For the Court, Security Council decisions raised questions of political judgment not judicial determination. Unlike the ECJ decision in *Kadi* case, the ICJ was not particularly troubled by the fact that the sanctions on Libya were directed at securing the extradition of individuals and therefore required heightened scrutiny to ensure consist-

of individual member states; *Certain Expenses of the United Nations, Advisory Opinion*, ICJ Reports 1962, 151, 168. In the 1971 Namibia opinion the Court explicitly confirmed that it lacked the power to review or appeal the decisions of the political organs, See *Legal Consequences for States of the Continued Presence of South Africa in South West Africa Namibia (South West Africa), notwithstanding Security Council Resolution 276 (1970), Advisory Opinion*, ICJ Reports, 1971, 16, para 89.

30 *Questions of Interpretation and Application of the 1971 Montreal Convention arising from the Aerial Incident at Lockerbie (Libyan Arab Jamahiriya v United Kingdom) Provisional Measures*, ICJ Reports 1992, 3. For a discussion see K Skubiszewki, 'The International Court of Justice and the Security Council' in V Lowe and M Fitzmaurice, *Fifty Years of the International Court of Justice* (Cambridge, Cambridge University Press, 1996) 606.

31 Under Resolution 748 of (1992), the Council decided that Libya had failed to comply with the terms of the resolution requiring it to hand over the Lockerbie suspects.

32 Convention for the Suppression of Unlawful Acts Against the Safety of Civil Aviation done at Montreal on 23rd September 1971, (1971) 10 *International Legal Materials* 1151.

33 C Gray and B Kingsbury, 'Developments in Dispute Settlement: Interstate Arbitration Since 1945' (1992) 63 *British Yearbook of International Law* 97.

ency with fundamental human rights.[34] In both cases the decisions of the political organs had profound implications for individual liberty, making it even more remarkable that the approaches were so radically different. One could even go further and argue that the sequestration of property rights at the centre of the *Kadi* decision, entailed lesser harm than the potential loss of personal liberty if an individual is extradited, the eventual outcome in the *Lockerbie* case.[35] To the extent that the resolutions were ultra vires, it is suggested that in both cases they implicated the responsibility of the Security Council as a matter of principle. In the *Bosnia Genocide* case, the Court was again indirectly invited to consider the legality of Security Council Resolution 713 of 25 September 1991 which imposed an arms embargo on Bosnia. The resolution passed by the Council under Chapter VII directed all states to observe 'a complete embargo on all deliveries of weapons and military equipment to Yugoslavia, until the Security Council decides otherwise'. Bosnia and Herzegovina opposed the embargo as incompatible with their right to self-defence under Article 51 of the Charter of the United Nations, and sought interim measures from the Court. It asked the Court to adjudge and declare that it had a right to defend itself and that the weapons embargo imposed by Security Council Resolution 713 (1991) was inconsistent with its right of 'individual or collective self-defence'.[36] The Court was thus indirectly called upon to assess the compatibility of Resolution 713 with right of a state to self-defence under Article 51 of the Charter of the United Nations.[37] If the resolution was ultra vires there was again room for the argument that it could in principle attract the normal consequences of responsibility. In both cases it is clear that the Court's task was complicated by the

[34] See n 3 and see G de Burca, 'The European Court of Justice and the International Legal Order After Kadi', available at www,judicial studies.unr.edu/js-summer09/JSP.

[35] See Separate Opinion of Judge Shahabuddeen in *Questions of Interpretation and Application of the 1971 Montreal Convention arising from the Aerial Incident at Lockerbie (Libyan Arab Jamahirya v United Kingdom)*, ICJ Reports 1992, 3, 31; see also *Questions of Interpretation and Application of the 1971 Montreal Convention arising from the Aerial Incident at Lockerbie (Libyan Arab Jamahirya v United States of America)*, ICJ Reports 1992, 114, 14.

[36] *Application of the Convention on the Prevention on the Prevention and Punishment of the Crime of Genocide, Provisional Measures, Order of 8 April 1993*, ICJ Reports 1993, 3 and 325.

[37] In its application, Bosnia argued that Resolution 713 (1991) should be interpreted in light of Bosnia's inherent right of self-defence and that as a result it should not be regarded as imposing an arms embargo on Bosnia-Herzegovina (see n 22 Preliminary Objections), para 13. Prior to the Court's decision, the UN General Assembly had overwhelmingly recommended that Bosnia and Herzegovina should be exempted from the arms embargo imposed by the council in UNGA Res 47/121 (18 December 1992). In its judgment in the Provisional Measures phase the Court had declined to rule on the specific question on the grounds that a review of the Council's decision was not within its mandate. See *Application of the Convention on the Prevention and Punishment of the Crime of Genocide, Order of 8 April 1993*, ICJ Reports 1993, 3, 5. See also C Gray, 'Application of the Convention on the Prevention and Punishment of the Crime of Genocide, Order of 8 April 1993' (1994) 43 *International & Comparative Law Quarterly* 704.

fact that it was implicitly being invited to carry out judicial review against organs that could not be parties to the dispute before it.

The extreme reticence shown by the International Court in these cases been much criticised and very little effort has been made to defend the position in the literature. It has been argued that the rule of law as a value permeating the Charter and its institutions requires that those who exercise power under it should not have their decisions totally immune from scrutiny.[38] The point is made by James Crawford that 'in the absence of an ultra vires doctrine, and some institutional expression of it, the Security Council under Chapter VII has the appearance of an unconstrained collective executive power. That is dangerously close to the definition of a tyranny, limited only by the possibility of disagreement between the collective bearers of the power, the permanent and temporary members of the Security Council'[39] Bowett has further suggested that those states not represented on the Council ought to presented with a mechanism for ensuring that what is done in their name is constitutional. He goes on to reject the argument that review of Council decisions would result in a Court substituting its own judgment for that of a political organ whose remit entails wide discretionary powers.[40] As the practice in national democracies show, accountability is not a hindrance but in fact plays an important role in promoting the rule law. Of course the International Court would have to show some deference, especially since in most cases the Council has to react quickly to highly volatile political conflicts. However, the exercise of unfettered discretion not only leads to abuse but also the loss of good faith on the part of those whose co-operation is necessary if the Council is to succeed. The Court has tried to justify the deference as a matter of constitutional principle, necessitated by the separation of powers between itself and the political organs of the United Nations. Clearly the rationale for such deference is on the face of it inapplicable to any putative review of organisations such as the EU that are not in a constitutional relationship with the ICJ, a concern which for now is wholly theoretical.

B. Responsibility of States for Acts of Insurgents and Non-State Groups

(i) Relations of Agency

One of the ILC's contributions to the law on state responsibility was to clarify the circumstances under which states could be held responsible

[38] DW Bowett, 'The ICJ and International Organisations' in Lowe and Fitzmaurice, above n 30, 190.

[39] J Crawford, 'Negotiating Global Security Threats in a World of Nation States: Issues and Problems of Sovereignty' in J Crawford, *International Law as an Open System* (London, Cameron & May, 2002) 106–07.

[40] See n 38, 191.

for the conduct of insurgents and other state groups. Much of this was *lex lata* and the Commission was able to rely on a rich body of arbitral practice, mostly pre-dating the UN Charter to support the propositions it put forward.[41] The International Court has in a series of cases beginning with the *Nicaragua* case[42] amplified the applicability of these provisions in a modern context. In that case, the Court had to decide whether the Nicaragua Contra rebels who had received substantial financial aid from the United States in their long campaign to overthrow Nicaragua's Socialist government of Daniel Ortega, could be treated as United States agents on account of that support, with the result that the United States would assume responsibility for their conduct. In support of its claim, Nicaragua provided evidence that US trained mercenaries were responsible for the torture, rape, killing of prisoners and civilians, in circumstances that could not be justified by military necessity. Furthermore, that the Contras had no real autonomy and that any offences committed by them should be directly attributed to the United States. There was plenty of evidence before the Court and elsewhere that the United States had supplied the Contras with financial and logistical support. However, the nexus between this support and the atrocities committed by the contras was not immediately apparent.

On the evidence, the ICJ rejected Nicaragua's argument that the degree of involvement was such as to make the Contras equivalent to the agents of the United States for the purpose of responsibility. It noted that for the Contras to be treated as approximate to internal organs of the United States, it was necessary to show that the relationship was one of dependence on the one side and control on the other. The Court concluded that as the evidence did not reveal complete dependency on the United States, it was inappropriate to conclude that the Contra forces could be equated for legal purposes with the forces of the United States. Thus, even where there has been extensive third state involvement in the activities of rebels, they are unlikely to be regarded as agents unless the state completely took over the detailed management of their strategy and operations.

In the *Bosnia Genocide* case, the International Court amplified this point and observed that:

> Persons, groups of persons or entities may for purposes of international responsibility be equated with state organs even if that status does not follow from internal law, provided that in fact the persons, groups or entities act

[41] ILC Articles on Responsibility of States for Internationally Wrongful Acts (2001), Report of the ILC, 53rd Session, *ILC Yearbook 2001*, vol II(2), 26 Art 8.

[42] *Military and Paramilitary Activities In and Against Nicaragua (Nicaragua v United States of America) (merits)*, ICJ Reports (1986) 14, paras 102–06; see also Judgment in the *Bosnia Genocide* case, above n 22; Preliminary Objections Judgment in the *Application of the Convention on the Prevention and Punishment of the Crime of Genocide (Croatia v Serbia)*, above n 22.

> in complete dependence on the state of which they are ultimately merely an instrument. In such a case, it is appropriate to look beyond legal status alone, in order to grasp the reality of the relationship between the person taking action, and the State to which he is so closely attached as to appear to be nothing more than its agent: any other solution would allow states to escape their international responsibility by choosing to act through persons or entities whose supposed independence would be purely fictitious[43]

In relation to the specific case before it, the Court concluded that the applicant Bosnia had not been able to show that *Republika Sprska and VRS* lacked real autonomy but were mere instruments through which the Federal Republic of Yugoslavia was acting.[44] It observed that although the ties between the authorities in Belgrade and the Bosnian Serb political and military organisations were close, they were not such that the latter could be equated with organs of the FRY. As a result it was unable to find in favour of the applicant that the acts of genocide at Srebrenica could be attributed to Serbia as having been committed by its organs or by persons or entities wholly dependant on it in circumstances that would entail responsibility.[45]

In truth and as the Court in the *Bosnia Genocide* case pointed out, responsibility under this head is likely to be exceptional. Paramilitary groups with aspirations of their own are unlikely to countenance a relationship of complete dependency in which they would be regarded as the de facto agents of a third state, Moreover, the situation envisaged is one that most governments would shy from. It potentially entails long term political costs for both third states and insurgents with very few strategic benefits.

(ii) Responsibility on the Basis of Direction and Control

The International Court has also clarified the circumstances under which a state could beheld responsible for the conduct of insurgents, which although not part of its internal organs, or qualifying as its agents, were nevertheless acting under its direction and control and in circumstances that make it possible to infer governmental complicity. It is precisely this situation that was envisaged by the ILC in Article 8 of the Articles adopted in 2001. That Article provides that: 'the conduct of a person or group of persons shall be considered an act of state under international law if the person or group of persons is in fact acting on the instructions of or under the direction or control of the state in carrying out that conduct.[46]

The covert nature of third party participation in internal conflicts

[43] See n 22, para 192.
[44] Ibid, paras 393–95.
[45] Ibid, paras 386–94.
[46] ILC Draft Articles (2001) in Crawford, above n 1, 110–13.

presents significant evidential problems in almost all cases, where the responsibility of a state is raised on the basis of direction and control. The precise test to be employed in attributing responsibility has been a matter of conjecture and the decisions of international tribunals on this point are far from a model of clarity.[47] Second, even assuming governmental involvement, it is still unclear which aspects of rebel conduct are attributable to the state. Moreover, the nature and extent of the responsibility of the sponsoring state has never been properly clarified in the literature. Responsibility on the basis of direction and control was explicitly put forward in the Nicaragua pleadings before the International Court. The Court was not persuaded by Nicaragua's arguments of United States complicity. It noted that for responsibility to arise on the basis of direction and control 'it would in principle have to be proved that the state had effective control of the military or paramilitary operations in the course of which the alleged violations were committed'.[48] The International Criminal Tribunal for Yugoslavia accepted the point of principle that responsibility could arise on the basis of direction and control, although it regarded the applicable standard as 'overall control' not effective control.

This approach to the question of state responsibility on the basis of complicity has been followed in other recent decisions and dicta. In these cases too the International Court has been categorical that states sponsoring insurgencies may incur responsibility for their conduct as a matter of principle but it has also exhibited a particular reluctance to make a finding of responsibility on the facts of the cases.

In the *Bosnia Genocide* case, the International Court had to consider the argument put forward by Bosnia that Yugoslavia should be held responsible for the acts of *Bosnia-Serb* militia groups on the grounds that these groups had acted under Yugoslavia's direction and control. The alleged atrocities attributable to *Bosnia–Serb* paramilitaries included massacre at Srebrenica in July 1995. In giving its response to this question the court had to confront the apparently contradictory tests employed in the *Nicaragua* and the *Tadic* decisions respectively: Nicaragua it will be recalled had required that the groups in question should have acted under the direction and control of the sponsoring state; *Tadic* on the hand was satisfied with the much lower standard of overall control.[49] The Court categorically rejected the approach taken by the Yugoslav tribunal in the *Tadic* case noting that although the test may have been appropriate for purposes of classifying a conflict in order to establish criminal responsibil-

[47] See n 19 in this context the decision of the International Court of Justice in Nicaragua, and that of the International Criminal Tribunal for Yugoslavia in the case of *Prosecutor v Tadic*, Case No IT-94-1-A, ICTY Appeals Chamber, Judgment (1999) 38 *International Legal Materials* 1518; For commentary see S Talmon, 'The Responsibility of Outside Powers for Acts of Secessionist Entities' (2009) 58 *International & Comparative Law Quarterly* 493.

[48] *Nicaragua* case, above n 19, para 65.

[49] See n 47.

ity, it could not be regarded as determinative for purposes of attributing responsibility under general international law. The Court emphasised that:

> the degree and nature of a State's involvement in an armed conflict on another state's territory which is required for the conflict to be characterised as international, can very well, and without logical inconsistency, differ from the degree and nature of involvement required to give rise to that state's responsibility for a specific act committed in the course of the conflict.[50]

State responsibility for the conduct of insurgents formed a central part of the parties' arguments in the case brought by the Democratic Republic of Congo against Uganda.[51] The Democratic Republic of Congo accused Uganda of supporting Congolese insurgencies, and of maintaining de facto administrative control through these insurgent groups in two provinces in eastern Congo. For its part, Uganda counter claimed, accusing successive Congolese governments of extending support and giving sanctuary to the two Ugandan rebel groups, Lord's Resistance Army (LRA) and Allied Democratic Forces (ADF), and that as a result the Congo too should be held responsible for the conduct of these insurgencies. The court found in favour of the Congo, and Uganda was in effect held responsible under the law of belligerent occupation for the conduct of the rebels, which on the facts, the Court found had been exercising de facto control on behalf of the Ugandan authorities. Although it accepted that Uganda had faced particularly vicious attacks from Ugandan insurgents based in eastern Congo, it was unable to find on the facts any evidence of Congolese complicity. Leaving aside the question of responsibility under the law of belligerent occupation, it is implicit in the judgment that the Court regarded the question of responsibility on the basis of direction and control as well founded in principle.

Responsibility on the basis of direction and control was also central to the dispute brought by Georgia against Russia.[52] On 1st April 2011, the ICJ upheld Russia's preliminary objections in the case brought against it by the Republic of Georgia and decided that it was no longer called upon to proceed to the merits. Several controversial themes underlay the application and the arguments of the parties as developed in both the request for provisional measures and the preliminary objections submitted by Russia.

Central to the dispute was the alleged Russian sponsorship of the insurgents in Abkhazia and Ossetia. Georgia maintained that the atrocities committed by these groups, in particular serious human rights violations directed at ethnic Georgians were directly attributable to Russia as the sponsoring state. Thus, the dispute again brought to the fore the question

[50] *Bosnia Genocide* case, above n 19, para 405.

[51] For an extended commentary see P Okowa, 'Congo's War: The Legal Dimension of Protracted Conflict' (2006) 77 *British Yearbook of International Law* 203.

[52] See n 21.

of state complicity in the acts of armed rebel groups and the circumstances under which the activities of such groups can engage the responsibility of a state or its institutions as well as the consequences of such attribution.[53]

The dispute also raised the question of the extra-territorial application of treaty obligations and whether a state continued to be bound by treaty commitments it had entered when it acted outside its territory. Russia argued that obligations under the CERD did not apply outside of its territory and specifically that the provisions contained in Articles 2–4 did not have extra-territorial application. Russia claimed that the violation of the obligations under the CERD rested primarily with the separatist authorities in Abkhazia and South Ossetia. These authorities it asserted were neither its organs nor were they acting under its direction and control.

As a strategy for promoting accountability, responsibility on the basis of complicity has several advantages. First, it provides a useful medium for circumventing the jurisdictional barrier in Article 34 that only states can be parties to a dispute by making the conduct of rebels and other non-state groups justiciable. Second, it expands the spatial reach of a state's obligations by making these obligations applicable to conduct outside its territorial jurisdiction. This is particularly useful since in many contexts where rebels act there is a power vacuum at the centre of government, making treaty regimes redundant for all practical purposes. In this way responsibility on the basis of complicity serves a useful function by closing the accountability gap.

It may be surmised that the Court clearly wanted responsibility on this basis to be exceptional and only applicable where the level of state complicity was tangible and well demonstrated. In the *Nicaragua* case, the Court on the facts, declined to find that the Contra rebels were sufficiently affiliated to the United States government, as to make them agents of the United States. It nevertheless clarified that non-state groups may nevertheless engage the responsibility of the sponsoring state, if that state had assumed 'effective control' over their activities. This pronouncement has had a lasting impact on the decisions of the International Criminal Tribunal for Yugoslavia and those of the European Court of Human Rights when faced with questions of state responsibility for armed groups operating in the areas under their control.[54] As noted, although the International Criminal Tribunal for Yugoslavia, in *Tadic* regarded the applicable standard as one of 'overall control', it did not cast any shadow of doubt on the point of principle laid down in Nicaragua. On the face of it, responsibility on the basis of complicity does not have any particular resonance

[53] See S Talmon, 'The Responsibility of Outside Powers for Acts of Secessionist Entities' (2009) 58 *International & Comparative Law Quarterly* 493. The dispute was based on Art 22 of the Convention on the Elimination of Racial Discrimination.

[54] *Ilascu and others v Moldova and Russia* [GC], no 48787/99, ECHR 2004-VII, para 384; *Loizidou v Turkey*, judgment of 18 December 1996, merits, RJD 1996-VI, para 56.

for international organisations and is therefore hardly of relevance to the present enquiry on the responsibility of the EU in an international context. States giving support to insurgent groups in these circumstances usually have collateral political objectives. But it is possible to envisage an international organization say with peacekeeping roles incurring international responsibility for failing to prevent the commission of an international crime in its power to prevent. If governments can incur responsibility when they act or fail to act for that matter, there is no reason why their collective decisions or omissions taken under the auspices of an international organisation should also not attract responsibility. It is suggested that the Court's pronouncements on extra-territorial application of treaty obligations is putatively of relevance to the EU and its Member States. In this context it has been suggested that the sustainability objectives which informs the EU's common fisheries policy applies too when Member States engage in fishing activities outside EU's territorial waters.[55] It, however, remains uncertain whether responsibility in these cases is visited on the EU or on the Member State's whose conduct falls short of the agreed policy.

D. State Responsibility for International Crimes

For much of the period that it was involved in the long project on state responsibility, the ILC was embroiled in a controversy on whether in addition to delictual responsibility, international law should also develop a separate regime of criminal responsibility for egregious state conduct. In part, this was a reaction to the increased public sensitivity to the importance of human rights values that has been a feature of developments since the Second World War. One immediate appreciable consequence was the recognition that certain fundamental obligations such as those in the human rights field were not discretely bilateral but were in fact owed *erga omnes* to the entire international community. The modalities of giving effect to these hierarchically important obligations were the source of much dissension. The traditional understanding of international law on the nature of state responsibility was that it was essentially delictual, and international law did not as such attach penal consequences for breach of its rules. Yet there was a feeling that the law should in some form give recognition to the importance of these obligations by attaching more serious consequences for their breach. It was in this context that the ILC included in the draft articles it was working on a separate regime for state crimes, intended to be conceptually different from the normal regime of delictual responsibility. The feasibility of a penal regime was to

[55] See E Witbooi, *Fisheries and Sustainability: A Legal Analysis of EU and West African Agreements* (Leiden, Brill, 2012) ch 5.

occupy the commission for more than two decades. As is well known, it became one of the most contested and divisive issues in the context of an already complex and controversial project.[56]The regime on state crimes was finally expressed in Article 19 of draft articles provisionally adopted in 1996. It said that:

> (2) An internationally wrongful act results from the breach by a state of an international obligation so essential for the protection of the fundamental interests of the international community that its breach is recognised as a crime by the community as a whole constitutes an international crime.
>
> (3) Subject to para 2 and on the basis of the rules of international law in force, an international crime may result, inter alia from
> (a) a serious breach of an international obligation of essential importance for safeguarding the maintenance of international peace and security such as prohibiting aggression.
> (b) A serious breach of an international obligation of essential importance for the safeguarding and preservation of the human environment, such as those prohibiting massive pollution of the atmosphere or of the seas.
>
> (4) Any internationally wrongful act which is not an international crime in accordance with para 2 is a state delict.

The categories on the whole were illustrative, and it was hoped by its proponents that other examples would be added as international law developed. In the event, there was never any consensus on candidate categories or modalities of giving effect to them. In fact, it immediately became apparent that the consequences would in the main be no different from those that attach to civil wrongs. As James Crawford, the ILC's last Special Rapporteur on the project remarked:

> if there are to be state crimes, in the proper sense, there has to be a proper collective approach. It cannot be that such a fundamental notion as crimes of state can be resolved by disaggregated responses of individual states. Thus it occurred that the Draft Articles as adopted on first reading in 1996 contained no significant collective element for the consequences of Article 19. There was no procedure at all whether a crime has been committed, or for co-ordinating the individual reactions of 'injured states' (by definition, all states) to a crime. The material consequences of crimes were minimal, and did not even extend to punitive damages.[57]

[56] It also generated a vast literature. See for instance, A Pellet, 'Can a State Commit a Crime, Definitely Yes! (1999) 10 *European Journal of International Law* 425; N Jorgensen, 'A Reappraisal of Punitive Damages in International Law' (1997) 68 *British Yearbook of International Law* 247; B Graefrath, 'International Crimes and Collective Security' in K Wellens (ed), *International Law: Theory and Practice* (The Hague, Martinus Nijhoff, 1998) 237; S Rosenne, 'State Responsibility and International Crimes: Further Reflection on Article 19 of the Draft of the Draft Articles on State Responsibility' (1998) 30 *New York University Journal of International Law and Policy* 145.

[57] Crawford, above n 39, 390–91.

As a result the Commission decided to shelve this aspect of the project and it was never included in the draft articles adopted in 2001. The question whether international law recognised a heightened regime of criminal responsibility was left lurking in the background.

The debate in the ILC on the nature of state responsibility for international crimes was largely theoretical. No actual instances of state responsibility, at any rate for international crimes had been the object of proceedings in an international tribunal since Nuremberg. Indeed it was only in the 1990s, in the immediate aftermath of the Balkan conflicts, that the debate assumed a practical perspective when cases were brought against Serbia for state responsibility. State responsibility for international crimes was central to the case brought by Bosnia against Serbia and Montenegro. It equally formed an important element of the case brought by Croatia against Serbia.

In the *Bosnia Genocide* case, Bosnia sought a declaration that Serbia was in violation of its obligations under the Genocide Convention by failing to prevent and punish genocide committed by Bosnia Serb militia, who it will be recalled, it had contended were acting on behalf of Serbia. Neither party had argued that should Serbia be found responsible the consequences would be anything other than those which attach to delictual responsibility. On this point the pleadings submitted by Bosnia were unequivocal; that the regime contemplated was civil not criminal. It said:

> the Genocide Convention in describing genocide as a crime in international law does so for a limited, specific purpose: to assert that States, in ratifying the Convention, 'undertake to prevent and to punish' the persons who commit such crimes. This provision does not purport to criminalise violations by States against other States . . . under the terms of the genocide convention and the Court's statute, this is a civil action. The *travaux* make this clear . . . most delegates were willing to endorse the introduction of 'responsibility of a state' only in so far as this was understood to extend to civil rather than criminal responsibility.[58]

Yet the question of state criminality arose for the Court's consideration indirectly. Serbia had argued that the regime of responsibility envisaged in the Genocide Convention did not contemplate state responsibility but was limited to the prosecution of individuals. Serbia relied extensively on the Convention's drafting history to support the contention that only physical persons could be subject to punishment. Specifically, that genocide was a crime that required specific intent and that this intent could be attributed to individuals not states.[59]

The international court rejected the substance of Serbia's argument. It observed that the obligation to prevent the Commission of genocide

[58] Memorial of the Republic of Bosnia, paras 5.1.2.5, 5.2.2.2 and 5.2.2.3.
[59] Counter-Memorial of the Republic of Serbia, paras 4.1.1.2, 4.10.1.2 and 4.10.1.1.9.

by implication also entailed an obligation on the part of a state not to commit genocide. It is significant that on the on the specific question of whether the responsibility contemplated by the convention was civil or Criminal, the Court was unequivocal. It said:

> the obligations in question in this case, arising from the terms of the convention and the responsibilities of states that would arise from breach of such obligations are obligations and responsibilities under international law. They are not of a criminal nature. This argument can accordingly not be accepted.[60]

The passage is significant for in it the Court was able to confirm in bold terms what the ILC had prevaricated on for nearly two decades, namely that the imposition of criminal responsibility was not a feature of the international system of justice as it stands at present. It is of course possible to argue that a distinct regime of criminal responsibility remains feasible at the regional level. The regime of state crimes envisaged in article 19 of the ILC draft articles also included serious pollution by a state. There is nothing to prevent a regional body such as the EU from imposing penalties for particularly egregious violations regarded as important at the regional level. The imposition of fines is increasingly a feature of EU enforcement strategy and although not described as punitive, their desiderata is in most cases deterrence rather than compensation and therefore more closely aligned to criminal responsibility.[61] That said, it is doubtful that the International Court will impose penalties on a state before it simply because it is a member of a regional body that recognises particular forms of penalties.

E. Standing to Bring International Claims

In one of its most famous and frequently cited passages, the International Court in the *Barcelona Traction* case drew a distinction between bilateral obligations and those owed to the international community as a whole. In its words:

> an essential distinction should be drawn between the obligations of a State towards the international community as a whole, and those arising vis-a-vis

[60] *Bosnia Genocide* case, judgment, above n 19, para 170.

[61] In the context of enforcement proceedings and non-compliance with a judgment of the Court of Justice, see Case C-387/97 *Commission v Greece* [2000] ECR 2000 I-5047 where sanctions were imposed under Art 260(2) TFEU for the first time. See also Commission Communication SEC (2010) 923/3 Application of Article 260 TFEU—Up-dating of data used to calculate lump sum and penalty payments to be proposed by the Commission to the Court of Justice in infringement proceedings (www.ec.europa.eu/eu_law/docs/docs_infringements/sec_2010_923_en.pdf). In addition, the Lisbon Treaty provides for the first time for the possibility of financial sanctions in case where a Member State has failed to notify measures transposing a directive (Art 260(3) TFEU).

> another State in the field of diplomatic protection. By their nature the former are the concern of all States. In view of the importance of the rights involved, all states can be held to have a legal interest in their protection; they are obligations erga omnes. Such obligations derive, for example, in contemporary international law from the outlawing of acts of aggression, and of genocide, as also from the principles and rules concerning the basic rights of the human person, including protection from slavery and racial discrimination. Some of the corresponding rights of protection have entered into the body of general international law . . . others are conferred by international instruments of a universal or quasi-universal character.[62]

This passage has been much discussed not least because it was subsequently taken as supporting the case for an *actio popularis*, entitling any member of the international community to bring an action in the public interest. In many contexts, it was also seen as a corrective to the Court's controversial decision in the *South-West Africa* cases, where it reached the conclusion that the applicant states, Liberia and Ethiopia had no legal interest to seek a declaration that South Africa was in breach of the terms of the mandate in so far as the obligations in question were owed to the League of Nations and not to its individual members.[63]

Yet the subsequent history of the passage in terms of concrete enforcement has been disappointing and the Court has taken the opportunity (on the few occasions when the issue has arisen) to deny the recognition of any general right of *actio-popularis*. In the *East Timor* case for instance, the Court observed that it could not entertain a claim on the basis of the *erga omnes* character of an obligation where the parties had not expressly accepted the Court's jurisdiction under the relevant instruments.[64] In that case it will be recalled that Portugal brought an action against Australia arguing that the 1989 treaty concluded between Portugal and Indonesia in relation to delimitation of the East Timor's continental shelf was a violation of the right of the East Timorese to self-determination; a dispute which the court could not determine without first deciding on the legality of Indonesia's invasion of East Timor in 1974. Standing in the way was the *Monetary Gold* rule, where the International Court had held that it could not decide on a dispute if it involved the assessment of the rights and obligation of a third state that had not accepted the Court's jurisdiction. Portugal argued that the limitations on the Court's jurisdiction under the *Monetary Gold* principle had no application in view of the *erga omnes* character of the obligations involved. The Court rejected the claim and observed that:

> Portugal's assertion that the right of people's to self-determination as it evolved from the Charter and from the UN practice has an erga omnes character

[62] See n 23, paras 33–35.
[63] See n 25.
[64] See n 29.

> is irreproachable. The principle of self-determination of peoples has been recognised in the United Nations Charter and in the Jurisprudence of the Court. It is one of the essential principles of contemporary international law. However, the Court considers that the *erga omnes* character of a norm and the rule of consent are two different things. Whatever the nature of the obligations invoked, the Court could not rule on the lawfulness of the conduct of a State when its judgment would imply an evaluation of the lawfulness of the conduct of another State which is not a party to the case. Where this is so, the Court cannot act even if the right in question is a right *erga omnes*'.[65]

In *DRC* v *Rwanda*, the Court again denied that the *erga omnes* character of an obligation could confer jurisdiction in face of a clear reservation depriving the Court of jurisdiction.[66] In the *Bosnia Genocide* case, Bosnia argued that the obligations imposed on Serbia were not bilateral but were owed to the international community. It submitted that as a result, 'the right to seize the Court for such disputes, even when the claimant state or its nationals are not direct victims of the genocidal act, is nothing but the logical consequence of the fact that the 'rights and obligations enshrined by the convention are rights and obligations *erga omnes*'.[67]

It supplied evidence that Serbia had committed acts of genocide not only on the territory of Bosnia but also elsewhere on the territory of the former Yugoslavia. In particular, that the atrocities were committed not only on the citizens of Bosnia and Herzegovina but also on Albanians, Sandzak Muslims, Croats, Hungarians, and other minorities. It is true that some of these minorities were nationals of Bosnia, but Bosnia also made it clear that it was bringing a claim in respect of acts of genocide against persons who were nationals of Yugoslavia itself and that the nature of the obligations involved entitled it to bring claims on behalf of third state nationals.[68]

The Court found it unnecessary to give a definitive judgment on this point. It noted that genocide was a crime that required a specific intent to eliminate a targeted group and that as a result the group had to be identified positively, a burden that the applicant had failed to discharge.[69] Moreover, as the Court had reached the conclusion that Serbia had not been involved in the direct commission of acts of genocide, it was not necessary for it to speculate as to which groups would fall within the ambit of protection. It is possible to read from this passage that the Court was not contesting the applicant's right to bring a claim in respect of atrocities committed against persons who are not its nationals. The Court was

[65] Ibid.

[66] *Armed Activities on the Territory of the Congo (New Application: 2002) (Democratic Republic of Congo v Rwanda), Jurisdiction and Admissibility, Judgment*, ICJ Reports 2006, 6.

[67] Judgment, above n 22, para 185.

[68] *Reply of the Government of Bosnia and Herzegovina* (23rd April 1998) 972.

[69] Judgment, above n 22, para 185.

merely concerned that on the specific facts before it, the applicant had been unable to prove that these nationals of a third state were victims of genocide. The opportunity to clarify the nature of *actio popularis* and the extent to which such a right was recognised under contemporary international law in a clear and decisive manner was nevertheless missed.

The Articles finally adopted by the ILC in 2001 explicitly recognise the right of states other than those directly injured to bring an action by way of enforcing the collective interest. The Special Rapporteur in the commentary to Article 48 acknowledged that in so far as the article contemplated the rights of any state to bring an action in the public interest the Article was the expression of a right *de lege ferenda*.[70] The articles and the commentary that accompanied it did not speculate that this putative *actio popularis* was also exercisable by international organisations. The right is largely seen through prism of states.

III. STATE RESPONSIBILITY IN THE JUDICIAL WORK OF THE INTERNATIONAL TRIBUNAL ON THE LAW OF THE SEA

A. Introduction

ITLOS exercises a complex web of jurisdictional competencies[71] but until recently it had decided relatively few cases.[72] Its case load to date has largely been dominated by two questions. Five cases have concerned the award of provisional measures,[73] in three of which the merits were to be

[70] See Commentary on ILC Draft Article 48, in Crawford n 1) 276–80.

[71] The ITLOS was created by, and forms a part of, the dispute settlement mechanisms established under Part XV of the 1982 UN Convention on the Law of the Sea, Annex VI of which comprises the Statute of the Tribunal. Under Art 287 of UNCLOS, states parties may opt for ITLOS as one of four potential dispute settlement mechanisms within the Convention framework. Some 30 states have currently done. In addition, the ITLOS exercises jurisdiction with regard to applications for provisional measures in cases brought before Arbitral Tribunals under the Convention Framework (Art 290(5)), for 'prompt release' of vessels arrested within the EEZ (Art 292) and also as regards disputes concerning the Deep Seabed (heard by a Chamber of the Tribunal, which can also issue Advisory Opinions). Ten other multilateral conventions (five of which are currently in force) also confer jurisdiction on ITLOS. For an overview see J Merrills, *International Dispute Settlement*, 5th edn (Cambridge, Cambridge University Press, 2011) ch 8; R Mackenzie, C Romano, Y Shany and P Sands, *Manuel on International Courts and Tribunals*, 2nd edn (Oxford, Oxford University Press, 2010) ch 2; N Klein, *Dispute Settlement in the International Law of the Sea* (Cambridge, Cambridge University Press, 2009).

[72] It has had a total of 19 cases brought before it, concerning 17 separate situations, one of which was discontinued.

[73] See *M/V Saiga (No 2) (Saint Vincent and the Grenadines v Guinea-Bissau), Provisional Measures, Order of 11 March 1998*, ITLOS Reports 1998, 24; *Southern Bluefin Tuna (New Zealand v Japan; Australia v Japan), Provisional Measures, Order of 27 April 1999*, ITLOS Reports 1999, 280; *MOX Plant (Ireland v United Kingdom), Provisional Measures, Order of 3 December 2001*, ITLOS Reports 2001, 95; *Land Reclamation by Singapore in*

heard by an Annex VII Arbitral Tribunal rather than ITLOS itself[74] and such cases tend not to give rise to many issues concerning responsibility as such.[75] Numerically, the largest single category of cases considered by ITLOS—nine—have concerned its particular jurisdiction under Article 292 to consider applications for 'prompt release' of vessels detained by a state for allegedly committing offences related to fisheries jurisdiction within the EEZ of the arresting state.[76] Cases of this nature are particularly prone to raise questions which fall within the traditional purview of the state responsibility, including issues such as determining nationality of vessels, the exhaustion of local remedies, etc and such issues have also arisen in the few cases[77] it has considered on the merits. As a result, the ITLOS jurisprudence touches on numerous issues significant for determining the capacity to bring an international claim. By way of example, its first merits judgment, *M/V Saiga (No 2)* considered in detail a whole range of core questions, including the primacy of flag state jurisdiction,[78] the relevance (or, rather, irrelevance) of the 'genuine link' for the purposes of recognizing grants of nationality,[79] the need (in this case the lack of need) to exhaust local remedies,[80] as well as nationality of claims.[81] It also considered

and around the Straits of Jahore (Malaysia v Singapore), Provisional Measures, Order of 8 October 2003, ITLOS Reports 2003, 10; *The M/V Louisa Case (St Vincent and the Grenadines v Kingdom of Spain), Provisional Measures, Order of 23 December 2010*, ITLOS Reports 2008–10, 52.

[74] The exceptions being the first, *M/V Saiga (No 2)* and the most recent, the *M/V Louisa*.

[75] See, eg the remarks of Judge Laing in his dissenting Opinion in *M/V Saiga (No 2), Provisional Measures*, above n 73, para 9, who, concerning the exhaustion of local remedies, remarked that 'it would appear that such matters . . . are not appropriate for decision at the stage of provisional measures'.

[76] See *M/V 'Saiga' (Saint Vincent and the Grenadine v Guinea), Prompt Release, Judgment*, ITLOS Reports 1997, 16; *'Camouco' (Panama v France), Prompt Release, Judgment*, ITLOS Reports 2000, 10; *'Monte Confurco' (Seychelles v France), Prompt Release, Judgment*, ITLOS Reports 2000, 80; *'Grand Prince' (Belize v France), Prompt Release, Judgment*, ITLOS Reports 2001, 17; *'Chaisiri Reefer 2' (Panama v Yemen), Prompt Release, Order of 13 July 2001*, ITLOS Reports 2001, 82 (discontinuing proceedings); *'Volga' (Russian Federation v Australia), Prompt Release, Judgment*, ITLOS Reports 2002, 10; *'Juno Trader' (Saint Vincent and the Grenadines v Guinea-Bissau), Prompt Release, Judgment*, ITLOS Reports 2004, 17; *'Hoshinmaru' (Japan v Russian Federation), Prompt Release, Judgment*, ITLOS Reports 2005–07, 18; *'Tomimaru' (Japan v Russian Federation), Prompt Release, Judgment*, ITLOS Reports 2005–07, 74.

[77] Principally in its first merits decision in *M/V Saiga (No 2) (Saint Vincent and the Grenadines v Guinea), Judgment, ITLOS Reports 1999*, 10. Its only other substantive judgment to date has been in *Delimitation of the Maritime Boundary in the Bay of Bengal (Bangladesh/Myanmar), Judgment*, ITLOS Reports 2011, nyr.

[78] *M/V Saiga (No 2)*, above n 77, para 45.

[79] Ibid, paras 83, 86.

[80] Ibid, paras 98, 100.

[81] Ibid, para 106. It had been argued that Saint Vincent and the Grenadines could bring the claim on behalf of the ship and ship owners but not in respect of foreign crew members. The Tribunal rejected this, saying that 'the ship, everything on it, and every person involved or interested in its operation are treaty as an entity linked to the flag state. The nationalities of these persons are not relevant'.

defences (here, that of necessity[82]) and reparation.[83] Subsequent cases have considered these issues in yet further detail.[84]

Interesting though all this is, it does not cast a great deal of light on the central focus of our current inquiry,[85] save to underline the extent to which the ITLOS has tended to largely mirror the more conservative approaches found in international legal debate on these questions. It should, then, come as no surprise to find that the ITLOS has also tended followed the direction of travel found in the ILC's Articles on State Responsibility whenever it has had occasion to do so. It is, however, interesting that

[82] Ibid, paras 133–34, where the Tribunal endorsed the approach of the ICJ in *Gabcikovo/Nagymaros Project (Hungary/Slovakia), Judgment*, ICJ Reports 1997, 7, paras 51, 52.

[83] Ibid, paras 170–72, where the Tribunal endorsed the famous approach of the PCIJ in the *Factory at Chorzow, Merits,* judgment no 13, 1929 PCIJ, Series A, No 17, 47), as well as the view of the ILC in its then Draft Article 42 of its Articles on the State Responsibility, that 'reparation may be in the form of restitution in kind, compensation, satisfaction, assurances and guarantees of non-repetition'. 'Assurances and guarantees of non repetition' are, however, not included as a form of reparation in equivalent Articles (Arts 34–39) as finally adopted by the ILC in 2001. They are, however, included in Art 30(b) as an obligation of a state responsible for a wrongful act, if the circumstances so require. See generally Crawford, above n 1, 31–34. See also S Barbier 'Assurances and Guarantees of Non-Repetition' in J Crawford, A Pellet and S Olleson, *The Law of International Responsibility* (Oxford, Oxford University Press, 2010) 551–61.

[84] The issue of determining the nationality of vessels has proven particularly interesting. See, for example, *Grand Prince*, above n 76, in which the Tribunal concluded that the vessel's provisional registration, valid at the time of the arrest, had subsequently lapsed and, since it was therefore not registered in Belize at the time of the application, it could not hear the case. See also *Juno Trader*, above n 76, where the Tribunal added that the confiscation order by a court of the arresting state did not automatically result in a change of nationality for the purposes of bringing a claim. In *Tomimaru*, above n 76, the Tribunal confirmed this, but added that where a confiscation was final, then indeed there was no longer any object to proceedings for prompt release as a judgment would no longer be pending. Of course, this does not prevent the flag state/applicant from instituting separate proceedings concerning the confiscation, provided there is an alternative jurisdictional basis outside of Art 292 for this.

[85] It must be recalled that this concerns questions of responsibility, and not the equally difficult question of the jurisdictional competence of the ITLOS (or Annex VII Arbitral Tribunals) in cases concerning disputes which also involve obligations under other conventions and which are subject to their own dispute settlement mechanisms (including questions of allocation of competences between states and institutions). It is beyond the scope of this footnote to set out and explore even in brief this large and difficult topic. It suffices to say that the two cases which have been raised under the UNCLOS provisions and which involve the European Community have both been of this nature and so, although of great interest, are not directly relevant to the current inquiry and so will not be considered further. These cases are the *MOX Plant Case (Ireland v United Kingdom), Provisional Measures* and the case concerning the *Conservation and Sustainable Exploitation of Swordfish Stocks in the South-Eastern Pacific Ocean (Chile/European Union)*, which was discontinued at the request of the parties following an agreement between them (see Order of 16 December 2009, ITLOS Reports 2008–10, 13). They do, however, in their own way, illustrate—from the jurisdictional perspective—the same tensions concerning the 'architectures of protection' which are being explored in this contribution from the perspective of state responsibility. For a consideration of the interplay between international dispute settlement and EU law, see I Govaere, 'Beware of the Trojan Horse: Dispute Settlement in (Mixed) Agreements and the Autonomy of the EU Legal Order' in C Hillion and P Koutrakos (eds), *Mixed Agreements Revisited* (Oxford, Hart Publishing, 2010) 187.

its endorsement of those Articles is not perhaps quite as fullsome or as unqualified as might have been expected in its most recent consideration of them. This is to be found in its first ever Advisory Opinion, given by its Seabed Disputes Chamber, on *Responsibilities and Obligations of States Sponsoring Persons and Entities with Respect to Activities in the Area* (hereafter referred to as the 'Advisory Opinion').[86]

B. The Advisory Opinion

It is important to set out the reason why the request for the Advisory Opinion was made in the first place. The Council of the International Seabed Authority made the request at the behest of Nauru, which—in a nutshell—wanted to engage in deep seabed exploration but did not want to bear the full financial risks that might flow from this. In the view of Nauru, the system of state sponsorship provided for under the Convention framework facilitated this by permitting a state to sponsor a commercial entity (doubtless on terms beneficial to the state[87]) whilst ensuring that liability for damage caused would be the responsibility of the sponsored entity and not the responsibility of the state. This was made clear by Nauru, which argued that:

> Nauru, like many other developing states, does not yet possess the technical and financial capacity to undertake seafloor mining in international waters. To participate effectively in activities in the Area, these States must engage entities in the global private sector . . . Not only do some developing States lack the financial capacity to execute a seafloor mining project in international waters, but some also cannot afford exposure to the legal risks potentially associated with such a project. Recognising this, Nauru's sponsorship of Nauru Ocean Resources Inc. was originally premised on the assumption that Nauru could effectively mitigate (with a high degree of certainty) the potential liabilities or costs arising from its sponsorship. This was important, as these liabilities or costs could, in some circumstances, far exceed the financial capacities of Nauru . . . [I]f a developing State[88] can be held liable for activities in the Area the State may potentially face losing more than it actually has . . .

[86] *Responsibilities and Obligations of States with Respect to Activities in the Area, Advisory Opinion, 1 February 2011*, ITLOS Reports 2011, nyr.

[87] The text of the Agreement between Nauru and Nauru Ocean Resources Inc is appended to its Written Statement to the Chamber, though the financial details set out in Appendix 1 are omitted, presumably for commercial reasons. Nevertheless the terms of the agreement give a general feel for the nature of the relationship and the aspirations of those a party to it.

[88] One strand of argument advanced was that developing states ought to be in an advantageous position under the general framework established by Part XI. Whilst the Chamber noted the existence of preferential rights for developing states within the Convention is was clear that 'the general provisions concerning the responsibilities and liability of the sponsoring State apply equally to all sponsoring States, whether developing or developed' (ibid, para 158).

> . . . Nauru considers it critical that guidance be provided on the interpretation of the relevant sections on Part XI pertaining to responsibility and liability, so that developing States can assess whether it is within their capabilities to effectively mitigate such risks and in turn make an informed decision on whether or not to participate in activities in the Area'.[89]

The Chamber, in rather more nuanced language, basically accepted the central thrust of this argument[90] and set out in some detail its view on the nature and scope of the obligations assumed by sponsoring states under Part XI in a fashion which facilitates the entry of developing states into the deep seabed exploration in this fashion. This will be briefly outlined, highlighting the elements of its reasoning which concern the interplay of liability of the state for the acts of the sponsored entity which may have some resonances for the interplay between responsibility in the EU/Member State context. It should, however, be stressed at the outset that there is no intention of suggesting that there is an equivalence between the position of sponsoring states and sponsored entities on the one hand, and that of the EU (or any other international organisation) and its Member States on the other. These are very different sets of relationships. Nevertheless, there are 'resonances', and it is these which form the background to, and provide the justification for, this enquiry.

This Advisory Opinion also gives some clues as to how the issue on which guidance is sought might be approached were it to arise and this will be the primary focus of the remainder of this section. Issues of responsibility and liability lie at the heart of the issue addressed in the Advisory Opinion. Article 153(2)(b) of UNCLOS requires that those legal or natural persons who wish to carry out activities in the 'Area' (the deep sea bed beyond national jurisdiction) must be nationals of a state party or effectively controlled by it or its nationals and they must also be 'sponsored by such States'. The Chamber explains the purpose of this is to 'achieve the result that the obligations set out in the Convention, a treaty under international law which binds only States Parties thereto, are complied with by entities that are subject of domestic legal systems'.[91] This is important because such entities are not subject to international law per se.

[89] ISBA/16/C/6 (1 March 2010), paras 1 and 6, quoted in Advisory Opinion, para 4. See also the Written Statement of Nauru submitted to the Chamber, which makes its reasons for seeking the submission of the request patently clear. For further details of the background see D Freestone, 'Responsibilities and Obligations of States Sponsoring Persons and Entities with Respect to Activities in the Area' (2011) 105 *American Journal of International Law* 755.

[90] As did most, but not all, of those states and other bodies which submitted Written Statements to the Chamber. At the same time, the Chamber identified a countervailing concern which seems to have weighed quite heavily with it—this being that facilitating access in which fashion might result in 'The spread of sponsoring States "of convenience"' which would 'jeopardise the highest uniform application of the highest standards of protection of the marine environment, the safe development of activities in the Area and the protection of the common heritage of mankind' (ibid, para 159).

[91] Advisory Opinion, para 75.

Of course, the requirement of sponsorship alone hardly serves to ensure this outcome: what it does is ensure that there is a state—the sponsoring state—which is 'responsible' for the entity having the legal capacity to engage in deep seabed mining. Article 139(1) then takes this further by providing that 'States Parties shall have the responsibility to ensure that activities in the Area . . . shall be carried out in conformity with this Part' [Part XI of UNCLOS].

A full analysis of these complex provisions is beyond the scope of this chapter,[92] as is a full presentation and analysis of the Advisory Opinion itself.[93] For current purposes it is sufficient to outline the general approach of the Seabed Dispute Chamber to the provisions in question, to the extent that this sheds light on the question of who bears responsibility for acts not in conformity with the obligations provided for in the convention framework.

Critically, the Chamber drew a clear distinction between 'responsibility' and 'liability'. In a rare criticism, it noted that the English version of the ILC's Articles on State Responsibility causes some confusion by using the same word—'responsibility' for both.[94] In the view of the Chamber, when interpreting the relevant UNCLOS articles, 'the term 'responsibility' refers to the primary obligation whereas 'liability' refers to the secondary obligation, namely, the consequence of a breach of the primary obligation.[95] Since for the ILC the entire corpus of rules of state responsibility are secondary rules and not a source of substantive legal obligations,[96] there is no contradiction here, but it does serve as a useful warning that one must be careful when transporting the language of the Articles on State Responsibility into legal contexts where both primary and secondary obligations are at issue.

It is, then, noteworthy that the Chamber was itself careful not to endorse the ILC's Articles on State Responsibility en bloc. Rather, it observed

[92] The complex drafting histories of these Articles is set out in MH Nordquist, SN Nandan, S Rosenne, MD Lodge, *United Nations Convention on the Law of the Sea 1982: A Commentary*, vol VI (The Hague, Martinus Nijhoff, 2002) 118–28 (Art 139) and 293–312 (Art 153).

[93] See generally DK Anton, A Makgill and CR Payne, 'Advisory Opinion on Responsibility and Liability for International Seabed Mining (ITLOS Case No 17): International Environmental Law in the Seabed Disputes Chamber' available at www.ssrn.com/AuthorID=371838 (accessed May 28, 2012); Freestone, above n 89; D French, 'From the Depths: Rich Pickings of Principles of Sustainable Development and General International Law on the Ocean Floor—the Seabed Disputes Chamber's 2011 Advisory Opinion' (2011) 26 *International Journal of Marine and Coastal Law* 525; I Plakokefalos, 'Analysis: Seabed Disputes Chamber of the International Tribunal for the Law of the Sea, Responsibilities and Obligations of States Sponsoring Persons and Entities with Respect to Activities in the Area, Advisory Opinion' (2011) *Journal of Environmental Law* doi:10.1093/jel/eqr021.

[94] Ibid, para 66.

[95] Ibid, para 65.

[96] For the centrality of this distinction, and the background to it, see Crawford, above n 1, 14–16. For a somewhat more sceptical view see E David, 'Primary and Secondary Rules' in Crawford et al, above n 11, 27–33.

that UNCLOS Article 304 referred to 'the application of existing rules and the development of further rules regarding responsibility and liability under international law' and that, in consequence 'account will have to be taken of such rules under customary law, especially in the light of the ILC Articles on State Responsibility'.[97] It further noted that 'Several of these articles are considered to reflect customary law', and that 'Some of these, even in earlier versions, have been invoked as such by the Tribunal . . . as well as by the ICJ'.[98] As will be seen later, in its Opinion the Chamber drew on a number of these Articles to support its position but it remains the case that there is a degree of ambivalence towards them, possibly because the distinction which the Chamber drew between responsibility and liability was critical to its ability to be able to deal clearly and effectively with the particular questions which had been put before it.

(i) Question 1

The first question put to the Chamber was 'What are the legal responsibilities and obligation of State Parties to the Convention with respect to the sponsorship of activities in the Area in accordance with the Convention . . .?'.

As has already been seen, the Chamber noted that the sponsoring state must exercise effective control over the sponsored entity, this being a necessary pre-requisite to their being able to fulfil their obligations under the Convention in respect of them.[99]

Article 139 (1) provides that 'States Parties shall have the responsibility to ensure' that sponsored entities carry out activities in the area are carried out in accordance with the Convention framework. The Chamber saw this as establishing 'a mechanism through which the rules of the Convention concerning activities in the Area, although only treaty law and this binding only on the subjects of international law that have accepted them, become effective for sponsored contractors which find their legal basis in domestic law'.[100] It stressed, however, that 'the sponsoring State's obligation 'to ensure' is not an obligation to achieve . . . the result that the contractor complies with the aforementioned obligations. Rather, it is

[97] Advisory Opinion, para 169.

[98] Ibid.

[99] The Chamber points out that the mere fact of nationality, or even effective control, is not a sufficiently robust guarantee of compliance by the entity with the Convention framework, hence 'it requires a specific act emanating from the will of the State or States of nationality and of effective control. Such act consists in the decision to sponsor' (Advisory Opinion, para 78).

[100] Advisory Opinion, para 108. It might be noted that the Chamber suggests here that the rules pertaining to activities in the area are not reflective of customary international law. This ought to be distinguished from the principle that the Area is the common heritage of mankind, which is generally considered to be customary in nature and, as such, binding on all states, including those not parties to the Convention.

an obligation to deploy adequate means, to exercise best possible efforts, to do the utmost, to obtain this result',[101] a melange which it synthesised into an obligation of 'due diligence', the precise implications of which are explored in some detail but need not be considered here.[102]

What is interesting is the observation that

> The expression 'to ensure' is often used in international legal instruments to refer to obligations in respect of which, while it is not considered reasonable to make a State liable for each and every violation committed by persons under its jurisdiction, it is equally not considered satisfactory to reply on mere application of the principle that the conduct of private persons or entitles is not attributable to the State under international law (see ILC Article on State Responsibility, Commentary to article 8(1)).[103]

This points to the need to look beyond an approach predicated upon a dichotomy between 'state' and 'private', with rules of attribution determining when the former becomes responsible for the latter. It suggests—as does so much else within the Advisory Opinion—that in the applied context of a convention regime, the formal structure of the Articles on State Responsibility may fail to capture the essence of the exercise which the states parties are attempting to engage in.[104]

In addition to the 'responsibility to ensure'—understood in the sense of exercising due diligence—the Chamber also identifies a number of direct obligations for which the state itself is responsible, including the obligation to assist the Authority and to take a precautionary approach, to itself conduct, and to ensure that the Contractor conducts, appropriate Environmental Impact Assessments[105] and make available domestic processes for seeking compensation in respect of damage.[106] This links into

[101] Ibid, para 110. The Chamber also uses the language of 'obligations of conduct' rather than of 'result', echoing the language of the ICJ in the *Bosnia Genocide* case, above n 22, para 430.

[102] Advisory Opinion, paras 111 and 117–20, setting out the 'content of the due diligence obligation to ensure'. In this regard, ITLOS drew on the approach of the ICJ in *Pulp Mills on the River Uruguay (Argentina v Uruguay), Judgment*, ICJ Reports 2010, para 187. See also French, above n 93, 538–42.

[103] Advisory Opinion, para 112.

[104] See also French, above n 93, 538, who argues that 'the "responsibility to ensure" is relied upon when, although the traditional principle of state responsibility for private behaviour, above namely, that the actions of a private individual are not attributable to the state) is "not considered satisfactory", the notion that the state would be held responsible for "each and every violation" by a private actor would equally be the wrong response to the situation. In other words, neither the laissez-faire nor the complete attribution approach is appropriate'.

[105] Advisory Opinion, paras 141–50. The Chamber, quoting the *Pulp Mills on the River Uruguay* case, took the view that this was not only so under the Convention but was now required as a matter of customary international law, though acknowledging that its scope and content were not well delineated.

[106] Ibid, paras 139–40.

the question of liability, which was the key issue, and the subject of the second question to which we now turn.

(ii) Question 2

The second question put to the Chamber was 'What is the extent of liability of a State Party for any failure to comply with the provisions of the Convention . . . by an entity whom it has Sponsored . . .?'

This was the crux of the issue as originally presented by Nauru: would the state end up liable for the actions of the entity it sponsored? For all its complexity, the position seems at first sight fairly clear under the Convention framework, and is set out in Article 139(2) which provides as follows:

> Without prejudice to the rules of international law and annex III, article 22, damage caused by the failure of a State Party of international organisation to carry out its responsibilities under this Part shall entail liability; States Parties or international organisations acting together shall bear joint and several liability. A State Party shall not, however, be liable for damage caused by any failure to comply with this Part by a person whom it has sponsored under article 153(2)(b), if the State Party has taken all necessary and appropriate measures to secure effective compliance under article 153(4) and Annex III, Article 4(4).

As the Chamber points out, the result is fairly straightforward,[107] though not without complex implications. If the state party is in breach of its own direct obligations, it will be liable for any resulting damage. It is not liable for the failure of the contractor to undertake its own obligations under the Convention framework[108] and will only be liable for damage resulting from the activities of a sponsored entity if it, the sponsoring state, has failed in its own obligation of due diligence in constructing and implementing an appropriate domestic regulatory and compliance framework. In short, the sponsoring state is only liable for damage caused by the sponsored entity if it, the sponsoring state, fails to exercise its obligation to exercise due diligence in ensuring that the entity operates in accordance with the provisions of the Convention. This is clear enough.

The problems are as follows. First, the Convention makes the liability of the state party for breach of its direct obligations conditional on there being actual damage.[109] This is not the case under the Article 2 of

[107] Even if the language used is not: see UNCLOS Commentary vol VI, above n 92, 126, which observes that Art 139 'addresses the responsibility and liability of States Parties and International Organisations with respect to activities in the area . . . In somewhat obscure terms which . . . creates unnecessary confusion'.

[108] This is as a result of Annex III, Art 22, for which see Advisory Opinion, paras 199–201.

[109] The Convention does not make it clear to whom the sponsoring state is liable, however. The Chamber argues that, by implication, the Authority would be able to bring such a claim. It also argues that the obligation may be of an *erga omnes* nature (in the light of its affecting the enjoyment of the common heritage of mankind, meaning that any state

the Articles on State Responsibility where there is no need for damage to have occurred before responsibility is engaged: it is sufficient that there is a breach of a primary obligation.[110] However, the Chamber points out that Article 139(2) is 'without prejudice to the rules of international law' and, as a result, it took the view that the principles of responsibility as set out in Articles on State Responsibility remained applicable as a matter of customary international law. Thus the state party remains liable under the rules of customary international law for breach of its direct obligations even if this has not resulted in damage.[111] To the extent that there was a potential liability gap[112] here, it was therefore closed.

This was not the case as regards the second area of difficulty, which concerns the gap in liability opened up by the liability of the sponsoring state for damage caused by the sponsored entity being limited to situations in which it had failed to fulfil its due diligence obligation to secure compliance. The Chamber was clear that the Convention 'does not provide for the attribution of activities of sponsored contractors to sponsoring States'.[113] The sponsoring state is not liable for the damage caused by the contractor, but for damage resulting from its own failure to exercise due diligence. As a result, the Chamber thought there also had to be a causal relationship between the failure to exercise due diligence and the damage caused by the operator, and that 'such a causal link cannot be resumed and must be proven'.[114] This means that if the state has fulfilled its due diligence obligations and nevertheless the sponsored contractor causes damage (or even if the due diligence obligations have not been fulfilled but the damage was not attributable to this failure), then the only option is to take action against the sponsored entity.

It is far from obvious that the sponsored entity will have the resources to meet such costs. Yet rather than fall back on the residual liability of the state, which might be justified on the basis of its sovereign act of 'enabling' the entity over which it exercises effective control to engage in

party might bring a claim. The Chamber draws on Art 48 of the ILC's Articles on State Responsibility in support of this proposition. See further French, above n 93, 546, who points out that this amounts to an *actio popularis* in international environmental law, and Anton, et al, above n 93, 10–11.

[110] The ILC said that 'whether such elements are required depends upon the content of the primary obligation, and there is no general rule in this respect. For example, the obligation under a treaty to enact a uniform law is breached by the failure to enact the law, and it is not necessary for another state party to point to any specific damage it has suffered by reason of that failure'. (Commentary to Art 2, para 9, for which see Crawford, above n 1, 84. The question of damage may, however, be relevant to the question of who can invoke the responsibility of the state in breach.

[111] Advisory Opinion, para 210. This does make one wonder what the Chamber thought the point of the inclusion of the requirement of damage at this point actually was.

[112] The danger of there being such a 'liability gap' was stressed by Australia in its Written Statement to the Chamber, para 35.

[113] Advisory Opinion, para 183.

[114] Ibid, para 182.

the activity, the Chamber fell back on what might be termed the 'allocation of competences' approach and accepted that the division of liability as provided for in the Convention framework should be allowed to lie—something it was not prepared to let happen in relation to the state's own direct obligations.[115] Why did it do so? For policy reasons, one presumes. It is clear that the Chamber was sympathetic to the need to facilitate the participation of developing states in activities in the area and clearly understood that allowing residual liability for damage flowing from the activities of sponsored entities would be a significant stumbling block for them. But it was also alert to potential dangers in its approach.[116] Thus it was content to suggest a variety of expedients which could be used to 'plug the liability gap', including the possible establishment of a trust fund 'to compensate for damage not covered'.[117] It was also quick to point out that the law regarding responsibility and liability is not static and thus the liability regime set out in the Convention 'may either be developed in the context of the deep seabed mining regime[118] or in conventional[119] or customary law'.[120] For all, this, it remains the case that the Chamber was not prepared to fall back on the more general rules of international law to 'fill the gap' as it had done in relation to the situation regarding the lack of damage flowing from the breach of the direct obligation of the sponsoring state. As regards damage caused by the sponsored entity, the Chamber did not think it appropriate to tamper with the allocation of liability provided for under the Convention framework.

(iii) Question 3

The final question posed was 'What are the necessary and appropriate measures that a sponsoring state must take in order to fulfil its responsibility under the Convention . . .?

[115] The justification given for doing so in para 209 was that the damage was the result of a lawful act and the ILC had not pursued the issue of damages resulting from acts not prohibited under international law, the relevance of which is not obvious. The acts giving rise to the damage may well have been prohibited under international law. The point is that the Chamber excludes the liability of the sponsoring state for damage which, but for its sponsorship, the entity would not have been in a position to cause. The legal or illegal nature of the act is not really the point: the point is the damage.

[116] See, eg para 159 on the pitfalls of 'sponsoring States of convenience'.

[117] See ibid, paras 205, 209. Doubtless the expectation would be that developed countries and those entities engaged in activities in the area would be the contributors to such a fund.

[118] *Cf* Freestone, above n 93, 759, who suggests that such developments could provide a means of plugging the 'liability gap'.

[119] *Cf* Plakokefalos, above n 93, 10, who points out that as regards oil pollution an alternative convention regime has been erected based upon strict but limited liability, based on International Convention on Civil Liability for Oil Pollution Damage (1969) 973 UNTS 3 (amended by the Protocol to Amend the International Convention on Civil Liability for Oil Pollution Damage, LEG/CONF.9/15, 2 December 1992).

[120] Advisory Opinion, para 211.

It is not necessary to explore the answer here, other than to make it clear that in answering this the Chamber was aware that it was, in effect, giving guidance as to the practical measures which, if undertaken, might relieve the sponsoring state from liability for damage caused by the contractor. At the same time, it was clear that, whilst not having an unfettered discretion, the actual content of such measures was ultimately something for the sponsoring state to determine rather than for Chamber to proscribe.[121]

C. Potential Lessons

It is difficult and probably disingenuous to over extrapolate from this Advisory Opinion, which is concernd with a complex legal regime of relationships, obligations and liabilities embedded within a politically sensitive framework. What it does suggest, however, is that the ITLOS is prepared to understand and apply the rules of responsibility and liability in a manner which respects the 'architecture' of the treaty regime, even if this results in a 'lacuna'. At the same time, where a state has failed in its own obligations under the treaty regime and would be responsible for that breach under the principles set out by the Articles on State Responsibility, then ITLOS also seems prepared to recognise liability on the basis of customary international law. This seems right. It is not really so much a question of 'architecture' or 'competence' but of ensuring that a state is unable to evade liability for its own failings merely because those failings have not (yet) resulted in damage caused by a third party.

Nevertheless, the entire point of the sponsorship regime is to permit the state to involve itself in seabed activities through the medium of a third party. As the Chamber makes clear, the sponsoring state must have effective control over the sponsored entity and must make an exercise of sovereign will in order that it might undertake such activities at all. In which case, one might ask, why are its acts not attributable to the state, at least residually?[122] There may be good policy reasons concerned with the participation of developing states in activities within the Area to justify

[121] Ibid, para 227. Again, this might allow for some leeway for determining whether the liability of the sponsoring state is in fact excluded. The Chamber says that the sponsoring state is to take measures which are 'reasonably appropriate' and that such measures may be justified 'only if they are agreeable to reason and not arbitrary' (ibid, para 229). Fortunately, it is not necessary attempt to interpret this most opaque of paragraphs, the upshot of which is that there is considerable room for manoeuvre concerning the reasonableness of the measures and thus the applicability of the liability regime.

[122] Obviously, a state is not liable for the acts of private entities which fall under its effective control. If it were, then it would have residual liability for all its nationals and attribution could be a redundant concept. The point is that without the support of the sponsoring state the entity would be unable to operate within the Area at all. Taken from this perspective, attribution seems hardly the right question to be asking.

the difference of approach but it is difficult to deny that there does seem to be a different approach taken in relation to the two critical 'gaps' in liability which the Chamber identifies.

In the first, it plugs the gap by reference to the traditional and customary principles of responsibility, based as they are on attribution and sovereign authority. In the second it fails to do so, based on respect for the architectural design of a regime. But it is not only because of that design. There is a very clear justification for the liability regime—encouraging participation by developing states in activities in the Area—which reflects a major strand of thinking within international law itself, the common heritage of humankind. Though not set out in these terms, this may provide an additional reason for the Chamber's accommodating approach: the 'institutional' architecture' provides not only a reinforcement of, but arguably a better means of achieving, a goal of the more general international law framework as well.

There may well be an important lesson for the EU—and any other similar organisation—here. Internal allocations of competence which serve to strengthen the realisation of general goals of the international community may be more likely to be respected than those which serve only the interests of the organisation itself, and particularly if they serve the organisational interest at the expense of the broader international community interest.

IV. CONCLUSION

The purpose of this contribution has been to highlight some salient points concerning the approaches of two international judicial bodies to issues of state responsibility in a manner which allows for some reflection on the way in which, from an international lawyers' perspective, the 'eternal conundrum' of who is to be held responsible and liable for activities when a multiplicity of actors are involved might be approached. The 'traditional' approach, illustrated and exemplified by the ICJ, focuses on questions of attribution and nationality of claims, underpinned, as those approaches are, by concepts of state sovereignty and hierarchical responsibility for those acting within or under the scope of that authority. It is as one might expect: in the final analysis, states are held internationally responsible—and accountable—for those acts which are, or which may be considered to be, a projection or reflection of their sovereign authority or power. This is faithfully reflected in the ILC's Articles on State Responsibility and mirrored in the Articles on Responsibility of International Organisations.

But how well does this transpose to institutional settings in which the site of sovereign authority or power has been, in practice, impacted upon by the adoption of alternative relational structures? Turning to the recent work of the ITLOS, one finds a degree of ambivalence to the approach found within the ILC's Articles on State Responsibility which suggests that the EU does well to stress the need for the responsibilities (and liabilities) of international organisations not to be modelled so strictly upon them and for allowing some scope for the internal 'architecture' and the purpose of institutional design to drive the question of international liability. It seems that the approaches from both the international law and EU law perspectives—either 'inside out', or 'outside in'[123]—both point in the same direction. Turning to the work of the ICJ, the possibility of international organisations such as the EU assuming responsibility in a litigation context before the ICJ is in principle feasible. However, as things stand, it remains a very distant prospect since there is little political appetite for expanding the category of entities that may appear as litigants before the ICJ beyond the Westphalian State.

[123] See Kuijper and Passivirta, above n 3.

5

International Responsibility of the EU and the European Court of Justice

ALLAN ROSAS

I. INTRODUCTION

THE MAIN FUNCTION of the European Court of Justice (ECJ)[1] is to adjudicate matters of an internal rather than an international nature. This is the case independently of what view one takes in the never-ending discussion about the constitutional nature of the European Union (EU), in other words, whether it is a federation, a confederation or something else.[2] The importance of the distinction to be made between the internal and the external stems from the simple fact that the basic Treaties and, to an even greater extent, the legislative and other legal acts of the EU which apply within the Union are fundamentally different from the legal relations between the EU and third states, which are governed notably by customary international law and international agreements concluded by the EU. Only the latter relations are wholly governed by public international law, whereas this law is of more limited relevance for EU law proper,[3] with its special characteristics of internal hierarchy, primacy, direct applicability and direct effect and Member States' liability vis-à-vis individuals.[4]

The Member States are certainly responsible for the fulfilment of their

[1] Unless otherwise stated, this article will deal with the case law of the Court of Justice rather than the General Court or the Civil Service Tribunal, all three courts comprising the Court of Justice of the European Union. See Art 19(1) of the Treaty on European Union (TEU).

[2] See, eg A Rosas and L Armati, *EU Constitutional Law: An Introduction* (Oxford, Hart Publishing, 2010) 3, 7–8.

[3] A Rosas, 'Relations entre les États members de l'Union européenne: Le droit international public a-t-il encore sa place?' in *L'État souverain dans le monde d'aujourd'hui; Mélanges en l'honneur de J-P Puissochet* (Paris, Éditions A Pedone, 2008) 255.

[4] See, eg Rosas and Armati, above n 2, chs 1–5.

obligations under EU law,[5] but there does not seem to be much sense in analysing these questions of responsibility and liability under EU law in the same way as questions of responsibility under public international law. This observation also applies to the extremely rare cases of litigation between the EU Member States before the ECJ,[6] as the applicable law, of course, remains Union law.

These observations are not called into question by the fact that the ECJ may, under certain special circumstances, be asked to apply, or interpret, rules applicable between the EU and a third state in a manner which goes beyond its normal function of ruling on international agreements concluded by the EU as integral parts of the Union legal order. One such example is the EU–Turkey Association Agreement of 1963, which provides for the possibility to submit to the ECJ a dispute between the two parties when it cannot be resolved by the bilateral Council of Association.[7] However, in practice such disputes are unlikely to be submitted to the ECJ.

This chapter will focus on the possible contribution of the ECJ, in the course of its normal adjudicatory activities, to the question of the responsibility of the Union vis-à-vis third states and other subjects of international law, rather than the adjudication of matters of responsibility and liability under EU law, or of disputes between the EU and third states in the particular instances where the ECJ itself would be acting as an international dispute settlement mechanism. Other contributions in this volume will deal with issues relating to the international responsibility of the EU more generally,[8] including issues with which international courts[9] and other international dispute settlement mechanisms such as the World Trade Organisation (WTO) system are confronted.[10]

The present chapter will thus look at the specific contexts in which

[5] Including not only the responsibility which may be brought to bear by the European Commission in so-called infringement proceedings under Art 258 of the Treaty on the Functioning of the European Union (TFEU) or by another Member State under Art 259 TFEU, but also the liability which, according to the famous *Francovich* case law of the ECJ, a Member State may incur for breaches of EU law in relation to private parties. On the latter form of liability, see, eg P Aalto, *Public Liability in EU Law: Brasserie, Bergaderm and Beyond* (Oxford, Hart Publishing, 2011).

[6] According to Art 259 TFEU, a Member State may bring an action against another Member State for an alleged infringement of an obligation under the Treaties (including here so-called secondary law such as legislative acts). The only cases which have led to a judgment are Case 141/78 *France v United Kingdom* [1979] ECR 2923; Case C-377/95 *Belgium v Spain* [2000] ECR I-3123; Case C-145/04 *Spain v United Kingdom* [2006] ECR I-7917. One case is pending, Case C-364/10 *Hungary v Slovakia* (the oral hearing took place on 1 February 2012).

[7] Art 25, paragraph 2, of the Agreement establishing an association between the European Economic Community and Turkey of 23 December 1963, [1964] OJ L217. See more generally A Rosas, 'International Dispute Settlement: EU Practices and Procedures' (2003) 46 *German Yearbook of International Law* 284, 289–91.

[8] See also ch 2 by Kuijper and Paasivirta in this volume.

[9] See also ch 4 by Evans and Okowa, ibid.

[10] See also ch 10 by Delgado-Casteleiro and Larik, ibid.

issues of responsibility have arisen in the case law of the ECJ (and to some extent the General Court[11]) in its capacity as the principal Union Court. According to Article 2 of the Articles on State Responsibility adopted by the United Nations (UN) International Law Commission (ILC)[12]—and, with respect to international organisations, Article 4 of the draft articles on the responsibility of international organisations adopted in 2011[13]—there is an internationally wrongful act which may entail the international responsibility of a state (or, as the case may be, an international organisation) when conduct consisting of an act or an omission (a) is attributable to the state (or international organisation) under international law and (b) constitutes a breach of an international obligation. In the following section, I shall examine how the ECJ may contribute to the avoidance of responsibility by minimising the risk that the EU might violate its international obligations, in other words, by minimising the risk of a material breach.

II. AVOIDANCE OF MATERIAL BREACH

It would go far beyond the remits of this chapter to try to cover the different situations in which the EU may incur responsibility for breach of its international obligations. As the Union has become an important actor on the international scene such responsibility may occur in many different contexts. The ECJ has repeatedly confirmed that the EU, including the Communities which ceased to exist in 2002 (Coal and Steel Community) and 2009 (European Community), must, as a subject of international law, respect international law in the exercise of its powers.[14] This is

[11] See n 1.

[12] Adopted by the ILC on 9 August 2001, ILC Yearbook 2001, vol II (part two). See also UN General Assembly resolution 56/83 of 12 December 2001, and UN doc. A/56/49(vol II)/Corr 4 and J Crawford, *The International Law Commission's Articles on State Reponsibility: Introduction, Text and Commentaries* (Cambridge, Cambridge University Press, 2002).

[13] Adopted at the sixty-third session of the ILC and submitted to the UN General Assembly as part of the ILC report, UN doc A/66/10. On the possible relevance of these draft articles for the EU see S Talmon, 'Responsibility of International Organizations: Does the European Community Require Special Treatment?' in M Rangazzi (ed), *International Responsibility Today: Essays in Memory of Oscar Schachter* (Leiden, Martinus Nijhoff Publishers, 2005) 405; E Paasivirta and PJ Kuiper, 'Does One Size Fit All? The European Community and the Responsibility of International Organizations' (2005) XXVI *Netherlands Yearbook of International Law* 169; PJ Kuijper, 'International Responsibility for EU Mixed Agreements' in C Hillion and P Koutrakos, *Mixed Agreements Revisited: The EU and Its Member States in the World* (Oxford, Hart Publishing, 2010) 208; F Hoffmeister, 'Litigating against the European Union and Its Member States: Who Responds under the ILCs Draft Articles on International Responsibility of International Organizations?' (2010) 21 *European Journal of International Law* 723.

[14] With respect to general or customary international law: Case C-286/90 *Poulsen and Diva Navigation* [1992] ECR I-6019, paras 9–10; Case C-162/96 *Racke* [1998] ECR I-3655, paras 45–46; Case C-366/10 *The Air Transport Association of America*, judgment of 21

contingent on the EU being bound by the public international law rule in question, or, as stated in Article 2 of the Articles on State Responsibility referred to above, that the conduct of the EU constitutes a breach of 'an international obligation'.

With respect to international agreements in particular, the Court has also consistently held that, if binding on the EU, they form an integral part of the Union legal order.[15] No separate act of internal implementation is required (assuming that the agreement is sufficiently exhaustive to lend itself to direct application) and the agreement is thus directly applicable (which does not necessarily mean that it has direct effect, see below).[16] In this respect, the EU system can be seen as monist rather than dualist. The question of responsibility for the fulfilment of mixed agreements (agreements concluded by both the Union and some or all of its Member States) and certain agreements concluded by EU Member States will be considered in Section III below.

If the EU has concluded the agreement or is otherwise internationally bound by it, the agreement is, according to Article 216(2), binding upon both the Union institutions and the Member States. The ECJ has underlined that in ensuring respect for the agreement, as provided for in Article 216, paragraph 2, TFEU, the EU Member States are fulfilling an obligation in relation to the Union, 'which has assumed responsibility for the due performance of the agreement'.[17] This consideration seems, at least implicitly, to run through much of the case law of the ECJ. The Court, in other words, attempts to facilitate, or at least not to render more difficult, the fulfilment of the international treaty obligations entered into by the EU so as to avoid the EU becoming responsible for a material breach vis-à-vis third states.

The question, then, arises as to what specific means are available to the ECJ to minimise the risk that the EU might incur such international responsibility. Three devices, in particular, stand out in this respect: the

December 2011 nyr, para 101. See also, eg A Gianelli, 'Customary International Law in the European Union' in E Cannizzaro, P Palchetti and RA Wessels (eds), *International Law as Law of the European Union* (Leiden, Martinus Nijhoff Publishers, 2012) 93. With respect to treaty law see, eg Case C-344/04 *IATA and ELFAA* [2006] ECR I-403, para 35.

[15] The judgment in Case 181/73 *Haegeman* [1974] ECR 449 has been followed by an extensive case law, see, eg J Wouters, A Nollkamper and E de Wet (eds), *The Europeanisation of International Law: The Status of International Law in the EU and its Member States* (The Hague, TMC Asser Press, 2008); P Eeckhout, *EU External Relations Law*, 2nd edn (Oxford, Oxford University Press, 2011) 321ff; Cannizzaro et al, above n 14.

[16] For a clear distinction, as far as international agreements are concerned, between direct applicability and direct effect see Case C-238/06 P *Develey Holding* [2007] ECR I-9375, para 43. See also Rosas and Armati, above n 2, 49.

[17] The first time this formula appears seems to be Case 104/71 *Kupferberg* [1982] ECR 3641, para 13. See also Case 127/6 *Demirel* [1987] ECR 3719, para 11; Case C-13/00 *Commission v Ireland* [2002] ECR I-2943, para 15; Case C-239/03 *Commission v France* [2004] ECR I-9325, para 26.

control of the validity of Union acts, the principle of direct effect and the principle of consistent interpretation. And in all these contexts, the Court is faced with the challenge of 'finding' the applicable public international law norm and of arriving at the 'right' interpretation of the norm thus found. It would go beyond the confines of this contribution to analyse in depth the relevant case law of the ECJ. What follows is a brief summary of the case law as it would appear to stand today.

Concerning control of validity, the Court has, by and large, maintained its approach first sketched out in *International Fruit*.[18] This means that, while, in the hierarchy of norms, international agreements prevail, in principle, over other (internal) Union acts of secondary law, such as regulations and directives,[19] there are three main conditions for the control of the validity of such acts: 1) that the international agreement is binding on the Union; 2) that, having regard to its nature and structure, it is in principle among the rules which can be invoked by individuals as grounds of invalidity, and 3) that the provision of the agreement actually invoked is sufficiently precise and unconditional to have direct effect.[20]

The second condition is not considered to have been fulfilled with respect to the WTO agreements,[21] the UN Convention on the Law of the Sea of 1982,[22] the Kyoto Protocol to the United Nations Framework Convention on Climate Change of 1997[23] and, it would seem, the Council of Europe-sponsored European Convention on the Protection of Animals Kept for Farming Purposes of 1976.[24] Many other agreements have been considered to fulfil the conditions, including some multilateral conventions such as Yaounde/Lomé/Cotonou agreements between the EU and African, Caribbean and Pacific countries[25] and the Montreal Convention for the Unification of Certain Rules for International Carriage by Air.[26]

Until recently, doubts persisted as to whether customary international law could be relied upon for the purpose of examining the validity of Union legal acts. While a case decided by the ECJ in 1998 certainly sug-

[18] Joined Cases 21–24/72 *International Fruit Company v Produktschap voor Groenten en Fruit* [1972] ECR 1219.

[19] Rosas and Armati, above n 2, 48–49.

[20] See, eg *The Air Transport Association of America*, above n 14, paras 52–54. See, more generally P Eeckhout, above n 15, 292–98, 331–55.

[21] See, eg *International Fruit*, above n 18; Case C-149/96 *Portugal v Council* [1999] ECR I-8395; Case C-377/02 *Van Parys* [2005) ECR I-8465. See also Rosas and Armati, above n 2, 48–49, 70–71; Eeckhout, above n 15, 292–97, 343–50.

[22] Case C-308/06 *Intertanko* [2008] ECR I-4057, paras 61–64.

[23] *The Air Transport Association of America*, above n 14, 73–78.

[24] See Case C-1/96 *Compassion in World Farming* [1998] ECR I-1251, paras 30–37, which is not entirely clear as to whether the Court relied on the second or third condition mentioned above.

[25] Case 85/75 *Bresciani* [1976] ECR 129; Case C-469/93 *Chiquita Italia* [1995] ECR I-4533.

[26] *IATA and ELFAA*, above n 14, para 39.

gested that such validity control was not excluded,[27] its contours remained largely an open issue. The question has been at least partly settled by a recent judgment concerning the validity of the EU scheme for greenhouse gas emission allowance trading and the inclusion of international aviation in that scheme.[28] The Court formulated two basic conditions for validity control: first, that the relevant principles of customary international law 'are capable of calling into question the competence of the [EU] to adopt that act' and, second, that the act in question 'is liable to affect rights which the individual derives from [EU] law or to create obligations under [EU] law in his regard'. However, the Court added a reserve on the intensity of validity control: since, according to the Court, a principle of customary international law does not have the same degree of precision as a provision of an international agreement, judicial review must necessarily be limited to the question whether, in adopting the act in question, 'the institutions of the EU made manifest errors of assessment concerning the conditions for applying those principles'.

If a given international norm (whether of a treaty or customary nature) cannot be invoked as grounds for invalidity, there is obviously a risk that because of the continued application of the internal Union act in question, the Union will be considered in breach of an international obligation. Such a conclusion adopted by an international dispute settlement body (such as a WTO panel or the WTO Appellate Body) might lead the Union to abrogate or amend the act or alternatively, to face the legal consequences of an internationally wrongful act, such as to make reparation for the injury caused. On the other hand, the risk of such a situation of non-compliance will be mitigated if the international norm in question allows for different ways of implementation and/or different interpretations of particular provisions, as it is precisely such agreements (or customary international rules) which often, according to case law, may not be invoked as grounds for invalidity. Thus, the finding of a violation by a dispute settlement body would arguably be less likely.

The WTO agreements are an example. The WTO Dispute Settlement Understanding (DSU) provides for three optional ways of implementation of recommendations and rulings adopted by the dispute Settlement Body (and based on a decision of a panel or the Appellate Body): 1) so-called direct implementation; 2) compensation and 3) tolerance of trade sanctions (termed suspension of concessions) undertaken by a trade partner which has invoked the dispute settlement procedures. While direct implementation is to be 'preferred',[29] it seems unlikely that choosing compensation or compliance with trade sanctions (which would enable maintaining in force, at least for the time being, the internal EU act found

[27] *Racke*, above n 14.
[28] *The Air Transport Association of America*, above n 14, paras 107–10.
[29] See Art 22(1) DSU.

to be in violation of a WTO agreement) would trigger a new finding of violation of WTO rules. These alternative ways of implementation, in fact, offer one explanation (in my view the most relevant explanation) why the ECJ has held that the nature and structure of the WTO system precludes validity control of internal Union acts.[30]

That said, if, as in the *Bananas* and *Hormones* cases, the EU measures are incompatible with WTO agreements,[31] and these measures are not repealed by the Union legislator or stricken down by the Union Courts, and if the parties cannot agree on compensation, the EU may have to endure trade sanctions (suspension of concessions). This, again, may cause various inconveniences both for private traders and in the trade relations between the EU and third states, as was the case specifically with regard to the Banana dispute.[32] On the other hand, one can ask whether the Union Courts are well placed to judge such highly complex and difficult questions of WTO law or whether, for the functioning of the WTO system, this task should better be left to its dispute settlement mechanism.

In this context the particular problems relating to the *Kadi* case law of the ECJ should be mentioned.[33] The situation with which the Court was faced in *Kadi* differs, however, from the question of control of validity of Union acts in relation to international agreements concluded by the EU. First, the EU is not a contracting party to the international agreement in question (the United Nations Charter). Second, the case, on appeal from the General Court,[34] did not concern the validity of a Union act in the light of an international agreement, but the validity of a Union act in the light of Union primary law, in a situation where the Union act constituted a faithful implementation of an international obligation, that is, a binding sanctions decision (freezing of funds) by the UN Security Council with regard to alleged terrorists. The Court annulled the Union act as it considered that it had been approved in violation of Union fundamental

[30] See *Van Parys*, above n 21, paras 42–48; A Rosas, 'Case Note on Case C-149/96 *Portugal v Council*' (2000) 37 *Common Market Law Review* 797, 810–11; A Rosas, 'Implementation and Enforcement of WTO Dispute Settlement Findings: An EU Perspective' (2001) *Journal of International Economic Law* 131, 139; Rosas and Armati, above n 2, 71.

[31] *EC—Regime for the Importation, Sale and Distribution of Bananas*, WT/DS15, WT/DS27/R and /AB, WT/DS105, WT/DS158; *EC—Regime for the Importation of Bananas*, WT/DS361, WT/DS364; *EC—Measures Concerning Meat and Meat Products (Hormones)*, WT/DS26/R and /AB, WT/DS48/R and /AB; *US—Continued Suspension of Obligations in the EC—Hormones Dispute*, WT/DS320/R and /AB.

[32] It is impossible here to give a full account of the 'banana saga' which for a long time weighed heavily on the trade relations between the EU, on the one hand, and the United States and some Latin American countries, on the other. A summary is given in the ECJ judgment in Joined Cases C-120/06 P and C-121/06 P *FIAMM* [2008] ECR I-6513, paras 13–28. See also Rosas 'Implementation and Enforcement of WTO Dispute Settlement Findings', above n 30, 137–38.

[33] Joined Cases C-402/05 P and C-415/05 P *Kadi and Al Barakaat International Foundation v Council* [2008] ECR I-6351.

[34] Case T-306/01 *Yusuf and Al Barakaat International Foundation* [2005] ECR II-3533; Case T-315/01 *Kadi* [2005] ECR II-3649.

rights and rule of law principles, notably the right to an effective remedy and the right to property.

The outcome, which diverges from the judgment of the General Court, has been criticised for putting the Union and its Member States in a situation of disrespect for their international obligations (the UN Charter).[35] The judgment certainly confirms that EU primary law prevails over international agreements, even in cases where they are directly binding on the Union (and thus, a fortiori, over agreements such as the UN Charter to which the Union is not a contracting party). In this regard, the conclusion is well grounded in EU constitutional law (and the same conclusion, if the case had been decided by a national court, would follow from the constitutional law of many of the Member States). *Kadi* thus relates to the internal hierarchy of EU norms and more precisely, the relation between primary law and one particular category of secondary law (international agreements) rather than to the question of monism versus dualism.[36] However, the outcome of the case is arguably also in line with a reasonable interpretation of the UN Charter: It is not to be assumed that the Charter, one of the cornerstones of a post-Second World War system of promotion and protection of human rights, would authorise a sanctions regime which, because of its rather draconian nature, including lack of any judicial or similar control, would run counter to the most fundamental values and principles of this system.[37]

In this context a brief word should also be said on the possibility that the ECJ is called upon to rule, not on the validity of a Union internal act in the light of an international agreement, but on the validity of the Council decision concluding the international agreement itself (eg because it is argued that the choice of legal basis was inappropriate or that the contents of the agreement is contrary to EU primary law). A judgment finding the decision invalid could, of course, create a problem for the Union's ability to continue honouring its international obligations. To minimise this risk, the Court may decide to preserve the effects of a decision for a transitional period allowing the Commission and the Council to take the necessary measures (for instance, to withdraw from the agreement).[38]

[35] See A Rosas, 'Counter-Terrorism and the Rule of Law: Issues of Judicial Control' in AM Salinas de Frías, K Samuel and N White (eds), *Counter-Terrorism: International Law and Practice* (Oxford, Oxford University Press, 2012) 83.

[36] *Cf* Gianelli, above n 14, 99–101, who claims that the Court 'appears to have followed Advocate General Poiares Maduro's strictly dualist approach' (100). In our terminology, monism relates to direct applicability of international norms rather than internal norm hierarchy and thus does not necessarily imply that international norms, in the internal hierarchy of norms, prevail over any other norm, including a norm of a constitutional character (Union primary law), Rosas and Armati, above n 2, 49.

[37] Rosas, above n 35, 106–10.

[38] See, eg Case C-360/93 *Parliament v Council* [1996] ECR I-1195; Joined Cases 317/04 and C-318/04 *Parliament v Council and Commission* [2006] ECR I-4721, where the effects

Apart from the question of the nature and structure of the agreement, there is the question of whether its individual provisions have direct effect, implying that they may be invoked by individuals before courts and authorities. Direct effect presupposes that the provision in question is sufficiently unconditional and precise. As already noted above, many agreements have been considered to have such an effect. This is particularly the case with respect to bilateral agreements such as association agreements and trade and cooperation agreements. Other agreements (examples were mentioned above), or at least their individual provisions, have been considered to lack direct effect, which is not to say that they are not directly applicable.[39]

Direct effect may help to reduce the risk of incurring international responsibility, although it cannot, of course, be ruled out that the interpretation given by the ECJ to a particular provision will be subsequently contradicted by the decision of an international adjudicatory body. Moreover, in the EU judicial system, where the national courts of Member States play an important role as integral parts of the system,[40] the direct applicability and direct effect of an agreement binding upon the Union may well be a matter for the national judge. While national judges may, and sometimes must, refer questions of interpretation to the ECJ, one cannot exclude that the case will be decided by the national judge, without a reference to the ECJ. In any case, given the high number of national legal systems in the EU, there would be an obvious risk that different national judges would come to different conclusions as to direct effect and, especially if direct effect is granted (whether by the ECJ or the national court), as to the material interpretation of the international norm applied. In such a scenario, direct effect might even, paradoxically, increase the risk that the EU might incur international responsibility for violation of the international norm.

Whether or not an international agreement has direct effect, the principle of consistent interpretation[41] instructs Union organs, including the Union Courts, to interpret, as far as possible, Union acts in conformity with the international obligations of the Union. This principle becomes particularly relevant with respect to agreements or customary norms which cannot serve as grounds for the control of validity and/or do not have

of a Commission decision closely linked to the application of an agreement with the United States on passenger name records of air passengers were maintained for a few months. See also Rosas and Armati, above n 2, 226.

[39] Rosas and Armati, ibid, 70–72; Eeckhout, above n 15, 290.

[40] See Art 267 TFEU and Opinion 1/09 of 8 March 2011, *Draft Agreement on the European and Community Patents Court*, nyr. See also A Rosas, 'The National Judge as EU Judge: Opinion 1/09' in P Cardonnel, A Rosas and N Wahl (eds), *Constitutionalising the EU Judicial System* (Oxford, Hart Publishing, 2012) 105.

[41] Rosas and Armati, above n 2, 61–62.

direct effect, such as the WTO agreements.[42] As is also the case with respect to EU directives, consistent interpretation may often lead to a result which, in essence, resembles that of a finding of invalidity or direct effect.[43]

When the ECJ is called upon to rule on such issues of validity, direct effect and consistent interpretation, it should seek an interpretation which does not conflict with a reasonable interpretation of the applicable international norm, and which does not run the risk of being overturned by an international dispute settlement mechanism. In the application and interpretation of a Union act, the ECJ has, from time to time, referred to not only a WTO agreement but also decisions of a WTO panel, or of the WTO Appellate Body, in order to support a given interpretation of the WTO agreement in question.[44] More generally, the Union Courts may refer to the case law of international adjudicatory bodies, including not only the WTO bodies but also the European Court of Human Rights (ECtHR) and the International Court of Justice (ICJ), as authoritative sources for the interpretation of an international agreement.[45]

With respect to international dispute settlement mechanisms, and that of the WTO in particular, one should question the extent to which Union Court judgments have been cited by the international dispute settlement body, either in support of the conclusion that the EU has not violated the international norm applied, or as Union measures which, on the contrary, are in violation of the applicable international norm. As it is not possible here to embark on such a systematic study of WTO practice, I will limit myself to two examples, taken from WTO case law. In one customs case, the WTO panel held that an ECJ judgment could constitute a relevant circumstance as a supplementary means of interpretation, under

[42] See, eg Case C-53/96 *Hermès* [1998] ECR I-3603, para 35; Case C-300/90 *Dior and others* [2000] ECR I-11307, para 47; Case C-373/08 *Hoesch Metals and Alloys* [2010] ECR I-951, para 40; Case C-428/08 *Monsanto Technology* [2010] ECR I-6761, paras 70–73; Case C-240/09 *Lesoochranárske zoskupenie*, judgment of 8 March 2011 nyr, paras 49–51; Opinion of Advocate General Trstenjak of 29 June 2011 in Case C-135/10 *SFC Consorzio Fonografici*, paras 80–83. For more references to case law see Rosas and Armati, ibid, 62 (fn 37).

[43] Rosas and Armati, ibid, 59–63.

[44] See, eg Case C-245/02 *Anheuser Busch* [2004] ECR I-10989, paras 49 and 67; Case C-2 60/08 *HEKO Industrieerzeugnisse* [2009] ECR I-11571, para 22. For examples of judgments which refer to the WTO agreements without citing a panel or Appellate Body decision see Case C-335/05 *Rizeni Letového Provozu* [2007] ECR I-4307, para 16; Case C-373/08 *Hoesch Metals and Alloys* [2010] ECR I-951, para 40; *Monsanto Technology*, above n 42, paras 71–73.

[45] For two recent examples see *The Air Transport Association of America*, above n 14, para 104, and Case C-347/10 *Salemink*, judgment of 17 January 2012, para 32 (which refer to ICJ case law). For more examples from ECJ case law see A Rosas, 'With a Little Help from My Friends: International Case-Law as a Source of Reference for the EU Courts' (2005) 5 *The Global Community: Yearbook of International Law and Jurisprudence* (Oxford, Oxford University Press, 2006) vol I, 203.

Article 32 of the Vienna Convention on the Law of Treaties of 1969.[46] More importantly, in another customs case the panel held that ECJ preliminary rulings, as they are binding on not only the national judge who made the reference, but all courts of the EU Member States, clarified the correct classification of the products in question. This ensured the necessary uniform application of customs law on a question that hitherto had seen divergences in the tariff classifications operated by EU national customs authorities.[47] I am not aware of a WTO case where a panel or the Appellate Body have ruled that a Union Court decision is, in itself, a measure incompatible with a WTO agreement.

As far as the ECtHR is concerned, the EU is not a contracting party to the European Convention on Human Rights.[48] However, the Charter of Fundamental Rights of the European Union refers to the Convention and even instructs the Union to give Charter provisions which correspond to a right recognised in the European Convention the same meaning and scope as those laid down by the Convention.[49] While the Union cannot become a respondent before the ECtHR in Strasbourg, the latter Court has not excluded the possibility that Member States become individually or collectively responsible for acts or omissions which are primarily attributable to the Union.[50] The ECJ case law, which pays considerable attention to not only the Convention but also the case law of the Strasbourg Court,[51] thus reduces the risk that EU Member States incur such international responsibility. In the same vein, the risk is reduced that the Union be more or less compelled to adjust its internal legislation in the light of a Strasbourg judgment finding that an EU Member State has violated the Convention in applying the relevant Union legislation.

[46] Although in the case at issue, the judgment had been superseded by a new Union legal act, *EC—Frozen Boneless Chicken*, WT/DS269/R, paras 7.373–7.405. The most relevant ECJ judgment was Case C-33/92 *Gausepohl-Fleisch* [1993] ECR I-3047.

[47] *EC—Selected Customs Matters*, WT/DS315/R, paras 7.200–7.206. The ECJ judgments were in Case C-339/98 *Peacock* [2000] ECR I-8947 and Case C-463/98 *Cabletron Systems* [2001] ECR I-3495.

[48] But see Art 6(2) TEU, which provides that the EU 'shall accede' to the European Convention. A draft accession agreement was negotiated in 2010–11 between the European Commission and Council of Europe Member States (including EU Member States) but at the time of writing, the EU Council has not been able to reach agreement (according to Art 218(8) TFEU, the Council shall act unanimously when adopting a decision concluding this accession agreement).

[49] See Art 52 of the Charter of Fundamental Rights of the European Union. On the binding character of the Charter see Art 6(1) TEU.

[50] Case of *Bhosporus v Ireland* [GC], Application No 45036/98, judgment of 30 June 2005, ECHR 2005-VI; Case of *Kokkelvisserij v Netherlands*, Application No 13645/05, judgment of 20 January 2009.

[51] See, eg A Rosas, 'The European Union and International Human Rights Instruments' in V Kronenberger (ed), *The European Union and the International Legal Order: Discord or Harmony?* (The Hague, TMC Asser Press, 2001) 53; A Rosas, 'Fundamental Rights in the Luxembourg and Strasbourg Courts' in C Baudenbacher, P Tresselt and T Örlygsson (eds), *The EFTA Court: Ten Years On* (Oxford, Hart Publishing, 2005) 163, 168–71.

As to the ECtHR, it refers increasingly to ECJ case law in at least the following contexts:[52] (i) it is seen as an indication of the general level of protection which has developed within the Union legal order in order to assess whether that level of protection is equivalent to the one offered by the European Convention system;[53] (ii) individual judgments are considered with a view to assessing whether an act or omission of an EU Member State is in compliance with the Convention;[54] and (iii) ECJ case law is used as a source of inspiration to support a specific interpretation of the European Convention.[55]

Outside the specific framework of the European Convention on Human Rights, there may be a Union law obligation to 'take into account' an international agreement binding on the EU Member States, but not directly on the Union as such, but this obligation is arguably of a weaker nature than the principle of consistent interpretation pertaining to agreements to which the Union is a contracting party.[56] Especially with respect to agreements that are binding on the Member States but which enjoy no particular status in Union law, the risk is obviously greater that a judgment of the ECJ, applying Union law proper, will somehow contribute to a situation where a Member State, obliged to give priority to the applicable Union norms, incurs international responsibility for violation of the agreement it has concluded with a third power.[57] While such a situation would be regrettable,[58] it is difficult to envisage that Union law could, outside the specific context of Article 351 TFEU (agreements concluded by Member States before they became EU members), tolerate derogations from the principle of the primacy of Union law—in other words tolerate that Member States could circumvent their Union law obligations by

[52] *Cf* Rosas, above n 51, 171–72.

[53] See, in particular, the judgment in *Bosphorus*, above n 50, where the Strasbourg Court made extensive references to ECJ case law in the field of fundamental rights, holding that the EU system guaranteed an equivalent level of protection and that therefore was a presumption that Member States' measures to implement Union law were in conformity with the Convention.

[54] For instance in the case of *Dangevill v France*, judgment of 16 April 2002, Reports of Judgments and Decisions 2002-III, paras 31–37, 53–58, the Strasbourg Court, in concluding that there was a violation of the Convention, took into account the fact that national legislation and case law, by virtue of ECJ case law, was also in violation of Union law.

[55] For two examples see *Scoppola v Italy [GC]*, Application No 10249/03, judgment of 17 September 2009, paras 38 and 105; *Micallef v Malta [GC]*, Application No 17056/06, judgment of 15 October 2009, paras 32 and 78.

[56] A Rosas, 'The Status in EU Law of International Agreements Concluded by EU Member States' (2011) 34 *Fordham International Law Journal* 1304 at 1341.

[57] See Case C-188/07 *Commune de Mesquer* [2008] ECR I-4501 and *The Air Transport Association of America*, above n 14, where the ECJ held that the Union is not bound by certain oil pollution conventions or the Chicago Convention on International Civil Aviation, respectively, concluded by the Member States. In such situations, one cannot exclude that respecting the ECJ judgment may put the Member State concerned at risk of breaching the international agreement it has concluded.

[58] See, eg J Klabbers, *Treaty Conflict and the European Union* (Cambridge, Cambridge University Press, 2009).

concluding agreements with third countries.[59] This question is related to the question of who is responsible for what (subjects of obligations and attribution), to which I shall now turn.

III. SUBJECTS OF OBLIGATIONS AND ATTRIBUTION

As noted above, Article 2 of the ILC Articles on State Responsibility,[60] and Article 4 of the draft articles on responsibility of international organisations adopted by the ILC in 2011,[61] provide that there is an internationally wrongful act which may entail the international responsibility of an international organisation when conduct consisting of an act or an omission both constitutes a 'breach of an international obligation' and is 'attributable' to the international organisation under international law.

Article 216, paragraph 2, TFEU, as well as ECJ case law, is based on the assumption that the obligation of the EU to respect the agreement in question is, in principle, limited to agreements to which the Union is a contracting party (Article 216, paragraph 2, speaks of agreements 'concluded by the Union'). If the Union is the only contracting party on the EU side (in other words, the EU Member States are not parties in their own right), a situation which normally occurs in the case of Union exclusive competence, there can be no doubt that it is responsible for the acts or omissions of its institutions, bodies, offices and agencies, including the conduct of the Union Courts.[62]

With respect to such agreements concluded by the Union alone, and especially if the matter falls within its exclusive competence, the Union is arguably also responsible for the acts or omissions of its Member States, which, according to Article 216(2) TFEU, are bound by the agreement concluded by the Union.[63] Whether in such a situation the Member States, too, may incur responsibility is a more complex question which cannot receive a definitive answer here. While there is a tendency in international case law to channel responsibility to the Union even for the fulfilment of mixed agreements, especially concerning parts of the agreement which fall under a Union exclusive competence (such as fisheries and trade in goods),[64] this question does not seem to have been addressed head-on by

[59] Rosas, above n 56, 1314–15.

[60] Hoffmeister, above n 13, 731–44.

[61] Ibid.

[62] See Art 4 of the ILC Articles on State Responsibility, according to the conduct of any state organ shall be considered an act of that state, 'whether the organ exercises legislative, executive, judicial or any other functions'.

[63] Hoffmeister, above n 13.

[64] See, eg *Case Concerning the Conservation and Sustainable Exploitation of Swordfish Stocks in the South-Eastern Pacific Ocean (Chile v European Community)*, Case No 7, which was pending before the International Tribunal for the Law of the Sea since 2000 but was subsequently settled out-of-court (Order 2009/1 of the Tribunal of 16 December

the ECJ. Nor do the draft articles on responsibility of international organisations adopted by the ILC in 2011 adequately answer such questions specifically arising for the EU (as was noted above, the relations between the Union and its Member States are governed by Union law, which in many respects is different from the public international law which regulates intergovernmental organisations).[65]

In an earlier judgment concerning a Union agreement, the Court noted that in respecting the agreement, Member States fulfilled an obligation 'in relation to the non-member country concerned' (although the Court added that they 'also and above all' fulfilled an obligation in relation to the Community, which had assumed international responsibility for the performance of the agreement).[66] The reference to third states has been dropped in subsequent case law (albeit concerning mixed agreements), the Court observing that the Member States 'fulfil, within the Community system, an obligation in relation to the Community'.[67] This could possibly indicate that the Court views the obligation of Member States as an internal obligation only and that it is the Union which is solely responsible vis-à-vis third states (but with respect to mixed agreements, not necessarily concerning the whole agreement, see below). These considerations would apply, a fortiori, to agreements concluded by the Union alone (non-mixed agreements).

Quite specific problems arise with regard to mixed agreements, as, on the one hand, they clearly fulfil the condition of Article 216(2), that is, are concluded by the Union, but, on the other hand, may cover areas

2009 ordering that the case be removed from the list of cases), and which concerned the responsibility of the EU for the activities of Spanish fishing vessels outside the coast of Chile; Rosas, above n 7, 301–02. See further a fairly extensive (by now) case law of the WTO dispute settlement system: Panel Report, 'European Communities—Customs Classification of Certain Computer Equipment', WT/DS62/R, DS67/R and DS68/R; Panel Report, 'European Communities—Measures Affecting Asbestos and Products Containing Asbestos', WT/DS135/R; Panel Report, 'European Communities—Geographic Indications', WT/DS174/R, para 7.725; Panel Report, 'European Communities—Biotech', WT/DS291/R, DS292/R and DS293/R, para 7.101; Panel Report, 'European Communities—Selected Customs Matters', WT/DS315/R, and Appellate Body Report, WT/DS135/AB/R, paras 122–37, 154, 210, 218–27. *Cf* Panel Report, 'European Communities—Tariff Treatment of Certain Information Technology Products', WT/DS375/R, DS 376/R, DS377/R, which was first registered with the 'European Communities and its Member States' as respondent but which figures on the WTO list of cases as cited, www.wto.org/english/tratop_e/dispu.status_e.htm (accessed on 4 February 2012).

[65] It is not possible here to enter into a detailed critique of the draft articles to the extent that they are meant to apply to the EU. A *lex specialis* clause (Art 64) inserted into the draft articles in 2009 (Report of the International Law Commission, sixty-first session (2009), UN doc A/64/10) with the special situation of the EU in mind seems to mitigate the problem. See also Kuijper, above n 13, 217–24; Hoffmeister, above n 13.

[66] *Kupferberg*, above n 17, para 13. See also M Björklund, 'Responsibility in the EC for Mixed Agreements: Should Non-Member Parties Care?' (2001) 70 *Nordic Journal of International* 373, 396–98.

[67] *Demirel*, above n 17, ECR 3719, para 11; *Commission v Ireland*, above n 17, para 15; *Commission v France*, above n 17, para 26.

which either fall outside the competence of the Union or where the Union has not (yet) exercised its competence, notably by adopting legislative or other legal acts. The question of 'mixity', which is highly complex and also controversial, cannot be fully analysed in this context.[68] I shall not only limit myself to the question of responsibility for mixed agreements[69] but also examine this question mainly from the point of view of ECJ case law only.

Particularly in the context of preliminary ruling requests under Article 267 TFEU, but also in the context of some infringement procedures under Article 258 TFEU, the ECJ has been confronted with the question of whether a specific provision of a mixed agreement constitutes Union law to the extent that it falls within the jurisdiction of the Court to apply it (in infringement proceedings) or interpret it (in preliminary ruling proceedings). While this by now fairly extensive case law cannot be analysed fully here, what deserves special attention is whether or not the ECJ, in arriving at a conclusion about the Union law status of a particular part of the mixed agreement, has explicitly or implicitly taken into account the question of international responsibility.

Reference has already been made above to a formula used in many judgments stating that, in ensuring respect for Union or mixed agreements, EU Member States fulfil an obligation in relation to the Union, 'which has assumed international responsibility for the performance of the agreement'.[70] This formulation could imply that, according to the ECJ, and also with respect to mixed agreements, the Union has undertaken an obligation vis-à-vis third states with regard to the entire agreement. It would appear that this approach also underpins the outcome of the cases, in which the Court concluded in favour of the Community (now Union) law status of the part of the agreement at issue.

The view of the Court concerning the Lomé Convention, concluded in 1989 between the then European Economic Community (EEC) and the ACP (African, Caribbean and Pacific) countries, was indeed that the Community was responsible for the fulfilment of the entire agreement. The Court observed that the Convention 'established an essentially bilateral ACP-EEC cooperation' and that, in the absence of derogations expressly laid down in the Convention, the Community and its Member States are

[68] See, generally, eg A Rosas, 'The European Union and Mixed Agreements' in A Dashwood and C Hillion (eds), *The General Law of EC External Relations* (London, Sweet & Maxwell, 200) 200; J Heliskoski, *Mixed Agreements as a Technique for Organizing the International Relations of the European Community and its Member States* (The Hague, Kluwer Law International, 2001); C Hillion and P Koutrakos (eds), *Mixed Agreements Revisited: The EU and Its Member States in the World* (Oxford, Hart Publishing, 2010).

[69] For a more complete discussion of the question of EU responsibility for the fulfilment of mixed agreements see, eg Björklund, above n 66; Heliskoski, above n 68, 121ff; Kuijper, above n 13; Hoffmeister, above n 13.

[70] See above n 17.

'jointly liable' to the ACP States for the fulfilment of 'every obligation' arising from the commitments undertaken.[71] According to the Advocate General, under a mixed agreement 'the Community and Member states are jointly liable unless the provisions of the agreement point to the opposite'.[72]

It should be noted that in the cases considered so far, there had been no declaration of competence, attempting to delimit Union from Member States competence. It should also be noted that these dicta do not exclude a responsibility on the part of the Member States; the Lomé judgment in fact explicitly foresees joint responsibility and this would apply to the entire agreement.

While this case law seems to be based on the idea of a global approach, seeing a Union interest in the uniform application and interpretation of a mixed agreement, including at the national level,[73] the picture somewhat changes when looking at a string of judgments mainly concerned with one of the WTO agreements, the Agreement on Trade-Related Aspects of Intellectual Property Rights (TRIPS). Similarly in TRIPS there is no declaration of competence; however, this case law, perhaps as a result of the ECJ's Opinion 1/94 stressing the relevance of internal EU legislation to establish a Union competence,[74] is essentially based on the idea of a division of competence and the non-Union law character of the fields of the agreement where the Union has not yet legislated, that is, exercised its competence.[75]

In both the first and the latest of these cases related to TRIPS, the Advocate General of the Court emphasised the importance of international responsibility also for the question of whether the Court had jurisdiction to rule on the interpretation of a given provision.[76] Their conclusion, based on both considerations relating to international responsibility and the principle of cooperation and the requirement of unity in the inter-

[71] Case C-316/91 *Parliament v Council* [1994] ECR I-625, para 29. See also Kuijper, above n 13, 209–10.

[72] Opinion of Advocate General F Jacobs of 10 November 1993 in *Parliament v Council*, ibid, para 69.

[73] See, eg *Commission v France*, above n 17, para 29, where the Court noted that the agreements at issue created rights and obligations 'in a field covered in large measure by Community legislation', and that there was thus 'a Community interest in compliance by both the Community and its Member States with the commitments concerned'.

[74] Opinion 1/94 *WTO Agreement* [1994] ECR I-5267.

[75] *Hermès*, above n 42; *Dior and others*, above n 42; Case C-89/99 *Schieving-Nijstad and others* [2001] ECR I-5851; Case C-431/05 *Merck Genéricos Produtos Farmacêuticos* [2007] ECR I-7001. See also Björklund, above n 66; Heliskoski, above n 68, 46–48, who argue that the presumption should not be joint and several liability but rather the idea that Union competence is limited to the part of the agreement on which the Union has already decided to exercise its competence by an internal legal act.

[76] Opinion of Advocate General G Tesauro of 13 November 1997 in *Hermès*, above n 42; opinion of Advocate General D Ruiz-Jarabo Colomer of 23 January 2007, paras 54–57, in *Merck Genéricos Produtos Farmacêuticos*, above n 75.

national representation of the Union,[77] was that the Court should have jurisdiction to give preliminary rulings on all the provisions of TRIPS. With respect to responsibility, the Advocate General argued that, when the Union is a contracting party vis-à-vis third states and that by virtue of Article 216(2) the agreement is binding on both the Union institutions and the Member States, 'this inevitably means that the Community is responsible vis-à-vis every party to the agreement' and that the Court has jurisdiction in order to ensure uniformity of interpretation and application 'throughout the Community and also to protect the Community's interest in not being obliged to assume responsibility for infringements committed by one or more Member States'.[78]

The Court did not base its decisions on this line of reasoning, although it mitigated the division of competence which it seemed to insist on in principle, by ruling that where a provision of TRIPS can apply both to situations falling within the scope of national law and to situations falling within the scope of Community law, 'it is clearly in the Community interest that, in order to forestall future differences of interpretation, that provision should be interpreted uniformly, whatever the circumstances in which it is to apply'.[79] The Court has also mitigated the division of competence in two further ways: first, it has held that a specific issue may become part of Union law even if it has not yet been the subject of Union legislation if the issue concerns a field 'in large measure' covered by such legislation.[80] Second, the Court seems to consider that if the Union's competence, although shared with Member States, is not implicit but is expressly provided for in the Treaties, this could be a factor lending support to the Union law character of the entire agreement.[81]

As to declarations of competence, in some judgments considerable importance is accorded to their wording, with a view to assessing the Union versus national law character of a given provision of the mixed

[77] The principle of cooperation has been established by the ECJ with regard to the area of shared competence, see, eg Case C-246/07 *Commission v Sweden* [2010] ECR I-3317 with references to earlier case law.

[78] Opinion of Advocate General Tesauro, above n 76, para 20. See also the Opinion of Advocate General Ruiz-Jarabo Colomer in *Merck Genéricos*, above n 76.

[79] *Hermès*, above n 42, para 32. For a recent affirmation see *Lesoochranárske zoskupenie*, above n 42, para 42.

[80] The quotation is from *Lesoochranárske zoskupenie*, ibid, para 36. See also *Commission v France*, above n 17, paras 29–31. See also Opinion 1/03 *Lugano Convention on Jurisdiction and the Recognition of Judgments in Civil and Commercial Matters* [2006] ECR I-7183, paras 120 and 126, where the Court, as one of the criteria for determining the existence of an exclusive competence, referred to 'an area which is already covered to a large extent by [Union] rules'.

[81] *Commission v France*, ibid, para 30; Case C-459/03 *Commission v Ireland* [2006] ECR I-4635, paras 94–95 (but see para 96 and note 82); *Lesoochranárske zoskupenie*, ibid, para 35.

agreement.[82] A recent judgment seems to downplay considerably the relevance of such a declaration,[83] but this may be due to the fact that, in the case at issue, the wording of the declaration was not clear. It goes without saying that if a declaration of competence is, as is sometimes the case, required by the agreement in question, and if, which is much less often the case, its meaning is clear, the declaration may reduce the possibility of third states invoking the responsibility of the Union for the fulfilment of the whole agreement.

To sum up, while the ECJ did not, in its case law relating to TRIPS, confirm expressly the approach recommended by one of its Advocates General, according to whom the existence of international responsibility (arguably for the entire agreement) is an important argument in favour of the Court's jurisdiction, the Court has, in another string of case law, itself referred to the fact that the Union has assumed international responsibility for the fulfilment of the agreement and in one judgment, it was explicitly said that this responsibility covered the whole agreement (but was shared with the Member States).[84] Moreover, in the judgments where responsibility has not been mentioned, there has been a tendency to qualify or nuance the requirement that, concerning a mixed agreement, the competence of the Union must have been exercised by internal legislative measures. This, again, is susceptible to broaden somewhat the scope of what is considered to be Union law and thus also the scope of the jurisdiction of the Court. It is arguable that also with regard to the latter category of cases, responsibility has, after all, played a certain role in the overall assessment of the situation.

Finally, a word should be said about international agreements concluded by the Member States to which the Union is not a contracting party. The starting point is that such agreements are to be regarded as part of the national law of the Member States concerned[85] and that accordingly the ECJ lacks jurisdiction to interpret them.[86]

The only clear exception to this principle is that the Union may become responsible for the fulfilment of an agreement concluded by its Member States which has become binding on it by way of succession. In the only case where the ECJ has accepted the existence of such a succession, *International Fruit* concerning the provisions of the General Agreement on Tariffs and Trade (GATT 1947),[87] the Court cited two principal elements:

[82] See, eg Case C-29/99 *Commission v Council* [2002] ECR I-11221, paras 67–71; *Commission v Ireland*, above n 81, paras 96–109.

[83] *Lesoochranárske zoskupenie*, above n 42, para 39.

[84] *Cf* Annex IX, Art 6(2), of the UN Convention on the Law of the Sea, according to which failure, on the part of the Union or a Member State, to clarify on demand the division of competence between the two shall result in joint and several liability.

[85] Rosas, above n 56, 1314.

[86] See, eg Case C-533/08 *TNT Express Nederland* [2010] ECR I-4107, para 61.

[87] *International Fruit*, above n 18.

that the then Community had assumed the powers previously exercised by the Member States in the area covered by GATT (trade in goods, and thus an area of exclusive Union competence[88]) and that the transfer of powers from the Member States to the Community had been recognised by the other contracting parties.[89] Ensuing case law, which has rejected the idea that the Union has succeeded the Member States with respect to several other international conventions than the GATT,[90] suggests that succession may occur only in exceptional circumstances.

Apart from the very special case of succession, agreements concluded by EU Member States do not, in principle, constitute an integral part of the Union legal order, but are part of the national legal orders of the Member States party to such agreements. That said, some of these agreements may become relevant also from a Union law perspective, for instance, if a Union legislative act incorporates or refers to their provisions, and the ECJ has held that, under certain circumstances, they should be applied (in case of incorporation) or account should be taken of them (in the case of more general references) in the interpretation of the EU act in question.[91] In such instances, however, the Union arguably does not become bound by the agreement in its relation with third states, but the legal effects of the agreement are limited to the EU and its Member States and issues of Union responsibility vis-à-vis third states normally do not arise.[92]

In this connection it should also be noted that the derogation from the principle of primacy of EU law, which is provided for in Article 351 TFEU concerning agreements concluded by EU Member States prior to EU membership, does not constitute an exception to what has just been said. While the ECJ has observed that this provision would not achieve its purpose if it did not imply a duty on the part of the Union institutions not to impede the performance of the obligations of Member States that stem from such a prior agreement, the Court has also recognised that

[88] See Art 3(1) TFEU, which list the common commercial policy as one of the areas of exclusive Union competence, and Art 207 TFEU on the scope of the common commercial policy. On the case law leading up to these provisions see, eg Rosas and Armati, above n 2, 19, 205–06.

[89] *International Fruit*, above n 18, paras 15–16.

[90] International Convention for the Prevention of Pollution from Ships (Marpol 73/78), Case C-379/92 *Peralta* [1994] ECR I-3463, para 16; *Intertanko*, above n 22, para 48; International Convention on Civil Liability for Oil Pollution Damage of 1969 and International Convention on the Establishment of an International Fund for Oil Pollution Damage of 1971, *Commune de Mesquer*, above n 57, para 85; Warsaw Convention for the Unification of Certain Rules Relating to International Carriage by Air of 1929, Case C-301/08 *Bogiatzi* [2009] ECR I-10185, paras 27–32; Chicago Convention on International Civil Aviation of 1944, *The Air Transport Association of America*, above n 14, paras 57–72.

[91] See, notably, Case C-439/01 *Cipra* [2003] ECR I-745, para 24 (concerning a situation of incorporation) and *Intertanko*, above n 22, para 52 (concerning a situation of a weaker reference). See also *Kadi and Al Barakaat International Foundation v Council*, above n 33, paras 292–96 (concerning the special case of the United Nations Charter). See more generally Rosas, above n 56, 1324 et seq.

[92] Rosas, ibid, 1330, 1333–34.

the immediate effects of Article 351 are limited to the Union law framework (they constitute, in fact, an exception to the principle of primacy of Union law over the national laws of Member States) and that the possibility offered by this provision to Member States to honour, at least for a transitional period, their previous international legal obligations does not bind the Union vis-à-vis the third state in question.[93]

IV. CONCLUDING REMARKS

The ECJ is mindful of the fact that the EU, as a subject of international law, must respect this law in its dealings with the rest of the world. Article 3(5) TEU, as amended by the Treaty of Lisbon, underlines this necessity in providing that the Union shall contribute to, inter alia, the 'strict observance and the development of international law, including respect for the principles of the United Nations Charter'. An important factor in this regard is that, if Union acts or omissions are not in conformity with public international law binding on the EU, the Union may incur international responsibility.

That being said, the ECJ is also committed to honouring Union primary law, including fundamental rights and other general principles of Union law. The Court has recognised that in the internal hierarchy of norms, primary law prevails over international agreements concluded by the Union. While the latter, in principle, prevail over internal legislation such as regulations and directives, it will depend on their nature and structure whether they may be invoked in order to challenge the validity of a legislative act or, with respect to the nature and formulation of individual provisions, be given direct effect. As to customary international law, the Court has recently confirmed that validity control may enter into the picture but has, on the other hand, due to the often uncertain and indeterminate nature of unwritten law, set a rather high threshold for the determination of invalidity.

It is submitted that, despite these qualifications, the case law of the ECJ shows a great deal of openness and friendliness towards international law and, at any rate, is not 'less friendly' than most national courts would be in the EU Member States or elsewhere. Direct effect is not a panacea which would always guarantee that international law be respected. It might even, in some instances, make it more difficult to maintain a uniform interpretation of Union law rules which have been granted direct effect. The principle of consistent interpretation seems a more important

[93] See, eg Case 812/79 *Burgoa* [1980] ECR 2787, paras 8–9; *The Air Transport Association of America*, above n 14, para 61; Opinion of Advocate General N Jääskinen of 15 March 2011, para 77, in Case C-264/09 *Commission v Slovakia*, judgment of 15 September 2011 nyr. See also Rosas, ibid, 1321.

device to ensure harmony between Union internal law and public international law.

The question of international responsibility has also been an issue in the context of determining the scope of Union competence, particularly as far as mixed agreements are concerned. The Court has several times referred to the fact that the Union has assumed international responsibility for the performance of an agreement, including a mixed agreement. On the other hand, in cases relating to TRIPS, in particular, the Court, unlike two of its Advocates General, does not seem to have paid much attention to the existence of responsibility as a criterion for the question of division of competence between the Union and its Member States. It appears that the Court's case law in this area is not entirely settled.[94]

Finally, it should be recalled that the ECJ, or the other EU courts, including the national courts of the Member States, are not international courts primarily called upon to deliver authoritative interpretations of public international law norms. This is the task of international dispute settlement mechanisms such as the International Court of Justice, the international criminal courts,[95] the International Tribunal for the Law of the Sea, the WTO panels and Appellate Body and arbitration tribunals. Issues related to the international responsibility of the EU will ultimately be decided in such fora, or tackled in negotiations between the Union and the third states concerned.

[94] See notably the judgment in *Lesoochranárske zoskupenie*, above n 42, which seems to be based on a more flexible approach to the question of the scope of Union law and of the jurisdiction of the Court in the case of mixed agreements.

[95] As the EU has become involved in missions and operations of a military character, it may have to apply not only international human rights law but also international humanitarian law applicable in armed conflicts, see A Rosas, 'Is the EU a Human Rights Organisation?', CLEER Working Paper 2011/1 (The Hague, Centre for the Law of EU External Relations, 2011), 14–16.

Part III

Tools for Determining Responsibility

6

Erga Omnes, Jus Cogens and Their Impact on the Law of Responsibility

CHRISTIAN J TAMS AND ALESSANDRA ASTERITI

I. INTRODUCTION

THE CONCEPTS OF obligations *erga omnes* and *jus cogens* fascinate international lawyers, who cannot, it seems, refrain from exploring ever new facets.[1] While both have a long pedigree, in their present 'incarnation', they were launched onto the international plane about four decades ago, and in rather dramatic fashion. In 1969, the Vienna Convention on the Law of Treaties (VCLT), after much debate, recognised that certain rules of international law (among which the drafters mentioned those outlawing the use of force, slavery, piracy or genocide) admitted of 'no derogation' and clarified that treaties violating

[1] Literature on both is vast. Important contributions include the following: P Picone, *Comunità internazionale e obblighi 'erga omnes'* (Naples, Jovene, 2006); C Tomuschat and J-M Thouvenin (eds), *The Fundamental Rules of the International Legal Order. Jus Cogens and Obligations Erga Omnes* (Leiden, Brill, 2006); A Orakhelashvili, *Peremptory Norms in International Law* (Oxford, Oxford University Press, 2006); S Villalpando, *L'émergence de la communauté internationale dans la responsabilité des Etats* (Paris, Presses Universitaires de France, 2005); C Tams, *Enforcing Obligations Erga Omnes in International Law* (Cambridge, Cambridge University Press, 2005, rev edn with new epilogue, 2010); PM Dupuy (ed), *Obligations multilatérales, droit impératif et responsabilité internationale* (Paris, A Pedone, 2003); R Kolb, *Théorie du Jus Cogens International* (Paris, Presses Universitaires de France, 2001); A Paulus, *Die internationale Gemeinschaft im Völkerrecht* (Munich, CH Beck Verlag, 2001); M Ragazzi, *The Concept of International Obligations Erga Omnes* (Oxford, Oxford University Press, 1997); JA Frowein, 'Reactions by Not Directly Affected States to Breaches of Public International Law' (1994) 248 *Recueil des Cours de l'Académie de Droit International*, 345; B Simma, 'From Bilateralism to Community Interest' (1994) 250 *Recueil des Cours* 217; D Alland, *Justice privée et ordre juridique international* (Paris, A Pedone, 1994); C Tomuschat, 'Obligations Arising for States With or Without Their Will'(1993) 241 *Recueil des Cours* 185; S Kadelbach, *Zwingendes Völkerrecht* (Berlin, Duncker & Humblot, 1992).

such 'peremptory norms' would be void.[2] One year later, the International Court of Justice (ICJ) adapted a similar idea to the field of law enforcement, by cryptically pointing to an 'essential distinction' between the regular obligations of a state and those 'towards the international community as a whole':[3] the latter, it went on, included obligations deriving 'from the outlawing of acts of aggression, and of genocide, as also from the principles and rules concerning the basic rights of the human person, including protection from slavery and racial discrimination', which were 'the concern of all States'.[4] And further: 'In view of the importance of the rights involved, all States can be held to have a legal interest in their protection; they are obligations *erga omnes*'.[5]

For many years, academic enthusiasm for the concepts of *jus cogens* and *erga omnes* met with a considerable degree of scepticism among those professing to concern themselves only with 'real law': theoretically interesting though they might have been, 'real lawyers' considered both concepts to be of very limited practical relevance at best. To mention just two prominent statements, Ian Brownlie at one point characterised *jus cogens* as a 'vehicle that hardly leaves the garage',[6] while Hugh Thirlway viewed obligations *erga omnes* as a 'purely theoretical category'.[7] Things have changed, though, and if anything, the problem today (even among courts or other players engaged in the business of the allegedly 'real law') is one of 'over-use'—of vehicles leaving garages all too often, as it were.[8] Whereas Articles 53, 64 VCLT indeed have hardly been invoked in practice, '*Jus Cogens* Beyond the Vienna Convention'[9] is of real relevance today: over the last decades, international and domestic courts have asserted an ever wider range of (often controversial) *jus cogens* effects, in

[2] Arts 53, 64 VCLT. The examples are mentioned in the ILC's Commentary to Draft Art 50 (the precursor to Art 53 VCLT): see *Yearbook of the International Law Commission*, 1966, vol II, 248.

[3] *Case Concerning the Barcelona Traction, Light and Power Co Ltd (New Application: 1962) (Belgium v Spain) (Second Phase)*, ICJ Reports 1970, 3, para 33.

[4] Ibid, paras 33–34.

[5] Ibid, para 33.

[6] I Brownlie, 'Comment' in J Weiler and A Cassese (eds), *Change and Stability in International Law-Making* (Berlin, de Gruyter, 1988) 108, 110.

[7] H Thirlway, 'The Law and Procedure of the International Court of Justice—Part One' (1989) *British Yearbook of International Law 60* at 102 (also describing it as 'an empty gesture', 100).

[8] With respect to *erga omnes*, see, eg *Legal Consequences of the Construction of a Wall in the Occupied Palestinian Territory*, ICJ Reports 2004, 136, Sep Op Higgins, para 57: 'The Court's celebrated dictum in Barcelona Traction, Light and Power Company, Limited, Second Phase (Judgment, ICJ Reports 1970, 32, para 33) is frequently invoked for more than it can bear . . . That dictum was directed to a very specific issue of jurisdictional locus standi . . . It has nothing to do with imposing substantive obligations on third parties to a case'.

[9] *Cf* G Gaja, 'Jus Cogens Beyond the Vienna Convention'(1981) 172 *Recueil des Cours*, 271.

fields as diverse as jurisdiction,[10] immunities,[11] diplomatic protection,[12] reservations to treaties,[13] prosecution of human rights abuses,[14] or extradition.[15] With respect to obligations *erga omnes*, a careful perusal of the ICJ's jurisprudence[16] suggests that the concept has become a legal *vademecum* prescribed to produce a wide array of legal effects: not only (as in the *Barcelona Traction* case) in the field of law enforcement, but also justifying third-party effects of treaties or resolutions,[17] an extensive

[10] There is considerable support for the proposition that all states are entitled to exercise universal jurisdiction over breaches of peremptory norms, see, eg ICTY, Trial Chamber, *Prosecutor v Furunzija*, Case IT-95–17/1-T (para 156); House of Lords, *Pinochet III* [2000] 1 AC 198 (per Lord Browne-Wilkinson); ibid, 275 (per Lord Millett); Brussels Court of First Instance, *Order In re Pinochet*, 119 ILR 356–57; US Court of Appeals (District of Columbia), *Princz v Germany*, Diss Op Judge Wald, 103 ILR 618; ICJ, *Arrest Warrant Case*, ICJ Reports 2002, 3, Diss Op van den Wyngaert (para 45). As regards 'European' jurisprudence, see especially Case T-306/01 *Yusuf and Al Barakaat International Foundation v Council and Commission*, judgment of the Court of First Instance of 21 September 2005, where the Court of First Instance declared that it was 'empowered to check, indirectly, the lawfulness of the resolutions of the Security Council in question with regard to *jus cogens*, understood as a body of higher rules of public international law binding on all subjects of international law, including the bodies of the United Nations, and from which no derogation is possible' (para 226). The CFI found no violations of jus cogens to have occurred, with regards to the imposition of sanctions. In 2008, the judgment was reversed on the merits Joined Cases C-402/05 P and C-415/05 P, *Kadi & Al Barakaat v Council of the European Union and EC Commission* (2008) 3 *Common Market Law Review* 41, with the Court, however, declaring that it had no power to review the lawfulness of resolutions of the Security Council adopted under Chapter VII, 'even if that review were to be limited to the examination of the compatibility of that resolution with *jus cogens*' (para 287). All in all, a victory for fundamental rights protection, but a defeat for jus cogens.

[11] See, eg the ICTY's *Furundzija* judgment (above) para 156; Judge Wald's dissent in *Princz* (103 ILR 618); House of Lords, *Pinochet III* [2000] 1 AC 278 (per Lord Millett) and 290 (per Lord Phillips); ICJ, *Arrest Warrant Case*, ICJ Reports 2002, 3, Diss Op Al-Khasawneh (para 7); Diss Op van den Wyngaert (para 23) (all controversially holding that international law precludes the plea of immunity in case of jus cogens breaches).

[12] See, eg Dugard, First Report on Diplomatic Protection, UN Doc A/CN 4, 506 and Add 1 (2000), paras 75–93, especially draft art 4 (1) (proclaiming a duty of states to exercise diplomatic protection in case of violations of jus cogens norms). *Cf* also the *Abbasi* case before the (English) Court of Appeal, [2002] EWCA Civ 159, paras 28, 41.

[13] See, eg UN Human Rights Committee, General Comment No 24 of 1994, UN Doc CCPR/C/21/Rev 1/Add 6; similarly the opinions of Judges Padillo Nervo and Tanaka and Judge ad hoc Sorensen in the *North Sea Continental Shelf Case*, ICJ Reports 1969, 3, 97, 182, and 248 respectively.

[14] In its *Furundzija* judgment (above), a trial chamber of the ICTY, for example, took the view that '[i]t would be senseless to argue, on the one hand, that on account of the jus cogens value of the prohibition against torture, treaties or customary rules providing for torture would be null and void ab initio, and then be unmindful of a State . . . condoning torture or absolving its perpetrators through an amnesty law' (para 155). See further the *Pinochet* case before the Spanish National Criminal Court (Audencia Nacional), 119 ILR 344.

[15] See, eg Swiss Supreme Court (Tribunal Fédéral), *Bufano et al, Recueil Officiel*, vol 108, I, 408–13 (para 8a); Lynas, ibid, vol 101, 541 (para 7b); Sener, ibid, vol 109, I, 72 (para 6aa) (all holding that where an individuals faced violations of jus cogens rights abroad, he/she could not be extradited).

[16] For details see Tams, above n 1, 97–116.

[17] See, eg *Legal Consequences for States of the Continued Presence of South Africa in Namibia (South West Africa) notwithstanding Security Council Resolution 276 (1970)*, ICJ Reports 1971, 56, para 126: 'the termination of the Mandate and the declaration

understanding of the territorial scope of obligations,[18] and alleged duties of non-recognition.[19]

As appears from this briefest of descriptions, the fascination of both concepts is some extent due to their 'mysterious' character, brought out not the least by the Latin terms denoting them.[20] As was recently noted by James Crawford, '[l]awyers have a habit of putting labels, especially Latin labels, on things . . . We tend to say "*jus cogens*" to a norm and everyone nods their heads sagely . . . Similarly with obligations *erga omnes*'.[21] Yet precisely because *erga omnes* and *jus cogens* are so often placed on a pedestal, it seems necessary to re-focus debates on the effects that the two concepts entail. This we attempt to do in the following sections, which single out three distinct areas in which the two concepts of *jus cogens* and *erga omnes* modify the regime of international responsibility applicable between states and international organisations—and thus affect the scope of responsibility potentially borne by the European Union (EU) and its ability to invoke the responsibility of other actors on the international plane.

Before proceeding with the analysis, two preliminary remarks may be called for. The first concerns our understanding of the term 'international responsibility'. As will become clear from the subsequent assessment, *jus cogens* and *erga omnes* do not alter the fundamentals of that regime. They modify aspects, and occasionally do so in important ways; yet they operate within the parameters of the regime of international responsibility shaped by the work of the International Law Commission (ILC), international practice and jurisprudence. In other words, neither concept affects the three basic propositions upon which the contemporary doctrine of responsibility rests: namely that (i) responsibility of states and international organisations (such as the EU) under international law

of the illegality of South Africa's presence in Namibia are opposable to all States in the sense of barring erga omnes the legality of a situation which is maintained in violation of international law'. This indeed is the traditional understanding of the term 'erga omnes', which had been common prior to the 1970 *Barcelona Traction* case: for details see Tams (2005/2010), 103–06.

[18] See, eg *Application of the Convention on the Prevention and Punishment of the Crime of Genocide (Bosnia and Herzegovina v Serbia and Montenegro)*, ICJ Reports 1996, 595, 616 (para 31), where the Court affirmed the erga omnes character of the 'the obligation each State . . . to prevent and to punish the crime of genocide' and then noted that it was 'not territorially limited'.

[19] *Legal Consequences of the Construction of a Wall in the Occupied Palestinian Territory*, ICJ Reports 2004, 136, paras 155–57. The point is taken up below, section IV.

[20] I Brownlie, 'To What Extent Are the Traditional Categories of Lex Lata and Lex Ferenda Still Viable?' in A Cassese and JHH Weiler (eds), *Change and Stability in International Law-Making* (Berlin, Walter de Gruyter, 1988) 66, 71 (describing the erga omnes concept as "very mysterious indeed").

[21] J Crawford, 'International Protection of Foreign Direct Investment: Between Clinical Isolation and Systemic Integration' in R Hofmann and C Tams (eds), *International Investment Law and General International Law* (Baden-Baden, Nomos, 2011) 17, 23.

is 'breach-based', ie triggered by attributable conduct violating international obligations;[22] (ii) that it is 'objective', ie not generally dependent on damage, or fault;[23] and (iii) that it gives rise to ensuing duties of cessation and reparation (plus, exceptionally, a duty to provide for guarantees and assurances of non-repetition).[24] What is more, the three effects assessed in the following have no direct impact on what seems to be—and certainly from the EU's perspective—the most controversial aspect of the 2011 Draft Articles, namely the delimitation between state and organisational responsibility in the context of joint activity.[25] It is within the basic parameters of the contemporary responsibility doctrine—as reflected in the ILC's texts of 2001 and 2011—that the concepts of *jus cogens* and *erga omnes* entail modifications. Put differently, they might be said to 'fine-tune' the application of international responsibility in instances involving particularly grave breaches of international law. The subsequent sections will assess three such instances of fine-tuning by inquiring whether *jus cogens* and *erga omnes*

(i) widen the potential for 'public interest enforcement' by the European Union (and other actors)
(ii) impose upon the EU and other actors a special regime of aggravated responsibility that would be triggered by breaches of fundamental interest obligations, and
(iii) affect the principles of international immunity that have long been perceived as obstacles to the invocation of responsibility.

The second preliminary remark is in the form of a caveat. For reasons of convenience, the subsequent sections treat *jus cogens* and *erga omnes* as sub-categories of a broader notion of norms protecting a 'fundamental interest of the international community', which we will refer to as 'fundamental interest obligations'. In treating them as part of a broader notion, we acknowledge the close nexus between the two concepts, which since the late 1960s, have largely developed 'in tandem' and which both describe categories of particularly important values. Given the increasing prominence of attempts to merge obligations *erga omnes* and *jus cogens* into a joint category,[26] we would, however, stress at the

[22] See Art 2 ASR and Art 4 DARIO. For comment on alternative approaches—eg explored under WTO law or in the field of liability—see C Tams, 'Unity and Diversity in the Law of State Responsibility' in A Zimmermann (ed), *Unity and Diversity in International Law* (Berlin, Duncker & Humblot, 2006) 437, 443–45.

[23] Art 2 ARS and Art 4 DARIO. For brief comment see paras 9–10 of the ILC's commentary to Art 2, in YbILC 2001, vol II, 36.

[24] Arts 30, 31 ARS and Arts 30, 31 DARIO.

[25] *Cf* Part Five DARIO, notably Art 62. See the chapters by Tomuschat and Kuijper and Paasivirta.

[26] See notably C Tomuschat, 'Reconceptualizing the Debate on Jus Cogens and Obligations Erga Omnes—Concluding Observations' in Tomuschat and Thouvenin, above n 1, 425; J Crawford, Foreword, in Tams, above n 1, xiii.

outset that there are sound reasons, both conceptual and pragmatic, to maintain the distinction between obligations *erga omnes* and norms of *jus cogens*. Notably, whereas *jus cogens* norms are characterised by their elevated hierarchical status, obligations *erga omnes* can well operate on an 'ordinary' hierarchical level. Whereas *jus cogens* status affects the validity of conflicting norms, *erga omnes* status affects the position of third states vis-à-vis the obligation. *Jus cogens* and obligations *erga omnes*—at least in their current 'incarnation'—thus may have entered the international legal discourse almost simultaneously, but follow different rationales. On that basis, they should not be merged; and our decision to deal with them 'en bloc' in the following sections should not be read as an attempt to support such a reading.

II. IMPLEMENTING RESPONSIBILITY FOR BREACHES OF FUNDAMENTAL INTEREST OBLIGATIONS

The first and most obvious impact concerns the legal rules governing the implementation of international responsibility. In essence, international law permits states and international organisations to invoke the responsibility of another state or international organisation for breaches of fundamental interest obligations even if they themselves have not been specially affected by the breach. This is the key aspect of the *erga omnes* concept, which following the *Barcelona Traction* case, has been understood primarily as a law enforcement doctrine permitting states to respond against breaches of obligations owed to the international community as a whole. Within the framework of international responsibility, this first impact concerns the 'enforceability' of international law—rather than the conditions under which responsibility is incurred, or the consequences of responsibility. In 2001, the International Law Commission sought to operationalise the *erga omnes* concept in Part Three of its Articles on the Responsibility of States for Internationally Wrongful Acts ('ARS'), notably Articles 42, 48 and 54. The 2011 Draft Articles on the Responsibility of International Organizations adopt these provisions with only minor modifications in Articles 43, 49 and 57.

Notwithstanding the ILC's work, the idea that international law should accept, within narrow boundaries, some form of 'public interest enforcement' continues to meet with occasional resistance. Perhaps this resistance is best explained as a 'rearguard action' by states and commentators clinging to the fiction of a system of international law based on synallagmatic pairs of reciprocal rights and duties running between pairs of states—or states and international organisations, for that matter. However, such rearguard actions belie the fact that international law has moved on to embrace multilateralism and global public interests: 'community interest is permeating the body of international law much more thoroughly than ever before',[27] and the ILC's attempt, in its work on responsibility, to spell out a regime of public interest enforcement, reflects that fact.[28] In fact, from the perspective of domestic or of European (Union) law, the notion of public interest enforcement in this sense is not alien at all. The public laws of many countries have in recent decades liberalised requirements of *locus standi* to allow individuals to challenge decisions that, while not injuring them in any special or individual sense, were of major relevance and thus ought to be scrutinised.[29]

Perhaps more pertinently, from the very foundations, the Treaty of Rome envisaged that EC/EU Member States should have standing to raise violations of other Member States in proceedings before the European Court of Justice—now enshrined in Article 259 TFEU.[30] If that route has hardly been travelled,[31] this should not be taken as a rejection of the concept, but reflects the fact that the treaties also enshrined the (much preferable) option of institutionalised enforcement at the instigation of the (European) Commission (as per Article 258 TFEU), as well as indirect mechanisms of enforcement based on actions brought by individuals and companies before national courts. If we move out of the realm of Union Law, then the same approach can be seen in the European Convention of Human Rights, which recognises the possibility of inter-state complaints in the public interest in Article 33[32]—and which has reduced the practical need for inter-state proceedings[33] by allowing for direct complaints by

[27] Simma, above n 1, 234.

[28] The ILC made the point very clearly when in para 4 of its commentary to Art 1 ARS, it cited the ICJ's *Barcelona Traction* dictum on obligations *erga omnes*, and went on to note: 'The consequences of a broader conception of international responsibility must necessarily be reflected in the articles which, although they include standard bilateral situations of responsibility, are not limited to them' (*Yearbook ILC* 2001, vol II, 33).

[29] See, eg Lord Diplock, in *Regina v Inland Revenue Commissioners ex parte Federation of Self-Employed and Small Businesses Ltd* [1982] AC 617, 644 E (professing his unwillingness to let 'technical rules of locus standi' prevent applicants from bringing legal matters to the attention of courts). For further details see C Tams and A Asteriti, 'Transparency and Public Interest Representation in Investment Arbitration' in S Schill (ed), *International Investment Law and Comparative Public Law* (Oxford, Oxford University Press, 2010) 787.

[30] Art 259(1) provides in clear-enough terms: 'A Member State which considers that another Member State has failed to fulfil an obligation under the Treaties may bring the matter before the Court of Justice of the European Union'.

[31] But see, eg ECJ, Case C-145/04 *Spain v UK* [2006] ECR I-7917; Case C-388/95, *Belgium v Spain* [2000] ECR I-3123; Case C-141/78, *France v UK* [1979] ECR 2923.

[32] Just as with Art 259 TFEU, the wording of that provision is clear: 'Any High Contracting Party may refer to the Court any alleged breach of the provisions of the Convention and the protocols thereto by another High Contracting Party'.

[33] But see the following inter-state complaints lodged with the Court or the (then) Commission: *Austria v Italy* (Application No 788/60); *Ireland v United Kingdom I and II* (Application Nos 5310/71 and 5451/72); *Cyprus v Turkey I-IV* (Application Nos 6780/74, 6950/75, 8007/77 and 25781/94); *Georgia v Russia I-III* (Application Nos 13255/07, 38263/08 and 61186/09); *Denmark v Turkey* (Application No 34382/97) as well as the different 'Greek cases' instituted by Denmark, Norway, Sweden and the Netherlands (Application Nos 3321/67, 3322/67, 3323/67; 3344/67, 4448/70). For a survey of inter-state applications

individuals (Article 34). In short, notions of decentralised 'public interest enforcement' which had to be progressively planted into general international law have been part of European (Union) law for decades. In general international law, they are important precisely because the options for institutionalised enforcement (equivalent to infringement proceedings instituted by the Commission) or direct recourse (along the lines of individual complaints to the Strasbourg court) are so limited.[34]

A. Public Interest Litigation

Even so, the practical implications of public interest concepts like obligations *erga omnes* have remained controversial.[35] For present purposes, it is important to note that the impact of the *erga omnes* concept depends on the character of the actors seeking to implement, or facing claims of, responsibility. In the traditional state responsibility context, obligations *erga omnes*—in line with the Court's *Barcelona Traction* jurisprudence—have primarily been considered in the context of litigation before international courts and tribunals, and more specifically with respect to the question of standing to institute proceedings (sometimes also referred to as problems of *locus standi*, *intérêt d'agir*, and so on).

While practice remains sparse, there is indeed good authority for the view that all states, irrespective of any individually sustained injury, have standing to bring contentious proceedings before the ICJ if, in their assessment, another state has failed to comply with what is required by an obligation *erga omnes*. Article 34 of the ICJ Statute—restricting party status (at least in contentious ICJ proceedings) to states—however closes the Court to proceedings brought by, or against, international organisations.[36] This means that with respect to judicial proceedings involving claims by or against

see F Voeffray, *L'actio popularis—ou la défense de l'intérêt collectif devant les juridictions internationales* (Paris, Presses Universitaires de France, 2004) 142–52; S Prebensen, 'Inter-State Complaints under Treaty Provisions—The Experience under the European Convention on Human Rights' (1999) 20 *Human Rights Law Journal* 446.

[34] As pertinently noted by Tomuschat, '[g]iven the dramatic lack of an adequate institutional framework', reliance on forms of private law enforcement in the public interest probably was 'the only viable way', above n 1, 365.

[35] The subsequent discussion focuses on law enforcement by way of legal proceedings, diplomatic claims and countermeasures. Other forms of law enforcement—such as military enforcement action, or the exercise of national or regional jurisdiction—are not addressed. For an attempt to survey a broader range of 'public interest enforcement measures' see C Tams, 'Individual States as Guardians of Community Interests' in U Fastenrath et al (eds), *From Bilateralism to Community Interest. Essays in Honour of Judge Bruno Simma* (Oxford, Oxford University Press, 2011) 379.

[36] If anything, their conduct can be addressed only indirectly, in the framework of proceedings directed against (or possibly instituted by) states. The Legality of Use of Force cases before the ICJ, brought by the Federal Republic of Yugoslavia against ten NATO states in response to NATO's bombing of Yugoslavia in 1999, are an example in point; however,

international organisations, the *erga omnes* concept is of lesser relevance than in the inter-state field. *Erga omnes*-inspired arguments might, however, be relevant in legal proceedings under agreements to which international organisations themselves are a party.

With respect to the EU, WTO proceedings provide one example in point, and in fact, in the *Bananas* saga, the Union has faced claims by a party—the United States—that had to rely on the broad notions of legal injury in order to establish standing.[37] By the same token, treaty-based versions of public interest arguments might become relevant in proceedings under the UN Convention on the Law of the Sea. All this, however, seems a rather remote possibility—and one which depends on the specific treaty rules as much as on general concepts like that of obligations *erga omnes*.

Not surprisingly, then, debates have moved on to other modalities of implementing responsibility. Two of these merit to be addressed in the following.

B. Diplomatic Claims outside Legal Proceedings

Formal diplomatic claims outside legal proceedings are the first category. Under the influence of the *erga omnes* doctrine, international law seems to have accepted that such claims could be brought in defence of interests of the international community as a whole. Article 48 ASR—recognising that 'in case of breaches of specific obligations protecting the collective interests of a group of states or the interests of the international community as a whole, responsibility may be invoked by states which are not themselves injured"' in any individual sense[38]—confirmed and consolidated[39]

the Court's decision not to entertain the case has meant that many crucial issues remain undressed. For details see ICJ Reports 1999, 124; ICJ Reports 2004, 279.

[37] See especially the Panel and Appellate Body Reports in the *Bananas III* dispute: WT/DS27/R (Panel), paras 7.49–7.51, and WT/DS27/AB/R (Appellate Body), paras 132–36. Both decisions recognised a right of all WTO members to bring violations complaints under article XXIII:1(a) GATT, irrespective of whether the impugned measure had had an impact on 'their' trade flows. In their reasoning, panel and Appellate Body did not rely on any 'public interest' argument, but noted that trade rules protected conditions of trade, not actual trade flows. However, commentators have noted that, in effect, WTO law recognises the legal interest of all members in seeing WTO law observed, and have qualified it as an '*erga omnes partes* regime': see, eg CA Günther, *Die Klagebefugnis der Staaten in internationalen Streitbeilegungsverfahren* (Berlin et al, Carl Heymanns Verlag, 1999) 142–44 and 242–47; C Tietje, *Normative Grundstrukturen der Behandlung nichttarifärer Handelshemmnisse in der WTO/GATT-Rechtsordnung: eine Untersuchung unter besonderer Berücksichtigung des Countertrade* (Berlin, Duncker & Humblot, 1998) 163–73; M Matsushita, Th Schoenbaum and P Mavroidis, *The World Trade Organization. Law, Practice, and Policy* (Oxford, Oxford University Press, 2003) 26–27.

[38] See ILC, para 2 of the commentary to Art 48 ARS, in *Yearbook ILC* 2001, vol II, 126.

[39] The ILC was rather cautious; in its view, Art 48(2) 'involve[d] a measure of progressive development', which it considered 'justified since it provides a means of protecting the community or collective interest at stake' (commentary to Art 48 ARS, para 12, in Yearbook

international law on this point.[40] While it did so in the inter-state setting, Article 49 DARIO applied this reasoning to claims brought against international organisations, to the extent the 'safeguarding the interest of the international community as a whole underlying the obligation breached is within the functions of the international organization invoking responsibility'.[41] By way of analogy, the same approach would apply in cases involving claims by an international organisation against a state breaching an obligation *erga omnes*.[42] Given the limited jurisdiction of international courts to adjudicate upon claims by and against international organisations, the recognition of such a *droit de regard* is of considerable importance.

C. Coercive Responses

Assertions of a right to implement responsibility through coercive measures are much more controversial and thus require a more detailed examination.[43] As long as international pressure remains intrinsically lawful—such as in the case of retorsions, or unfriendly acts—states or organisations seeking to react against *erga omnes* breaches need not establish any particular title to do so. However, matters are different if their response crosses the threshold of prima facie illegality. Examples in point include the suspension of treaty obligations in relation to the state or international organisation allegedly breaching an obligation *erga omnes*, or the imposition of countermeasures such as travel bans or economic boycotts. In this case, international law must strike a balance between, on the one hand, the need for effective enforcement action in defence of public interests, and, on the other, the importance of preventing abusive claims by self-proclaimed guardians of public policy.

Whether, as part of that balancing exercise, it should, exceptionally, recognize a right to take countermeasures in response to *erga omnes* breaches, is one of contemporary international law's great debates.[44] In

ILC 2001, vol II, 127). For details see J Crawford, 'Responsibilities for Breaches of Communitarian Norms: An Appraisal of Article 48 of the ILC Articles on Responsibility of States for Wrongful Acts' in Fastenrath et al, above n 35, 224.

[40] It should be noted that para 2 of Art 48 limits the scope of claims in the public interest to (a) cessation and possibly guarantees and assurances of non-repetition, and '(b) performance of the obligation of reparation in accordance with the preceding articles, in the interest of the injured State or of the beneficiaries of the obligation breached'.

[41] Art 49(3) DARIO.

[42] See below for references to international practice involving coercive responses.

[43] The following draws heavily on Tams, above n 1, 198–251.

[44] In addition to the works by Simma, above n 1, 293–301 and Frowein, above n 1, 417–23, see, eg M Akehurst, 'Reprisals by Third States' (1970) 44 *British Year Book of International Law* 1; J Charney, 'Third State Remedies in International Law' (1989) 10 *Michigan Journal of International Law* 57.

its work on responsibility, the ILC deliberately avoided to take a stance. Article 54 ARS adopted in 2001 left the matter open;[45] Article 57 DARIO followed suit.[46]

At least with respect to measures taken against states, practice suggests a more liberal approach. Since 1970, states and international organisations have taken countermeasures in response to grave and systematic breaches of fundamental interest obligations in a surprisingly large number of instances. They have not usually made express reference to the *erga omnes* character of the breach in question; but by and large seem to have responded against breaches of obligations that (like those protecting fundamental human rights or outlawing the use of force) are generally considered to be owed to the internationally community as a whole. In most instances, these assertions of a right to defend public interests of the international community have involved coercion of a limited degree—typically breaches of bilateral treaties of limited relevance; often political symbolism rather than actual pressure of relevance. Still, international practice—to be illustrated below—suggests that, when seeking to respond against grave breaches of fundamental interest obligations, states and international organisations have been prepared to act as 'guardians' of community values and, in that context, asserted a right to violate international law in order to 'induce the wrongdoing State to comply with its obligations under international law'.[47]

When focusing on the conduct of international organisations, it deserves to be noted that the European Community (and later the European Union) has been at the forefront of developments.[48] Three categories of EC/EU practice may serve to illustrate the point—and also shed light on the practice of coercive 'public interest enforcement'.[49]

(i) From the 1970s onwards, the EC/EU has responded to serious violations of international law by curbing, or threatening to curb, development assistance or economic co-operation. To the extent that early generations

[45] See Art 54 ARS, which provides: 'This chapter does not prejudice the right of any State, entitled under article 48, paragraph 1, to invoke the responsibility of another State, to take lawful measures against that State to ensure cessation of the breach and reparation in the interest of the injured State or of the beneficiaries of the obligation breached'.

[46] See especially para 2 of the ILC's Commentary, in *ILC Report* 2011, 89.

[47] ICJ, *Gabčikovo-Nagymaros Project (Hungary v Slovakia)*, ICJ Reports 1997, 7, para 85.

[48] By contrast, there does not seem to be any practice of countermeasures taken against international organisations (such as the EC/EU). In its commentary to Art 57 DARIO, the ILC acknowledged this lack of practice, and explained that it was in line with the relative absence of any form of coercive enforcement action against international organisations (whether in defence of public or individual interests): *cf* ILC Report 2011, 89.

[49] For much more detail, as well as context, on this point see, eg the chapters by Paasivirta/Rosas and Palchetti in E Cannizzaro (ed), *The European Union as an Actor in International Relations* (Dordrecht, Kluwer, 2002) 207 and 219, respectively; as well as P Koutrakos, *Trade, Foreign Policy and Defence in EU Constitutional Law* (Oxford, Hart Publishing, 2001).

of economic agreements such as Lomé I did not expressly recognise such a right, the early debates among the Commission and Member States revealed uncertainty about the legality of suspending treaty benefits. Still, the EC, after considerable hesitation, eventually suspended development assistance to Uganda during 1977-79 in response to that country's systematic disregard of human rights.[50] Having asserted a right of coercive 'public interest enforcement' once, in relation to Uganda, the EC responded in similar fashion when, in 1980, Liberia's new leader systematically repressed opposition groups in violation of fundamental rights.[51] In 1991, and outside the field of EC/ACP co-operation, the EC applied a similar sanction to Yugoslavia when it suspended, and subsequently denounced, the 1983 Co-operation Agreement[52] with immediate effect, so as to respond to the outbreak of the Yugoslav war.[53] These measures were incompatible with the terms of the agreement, and had to be based on a right to react coercively against grave breaches of fundamental interest obligations.[54] Finally, it should be noted that, from the 1980s onwards, the 'problem' faced by the EC in these early cases was solved rather elegantly when subsequent generations of economic co-operation agreements began to incorporate the notion of human rights conditionality:[55] Conventions such as Lomé II, III, IV, and most recently, the Cotonou Agreement recognised the EC/EU's right to adopt 'appropriate measures'—including, as a last resort, the suspension of the agreement—if another party 'has failed to fulfil an obligation stemming from respect for human rights, democratic principles, and the rule of law'.[56] Under these agreements, suspension of development aid or other forms of economic co-operation thus need no

[50] See EC Bull 1977, No 6, para 2.2.59. For many further references see F Hoffmeister, *Menschenrechts- und Demokratieklauseln in den vertraglichen Außenbeziehungen der Europäischen Gemeinschaft* (Berlin, Springer, 1998) 11–14; G Oestreich, *Menschenrechte als Elemente der dritten AKP-EWG-Konvention von Lomé. Sanktionsinstrumente oder Zielvorgabe einer Entwicklungszusammenarbeit im Dienste des Menschen?* (Berlin, Duncker & Humblot, 1990) 45–48, 304–07 and 442–43.

[51] See statement by Commissioner Cheysson, 8 July 1980, in: *Europe*, vol 28, no 2495, 11; see further Oestreich, ibid, 320–22 and 447–49

[52] [1983] OJ L41/1.

[53] [1991] OJ L315/1 (suspension); [1991] OJ L325/23 (denunciation).

[54] Rather curiously, the EC sought to justify its conduct by invoking the *clausula rebus sic stantibus* (rather than a right to take countermeasures in the public interest)—and more curiously still, the ECJ accepted this reasoning in Case C-162/96 *Racke GmbH and Cov Hauptzollamt Mainz* [1998] ECR I-3655, paras 52–59. Whatever the preferred legal explanation, though, it seems clear that the episode provides further evidence of the willingness, among the EC and its members, to construe treaties clauses in the light of fundamental interest obligations, and to recognise a right to respond coercively in defence of public interests.

[55] On the evolution of human rights clauses in the external relations of the European Community, see Hoffmeister, above n 50; B Brandtner and A Rosas, 'Human Rights and the External Relations of the European Community: An Analysis of Doctrine and Practice' (1998) 9 *European Journal of International Law* 468.

[56] Cotonou Agreement, [2000] OJ L317/3, Art 96, para 2(a); as for the scope of 'appropriate measures' see Art 96, para 2(c)(i). In Addition, Art 9 prescribes that respect for human rights is an 'essential element' of the EC–ACP co-operation.

longer be based on any general title (such as a right to enforce obligations *erga omnes* coercively), but is envisaged in the treaty itself.[57] The public interest of treaty parties in the protection of fundamental human rights has thus been elevated to the level of a treaty aim; and the economic agreement thus has been 'humanised'.[58]

(ii) Outside the field of EC economic co-operation, embargoes and flight bans have proved to be popular forms of exercising pressure on states responsible for grave violations of international law. To the extent that the states or international organisations concerned are parties to WTO agreements (or previously, GATT), import bans would prima facie be in violation of Article XI GATT and thus require justification. In a number of instances, states or international organisations seeking to respond against grave breaches of international law have, expressly or implicitly, asserted a right to violate Article XI in defence of public interest concerns. With respect to EC practice, the import bans imposed on Argentina during the 1982 Falklands crisis are the most prominent example.[59] Interestingly, these measures gave rise to considerable debate among GATT members.[60] During this debate, the EC and other GATT members conceded that the import embargo affected Argentina's rights under GATT, but asserted an 'inherent right' to impose an embargo in response to Argentina's occupation of the Falkland islands.[61]

As regards flight bans, European Member States—at times at the instigation of the EC/EU—have frequently responded to grave violations of fundamental interest obligations by suspending aviation agreements concluded with the responsible state. As in the instances addressed previously, such measures were not envisaged in the treaty, but had to be based

[57] Measures imposed on Zimbabwe from 2002, in response to the worsening human rights record of the Mugabe Government, provide an example in point: *cf* eg [2005] OJ L48/28, [2005] OJ L200/98 and [2006] OJ L26/28 (of 31 January 2006). For details see P Pillitu, 'Le Sanzioni dell'Unione e della Comunità Europea nei Confronti dello Zimbabwe e di Esponenti del suo Governo per Gravi Violazioni dei Diritti Umani e dei Principi democratici'(2003) 86 *Rivista di Diritto Internazionale* 55.

[58] A similar approach is followed under a number of multilateral agreements in the environmental field: thus the Kyoto Protocol (under its 'enforcement branch' established by Decision 27/CMP 1 in 2005) and CITES (Art VIII), to give just two examples, envisage trade sanctions in response to treaty breaches. Admittedly, however, these treaty sanctions typically presuppose an institutional decision. For comments and references see C Tams, 'Enforcement' in G Ulfstein et al (eds), *Making Treaties Work—Human Rights, Environment and Arms Control* (Cambridge, Cambridge University Press, 2007) 391, 388–399.

[59] See Regulations 877/82, [1982] OJ L102/1 and 1176/82, [1982] OJ L136/1; as regards the parallel measures adopted by the European Coal and Steel Community see Regulations 82/221/ECSC, [1982] OJ L102/3, and 82/320/ECSC, [1982] OJ L136/2.

[60] *Cf* GATT Doc C/M/157; PJ Kuijper, 'Community Sanctions Against Argentina: Lawfulness under Community and International Law' in D O'Keefe and H Schermers (eds), *Essays in European Law and Integration* (Deventer, Kluwer, 1982) 141, 151–54; MJ Hahn, *Die einseitige Aussetzung von GATT-Verpflichtungen als Repressalie* (Berlin, Springer, 1996) 328–34.

[61] For details and references see Tams, above n 1, 215–16.

on a general title to defend public interests. Examples in point include the suspension of aviation agreements with Poland following the 1981 crackdown on Solidarnosc; or with the Soviet Union following the shooting-down of a Korean airliner in 1983.[62] The Council of Ministers, during the Kosovo crisis of 1998, decided that Member States should impose an immediate flight ban on the Federal Republic of Yugoslavia[63]—which states like France and the United Kingdom implemented, albeit (in the latter case) after considerable debate about the legality of the sanction.[64]

(iii) More recently, responses against grave violations of fundamental interest obligations have become more targeted. Assets freezing and travel bans imposed upon individuals responsible for grave breaches of fundamental interest obligations have become rather common.[65] Such forms of 'smart coercion' in defence of public interests have for example been imposed on Iraq (following the invasion of Kuwait) and the Federal Republic of Yugoslavia (during the Kosovo crisis),[66] as well as more recently on members of the Zimbabwean Government,[67] and leaders of Belarus.[68]

These examples (which, it needs to be underlined, are illustrative only, and only reflect practice involving the EC/EU and its members) suggest that, contrary to concerns expressed by the ILC,[69] international practice relating to 'third party countermeasures' is 'far from scarce',[70] but surprisingly wide-spread. As noted above, 'third party countermeasures' typically

[62] For details see C Rousseau, 'Chronique des faits internationaux' (1982) 86 *Revue Générale de Droit International Public* 543, 607; GC Hufbauer, JJ Schott and KA Elliott, *Economic Sanctions Reconsidered*, 2nd rev edn, vol 1 (Washington, DC, 1990) 192–204 and the summary in Tams, ibid, 213–14 and 217.

[63] Common Position 98/326/CFSP, [1998] OJ L143/1, and Common Position 98/426/CFSP, [1998] OJ L190/3. For the implementation see Regulation 1091/98, [1998] OJ L248/1.

[64] For details see D Wibaux, 'A propos de Quelques Questions Juridiques Posées par l'Interdiction des Vols des Compagnies Yugoslaves'(1998) 44 *Annuaire Francais de Droit International* 262.

[65] As a coercive interference with another state's property, assets freezes are not just an unfriendly act, but require justification: *cf* OY Elagab, *The Legality of Non-Forcible Countermeasures in International Law* (Oxford, Clarendon Press, 1988) 214. For a more detailed examination of the measures mentioned in the text see M Dawidowicz, 'Public Law Enforcement without Public Law Safeguards? Analysis of State Practice on Third-Party Countermeasures and Their Relationship to the UN Security Council' (2006) 77 *British Year Book of International Law* 333, 394–98.

[66] For details see Tams, above n 1, 219 and 223.

[67] See, eg [2005] OJ L48/28 (of 19 February 2005); [2005] OJ L200/98 (of 30 July 2005); [2006] OJ L26/28 (of 31 January 2006).

[68] Actual and proposed measures are detailed eg in [2004] OJ L301/67 (of 28 September 2004); *EU Bulletin* No 3/2005 of 10 March 2005, 1.2.4, and *EU Bulletin* No 1–2/2006 of 16 February 2006, 1.32.26.

[69] See para 3 of the Commission's commentary to Art 54 (in *Yearbook ILC* 2001, vol II, 137); and further C Hillgruber, 'The Right of Third States to Take Countermeasures' in Tomuschat and Thouvenin, above n 1, 265.

[70] As rightly pointed out by G Gaja in his 'Second Report on Obligations and Rights *Erga Omnes* in International Law' (2005) 71 (I) *Annuaire de l'Institut de Droit International* 119, 200.

involve rather trivial breaches of international obligations, which in and of themselves are unlikely to induce a wrongdoing state back into compliance; it is often part of a 'sanctions mix' involving diplomatic pressure, unfriendly acts, sometimes UN action—and the occasional countermeasure. However, the brief survey suggests that, where this seemed opportune, the EC/EU and its Member States—just as other states—have not shied away from disregarding their obligations owed to states systematically violating fundamental interest obligations. On that basis, it does indeed seem possible to move beyond the cautious stance taken by the ILC, and to accept that, as noted by the Institut de Droit International, where "a widely acknowledged grave breach of an *erga omnes* obligation occur[s]", all states "are entitled to take non-forcible counter-measures" against the wrongdoing state.[71]

D. Interim Conclusions

All this suggests that the *erga omnes* concept has had an impact on the legal rules governing the implementation of responsibility. Influenced by the *erga omnes* concept, contemporary international practice has embraced different forms of 'public interest enforcement' in response to breaches of fundamental obligations of international law. This has broadened the circle of states, or international organisations, entitled to respond against an internationally wrongful act.

The European Union and its members have made occasional use of this option by asserting a right to respond against violations of fundamental interest obligations that did not specially affect them—and through their practice, have in fact paved the way for the slow, but steady, recognition of a right of 'third party countermeasures'. This is the first, and most obvious, field in which the concepts of *jus cogens* and obligations *erga omnes* have affected the regime of international responsibility.

III. A SPECIAL REGIME FOR 'AGGRAVATED RESPONSIBILITY'?

Two further instances of 'fine-tuning' may be addressed more briefly: the idea that breaches of fundamental interest obligations should trigger a special, 'aggravated', regime of responsibility; and the relationship between responsibility for such breaches on the one hand, and rules of immunity on the other.

[71] Institut de Droit International, Resolution on 'Obligations and Rights *Erga Omnes* in International Law' in 71 (II) *Annuaire de l'Institut de Droit International* (2006) 289 (Art 5).

The notion of 'aggravated responsibility' has been the subject of long-standing and protracted debates.[72] On the face of it, it seems difficult not to accept that breaches of fundamental interest obligations protecting core values should trigger particular consequences: an act of genocide is different from the violation of a bilateral trade agreement, and the rules on responsibility should be seen to reflect that difference.[73] They do so, of course, insofar as the regular consequences of the breach (restitution, compensation and so on) will differ, depending on the type and extent of injury suffered, or damage sustained. Yet many have felt that differentiation 'from within' (ie following from applying the regular rules to specific sets of breaches) was not enough, and that a categorical distinction between 'normal' and 'aggravated' regimes of responsibility would be required.[74]

At some point, the ILC felt the difference ought to be expressed as one between serious breaches (labelled 'crimes') and ordinary breaches (labelled 'delicts'), but the choice of 'criminal' terminology remained controversial, and terminological debates prevented the Commission from discussing the implications of the crime-delict-dichotomy.[75] Once the notion of 'crime of state' had been overcome, these implications could at least be discussed; however, the outcome of discussions turned out to be fairly disappointing: it can be found in Article 41 ASR and Article 42 DARIO respectively, which lay down special consequences triggered by "[s]erious breaches of obligations under peremptory norms of general international law".[76]

Following the ILC, these special consequences are superimposed on the regular regime of consequences. They are very special indeed, in that they only apply to a narrow group of doubly-qualified breaches of international law, namely 'gross or systematic failure[s]' to impose obligations flowing from *jus cogens* rules.[77]

Curiously, notwithstanding the narrow formulation of the category to which it applies, this 'special regime' of responsibility is rather underdeveloped and unbalanced. Article 41 of the ILC's Articles on State

[72] For an excellent summary see notably A Cassese, *International Law*, 2nd edn (Oxford, Oxford University Press, 2005) 262–77.

[73] See, eg A Pellet, 'Can a State Commit a Crime? Definitely, Yes!' (1999) 10 *European Journal of International Law* 425, 426: 'It is absolutely unacceptable to assimilate purely and simply a genocide and an 'ordinary' breach of international law, say a breach of a bilateral trade treaty'.

[74] Ibid, 426–27.

[75] See J Crawford, 'Introduction' in ibid (ed), *The International Law Commission's Articles on State Responsibility* (Cambridge, Cambridge University Press, 2002) 16ff, for a clear summary of the debate; and more briefly C Tams, 'All's Well That Ends Well?' (2002) 62 *ZaöRV* 759, 770ff.

[76] *Cf* Art 40 ASR, Art 41 DARIO. For a useful discussion of their background see Crawford, ibid, 35ff; for further comments see Tams, above n 1, 772ff.

[77] See Art 40(2) ASR, Art 41(2) DARIO.

Responsibility lists a set of obligations: (a) to co-operate to bring an end to the breach through lawful means; (b) not to recognize as lawful a situation created by the breach; and (c) not to render aid or assistance for the maintenance of said situation. Identical obligations are envisaged in Article 42 DARIO. Whatever the concrete meaning of the three special obligations mentioned, it is striking that, from the perspective of the lawbreaker, the ILC's regime of 'aggravated responsibility' is not at all special: the state or international organisation responsible for the serious breach is under the obligations imposed by the regular regime of responsibility (to make reparation, to cease ongoing breaches, and so on), but faces no special aggravated consequences. If the regime is aggravated, it is in the sense that it imposes special, ancillary, obligations on third states and international organisations: it seeks to prevent bystanders from being neutral. From the EU perspective, this is—at least in theory—important, as it restricts the policy space and may on occasion require the Union and its members to join international efforts against a law-breaker.

That said, the ancillary obligations imposed are either vague or not (yet) fully accepted as a matter of law. The positive duty of co-operation envisaged in paragraph 1 of Article 41 ASR, Article 42 DARIO does not seem to reflect the current state of customary international law for serious breaches of peremptory obligations, in the sense that there does seem to be, currently, a duty for states to positively co-operate in order to bring a breach to an end, and in that respect, constitutes an instance of the ILC acting *de lege ferenda*, rather than expressing *lex lata*.[78] Furthermore, there is no clear and consistent practice on what forms of co-operation are envisioned and if passive co-operation (eg not hindering international organisations or 'coalitions of the willing' from taking action in order to bring an end to a serious breach of a peremptory norm) constitutes a form of co-operation for the purposes of the provision.

The negative duties of non-recognition and non-assistance laid down in paragraph 2 of Article 41 ASR, Article 42 DARIO are more firmly grounded in international practice and supported by the necessary *opinio juris*.[79] For example, the non recognition of territorial annexation is well

[78] This without prejudice to any positive duties of intervention which might be expressed in international agreements, such as the duty 'to ensure respect for' the four 1949 Geneva Conventions (Common Art 1) or the obligation contained in Art 89 of Additional Protocol I (1977): 'In situations of serious violations of the Conventions or of this Protocol, the High Contracting Parties undertake to act, jointly or individually, in co-operation with the United Nations and in conformity with the United Nations Charter'. In the 2004 Advisory Opinion on the *Wall in the Occupied Palestinian Territory*, ICJ Reports 2004, 136, the Court drew a fine distinction between the duty not to recognise a certain situation (which it said was derived from the *erga omnes* concept) and the duty to take positive action against it: see ibid, paras 153–56.

[79] See S Talmon, 'The Duty not to "Recognize as Lawful" a Situation Created by the Illegal Use of Force or Other Serious Breaches of a *Jus Cogens* Obligation: An Obligation without Real Substance?' in Tomuschat and Thouvenin, above n 1, 99, 101ff.

established in international law and supported by state practice. In its Advisory Opinion on the Wall in the Occupied Palestinian Territory of 2004, the International Court of Justice expressed the view that: 'all States are under an obligation not to recognize the illegal situation resulting from the construction of the wall in the Occupied Palestinian Territory . . . They are also under an obligation not to render aid or assistance in maintaining the situation created by such construction'.[80] This statement exemplifies the application of these negative duties to actions by a state that create a situation on the ground comparable to annexation, even if brought about not by open aggression, but 'obliquely', through the partition of territory ostensibly for the purpose of self-defence.

However, the application of the negative duty of non-recognition outside the traditional realm of actions creating 'facts on the ground', such as the unlawful acquisition of territory,[81] jars with the difficulty of establishing what constitutes a 'situation' triggering the duty to abstention and what is the substantive content of the obligation (what counts as recognising as legal or lawful).[82] The progressive limitation of the obligation in the course of the negotiations over its wording, and particularly the acceptance that there would be qualifying circumstances allowing the recognition of 'neutral' conduct,[83] has resulted in a widespread scepticism.[84] As no rights arise from illegal acts, and a fortiori from violations of peremptory norms, what value is supposed to be given to 'non-recognition as legal'

[80] *Legal Consequences of the Construction of a Wall in the Occupied Palestinian Territory*, ICJ Reports 2004, 136, para 159. See also *Legal Consequences for States of the Continued Presence of South Africa in Namibia (South West Africa) notwithstanding Security Council Resolution 276 (1970)*, ICJ Reports 1971, 16. The Court incorrectly derived the obligation not to recognise from the *erga omnes* status of the obligations, while it is a well established duty in general international law that an illegal act is not to be recognised or aided, and that no legal rights are to be attached to it (*ex injuria jus non oritur*); for this, see Judge Higgins Separate Opinion, paras 37ff. The real question is how this non-recognition differs from the regular non-recognition of ordinary breaches.

[81] See already the 'Stimson doctrine', expressing the position taken by the US Secretary of State Henry Stimson, and followed by the majority of the state members of the League of Nations, with respect to the Japanese invasion of Manchuria in 1932. The principle of non-recognition of any territorial acquisition contrary to international law is expressed in GA Resolution 2625 (XXV)—Declaration on Principles of International Law concerning Friendly Relations and Co-operation among States. The application of this principle can also be seen in the international reaction to the annexation of Kuwait by Iraq in 1990 (SC Resolution 662).

[82] Talmon, above n 79, 103ff; Judge Kooijmans' Separate Opinion in *Wall in the Occupied Palestinian Territory*, ICJ Reports 2004, paras 43, 44.

[83] See para 10 of the commentary to Art 41 ASR. In the *Namibia* opinion, the ICJ noted that 'the non-recognition of South Africa's administration of the Territory should not result in depriving the people of Namibia of any advantages derived from international co-operation. In particular, while official acts performed by the Government of South Africa on behalf of or concerning Namibia after the termination of the Mandate are illegal and invalid, this invalidity cannot be extended to those acts, such as, for instance, the registration of births, deaths and marriages, the effects of which can be ignored only to the detriment of the inhabitants of the Territory' (ICJ Reports 1971, 16, para 125).

[84] See Talmon, above n 79, 108ff, for references.

may remain unclear.[85] For example, the ICJ in the *Namibia* Advisory Opinion extended the duty of non-recognition from the purely formal duty of de jure non recognition, to a prohibition against 'acts and dealings . . . implying recognition of the legality of [South Africa's] presence and administration [of Namibia]'.[86] One might also wonder whether a collective duty of non-recognition, as conceptualised by the ICJ in *Namibia*, might not constitute a form of co-operation for the purposes of Article 41(1) ASR. Finally, the relationship between the duty not to render aid of assistance in maintaining a situation created by a serious breach of a peremptory obligation (contained in Article 41(2) ASR and Article 42(2) DARIO) and the responsibility incurred by states aiding or assisting other states in the commission of an internationally wrongful act (Article 16 ASR and Article 14 DARIO) by which they are both bound, is not entirely clear, in view of the fact that some of the examples given in the Commentary to Article 16[87] actually concern breaches of peremptory norms (unlawful use of force, serious human rights violations), which should be within the scope of Article 41(2) ASR and Article 42(2) DARIO instead.[88]

The scope of these ancillary obligations with respect to breaches of peremptory norms is probably less clear when applied to serious breaches by international organisations. As the ILC observed, there was support for the view that they should apply;[89] however, it did not identify examples of relevant practice. Examples that might be taken to support the point

[85] Practice outside the territorial context is sparce, but new categories can be envisaged. Court judgments based on evidence obtained by torture should never be recognised as legal or have legal effects (as proposed by *A and others v Secretary of State for the Home Department (No 2)* [2004] EWCA Civ 1123, [2005] 1 WLR 414; this was overruled by the House of Lords in *A and others v Secretary of State for the Home Department (No 2)* [2005] UKHL 71, [2005] 3 WLR 1249). In the case of the Israeli illegal settlements, there should be no preferential tariff treatment for product originating from the settlements (as ruled by the Court of Justice of the European Union in C-386/08 *Brita GmbH v Hauptzollamt Hamburg-Hafen*, to the effect that Israeli goods produced in the Occupied Territories cannot benefit from the preferential treatment accorded to Israel by the 2000 EU-Israel Association Agreement). Equally, EU CAP funding should be withdrawn from countries, like Italy, allowing illegal conditions for agricultural immigrant workers, 'employed' by companies receiving EU subsidies (see www.espresso.repubblica.it/dettaglio/io-schiavo-in-puglia/1370307, in Italian).

[86] *Legal Consequences for States of the Continued Presence of South Africa in Namibia (South West Africa) notwithstanding Security Council Resolution 276 (1970), Advisory Opinion*, ICJ Reports 1971, 16, para 133.

[87] And in the Commentary to Art 14 DARIO, where the conduct of the UN Mission in the DRC (MONUC) in support of the actions of one of the factions in the war there might have assisted in violations of human rights, humanitarian and refugee law, see Commentary to the Draft Articles on the Responsibilities of International Organizations, with Commentaries, to appear in *Yearbook of the International Law Commission* (2011), vol. II, Part Two.

[88] Unless the difference lies in that Art 16 covers the responsibility in the commission of the unlawful act, and Art 41(2) in maintaining the situation resulting from the commission of the unlawful act. For a comprehensive assessment see H Aust, *Complicity and the Law of State Responsibility* (Cambridge, Cambridge University Press, 2011).

[89] See DARIO, Commentary to Art 42, para 5: 'not insignificant that these obligations were considered [by governments and organisations commenting on the text] to apply to international organizations when a breach was allegedly committed by a State'.

(while not providing clear guidance on the scope of the duty) would seem to include the ICJ's already-quoted *Wall Opinion*; Security Council Resolution 662 calling upon all states, international organisations and specialized agencies not to recognize Iraq's annexation of Kuwait[90] and to refrain from any action or dealing that might be interpreted as an indirect recognition of the annexation); and the EC's Declaration on Yugoslavia and the Guidelines on the Recognition of New States.[91]

As appears from these considerations, international law may well have come to recognise a regime of 'aggravated responsibility' triggered by grave breaches of *jus cogens* rules; however, this regime holds less than the notion of 'aggravated responsibility' suggests. From the specific perspective adopted in the present contribution, it seems the notion of fundamental interests has affected the consequences of international responsibility less than the regime of enforcement addressed in section II. As the concepts of obligations *erga omnes* and *jus cogens* continue to evolve, this may change, and nothing precludes the international community from agreeing on special consequences going beyond the rather meagre substance of Article 41 ASR, Article 42 DARIO—and notably special consequences imposed on the wrongdoing state or organisation. For the time being, however, the impact of *jus cogens* and obligations *erga omnes* on the consequences of responsibility has been rather marginal.

IV. FUNDAMENTAL INTEREST OBLIGATIONS AND QUESTIONS OF IMMUNITY

Finally, there is much discussion about the relationship between fundamental interest obligations on the one hand, and rules of immunity on the other. The question arises with respect to proceedings before domestic courts, in which foreign states and international organisations, as a matter of principle, are entitled to immunity from process and enforcement. Within that particular setting, rules of immunity may thus be viewed as precluding a particularly attractive avenue of invoking the responsibility of another state or of an international organisation.

To uphold immunity is certainly in line with the principle of sovereign equality of states (*par in parem non habet imperium*) and is often man-

[90] UN Doc S/RES/662 (1990).

[91] Specifically the European Community Declaration on Yugoslavia and on the Guidelines on the Recognition of New States, 16 December 1991, reproduced in (1992) 31 *International Legal Materials* 1485, 1487. On 14 December 2011, the European Parliament voted against the extension of the EU–Morocco Fisheries Agreement, following a critical report of MEP Carl Haglund and of the Committee on Development, on the possible role of the EU in ensuring compliance with international law with regards to the right of the population of Western Sahara, a Non-Self-Governing Territory, to benefit from exploitation of its natural resources (see www.europarl.europa.eu/news/en/pressroom/content/20111213IPR34070/html/Extension-of-EU-Morocco-fisheries-agreement-rejected-call-for-a-better-deal).

dated by documents setting up international organisations.[92] However, immunity has come under pressure in recent years when invoked as a shield in proceedings brought by victims of grave human rights violations such as torture or crimes against humanity. Among the many legal arguments that have been advanced to curb immunity/impunity, the *jus cogens* doctrine has been particularly attractive.[93] The reason for this may have been that, on the face of it, it seems to preclude the application of immunity rules almost by definition: in fact, if *jus cogens* rules—so the most prominent argument runs—are defined as admitting of no derogation, would they not 'trump' immunity, which after all can be waived? On that reasoning, the *jus cogens* concept would indeed facilitate the implementation of responsibility of foreign states or international organisations in the specific setting of domestic court proceedings.

Arguments based on *jus cogens* have been advanced in a range of proceedings implicating diverse forms of immunities recognised under international law. As regards the personal immunity enjoyed by Heads of States and Governments and Foreign Ministers, *jus cogens* has generally not made a difference: as confirmed in the *Arrest Warrant* case, these officeholders remain protected even in cases of gross violations of human rights.[94] As regards state immunity, as well as immunities enjoyed by other state officials, matters have—at least until recently—remained open. By and large the matter is left to the discretion of states and (if they can regulate the matter) possibly international organisations. While they have so far been considered free to restrict immunity from prosecution in cases involving gross violation of human rights, general international law does not require them to do so. The default international law position[95] is that states and international organisations are not obliged to lift immunity, even for breaches of peremptory norms of international law.[96] As this

[92] See for example Art 105 of the UN Charter and the Convention on the Privileges and Immunities of the United Nations. New York, 13 February 1946; Art IV European Space Agency Convention.

[93] Literature on this topic is abundant: see, eg A Bianchi, 'Immunity versus Human Rights: The Pinochet Case' (1999) 10 *European Journal of International Law* 237; W Adams, 'In Search of a Defence of the Transnational Human Rights Paradigm: May *Jus Cogens* Norms Be Invoked to Create Implied Exceptions in Domestic State Immunity Statutes?' in C Scott (ed), *Torture as Tort* (Oxford, Hart Publishing, 2001) 247.

[94] *Case Concerning the Arrest Warrant of 11 April 2000 (Democratic Republic of the Congo v Belgium)*, ICJ Reports 2002, 3, para 58.

[95] See *Princz v Federal Republic of Germany*, 26 F 3d 1166, 1170–71 (DC Cir 1994) and, more recently, *Germany v Italy* (www.icj-cij.org/docket/files/143/16556.pdf) and the *Distomo* case at the German Supreme Court (see www.cgerli.org/fileadmin/user_upload/interne_Dokumente/Judgments/bghz155279.htm).

[96] See, eg *Al-Adsani v United Kingdom* (2002) 34 EHRR 11; *Bouzari v Iran*, 71 OR 3d 675 (2004) 243 DLR (4th) 406 (CA); *Jones v Saudi Arabia* [2006] UKHL 26. For references and discussion see, eg T Giegerich, 'Do Damages Claims Arising from *Jus Cogens* Violations Override State Immunity from the Jurisdiction of Foreign Courts?' in Tomuschat and Thouvenin, above n 1, 203; and A Bianchi, 'Serious Violations of Human Rights and Foreign States' Accountability Before Municipal Courts' in LC Vorah et al (eds), *Man's Inhumanity*

is strictly a procedural, 'threshold' matter, if states decide against lifting immunity, the domestic courts are in effect declaring the claim inadmissible with no consideration of the merits.[97]

As noted above, the issue is often conceptualised as a conflict between *jus cogens* and state responsibility on the one hand and state immunity on the other hand.[98] However, read properly, it can also be seen as a conflict between rights: on the one hand, the right to immunity and on the other, the right to access to courts and to obtain redress for breaches of peremptory norms. What then needs to be assessed is the effect the regime of aggravated responsibility has on this set of rights and, specifically, whether this ancillary right to obtain redress for breaches of peremptory norm has itself acquired *jus cogens* status.[99] There are limited instances in which treaty law points towards the establishment of a duty to restrict immunity for certain gross violations of human rights. The duty to prosecute under the Convention against Torture has at times been interpreted as implying an obligation to lift the immunity of the alleged perpetrators, as otherwise (so the argument runs) it would lack substantive content.[100] National immunity statutes, by contrast, do not typically codify a *jus cogens*-based exception to immunity.[101] In the *Al-Adsani* case, a Grand Chamber of

to Man. Essays on International Law in Honour of Antonio Cassese (The Hague, Kluwer Law International, 2003) 149.

[97] See *Al-Adsani v United Kingdom* (ECHR), above n 96, para 48: 'The Court does not accept the Government's submission that the applicant's claim had no legal basis in domestic law since any substantive right which might have existed was extinguished by if the defendant state waives immunity operation of the doctrine of state immunity. It notes that an action against a state is not barred *in limine*, the action will proceed to a hearing and judgment. The grant of immunity is to be seen not as qualifying a substantive right but as a procedural bar on the national courts' power to determine the right'. See I Pingel, 'L'immunité des Etats' in Tomuschat and Thouvenin, above n 1, 239, 242.

[98] See, eg T Giegerich, above n 96, 203. One should also add the jurisdictional rights of territoriality, according to which a state is entitled to exert territorial jurisdiction. Giegerich proposes that denial of immunity might be allowed as a form of reprisal (countermeasure) for a previous violation of a *jus cogens* norm, including the failure to provide an effective judicial remedy.

[99] This point is indeed often side-stepped by commentators (and courts) presenting the debate as one between *jus cogens* and immunity: for brief comment *cf* C Tams, 'Well-Protected Enemies of Mankind'(2002) 61 *Cambridge Law Journal* 246.

[100] *Pinochet I* [1998] 3 WLR 1456; *International Legal Materials* 37 (1998), 1302; *Pinochet III* [1999] 2 All ER 97 [1999] 2 WLR 825. For comment, see C Chinkin, 'Case Note: *Pinochet III*' (1999) 93 *American Journal of International Law* 703. On Art 14 of the UNCAT, designed to ensure compensation, the Committee Against Torture criticised Canada for its failure to ensure the right to a remedy (Conclusions and recommendations of the Committee against Torture: Canada, 7 July 2005, CAT/C/ CR/34/CAN) in response of the judgment in *Bouzari v Republic of Iran*, above n 94, where a claim in tort was rejected by the Ontario Court of Appeal by application of the Canadian State Immunity Act. See finally the ITCY in *Prosecutor v Furundzija* (10 December 1998, Case No IT-95- 17/I-T (1999) 38 *International Legal Materials* 317).

[101] The US 1996 Foreign Sovereign Immunities Act introduced an exception for terrorism activities, which are not, of course, *jus cogens* violations, nor do they usually involve states directly (but they can be carried out by state agents). Equally, the 1992 Torture Victim

the European Court of Human Rights held that states were entitled to uphold immunity in cases of *jus cogens* breaches—such as acts of torture.[102] Many other national decisions—among them *Jones* and *Bouzari*, to name but two examples[103]—point in the same direction. Equally, the German *Bundesgerichtshof* refused to recognise a Greek judgment that would have obliged Germany to pay damages for massacres in the Greek village of Distomo.[104]

Things are not entirely uniform, though. In a case involving world war atrocities, the Italian Corte di Cassazione accepted the claim for damages against Germany brought in a trial against Max Josef Milde for the massacre at Civitella in Val di Chiana in June 1944.[105] In *Ferrini*, the same court had already excluded from the scope of immunity 'state activities which—even if considered as an exercise of sovereign powers (such as those performed in the course of war operations)—constitute a serious violation of the liberty and dignity of the human being, to the point that they amount to crimes under international law'.[106] In fact, referring, amongst other things, to *jus cogens*, the Italian Court expressly recognised an immunity exception. In a similar vein, a civil claim for damages for the Distomo massacre had initially been accepted by the Greek Supreme Court (Areios Pagos), invoking the *jus cogens* doctrine.[107]

By and large, however, cases like *Ferrini* and *Prefecture of Voiotia* have

Protection Act, and the Alien Tort Act, allow for damages for certain activities against the law of nations or torture but do not include rules on lifting immunity. The US Supreme Court in *Saudi Arabia v Nelson*, 113 S Ct 1471 (1993), declared that the alleged torture suffered by Mr Nelson, which he claimed had been covered by the commercial activity exception of the Act (he claimed the conduct had been associated and connected to his contract of employment by a Saudi hospital) was in fact not covered by the exception; by denying the application of the exception to immunity, the Court accepted that torture is protected by sovereign immunity if it is attributed to state agents (at 1480). On the UK Torture (Damages) Bill, see House of Lords—House of Commons Joint Committee on Human Rights, *Closing the Impunity Gap: UK Law on Genocide (and Related Crimes) and Redress for Torture Victims, Twenty-fourth Report of Session 2008–09*, HL Paper 153 HC 553 (London, The Stationery Office, 2009).

[102] *Al-Adsani*, above n 96.

[103] See n 96 for references.

[104] BGH, *Urteil vom 26 Juni 2003*—III ZR 245/98.

[105] Corte Suprema di Cassazione, Sezione I Penale, Judgment no 1072 of 21 October 2008, *Milde*, (2009)92 *Rivista di Diritto Internazionale* 618. For an analysis of the case, see A Ciampi, 'The Italian Court of Cassation Asserts Civil Jurisdiction over Germany in a Criminal Case Relating to the Second World War (The *Civitella* Case)' (2009) 7 *Journal of International Criminal Justice* 597.

[106] Corte Suprema di Cassazione, Sezioni Unite Civili, Judgment no 5044 of 6 November 2003, *Ferrini*, (2004) 87 *Rivista di Diritto Internazionale* 539. See P De Sena and F De Vittor, 'State Immunity and Human Rights: The Italian Supreme Court Decision on the *Ferrini* Case' (2005) 16 *European Journal of International Law* 89. For the limitation of immunity in criminal cases, see Corte Suprema di Cassazione, Sezione I Penale, judgment no 31171 of 19 June 2008, *Lozano*, (2008) 91 *Rivista di Diritto Internazionale* 1223.

[107] Areopag, *Prefecture of Voiotia v Federal Republic of Germany*, Case No 11/2000, judgment of 4 May 2000.

remained exceptional, if not isolated 'odd ones out'. Typically, courts willing to rely on *jus cogens* have been reigned in rather quickly. As regards damages awarded by the Areios Pagos, the Greek Government blocked the execution of the decision; this was upheld by the European Court of Human Rights.[108] *Ferrini*, for its part, gave rise to proceedings between Germany and Italy before the International Court of Justice,[109] in which the Court recently upheld state immunity in no uncertain terms:

> Accordingly, the Court concludes that even on the assumption that the proceedings in the Italian courts involved violations of jus cogens rules, the applicability of the customary international law on State immunity was not affected.[110]

As regards international organisations, the argument has largely evolved in parallel. International organisations enjoy immunity based on the principle of functionality rather than on doctrines of sovereign equality or jurisdictional territoriality[111] and on the basis of provisions contained in their incorporation instruments.[112] The immunity of the United Nations was at the basis of the series of cases brought in the Netherlands courts as a consequence of the Srebrenica massacre in 1995: in 2008, the Hague District Court ruled that it had no jurisdiction to hear the case against the United Nations (under whose command the Dutch troops were operating) as it found that no exception applied to Article 105 of the Charter, by analogy to similar cases decided in domestic courts with respect to civil liability of states for violations of peremptory norms.[113] In a similar case, the Hague Court of Appeal upheld the immunity from prosecution of the United Nations for the same set of events, but brought by a different plaintiff.[114] The Court did not accept that the right of access to justice could trump immunity from jurisdiction[115] and argued that the 'crime of omission' of failure to prevent genocide did not constitute a serious enough breach to lift immunity, apparently leaving open the possibility

[108] *Kalogeropoulou et al v Greece and Germany*, Admissibility Decision of 12 December 2002, available at: www.hudoc.echr.coe.int.

[109] *Case Concerning Jurisdictional Immunities (Federal Republic of Germany v Italian Republic)*, Application of the FRG of 23 December 2009.

[110] Ibid, judgment of 3 February 2012, para 97. For vigorous criticism see the dissent by Judge Cançado Trindade.

[111] See Art 105 of the Charter of the United Nations.

[112] On the topic, see recently A Reinisch (ed), *Challenging Acts of International Organizations before National Courts* (Oxford, Oxford University Press, 2011).

[113] District Court of The Hague, *Hasan Nuhanovic v The State of the Netherlands*, judgment of 10 September 2008, Case No 265615/HA ZA 06-1671. The Court of Appeal on 5 July 2011 reversed the judgment as concerns the attribution of responsibility for the facts, which it considered attributable both to the UN (whose immunity had been established by the lower court) and to the Dutch State: Court of Appeal of the Hague, *Hasan Nuhanovic v The State of the Netherlands*, judgment of 5 July 2011, Case No 200.020.174/01.

[114] Court of Appeal of The Hague, *Mothers of Srebrenica, et al v The State of the Netherlands & the United Nations*, judgment of 30 March 2010, Case No 200.022.151/01.

[115] As established by the ECtHR in *Beer and Regan v Germany* (Application No 28934/95) and *Waite and Kennedy v Germany* (Application No 26083/94).

that the UN might lose their immunity in cases involving graver violations of peremptory norms.

As is clear from these considerations, international law does not at the present stage require states to accept a *jus cogens*-based exception to immunity. Conversely, states (unless restrained by mandatory rules like those protecting Heads of States, and so on) retain some discretion: consequently, the possibility of real redress often depends on the attitude of domestic courts or legislators. Not surprisingly, victims of human rights abuses reaching the level of *jus cogens* violations have sought to bring claims in 'sympathetic' domestic legal systems—ie those that, jurisdiction being established, are willing to restrict immunity. But in the light of the recent ICJ judgment between Germany and Italy, the number of such sympathetic countries is likely to remain fairly limited. And on the basis of past experience, it seems that for every *Milde* court—which unequivocally stated that: 'It would be meaningless to state the primacy of the person's fundamental rights and, then, inconsistently therewith, to prevent the possibility of access to a court'[116]—there is more than one *Al-Adsani* court, pragmatically stating that 'there may be no international forum (other than the forum of the *locus delicti* to whom a victim of torture will be understandably reluctant to turn) where this terrible, if established, wrong can receive civil redress'.[117]

The debate about limits to state immunity thus shows the potential as well as the limits of concepts like *jus cogens*. They embody a claim to normative hierarchy, which could provide a powerful argument against upholding immunity. Yet, they need to be applied more cautiously than *jus cogens*-activists, seeking to move the concept outside the law of treaties, accept. The ongoing debate between courts and commentators on the matter suggests that to date, international law has not accepted that the right to have *jus cogens* breaches remedied should 'trump' immunity.

V. CONCLUDING OBSERVATIONS

The preceding considerations suggest that concepts like obligations *erga omnes* and *jus cogens* affect the application of international responsibility. They do so in rather particular ways, 'fine-tuning' rather than rewriting the law of responsibility. Yet the combined effect of the three instances of fine-tuning assessed in the preceding section should not be discarded.

The regime of enforcement, both national and international, and to some extent the rules governing consequences of wrongfulness, have gradually opened up to accommodate arguments based on fundamental

[116] Quoted in Ciampi, above n 104, 604.
[117] *Al-Adsani v Kuwait*, above n 96, para 18.

values of the international community. This process is at different stages of development: the regime of law enforcement laid down in Articles 42, 48 and 43, 49 of the ILC's texts on responsibility already goes some way in embracing the idea of public interest enforcement on which the *erga omnes* concept is based. From the perspective of the EU, this increases the potential for law enforcement: it allows the Union to take enforcement action in the public interest, irrespective of any individualised harm sustained. It bears recalling that the practice of European Member States and the EU/EC provides crucial evidence in support of this approach.

By contrast, the regime of special consequences triggered by serious breaches of *jus cogens* rules is still in its infancy. As regards immunity, the arguments have been advanced, and their relative merits are being weighed. In all three areas assessed, it seems that international law is still coming to terms with the launch onto the scene, in 1969 and 1970 respectively, of the two concepts of *erga omnes* and *jus cogens*. Contrary to what may have been expected at the time, the legal regime governing fundamental rules of the international legal order cannot simply be deduced from the 'nature' of the *erga omnes* and *jus cogens* concepts. There is in fact no 'mechanical link . . . between the breach of a fundamental rule of international law and the legal consequences deriving therefrom';[118] instead, the specific consequences need to be gradually accepted in international practice or jurisprudence. This may on occasion be a cumbersome process; however, the preceding sections suggest that concepts like *jus cogens* and obligations *erga omnes* have become part and parcel of the international discourse and are gradually being read into the regime of international responsibility. As an actor operating within the regime of international law, the EU is of course affected by this readjustment; and the examples addressed in the paper suggest that it has contributed considerably to the development of international law in the field.

[118] Tomuschat, 'General Conclusions' in Tomuschat and Thouvenin, above n 1, 436.

7

EU Declarations of Competence and International Responsibility

JONI HELISKOSKI*

I. INTRODUCTION

THIS ARTICLE EXAMINES 'declarations of competence' of the European Union (EU) from the perspective of the law of international responsibility. By 'declarations of competence' is meant declarations that the Union is required to submit pursuant to an international agreement at the time when it becomes a contracting party to the agreement. For instance, Article 5(1) of Annex IX to the United Nations Convention on the Law of the Sea (UNCLOS)[1]—which was the very first international agreement containing such a requirement—provides that:

> [t]he instrument of formal confirmation or of accession of an international organisation shall contain a declaration specifying the matters governed by this Convention in respect of which competence has been transferred to the organisation by its Member States which are Parties to this Convention.[2]

Today, the EU and (some or all of its) Member States are parties to some thirty international agreements containing a specific obligation to submit a

* While the author is an official of the Ministry for Foreign Affairs, Helsinki, the views expressed are personal.

[1] [1998] OJ L179/3.

[2] The provisions of the UNCLOS concerning declarations of competence are exceptional in two respects. First, Annex IX to the Convention requires a declaration from an international organisation also at the time of signature of the Convention (Art 2) and, secondly, upon ratification or accession, a member state of an international organisation is also required to make a declaration of competence of its own (Art 5(2)). No other agreement contains similar provisions. However, under Art 47(1) of Agreement for the implementing of the provisions of the UNCLOS relating to the conservation and management of straddling stocks and highly migratory fish stocks, [1998] OJ L189/17, Annex IX to the UNCLOS applies mutatis mutandis to participation international organisation in the Agreement, except where otherwise provided.

declaration of competence. The agreements concerned are all multilateral agreements, most of drawn up under the auspices of the United Nations. At the level of the EU institutions, the text of such declarations is usually adopted as an annex to the decision of Council concerning the conclusion of an agreement on behalf of the EU and then deposited, together with the instrument of ratification or accession, with the depositary of the given agreement.

Declarations of competence are supposed to serve a number of objectives arising from the specific context where the Union becomes a contracting party to an international agreement alongside some or all of its Member States. As preparatory documents of the UNCLOS demonstrate, one such objective is deemed to relate to the desire to address the question of the international responsibility of the Union and its Member State under such 'mixed agreements'.[3] In the case of the UNCLOS, the wording of Article 6(1) of Annex IX to the Convention makes an express link between the attribution of competence and the attribution of responsibility, as follows:

> Parties which have competence under Article 5 of this Annex shall have responsibility for failure to comply with obligations or for any other violation of this Convention.

The aim of the present chapter is to assess declarations of competence of the EU specifically as a tool of organising the question of the international responsibility of the Union and the Member States under mixed agreements.[4] A more general analysis of the various legal questions linked to such declarations would go beyond not only the thematic area of the present volume but also the space that is available. It is hoped, however, that a study focusing on the practice of declarations of competence from the point of the law of international responsibility might also be capable of contributing to the understanding of the rules and principles governing the international responsibility of the EU and its Member States in a more general fashion. In that regard, the fundamental question is whether declarations of competence should be conceived of as an appropriate, or useful, method of governing the question of the international responsibility

[3] See, eg President's note to Informal Plenary on Final Clauses, doc FC/13 (20 August 1979), reproduced in R Platzöder, *Third United Nations Conference on the Law of the Sea: Documents*, vol XII (Dobbs Ferry, Oceana, 1987) 386. According to the President, 'it was imperative that the sovereign parties to the Convention must know who is to be sued or who bears responsibility' (para 9).

[4] The literature on the international responsibility of the EU and its Member States, including under mixed agreements, is voluminous. For some of the most recent contributions, see PJ Kuijper, 'International Responsibility for EU Mixed Agreements' in C Hillion and P Koutrakos (eds), *Mixed Agreements Revisited* (Oxford, Hart Publishing, 2010) 208; F Hoffmeister, 'Litigating against the European Union and Its Member States—Who Responds under the ILC's Draft Articles on International Responsibility of International organisations?'(2010) 21 *European Journal of International Law* at 723; P Eeckhout, *EU External Relations Law*, 2nd edn (Oxford, Oxford University Press, 2011) 262–64.

of the EU—a technique that is to be welcomed and promoted in the actual practice. Finally, while declarations of competence certainly raise a multitude of issues EU law, the perspective of the present study will be predominantly that of public international law.

The analysis will be divided into four themes as follows: first, the relationship between, on the one hand, the rules of the attribution of competence and, on the other hand, the rules of general international law governing international responsibility; secondly, the provisions of mixed agreements determining the legal consequences of a declaration of competence; thirdly, the content and drafting of declarations of competence in practice; and, fourthly, the consequences of the evolving nature of the Union's external competence for the technique based on the use of declarations of competence.

It will have to be acknowledged at the outset, however, that no international dispute settlement practice concerning declarations of competence in the context of the international responsibility of the EU and its Member States currently exists.[5] In that sense, any conclusions on the topic will have to be qualified pending the emergence of relevant practice in future.

II. A PRELIMINARY EXCURSION: THE CONCEPTS OF 'COMPETENCE' AND 'RESPONSIBILITY'

An inquiry into declarations of competence, from the point of view of international law of responsibility, necessarily raises the preliminary question of the relationship between the concept of competence and the elements of international responsibility under general international law. It is often suggested that, in the context of mixed agreements, the incidence of international responsibility as between the EU and its Member States should, in principle, follow the distribution of competence between them especially where there is a declaration of competence.[6] As already noted, under Article 6(1) of Annex IX to UNCLOS responsibility for violations of the Convention appears to be attributed on the basis of the attribution of competence as between an organisation and its Member States.

[5] Mention must, however, be made of the Case No 7 before the International Tribunal for the Law of the Sea (established by the UNCLOS) between Chile and the EU concerning the conservation and sustainable exploitation of swordfish stocks in the South-Eastern Pacific Ocean. The fact that the case was brought against the EU in its own right (and not against the Member States) is probably explained by the European Community's declaration of competence where it is pointed out, inter alia, that the 'Member States have transferred competence to [the Community] with regard to the conservation and management of sea fishing resources'. The case was discontinued by agreement of the Parties (Order of 16 December 2009 of the Special Chamber). For the declaration of competence, see [1998] OJ L179/129.

[6] See, eg F Hoffmeister, 'The Contribution of EU Practice to International Law' in M Cremona (ed), *Developments in EU External Relations Law* (Oxford, Oxford University Press, 2008) 37, 65.

For the purposes of a study of declarations of competence from the perspective of international law of responsibility, it is crucial to ascertain whether the above understanding of the relationship between the two concepts is actually sustainable. The present author believes it is not. The problem is not that the distribution of competence may not always have been sufficiently clarified to the Union's treaty partners. The argument is rather that even if there had been a declaration of competence, however meticulously drafted, the relationship between the concepts of competence and responsibility is a much more nuanced one, so that, within the system of general international law of international responsibility, the incidence of competence should not be conceived of as providing an appropriate criterion for determining the incidence of responsibility. To make this point for present purposes does not require an in-depth conceptual analysis of the two notions and their meaning; it will be sufficient to look at the two concepts in their 'conventional' senses. Insofar as concerns 'competence', use will made of the meaning of that concept in the Union's constitutive Treaties, while insofar as concerns 'responsibility', reference will be made to the work of the work of the International Law Commission (ILC) on State Responsibility[7] and on Responsibility of International Organisations.[8] To make use of the work of ILC should not be considered problematic even though the EU has sometimes been regarded as a 'special case' by the Commission;[9] it is one thing to explore the relationship between the concepts of competence and responsibility and another thing to seek to postulate the rules governing the international responsibility of the EU.

Within the system of the EU's constitutive Treaties, the very essence of the concept of competence relates to the Union's legal authority to act pursuant to the relevant power-conferring provisions of the Constituent Treaties (Article 5 TEU), as well as the (residual) power, if any, of the Member States to act legally. More specifically, under Article 2 of the TFEU, the concept signifies a power 'to legislate and adopt legally binding acts' (paras 1 and 2); 'to provide [arrangements]' (para 3); 'to define and implement a [policy]' (para 4) or, 'to carry out actions' (para 5). The authority 'to conclude an agreement with one or more third countries or international organisations' (Art 216 TFEU) is of course particularly relevant for present purposes. In all cases, however, it follows unequivocally

[7] See Draft Articles on Responsibility of States for Internationally Wrongful Acts, with commentaries, adopted by the ILC at its fifty-third session in 2001 and submitted to the General Assembly (UN document A/56/10, 31).

[8] See Draft Articles on Responsibility of International organisations provisionally adopted by the Commission on first reading at its sixty-first session in 2009 (see UN document A/64/10 39).

[9] See, eg n 7. In the Commentary to Draft Article 47 on State Responsibility, for example, the responsibility of the EU and its Member States under mixed agreements is regarded as a 'special case'.

that the existence of competence is always potential in the sense that no action is necessarily implied.

So as to understand the relationship between the concepts of competence and that of responsibility, the meaning of the concept of responsibility will next have to be clarified. In that regard, the ILC has established an identical definition of the 'elements of an internationally wrongful act' of both states and international organisations. Article 2 of the Draft Articles on State Responsibility (as well as Article 4 of the Draft Articles on the Responsibility of International organisations) reads as follows:

> There is an internationally wrongful act of a State [international organisation] when conduct consisting of an action or omission:
> (a) is attributable to the State [international organisation] under international law; and
> (b) constitutes a breach of an international obligation of the State [that international organisation].

So, there are two necessary conditions for an internationally wrongful act of: first, conduct attributable to the state (or international organisation) under international law and, secondly, a breach by that conduct of an international obligation of the state (or international organisation) concerned. If the concept of competence signifies legal authority to act—for present purposes, to enter into international agreements with third parties under international law—it certainly has relevance for determining whether an organisation and/or its Member States may be regarded as being bound by the international obligation the breach of which is at issue.[10] In so far as concerns the question of attribution of the conduct to the organisation and/or its Member States, however, the relevance of the distribution of competence between the organisation and its Member States appears to be more uncertain. It is true that, according to Article 5(2) of the Draft Article on the Responsibility of International organisations, the rules of the organisation (including, the rules on the competence) apply to the determination of the functions of its organs and agents and, in that sense, may be relevant to the question of attribution. However, under Chapter II of the Draft Articles conduct exceeding the authority of an organ or agent may nonetheless be attributable to the organisation. In general, the Draft Articles provide little or no indication of the relevance of the distribution of competence between the organisation and its Member States to the question concerning the attribution of conduct as between them.

The same applies to the specific (and exceptional) situations where an

[10] Subject, of course, to the principle enshrined in Art 27 of the Vienna Convention on the Law of Treaties and the Vienna Convention on the Law Treaties between States and International Organisations or between International Organisations, respectively, that, without prejudice to Art 46 of the above Conventions, a state or an international organisation may not invoke the provisions of its internal law as justification for its failure to perform a treaty.

international organisation may incur international responsibility for an act attributable to its Member State (or Member States) governed by Chapter IV of Part Two of the Draft Articles, as well as the specific (and equally exceptional) cases concerning the responsibility of a state in connection with an act attributable to an international organisation (Part Five). As a matter of fact, the sole provision in the Draft Articles referring to the possession of 'competence' by an international organisation is Article 60 (Responsibility of a Member State seeking to avoid compliance) in Part Five. In particular, Article 16 (Decisions, authorizations and recommendations addressed to Member States and international organisations), which 'mirrors' Article 60 of the Draft Articles and concerns a situation where an organisation may incur responsibility for an act that is attributable to its Member State (or Member States), attaches no importance to the distribution of competence between the organisation and its Member States. The essential criterion for the purposes of establishing responsibility is rather the impact or influence that a measure undertaken by the organisation (decision, authorization, recommendation) is deemed to have upon the Member States. The mere possession of certain 'competence' by the organisation is not sufficient for that organisation to incur responsibility for an act attributable to its Member State. Even in the practice of the WTO dispute settlement, which is sometimes referred to in support of a 'special rule of attribution' concerning the European Union—that is, the attribution of conduct by EU Member States to the Union on the basis that the former are acting as 'organs' of the latter[11]—the scope of application of such a 'rule of attribution' appears to be limited to situations where actual use has been made of the Union's competence.[12] Thus, the

[11] See, eg para 4 of the Commentary to Draft Art 63 (*Lex Specialis*) on Responsibility of International organisations, above n 8, where the WTO approach is considered to imply the existence of such a special rule. Upon the first reading of the Draft Articles, however, the ILC remains inconclusive as to whether the special rule concerned should deemed to exist.

[12] See WT/DS62/R, WT/DS67/R, WT/DS68/R, European Communities—Customs Classification of Certain Computer Equipment (implementation of Commission Regulation (EC) No 1165/95 of 23 May 1995 concerning the classification of certain goods in the combined nomenclature, [1995] OJ L117/15–18); WT/DS174/R, European Communities—Protection of Trademarks and Geographical Indications for Agricultural Products and Foodstuffs (implementation of Council Regulation (EEC) No 2081/92 of 14 July 1992 on the protection of geographical indications and designations of origin for agricultural products and foodstuffs, [1992] OJ L208/1–8); WT/DS315/R European Communities—Selected Customs Matters (implementation of Council Regulation (EEC) No 2913/92 of 12 October 1992 establishing the Community Customs Code, including all annexes thereto, as amended (the 'Community Customs Code'), [1992] OJ L302/1; Commission Regulation (EEC) No 2454/93 of 2 July 1993 laying down provisions for the implementation of Council Regulation (EEC) No 2913/92 of 12 October 1992 establishing the Community Customs Code, including all annexes thereto, as amended (the 'Implementing Regulation'), [1993] OJ L253/1; Council Regulation (EEC) No 2658/87 of 23 July 1987 on the tariff and statistical nomenclature and on the Common Customs Tariff, including all annexes thereto, as amended (the 'Common Customs Tariff'), [1987] OJ L256/1; and the Integrated Tariff of the European Communities established by virtue of Article 2 of Council Regulation (EEC) No 2658/87 of 23 July 1987 on the tariff and statistical nomenclature and on the Common Customs

mere existence of a Union competence, even exclusive, would not seem to entail international responsibility of the Union for acts attributable to the Member States. Moreover, even if the organisation incurred responsibility for an act attributable to its Member States (or vice versa), this would not necessarily rule out the responsibility of the state or organisation that committed the internationally wrongful act (see Draft Articles 18 and 62).

However, it will have to be asked whether the above analysis needs to be qualified in two senses. The first point to be clarified is whether a distinction should be drawn between conduct consisting, on the one hand, of 'an action' and, on the other hand, of 'an omission'. If it is assumed that an omission is constituted by a failure to comply with an obligation to take some positive steps, it might be argued that the rules governing the distribution of competence between the Union and its Member States are relevant in identifying the responsible entity in the sense that compliance with the obligation may only be expected from the entity which has the requisite competence. Such reasoning would seem particularly appropriate in the case of the EU in the light of the fact that, in the areas of exclusive competence of the Union, the Member States may not adopt any legally binding acts, unless specifically empowered to do so, or for the implementation of acts of the Union—Article 2(1) TFEU. However, no provision of the ILC Draft Articles on the Responsibility of International organisations recognises the relevance of the distribution of competence as criterion for attributing an omission to either the international organisation or its Member States. Secondly, and following a very similar logic, it could be argued that the rules concerning the distribution of competence should determine the attribution of responsibility, for both actions and omissions, on the ground that the undoing of a breach presupposes the necessary competence. However, here, too, the ILC Draft Articles point to a somewhat different direction. The Commentary to Draft Article 31 (Irrelevance of the rules of the organisation) explains that '[i]n the relations between an international organisation and a non-Member State or organisation, it seems clear that the rules of the former organisation cannot per se affect the obligations that arise as a consequence of an internationally wrongful act'. So, even for the question of responsibility for wrongful conduct

Tariff, including all annexes thereto, as amended) and WT/DS291/R, WT/DS292/R, WT/DS293/R European Communities—Measures Affecting the Approval and Marketing of Biotech Products (relating, in part, to the implementation of Directive 2001/18/EC of the European Parliament and of the Council of 12 March 2001 on the deliberate release into the environment of genetically modified organisms and repealing Council Directive 90/220/EEC, [2001] OJ L106/1). While WT/DS135/R European Communities—Measures Affecting Asbestos and Asbestos-containing Products concerned the French Government Decree No 96–1133 of 24 December 1996 banning asbestos, the field in question is covered by several EU directives (including Council Directive 76/769/EEC of 27 July 1976 on the approximation of the laws, regulations and administrative provisions of the Member States relating to restrictions on the marketing and use of certain dangerous substances and preparations ([1976] OJ L262/201), as amended).

consisting of an omission, or for the consequences of an internationally wrongful act, there may not be a straightforward link between the attribution of competence and the attribution of responsibility.

III. THE LEGAL EFFECTS OF A DECLARATION OF COMPETENCE WITHIN THE FRAMEWORK OF A MIXED AGREEMENT: ON THE DIFFERENT WAYS OF LINKING THE DECLARATION TO THE AGREEMENT

While the concept of competence may not always be appropriate for the purposes of addressing the question of international responsibility, nothing prevents the inclusion of an express provision on the attribution of responsibility (and not conduct) in terms of the distribution of competence. As will be seen in the following, however, very few of mixed agreements laying down a requirement of a declaration of competence actually make provision to that effect. Even in Annex IX to the UNCLOS, the link between the requirement to submit a declaration and the question of the incidence of responsibility is a much more complex one than would appear in the light of the wording of Article 6(1) of the Annex.

From the specific perspective of the question concerning international responsibility, it emerges from the actual practice that there are three principal ways of linking a declaration of competence to the provisions of a mixed agreement. It is submitted that virtually every mixed agreement requiring the submission of a declaration of competence falls within one of the following categories.

A. Attribution of Responsibility by Reference to the Distribution of Competence

As already mentioned, under Article 6(1) of Annex IX to the UNCLOS international responsibility is attributed to an international organisation and its Member States by reference to their respective spheres of competence. This is rare, however. To date, the UNCLOS remains the only that includes a provision equivalent to Article 6(1) of Annex IX to the Convention.

Even in the case of the UNCLOS, the link between the attribution of competence and the attribution of responsibility is more complex than would appear on the basis of Article 6(1) of Annex IX alone. Like most other mixed agreements requiring a declaration of competence, Annex IX also lays down a requirement to notify of any changes to the distribution of competence between an international organisation and its Member States (Article 5(4)). Moreover, under Article 6(2), any contracting party may also request an international organisation and its Member States to provide information as to who has responsibility in respect of any specific matter, the organisation and its Member States concerned being under an obligation to provide this information. As a default position for cases where the information is not provided within a reasonable period of time, Article 6(2) then establishes a default position providing for a joint and several liability of the organisation and the Member States.

The above provisions therefore seem to negate the entitlement of the other contracting parties to rely upon the general declarations submitted by the organisation and its Member States under 5 of Annex IX and to postpone the question of the attribution of responsibility to specific cases as they emerge. As the present author has submitted elsewhere,[13] Articles 5 and 6 of Annex IX essentially create a procedural framework within which any possible doubts as to the attribution of responsibility can be addressed. The lesson for present purposes, however, is that the declaration of competence submitted by the organisation at the time when it becomes party to the Convention is not to be conceived of as decisive for the question of the attribution of responsibility. Annex IX rather recognises that the question of attribution may, by the very nature of the operation in question, only be addressed ex post facto, when an alleged breach of the Convention has taken place.

B. Express Limitation of Treaty Obligations by Reference to the Distribution of Competence

While UNCLOS is the only mixed agreement in which the attribution of international responsibility is addressed in terms of the distribution of competence, there are other mixed agreements where a link between the two concepts is made, albeit in a more indirect fashion; the clauses concerned expressly govern the question of attribution of treaty obligations (and not responsibility) as between an organisation and its Member States. However, if it is assumed that a breach of an obligation as an element of international responsibility concerns the compatibility of certain conduct with the relevant primary obligations,[14] the clauses in question actually amount to (special) rules governing the attribution of conduct to an international organisation or its Member States. On this assumption, the difference to the provisions of Annex IX seems to be rather a small one for all practical purposes.

In practice, two basic techniques have been applied in mixed agreements

[13] See J Heliskoski, *Mixed Agreements as a Technique of Organising the International Relations of the European Community and its Member States* (The Hague, Kluwer, 2001) 161–66.

[14] See Draft Articles on State Responsibility, above n 8, Commentary to cc III of pt I, para 2.

for the purpose of expressly attributing treaty obligations to an organisation and its Member States in terms of the distribution of competence. In the first technique, the status of an organisation as a contracting party to the agreement is confined to matters falling within the organisation's competence. In other words, the treaty rights and obligations are limited accordingly. Article 2(j) of the United Nations Convention against transnational organised crime,[15] for instance, provides as follows:

> 'Regional economic integration organisation' shall mean an organisation constituted by sovereign States of a given region, to which its membership States have transferred competence in respect of matters governed by this Convention and which has been duly authorized, in accordance with its internal procedures, to sign, ratify, accept, approve or accede to it; *references to 'States Parties' under this Convention shall apply to such organisations within the limits of their competence* (emphasis added).[16]

The second technique consists of confining the requirement of the fulfilment of 'responsibilities' by an organisation to matters within its competence, as communicated in a declaration of competence. Reference may be made Article 14(3) of the Convention on Customs Treatment of Pool Containers used in International Transport[17] that provides as follows:

> Any regional economic integration organisation may become, in accordance with the provisions of paragraph 1 of this Article, a Contracting Party to this Convention. Such organisation, Contracting Party to this Convention, shall inform the depositary of its competence and any subsequent changes thereto, with respect to the matters governed by this Convention. *The organisation concerned shall, for the matters within its competence,* exercise the rights and *fulfil the responsibilities which this Convention confers on States which are Contracting Parties to this Convention.* In matters within the competence of the organisation, of which the depositary has been informed, the Member States of the organisation, which are Contracting Parties to this Convention, shall not be entitled to exercise individually these rights, including inter alia the right to vote (emphasis added).[18]

An essentially similar approach is followed in the Convention on the Protection and Promotion of the Diversity of Cultural Expressions (20 October 2005);[19] Article 27(3) of the Convention requires a regional economic integration organisation to declare, in the instrument of accession

[15] [2004] OJ L261/70.

[16] See also Art 26(c) United Nations Convention against Illicit Traffic in Narcotic Drugs and Psychotropic Substances, UN document E/CONF.82/15, Corr 1 and 2, reprinted in 28 *International Legal Materials* 493 (1989).

[17] [1993] OJ L130/4.

[18] For a similar arrangement, see also Art 24(7) of the Convention relating to temporary admission (Istanbul Convention), [1993] OJ L130/4. Unlike in the case of UNCLOS, however, no corresponding limitation to the 'responsibilities' of the Member States of the organisation is provided for in either of the Conventions.

[19] [2006] OJ L201/17.

(ie, in the declaration of competence), the distribution of 'responsibilities' as between the organisation and its Member States with respect to matters governed by the Convention. There is, however, a presumption of the responsibility of the Member States: the latter shall be presumed to retain competence over all matters in respect of which transfers of competence to the organisation have not been specifically declared or informed to the depositary (Article 27(3)(d)).

C. Implicit Limitation of Treaty Obligations by Reference to the Concept of Competence

There is, finally, a third—and, in the light of the actual practice, most prevalent—category of clauses in mixed agreements of the EU and its Member States that is relevant for the purposes of assessing the role played by declarations of competence in respect of the question of international responsibility. These clauses, too, are based on what might be described as alternative performance of treaty obligations (and alternative exercise of treaty rights). In distinction to the two previous categories, however, the link between the question of attribution of treaty obligations and the distribution of competence as defined in the declaration of competence is a more implicit one. The following provisions were first included the Vienna Convention for the Protection of the Ozone Layer[20] (Article 13(2)–(3)) and have since then been 'carried over', almost word by word, to a number of other multilateral conventions drawn up under the auspices of the United Nations:

> 2. Any organisation referred to in paragraph 1 above which becomes a Party to this Convention or any protocol without any of its Member States being a Party shall be bound by all the obligations under the Convention or the protocol, as the case may be. In the case of such organisations, one or more of whose Member States is a Party to the Convention or relevant protocol, *the organisation and its Member States shall decide on their respective responsibilities for the performance of their obligations under the Convention or protocol*, as the case may be. In such cases, the organisation and the Member States shall not be entitled to exercise rights under the Convention or relevant protocol concurrently.
>
> 3. In their instruments of ratification, acceptance or approval, the organisations referred to in paragraph 1 above shall declare the extent of their competence with respect to the matters governed by the Convention or the relevant protocol. These organisations shall also inform the Depositary of any substantial modification in the extent of their competence (emphasis added).

The structure and wording of individual provisions may be different, but

[20] [1998] OJ L297/10.

the basic principle remains the same. While a declaration of competence is required, the organisation and its Member States may, independently of the declaration concerned, decide on their respective responsibilities for the performance of their obligations under this Convention.

It might be argued that the legal situation resembles the combined effect of Articles 5 and 6 of Annex IX to UNCLOS in the sense that the attribution of responsibility as between the organisation and its Member States does not necessarily follow the declaration of competence but is to be decided ex post facto. In some cases, such as the Customs Convention on the Temporary Importation of Private Road Vehicles[21] or the Customs Convention on the Temporary Importation of Commercial Road Vehicles,[22] the relevant provision even seems to set out the joint and several liability of the organisation and its Member States as a default position in manner similar to Article 6(2) of Annex IX, by stressing that the right of the organisation and its members to decide should not allow derogation from the obligations under the convention.

IV. THE CONTENT AND DRAFTING OF DECLARATIONS OF COMPETENCE: THE STANDARD REQUIRED BY NON-EU PARTIES AND THE ACTUAL PRACTICE

It was seen that, in most agreements requiring a declaration of competence, the link between the question of attribution of responsibility and the question of distribution of competence is an indirect one in the sense that the concept of competence is conceived of as a tool for the delimitation, expressly or by implication, of treaty obligations as between an international organisation and its Member States.

For the purposes of assessing declarations of competence as a technique of governing the question of the international responsibility, it is also necessary to examine the content and drafting of the declarations from the perspective of the above objective of delimitation of treaty obligations. Needless to say that, in this respect, a more specific and precise declaration is usually more appropriate than a more general and imprecise one. An analysis of the actual practice will show, however, that the drafters of declarations of competence rarely meet—or even intend to meet—the standard envisaged in agreements containing a requirement of such a declaration.

[21] [1994] OJ L56/3.
[22] [1994] OJ L56/28.

A. The Standard to be Observed under Agreements Requiring a Declaration of Competence

In general, agreements requiring a declaration of competence do not include detailed provisions on what such declarations should contain or look like. An overwhelming majority of the agreements in question follow, word by word, the formula contained in Article 13(3) of the Vienna Convention for the Protection of the Ozone Layer requiring an organisation to 'declare the extent of their competence with respect to the matters governed by the Convention'. So, the 'extent of competence'[23] ought to be declared 'with respect to the matters governed by the convention'.

An underlying assumption concerning the requirement to submit a declaration of competence is, however, that the declaration ought to be sufficiently precise and informative so as to serve the interest of the other contracting parties in legal certainty and predictability.[24] The clearest illustration of this assumption is, once again, provided by the drafting history of Annex IX to UNCLOS; at the Law of the Sea Conference, it was argued that international organisations that become contracting parties to the Convention should be placed under an obligation to inform the other parties of their competence, 'with indication of *the specific provisions of [the] Convention* which are affected'.[25] While this proposal was not accepted, and Article 5(1) of Annex IX nonetheless requires 'a declaration *specifying* the matters governed by this Convention in respect of which competence has been transferred to the organisation by its Member States',[26] the interest of the other contracting parties in legal clarity having been an essential consideration behind the introduction of the requirement of submitting a declaration of the competence into the Law of the Sea Convention.[27] The requirement of a sufficiently specific declaration of competence also featured prominently in the negotiation of the

[23] In Case C-29/99 *Commission v Council* [2002] ECR I-11211, concerning the accession of the European Atomic Energy Community to the IAEA Convention on Nuclear Safety ([1999] OJ L318/21), the Court of Justice held that by requiring that an international organisation to indicate 'the extent of its competence', Art 30(4)(iii) of the Convention seeks to ensure that it communicates to the depositary 'both *the fields covered by the Convention* in which it has competence to fulfil the obligations and exercise the rights which flow from it and *the extent of that competence*' (para 49, emphasis added).

[24] In Case C-29/99 *Commission v Council* [2002] ECR I-11211 the Court further emphasised that 'Article 30(4)(iii) of the Convention [on Nuclear Safety] must, in the interest of the other contracting parties, be interpreted to mean that the declaration of competences under that provision must be complete' (para 70). For a recent analysis from the perspective of the non-EU parties, see PM Olson, 'Mixity from the Outside: the Perspective from the Outside' in C Hillion and P Koutrakos (eds), *Mixed Agreements Revisited* (Oxford, Hart Publishing, 2010) ibid 335–37.

[25] Informal Proposal by the Group 77 (25 March 1981), reproduced in Platzöder, above n 2, 342 (emphasis added).

[26] Emphasis added.

[27] See M Ederer, *Die Europäische Wirtschaftsgemeinschaft und die Seerechtskonvention der Verainten Nationen von 1982* (Munich, Verlag V Florenz, 1988) 157.

amendments to the Constitution of the Food and Agriculture organisation of the United Nations (FAO) designed to enable the accession of the European Community to the organisation. The Council of the FAO insisted time and again that the competence of a regional economic integration organisation (in practice, the EC) would have to be defined in 'a very specific and complete manner' by means of 'a statement of competence as detailed as possible'.[28] This desire is currently reflected in Article II:5 of the FAO Constitution.[29]

As a 'guarantee' for the fulfilment of the above requirement of specificity, the agreements concerned also include a provision laying down a presumption of Member State competence; for instance, Article 5(3) of Annex IX to UNCLOS reads as follows:

> States Parties which are Member States of an international organisation which is a Party to this Convention shall be presumed to have competence over all matters governed by this Convention *in respect of which transfers of competence to the organisation have not been specifically declared, notified or communicated* by those States under this Article. (emphasis added).

B. The Content and Drafting of Declarations of Competence in Practice

While a certain degree of specificity and precision has certainly been expected from declarations of competence by the non-EU parties, a survey of the declarations actually submitted will readily illustrate that such declarations usually fall short of those expectations. The declarations are imprecise, incomplete and open-ended—and, without a slightest doubt, often deliberately vested with all of the above qualities. A number of aspects of the actual practice may be cited in support of this conclusion.

First of all, it is exceptional for declarations of competence to indicate the distribution of competence in respect of the individual provisions (or even parts) of agreement. The overwhelming majority of the declarations contain a description of the Union's competence in regard to a policy area or subject matter, with no precise link to the actual wording or structure of the agreement. The only cases where the Union's competence is defined in terms of the individual provisions of the agreement are the declarations submitted under the UN Convention against Illicit Traffic in Narcotic Drugs and Psychotropic Substances[30] and the UN Nations

[28] 'Report of the Council of the FAO, Ninety-eight Session (19 to 30 November 1990)', FAO document CL 98/REP, para 238.

[29] See *Basic Texts of the Food and Agriculture organisation of the United Nations*, vols I and II (2011).

[30] [1990] OJ L326/57. The declaration provides that 'the European Economic Community is at present competent for questions of commercial policy relating to the substances frequently used in the illicit manufacture of narcotic drugs and psychotropic substances, questions which are dealt with in Article 12 of the Convention'.

Convention against Transnational Organised Crime.[31] In relation to the Convention Relating to Temporary Admission the same result is reached through a declaration exhaustively enumerating the provisions for which the EU is not competent.[32]

Secondly, the link between the description of the Union's competence and the content of a given agreement is made ambiguous by a choice of language that is deliberately vague, imprecise and open-ended. Moreover, concepts that have no settled meaning (at least before the definition of the various categories of competence in Article 2 of the TFEU)—such as 'shared' or 'complementary' competence—are used. A paradigm is once again provided by the declaration made under the UNCLOS. While the text of the declaration is (alongside with the declaration submitted upon the Union's accession to the FAO) the longest and most detailed one to date, much room for interpretation is left by the use of expressions such as 'for a certain number of matters . . . there is shared competence'—'for example'—'inter alia'— 'in particular'—'competence relates mainly to' —'these policies may also have some relevance'.[33]

Thirdly, it is commonplace to describe, in a declaration of competence, the Union's competence by way of listing acts of Union's secondary legislation. However, as becomes clear either from the express wording of the declaration or from the way in which the listing is done, such lists are to be regarded merely as illustrative of the scope and nature of the Union's competence. Thus, insofar as concerns the list featuring in the declaration submitted under the UNCLOS, the declaration provides that:

> [a] list of relevant Community acts appears in the Appendix. The extent of Community competence ensuing from these acts must be assessed by reference to the precise provisions of each measure, and in particular, the extent to which these provisions establish common rules . . .

The implication of the above technique is that a declaration of competence is not a self-contained one but requires the precise scope and nature of the Union's competence to be construed by way of reference not only to the individual provisions of the legal acts cited—the total number of which, in the case of the UNLCOS, for example, is no less than 54 (!)—but also to the principles governing the existence and nature of the Union's implied external competence as they result from so-called AETR case law

[31] [2004] OJ L261/115. According to the declaration '[Community] competence relates to Articles 7, 9 and 31(2)(c) of the Convention. Moreover, Community policy in the sphere of development cooperation complements policies pursued by Member States and includes provisions to combat corruption. This competency relates to Article 30 of the Convention. Moreover, the Community considers itself bound by other provisions of the Convention to the extent that they are related to the application of Articles 7, 9, 30 and 31(2)(c), in particular the articles concerning its purpose and definitions and its final provisions'.

[32] [1993] OJ L130/75.

[33] [1998] OJ L179/129.

of the Court of Justice of the European Union, to which the concept of 'common rules' in the declaration is deemed to refer.[34] Therefore, given the difficulties inherent in such an operation, the description by the Court of Justice of the UNCLOS list of legal acts as 'a useful reference base'[35] for the purpose of determining the scope of the Union's competence within the areas covered by the Law of the Sea Convention may appear as an overstatement, at least for those less informed of the subtleties of the relevant principles of the Union legal order.

It is interesting, however, that some of the declarations specifically seek to address the question of the attribution of responsibility by way of a reference to legal acts adopted by the Union. The declaration concerning Cartagena Protocol on Biosafety to the Convention on Biological Diversity, for example, provides that 'The European Community is responsible for the performance of those obligations resulting from the Cartagena Protocol on Biosafety which are covered by Community law in force'.[36]

Such a statement would seem no more helpful than the one featuring in the declaration concerning the UNCLOS, however. The difficulty concerns not only the identification of 'Union law' that is deemed to cover certain obligations resulting from the agreement but also to the determination and application of the criteria to fulfilled by the relevant legislation so as for the Union's responsibility to be triggered.

An exceptional attempt to specify the above principle may, however, be found from the declaration submitted under the Convention on access to information, public participation in decision-making and access to justice in environmental matters (Århus Convention) which provides that:

> the legal instruments [adopted by the Community] in force do not cover fully the implementation of the obligations resulting from Article 9(3) of the Convention as they relate to administrative and judicial procedures to challenge

[34] Case 22/70, *Commission v Council* [1971] ECR 263, paras 17 and 22. See also Opinion 1/03 (Competence of the Community to conclude the new Lugano Convention on jurisdiction and the recognition and enforcement of judgments in civil and commercial matters) [2006] ECR I-1145, para 124 where the Court held that 'any [Community] competence, especially where it is exclusive and not expressly conferred by the Treaty, must have its basis in conclusions drawn from a specific analysis of the relationship between the agreement envisaged and the Community law in force and from which it is clear that the conclusion of such an agreement is capable of affecting the Community rules'.

[35] Case C-459/03 *Commission v Council (MOX plant)* [2006] ECR I-4635, para 109.

[36] Declaration concerning Cartagena Protocol on Biosafety to the Convention on Biological Diversity, [2002] OJ L201/50 See also the similar declarations in regard to the Convention on access to information, public participation in decision-making and access to justice in environmental matters (Århus Convention), [2005] OJ L124/4; the Protocol on Pollutant Release and Transfer Registers, [2006] OJ L32/56; the Stockholm Convention on Persistent Organic Pollutants, [2006] OJ L209/3; and the Rotterdam Convention on the Prior Informed Consent Procedure for certain hazardous chemicals and pesticides in international trade, [2006] OJ L299/25. Declaration concerning the Convention on Environmental Impact Assessment in a Transboundary Context (Espoo Convention) (30 *International Legal Materials* 800) provides, inter alia, that 'Member States are responsible for the performance of those obligations resulting from the Espoo Convention not currently covered by Community law'.

> acts and omissions by private persons and public authorities other than the institutions of the European Community as covered by Article 2(2)(d) of the Convention, and that, consequently, its Member States are responsible for the performance of these obligations at the time of approval of the Convention by the European Community and will remain so unless and until the Community, in the exercise of its powers under the EC Treaty, adopts provisions of Community law covering the implementation of those obligations.[37]

For obvious reasons, no comprehensive analysis of the reasons behind the above characteristics of the EU's declarations of competence—that is, their imprecise, incomplete and open-ended manner of drafting—can be made in the present context. However, as the present author has sought to demonstrate in another context, the above characteristics would clearly seem to relate to the very fundamental nature of the technique of concluding mixed agreements.[38]

The appeal towards the technique concerned appears to be based on the possibility of leaving the often difficult and controversial issues concerning the distribution of competence open at the time of the conclusion of agreement, to be decided on a case-by-case basis in future. The technique is thereby capable of sustaining both a broad interpretation of the Union' external competence and the right of the Member States to become contracting parties in their own right, without there being any need to define in detail the respective spheres of competence. It is not difficult to see, however, that any requirements of precise and detailed declarations of competence inevitably run against the above advantage of the mixed agreement formula. It is essentially the above contradiction that creates the tendency towards the submission of declarations that are drafted in imprecise, incomplete and open-ended fashion. The consequence, however, is that at least some of the objectives behind the requirement of such declarations, including the achievement of legal certainty and predictability in regard to the question of international responsibility, are, if not shattered, at least seriously compromised.

V. DECLARATIONS OF COMPETENCE AND THE EVOLVING NATURE OF THE EU'S EXTERNAL COMPETENCE

The problems caused by the imprecise, incomplete and open-ended nature of declarations of competence are further exacerbated by a well-known characteristic of the Union's external competence: the scope and nature of that competence evolves as a result of the development of Union

[37] See Case C-240/09 *Lesoochranárske zoskupenie*, judgment of 8 March 2011, nyr, paras 39–40.

[38] See, above n 13, 143–44.

legislation.[39] The corollary for declarations is that such declarations will either have to be constantly updated or risk becoming hopelessly out of date. In other words, the declarations in question are, by definition, of an interim or provisional nature—or, as one observer once put it, 'a snapshot of the [Union's] competences at a given moment in time'.[40]

It is therefore of no surprise that virtually every international agreement contains a requirement to update or renew the declaration should there be a change in the competence of an international organisation in question. Pursuant to Article 5(4) of Annex IX to UNCLOS, for example:

> [t]he international organisation and its Member States which are States Parties shall promptly notify the depositary of this Convention of any changes to the distribution of competence, including new transfers of competence, specified in the declarations under paragraphs 1 and 2.

To date, the sole exception is the Istanbul Convention relating to temporary admission which does not include an express provision requiring the Union to notify of changes to the distribution of competence. One might therefore be inclined to expect that the EU's declarations of competence are frequently updated so as to keep the other contracting parties informed of the changes in the scope and nature of the Union's competence at any given moment in time. In most declarations, including the one concerning the UNCLOS, an express promise on behalf of the Union to that effect has been made.

The truth of the matter is, however, that in practice, declarations of competence are only very rarely completed or amended. One of the very rare instances concerns the declaration submitted under the Rotterdam Convention on the Prior Informed Consent Procedure for certain hazardous chemicals and pesticides in international trade[41] which had to be renewed as a result of a judgement of the Court of Justice[42] annulling the Council Decision on the approval, on behalf of the European Community, of the Convention.[43] In particular, the present author is aware of no case where a declaration would have been formally updated as a result of a change in the secondary EU law. While there seem to have been notifications concerning amendments to the Union's constitutive Treaties, they seem to have been done in an incidental rather than a systematic

[39] Ie through the adoption of 'common rules' in the sense of the AETR case law, above n 34. It goes without saying that the scope and nature of the Union's competence may also evolve as a result of the amendment of the Constitutive Treaties (Art 48(2) TEU).

[40] KR Simmonds, 'The European Economic Community and the New Law of the Sea' (1989) 218 *Collected Courses of the Hague Academy of International Law* 130.

[41] [2003] OJ L63/29.

[42] Case C-94/03 *Commission v Council* [2006] ECR I-1.

[43] For the original declaration, see [2003] OJ L63/47, and for the revised one, [2006] OJ L299/25.

fashion.[44] Even after the entry into force of the Treaty of Lisbon—whereby important changes to the scope and nature of the Union's competence were introduced—the declarations submitted prior to the Treaty change remain in place as if nothing had happened.

The reasons behind this reluctance for providing updates to declarations would seem to be similar to the ones explaining the way the initial declarations are drafted. A requirement to complete or amend such declarations are deemed to run against the fundamental logic of mixed agreements, that is, the possibility of leaving questions concerning the distribution of competence between the Union and the Member States undecided.[45] However, the problems caused by 'out of date' declarations remaining in force would seem to be more severe than the ones arising from imprecise, incomplete or open-ended declarations: not only do the declarations fall short of the expectations of the non-EU parties insofar as concerns legal certainty and predictability, but also the evolving character of the EU's competence, including the AETR, risks having no effect at the level of international law.

VI. CONCLUSIONS AND EVALUATION

It emerges from the foregoing analysis that the arrangement of the question of the international responsibility of the EU and its Member States by means of declarations of competence is not an uncomplicated exercise. If, as one is led to believe, the introduction of a system based on such declarations for the first time (at the Law of the Sea Conference) had the aim of placing the contracting parties in a position where they would know, at any given moment in time, whether responsibility for a given breach of the Convention would lie within either the EU or it Member States, the aspirations of the inventors of the system have proved unrealistic. Declarations of competence are not capable of performing such a function.

This is not to say, however, that such declarations could serve no useful purpose as a technique of addressing the question of responsibility of the EU and its Member States. One simply has to acknowledge, and be conscious of, the legal and practical problems that are deemed to arise when declarations are used. The most critical ones would seem to include the following.

It is submitted, first of all, that the idea of addressing the question of international responsibility of an international organisation and its

[44] For one example, see the Communication from the Community to the Director-General of the FAO on the changes to the Community competence introduced by the Treaty on European Union, SEC(94) 437 (17 March 1994).

[45] See n 4 above and, further, n 13, 143–45.

Member States by means of declarations of competence is based on an over-simplified conception of the rules and principles governing the question of international responsibility. To adopt the distribution of competence as a (let alone *the*) criterion for determining the question of attribution of responsibility is fallacious for a number of reasons. It is clear that a given act may be attributable to an international organisation or some or all of its Member States irrespective of the distribution of competence as between them; one obvious example concerns ultra vires acts. It is equally evident that the logic whereby an organisation may incur responsibility for an act or omission attributable to its Member States is not necessarily based upon the possession of certain 'competence' but rather upon the influence or control exercised by the organisation over its Member States. Likewise, a Member State (or Member States) may be held responsible for an act attributable to the organisation notwithstanding the fact that the organisation is deemed to have competence in relation to the subject matter in question. These examples suffice to show that problems concerning the attribution of responsibility simply do not lend themselves to be governed by one 'trump card' of 'competence'; the picture is a much more nuanced one. In other words, the distribution of competence is but one criterion to be considered when the question of the attribution arises. One fundamental problem relates to the fact that the notion of 'competence' is deemed to signify a legal capacity, that is, something potential. The same does not necessarily apply to the prerequisites for the existence of an internationally wrongful act that may consist of either action or omission. For all these reasons, it would simply not seem appropriate to attribute responsibility solely on the basis of criteria relating to the distribution of competence.

Secondly, the agreement practice of the EU and its Member States provides no evidence in support of the view that the distribution of competence, as articulated in a declaration, should be regarded as decisive for the purposes of determining the attribution of responsibility. The analysis of the provisions defining the link between the agreement and the declaration shows that the relationship between the question of the distribution of competence and the attribution of responsibility is more indirect than one may be led to believe. Even in the case of Article 6 of Annex IX to the UNCLOS—paragraph 1 of which seemingly makes a direct link between the two questions—the significance of the declarations of competence for the purposes of governing the question of responsibility is, if not ruled out, considerably diminished by paragraph 2 of the provision concerned; the question of the attribution of responsibility is to be determined in respect of any specific matter within what essentially amounts to a procedural framework based upon exchange of information between the organisation (or its Member States) and the other contracting party concerned, with a default position of joint and several liability of the organisation and its Member States.

Thirdly, the declarations of competence submitted by the EU (and, in some cases, its Member States) only rarely meet up with the standard of precision and completeness that would be required for the declarations to serve the interest of non-EU parties to an agreement in legal certainty and predictability. Apart from a few exceptional cases (where the distribution of competence is defined in regard to individual provisions of an agreement), declarations of competence are imprecise, incomplete and open-ended. Moreover, the obligation contained in most agreements requiring a declaration of competence for such declarations to be updated or revised is not complied with in practice. Hence, the changes in the scope and nature of the Union's competence are not conveyed to the attention of the non-EU parties, the result being that the original declarations become out of date. As has been argued, the reasons behind the Union's reluctance to provide specific declarations with updates relate to the fact that the defining of the scope and nature of the Union's competence runs counter to one of the fundamental characteristics (some would argue, virtues) of mixed agreements; the technique enables questions of the scope and nature of the Union's competence to be postponed and to be decided on a case-by-case basis in a contextual fashion. This is why the EU in general and the European Commission in particular has traditionally been against the inclusion of an obligation to submit declarations of competence, which may explain why no bilateral mixed agreement concluded by the Union contains such an obligation. A requirement to submit a declaration of competence is something that the Union has been forced to accept in the multilateral context only, with Annex IX to the UNCLOS having served as an 'inconvenient' precedent.

The above conclusions notwithstanding, it would seem inappropriate to suggest that declarations of competence have absolutely no value whatsoever for the purposes of governing the question of the international responsibility. More than anything else, they should perhaps be conceived of as an instrument for providing the contracting parties of an agreement with information of the legal relationship between the EU and its Member States under European Union law—an element that may or may not prove relevant or even decisive for the determination of the question concerning the attribution of international responsibility. The fact remains, however, that in practice the information supplied has often proved to be not only incomplete but also clearly past its 'best before' or even 'use by' date.

VII. ANNEX: MIXED AGREEMENTS REQUIRING A DECLARATION OF COMPETENCE[46]

1. United Nations Convention on the Law of the Sea (10 December 1982) and the Agreement of 28 July 1994 relating to the Implementation of Part XI thereof, [1998] OJ L189/3.
2. Vienna Convention for the Protection of the Ozone Layer (22 March 1985), [1988] OJ L297/10.
   - Montreal Protocol on Substances that Deplete the Ozone Layer (16 September 1987), [1988] OJ L 297/21
3. United Nations Convention against Illicit Traffic in Narcotic Drugs and Psychotropic Substances (20 December 1988) Command Paper Cm 1927.
4. Convention on the Control of Transboundary Movements of Hazardous Wastes and their Disposal (Basel Convention) (22 March 1989), [1993] OJ L3/3.
5. Convention relating to temporary admission (Istanbul Convention) (26 June 1990), [1993] OJ L130/4.
6. Convention on Environmental Impact Assessment in a Transboundary Context (Espoo Convention) (25 February 1991), 30 I.L.M. p. 800.
7. Constitution of the Food and Agriculture Organization of the United Nations (16 October 1945, modified on 27 November 1991 in order to allow accession of REIOs), Basic Texts of the Food and Agriculture Organization of the United Nations, vols I and II (FAO, Rome, 1994).
8. Convention on the Transboundary Effects of Industrial Accidents (17 March 1992), [1998] OJ L326/6.
9. United Nations Framework Convention on Climate Change (9 May 1992), [1994] OJ L33/13.
   - The Kyoto Protocol to the United Nations Framework Convention on Climate Change (11 December 1997), [2002] OJ L130/4.
10. Convention on Biological Diversity (5 June 1992), [1993] OJ L309/3.
    - Cartagena Protocol on Biosafety to the Convention on Biological Diversity (29 January 2000), [2002] OJ L201/50.
11. Customs Convention on the Temporary Importation of Private Road Vehicles (4 June 1954, amended on 30 October 1992 in order to allow accession of REIOs), [1994] OJ L56/3.
12. Customs Convention on the Temporary Importation of Commercial Road Vehicles (18 May 1956, amended on 30 October 1992 in order to allow accession of REIOs), [1994] OJ L56/28.
13. Convention on Customs Treatment of Pool Containers used in International Transport (21 January 1994), [1995] OJ L91/46.

[46] List covers agreements to which the EC/EU has expressed its consent to be bound.

14. United Nations Convention to Combat Desertification in Countries Seriously Affected by Drought and/or Desertification, particularly in Africa (17 June 1994), [1998] OJ L83/3.
15. Agreement to Promote Compliance with International Conservation and Management Measures by Fishing Vessels on the High Seas (24 November 1994), [1996] OJ L177/26.
16. Agreement for the Implementing of the Provisions of the United Nations Convention on the Law of the Sea of 10 December 1982 Relating to the Conservation and Management of Straddling Stocks and Highly Migratory Fish Stocks (4 August 1995), [1998] OJ L189/17.
17. International Plant Protection Convention, as revised (17 November 1997), [2004] OJ L267/41.
18. Convention on Access to Information, Public Participation in Decision-making and Access to Justice in Environmental Matters (25 June 1998), [2005] OJ L124/4.
    - Protocol on Pollutant Release and Transfer Registers (21 May 2003), [2006] OJ L32/56.
19. Rotterdam Convention on the Prior Informed Consent Procedure for certain hazardous chemicals and pesticides in international trade (10 September 1998), [2003] OJ L63/29.
20. United Nations Convention against Transnational Organised Crime (15 November 2000), [2004] OJ L261/70.
    - Protocol Against the Smuggling of Migrants by Land, Sea and Air, supplementing the United Nations Convention Against Transnational Organised Crime (15 November 2000), [2006] OJ L262/36.
    - Protocol to Prevent, Suppress and Punish Trafficking in Persons, Especially Women And Children, supplementing the United Nations Convention Against Transnational Organised Crime (15 November 2000), [2006] OJ L262/53.
21. Stockholm Convention on Persistent Organic Pollutants (22 May 2001), [2006] OJ L209/3.
22. Athens Protocol of 2002 to the Athens Convention relating to the Carriage of Passengers and their Luggage by Sea, 1974 (1 November 2002), [2012] OJ L8/4.
23. WHO Framework Convention on Tobacco Control (21 May 2003), [2004] OJ L213/9.
24. United Nations Convention against Corruption (31 October 2003), [2008] OJ L287/3.
25. Convention on the Protection and Promotion of the Diversity of Cultural Expressions (20 October 2005), [2006] OJ L201/17.
26. International Tropical Timber Agreement, 2006 (27 January 2006), [2007] OJ L262/8.
27. Convention on the International Recovery of Child Support and

Other Forms of Family Maintenance (23 November 2007), [2011] OJ L192/51.

28. Statute of the International Renewable Energy Agency (IRENA) (26 January 2009), [2010] OJ L178/18.
29. International Rubber Study Group Constitution (14 July 2011), [2011] OJ L264/14.

Part IV

Responsibility of the EU in Substantive Policy Areas

8

Responsibility of the European Union in the Context of Investment

EILEEN DENZA

I. INTRODUCTION

FROM A STRICTLY practical point of view, potential plaintiffs—whether non-Member States or individuals—want two simple things when they seek to hold an international organisation responsible. First they want a defendant which is subject to the appropriate jurisdiction, either a domestic court of law or an international tribunal with relevant expertise. Secondly they want a defendant which has powers either to rectify the legal wrong of which they complain or in the alternative to provide appropriate financial compensation. Prior to the entry into force of the Treaty of Lisbon in 2009 both of these concerns posed major problems for plaintiffs seeking to hold the EU responsible if 'international legal personality' was imputed to the European Union in consequence of its expressly conferred and unchallenged treaty-making capacity. The extensive literature addressing the question of the Union's legal personality between 1999 and 2009 focused almost exclusively on its treaty-making capacity and on the *Reparations* case[1] and paid virtually no attention to the Union as a bearer of international legal responsibilities separate from those of its Member States or as a potential defendant in legal proceedings. The Union was never successfully sued before any domestic court and was clearly not capable of being sued before any international tribunal such as the European Court of Justice (given the absence of provision

[1] ICJ Reports 1949, 174. For a balanced discussion of the relevance of the case to the international legal personality of the Union prior to the Treaty of Lisbon see P Gautier, 'The Reparation for Injuries Case Revisited: The Personality of the European Union' (2000) *Max Planck Yearbook of United Nations Law* 331. For discussion of the problem of potential responsibility see E Denza, *The Intergovernmental Pillars of the European Union* (Oxford, Oxford University Press, 2002) 173–78, esp. 176–77.

for this in the Treaty on European Union), the International Court of Justice (whose Statute provides in Article 34 that 'Only states may be parties in cases before the Court'), or the International Centre for the Settlement of Investment Disputes (whose facilities for conciliation and arbitration are open only to contracting states and nationals of other contracting states). Particularly in the early days of the Union, before the improvements introduced by the Treaty of Amsterdam, its access to financing- even to meet its legal obligations—was somewhat dubious and subject to political agreement among its Member States. The matter of the absent single telephone number on which to phone Europe paled into insignificance by comparison with the difficulties of holding Europe as a single entity responsible for the wrongdoing of its institutions or for the unlawful consequences of its decisions.

The Treaty of Lisbon has endowed the European Union with indisputable international legal personality and the Council and Commission of the EU have sent 'letters of succession' informing their treaty partners and depositaries of multilateral agreements of the absorption of the EC by the Union.[2] This welcome simplification does not, however, in itself imply that the Union can be made subject to the jurisdiction of relevant courts or tribunals by non-Member States or by their investors seeking to make it responsible for default. Other changes to the Treaties should, however, at least ensure that if the European Union can be shown to be responsible for wrongdoing it will be better able to make appropriate amends either by rectifying the unlawful conduct or by providing financial reparation to those injured.

The European Union has not so far engaged in significant default on its financial obligations or obligations in the context of investment. But the potential difficulties in these areas are well illustrated by events which began 25 years ago when the International Tin Council ('the ITC') in effect went bankrupt. As the price of tin collapsed, the ITC in pursuance of its mandate to stabilise the price of this commodity continued to buy tin for its 'buffer stock' and to borrow money from banks in order to buy more tin. These stabilisation efforts ultimately failed, the coffers of the ITC were cleaned bare, and tin brokers and bankers were left with unsatisfied claims which collectively totalled £1,000 million. The ITC was not immune from the relevant legal actions in contract before UK courts, but it had no more money and the Member States were unwilling to provide it with any additional funds to meet its liabilities. The Member States were not immune either from the jurisdiction of UK courts in regard to claims for debt and contract default and they did have money, but they argued that because the ITC had 'the legal personality of a body corporate'

[2] F Hoffmeister, 'Litigating against the European Union and its Member States ... Who Responds under the ILC's Draft Articles on International Responsibility of International Organizations' (2010) 21 *European Journal of International Law* 723.

which had been given effect in UK domestic legislation, they could not be sued directly, and they were ultimately successful in the UK courts.[3] The Member States and their advisers did not accept that there was a rule of customary international law under which they were responsible for the debts or misdeeds of an international organisation which they had set up, but they were well aware that there were arguments to that effect even if they could not be effectively deployed in English courts. The existence of an international law rule of ultimate liability of the Member States for an organisation they had set up was never accepted by the English courts, far less that any such rule could be enforced at the national level. But it was in part due to these arguments that an overall settlement, with partial payment by states of the ITC debts against undertakings by banks and brokers to end all litigation, was reached.[4] Recollection of this sorry story no doubt had some influence on some of the draft Articles on Responsibility of International Organizations drawn up by the International Law Commission (for example Article 60 on the responsibility of a state which uses an international organisation of which it is a member and which has competence in relation to the subject matter to circumvent its own responsibility).[5]

II. GROWTH OF EU INVOLVEMENT IN INVESTMENT

Thirty years ago the EC began actively to involve itself in the regulation of foreign investment. There were three somewhat separate strands of activity:

(1) For a period of over ten years there were active negotiations for a multilateral Agreement on the promotion and protection of Investment within the framework of the Euro-Arab Dialogue. On both sides there were strong incentives for such an agreement. The Arab side—composed of all Members of the Arab League—included oil-rich states anxious to

[3] The leading case was *JH Rayner (Mincing Lane) v Department of Trade and Industry and the International Tin Council* [1990] 2 AC 418.

[4] For a comprehensive account of the litigation resulting from the collapse of the ITC, see C J Greenwood, 'Decisions of British courts during 1989 involving questions of public or private international law' (1989) *British Year Book of International Law* 461–79. See also I Cheyne (1987) *International & Comparative Law Quarterly* 931; (1989) *International & Comparative Law Quarterly* 417 and (1990) *International & Comparative Law Quarterly* 945.

[5] Art 60.1 provided 'A State member of an international organization incurs international responsibility if it seeks to avoid complying with one of its own international obligations by taking advantage of the fact that the organization has competence in relation to the subject matter of that obligation, thereby prompting the organization to commit an act that, if committed by the State, would have constituted a breach of the obligation'. A rather more tightly drafted version of the provision, limited to cases where the State 'circumvents that obligation by causing the organization to commit an act . . .' forms Art 61.1 of the draft articles adopted by the ILC in 2011, UN doc. A/CN4/L.778.

protect their large financial deposits and investments in Europe from freezing or penal measures as well as poorer states eager to attract inward investment. The European side believed that a multilateral agreement based on a balance of mutual financial advantage rather than one between developed and developing states (which was the usual kind) would have major value as an international precedent, and would help to establish acceptable rules on fair and equitable treatment, on limits to powers to expropriate foreign investment and on free transfer of investments and the returns from them. These negotiations led to quite systematic exchange of information both on policies and on particular negotiations among European Member States already active in the field. Those Member States– in particular Germany, France and the United Kingdom which had already negotiated many bilateral investment treaties (BITs) mostly with developing states—resisted the claim of the European Commission that foreign investment fell within the common commercial policy so as to give the EC exclusive competence. They were, however, prepared to accept that the EC should become a party to any agreement between the then nine (later ten) Member States of the EC and the 23 Member States of the Arab League (including Palestine) on the basis that the guarantees for certain external investments from the European Development Fund (which were themselves financed by Member States in agreed proportions) were a charge on the Budget of the Communities. So the proposed multilateral agreement with the Members of the Arab League—which in the mid-1980s came tantalisingly close to completion before running into primarily political obstacles—would have been mixed, with the European Community joining its Member States as a contracting party.[6]

(2) Within the framework of negotiations for a new Lomé III Convention between the EC and its Member States on the one hand and the African, Caribbean and Pacific States (ACP) on the other—almost all of them former dependencies of one of the European States—the suggestion was explored that Member States might in negotiating new BITs with contracting states to Lomé claim the benefit of terms in the BITs of other Member States (a kind of most-favoured nation provision). This was not accepted, on the basis that it was unrealistic and would fetter the sovereign right of states on both sides to conclude treaties on the best terms offered, or not to conclude them at all. Lomé III, however, signed in 1984, in its new provisions on investment promotion[7] laid strong emphasis on the conclusion of BITs, and they were seen as providing a springboard for

[6] On the importance of financing in the context of EC competence, see Opinion 1/78 *re International Agreement on Natural Rubber* [1979] ECR 2871.

[7] Cmnd. 9511, Title IV Chapter I on Investment, especially Arts 240 and 243 and the related Joint Declaration in Annex XXVI; P Juillard, 'Lome III et l'Investissement International' (1986) 296 *Revue du Marché Commun* 217; E Denza and S Brooks, 'Investment Protection Treaties: United Kingdom Experience' (1987) 36 *International & Comparative Law Quarterly* 914–15.

further investment. The importance of investment for stable development of the recipient country was increasingly being accepted, just as the traditional forms of development assistance—loans and grants—were beginning to come under challenge as too uncertain in their effects and encouraging continuing dependency, corruption and unsustainable burdens of debt. The provisions which were first agreed in Lomé III have been expanded and developed in the later Lome IV Convention[8] and in the Cotonou Agreement. In Article 1 of the 2000 Cotonou Agreement, which sets out the objectives of the partnership it was provided that:

Regional and sub-regional approaches which foster the integration of the ACP countries into the world economy in terms of trade and investment shall be encouraged and supported.

Articles 75 to 78 elaborate on this in terms of stable investment standards and proposed bilateral investment agreements.[9]

(3) The EC itself began to complement the BITs of the Member States—which did not cover any right of access for foreign investment but only post-admission treatment—by negotiating external agreements which gave non-discriminatory mutual rights of access for investors. The 1994 Cooperation Agreement on Partnership and Development between the European Community and the Republic of India,[10] for example, which replaced earlier and more limited agreements on commercial and economic cooperation, listed first among the objectives of cooperation 'further development and diversification of trade and investment in their mutual interest', set out a policy for improving access to each other's markets and emphasised the promotion of investments and joint ventures. In Article 10 on Investment, the parties agreed to encourage an increase in mutually beneficial investment, better conditions for transfer of capital, exchange of information on investment opportunities, cooperation between their financial institutions, and promotion and protection of investments between the EC and India on the basis of non-discrimination and reciprocity.

Much more specific provisions on investment were included in the 1997 Agreement on Partnership and Cooperation between the European Communities and their Member States and Russia.[11] The objectives of the new partnership included the promotion of trade and investment and harmonious economic relations between the parties based on the principles of market economy. Title IV of the Agreement on Business and Investment contained detailed obligations liberalising labour conditions of employees, most-favoured-nation treatment in regard to establishment and treatment

[8] Signed in December 1989, [1991] OJ L229/03, Arts 258–74 and Annex LIII.

[9] Signed in June 2000, OJ L317/3, 15.12.2000. The Agreement was amended in 2005 and in 2010. See also Hadfield, 'Janus Advances? An analysis of EC Development Policy and the 2005 Amended Cotonou Partnership Agreement' (2007)12 *European Foreign Affairs Review* 43.

[10] [1994] OJ L223/23.

[11] [1997] OJ L327/3

of companies, in particular banking, insurance and maritime transport service enterprises, with undertakings being required to avoid taking any measures to restrict the conditions of operation for each other's companies. Most-favoured-nation treatment was also provided for cross-border supply of services in specified sectors. Article 58 on Investment promotion and protection aimed to establish a favourable climate for investment and the transfer of capital, and envisaged the conclusion of agreements between EC Member States and Russia on investment promotion and protection as well as on double taxation.

Across the board, investment provisions in EC external agreements related at first mainly to services, but later also to establishment.[12] The General Agreement on Trade in Services (GATS) provided a framework for admission and treatment of investment in services which could be confirmed and amplified in specific bilateral agreements. With the growth in relevant internal Community rules, the area of implied competence of the EC gradually extended, but agreements containing significant new obligations on investment were invariably mixed.[13] These agreements always contained provisions which were within national competence—such as standards limiting expropriation of investments—in addition to provisions where the EC could claim either exclusive or shared competence.

III. RESPONSIBILITY PROVISIONS

Provisions on responsibility did not loom large in the early stages of the EC activities described above, which were mainly driven by the desire for more effective protection for EC investors in a period of widespread and arbitrary expropriation by newly independent states eager to assert their sovereign rights over their natural resources. There were, however, encouraging signs of acceptance by Europe of its responsibilities as a counterbalance to its increasing competence. In *European Parliament v Council of the European Union*,[14] in 1994, the European Court analyzed the commitments to development and financial assistance assumed under the fourth Lomé Convention by the EC and the Member States. In paragraph 29 the Court said:

[12] For an account of the varied bases for EC competence to include these provisions in external Agreements see R Leal-Arcas, *International Trade and Investment Law: Multilateral, Regional and Bilateral Governance* (Cheltenham, Edward Elgar, 2010) 224–29; A Dimopoulos, *EU Foreign Investment Law* (Oxford, Oxford University Press, 2011) 65–124. On the content and objectives of the agreements, see Dimopoulos (2011) 125–245.

[13] For an account of how Community rules, in particular on free movement of capital, increasingly affected powers of Member States to control inward investment, see F Benyon, *Direct Investment, National Champions and EU Treaty Freedoms* (Oxford: Hart Publishing, 2010) ch 8, 'Direct Investment from Third Countries'.

[14] [1994] ECR I 625.

The Convention was concluded, according to its preamble and Article 1, by the Community and its Member States of the one part and the ACP States of the other part. It established an essentially bilateral ACP-EEC cooperation. In those circumstances, in the absence of derogations expressly laid down in the Convention, the Community and its Member States as partners of the ACP States are jointly liable to those latter states for the fulfilment of every obligation arising from the commitments undertaken, including those relating to financial assistance.

It followed that the obligation to grant financial assistance fell on the Community and its Member States, considered together, that the competence to implement the responsibility was shared by the Community and its Member States and that it was for them to choose the source and methods of financing (paragraphs 33–35). This was a satisfactory result for non-Member States of the Community—who were thereby freed from any responsibility to investigate the complex and changing internal allocation of competence between the EC and its Member States—and it would apply to other mixed agreements in the absence of specific provisions on allocation of competence. Although the question of responsibility of the Community and its Member States to the ACP States was not central to this case, the above statement by the Court has not subsequently been called into question.[15] In the environmental field, the Court held that the Community had assumed external responsibility for the performance of non-pollution obligations under a mixed agreement to which France and some other Member States were parties together with the Community. In consequence of this, France was liable as a matter of Community law for non-performance of certain obligations even though these were not covered by any instrument of internal Community law.[16]

The Energy Charter Treaty signed in December 1994, and in force since 1998, is a multilateral and widely applied treaty on trade, transit and investment in the energy sector.[17] It contains strong provisions under which contracting parties give unconditional consent to submission of disputes with an investor of any other party either to their own national courts, under previously agreed settlement procedures or in accordance with international arbitration or conciliation procedures set out in the Treaty itself. Article 26 on Settlement of Disputes between an Investor and a Contracting Party required the EC as a regional economic integration organisation and a prospective separate party to the Treaty to 'provide a written statement of its policies, practices and conditions in this regard

[15] See also, to the same effect, A-G Tesauro in Case C-53/96 *Hermès International v FHT Marketing Choice BV* [1998] ECR I-3603, para 14, n 13.

[16] Case C-239/03 *Commission v France (Etang de Berre)* [2004] ECR I-9325, para 26.

[17] For a comprehensive analysis, see A Konoplyanik and T Wälde, 'Energy Charter Treaty and its Role in International Energy' (2006) 24 *Journal of Energy and Natural Resources Law* at 523; TW Wälde (ed), *The Energy Charter Treaty: An East–West Gateway for Investment and Trade* (London, Kluwer, 1996) esp chs 13 and 14.

to the Secretariat no later than the date of the deposit of its instrument of ratification, acceptance or approval' (para. 3(b)(ii)). The EC in accordance with this requirement made a declaration which inter alia stated:

The European Communities and the Member States have both concluded the Energy Charter Treaty and are thus internationally responsible for the fulfilment of the obligations contained therein, in accordance with their respective competences.

The Communities and the Member States will, if necessary, determine among them who is respondent party to arbitration proceedings initiated by an Investor of another Contracting Party. In such case, upon the request of the Investor, the Communities and the Member States will make such determination within a period of 30 days.

This provision may be contrasted with the earlier provisions in the 1982 UN Convention on the Law of the Sea[18] (UNLOSC) which under Annex IX entitled the EC to become a contracting party 'to the extent that it has competence in accordance with the declarations, communications or information or notifications' required to be submitted to the UN Secretary-General along with any instrument of ratification or approval. Article 6 of Annex IX on Responsibility and Liability provides that parties which asserted competence under its provisions 'shall have responsibility for failure to comply with obligations or for any other violation of this Convention'. On request, the EC and its Member States were required to provide information to any other state party as to who had responsibility for any specific matter, and failure to provide such information within a reasonable time or provision of contradictory information 'shall result in joint and several liability'. The EC was reluctant to make a Declaration of Competence—arguing that the demarcation between the EC and its Member States was complex and continually changing. This initial reluctance was supported by the European Court of Justice which maintained in Ruling 1/78 *International Atomic Energy Agency*[19] that it was not necessary for the EC to set out the division of competence between the EC and its Member States, particularly as it might change and was not a legitimate concern for non-Member States parties to the relevant treaty. The Community was, however, given no alternative by other states participating in the Conference if it wished to become a separate party to the Convention. It was argued that other parties would in the absence of any guidance find it difficult to know how to attribute liability in the event of a breach of the Convention by a European Member State or States.[20] The Declaration required prolonged and difficult negotiations among the

[18] Cmnd. 8941.

[19] [1978] ECR 2151, para 35. The Court altered its position in later cases.

[20] For a clear account of the attitude of non-Member States see P M Olson, 'Mixity from the Outside' in C Hillion and P Koutrakos (eds), *Mixed Agreements Revisited: the EU and its Member States in the World* (Oxford Hart Publishing, 2010) 331.

Member States and the Commission and the version submitted on formal confirmation in 1998 has never been updated to reflect the adoption of later relevant legislation by the Community.[21]

The Energy Charter Treaty differed from Article 6 in Annex IX to UNLOSC in that it contained no requirement for an initial express declaration of competences, and there was a precise time limit for determining any respondent to arbitration proceedings initiated by an investor. On the other hand there was no fall-back sanction of 'joint and several liability' to safeguard against non-compliance in the matter of clarifying who should be the appropriate respondent to any claim.[22] The provision is also criticised by Dimopoulos on the ground that while it provides a practical solution to the determination of responsibility, it does not allow third countries to know beforehand the contracting party assuming an obligation.[23]

By the late 1990s therefore, the position regarding responsibility of the European Union and its Member States from the practical standpoint of external investors might have been regarded as satisfactory. Mixed agreements covering entry of investment, non-discriminatory treatment and an increasing number of aspects of post-entry treatment were growing. Concurrently the large network of bilateral BITs concluded by EU Member States gave more precise rights in regard to post-entry treatment of investments, free transfer of capital and strong rights for private investors to invoke arbitration before ICSID. The ECJ had endorsed the proposition that for mixed agreements lacking precise provisions on allocation of competence, the EC and its Member States were jointly and severally responsible. The Energy Charter Treaty had set a precedent whereby non-Member States would not have to scrutinise and evaluate a declaration of competences by the EC in order to determine whom to sue, but could expect the EC—having all the relevant expertise and up-to-date knowledge—to nominate the appropriate respondent. Non-Member States and their investors could rely on invoking rights to access to domestic courts, or to international conciliation or arbitration under BITs with European Member States. Most of these BITs gave individual or corporate investors the right of access to the facilities of the International Centre for the Settlement of Investment Disputes (ICSID) for settlement of disputes with the host state. Where there was a European interest in the issues under

[21] The texts of the first Declaration, submitted on signature by the EC on 7 December 1984 and of the second Declaration, submitted on formal confirmation on 1 April 1998, are available on the website of the Treaty Section of the Office of Legal Affairs of the United Nations, 1998 UNTS 227 and at [1998] OJ L/179/1.

[22] A provision somewhat similar to that in the Energy Charter was put forward in the context of the unsuccessful negotiations for a Multilateral Investment Agreement, see Art D6 in draft text of 24 April 1998 and OECD Commentary in DAFFE/MAI (98) 7/REV 1.

[23] Dimopoulos, above n 12, 252. At 271, the Energy Charter provision is described as a successful example of a procedural mechanism for determining responsibility in a given case.

dispute, the Commission could file a written submission as a non-disputing party pursuant to the ICSID Arbitration Rules[24]—a course which it successfully followed in the ICSID Case *AES Summit Generation Ltd. and AES-Tisza Erömü v Hungary Kft.* Partnership and Cooperation Agreements or Association Agreements containing investment access or treatment provisions entitled non-Member States to proceed against the EC, its Member States or both under dispute settlement procedures offering varied possibilities for redress.

These provisions were from the standpoint of external investors more progressive than those to be found in most other agreements establishing international organisations. The wide-ranging survey of practice submitted by Germany to the International Law Commission shows that the constituent instruments of most organisations, to the extent that they make express provision regarding liability at all, do not provide for alternative or subsidiary liability of the Member States in addition to that of the organisation. Germany concluded from its survey of practice including case law that the responsibility of international organisations is distinct from that of their Member States and that there was no presumption in customary international law that either the organisations or their Member States were responsible for the actions of international organisations. The overall trend in German state practice was to deny member state responsibility for the actions of international organisations.[25] Much of the practice, however, related to actions of armed forces where it has been usual for any wrongdoing to be attributable to one particular national armed group and for the state in question to assume responsibility and offer compensation. It is not necessarily applicable or appropriate in the quite different areas of finance or investment.

The European Commission has submitted extensive comments on the International Law Commission's draft Articles on the Responsibility of international organisations.[26] In its general comments, the Commission emphasised that there significant differences between traditional international organisations and organisations such as the EU 'which has important law-based foreign relations powers that have a tendency to develop over time'. It was suggested that some of the ILC draft articles, even when taken with the relevant commentaries, were inadequate or inapplicable to the EU. The Commission stressed that under its treaties, the EU institutions were fully accountable to one another and to Member States for acts and failure to act. Under express provisions in international agreements, non-EU states had the possibility of seizing EU courts with alleged breaches by the Union, and could participate in preliminary reference pro-

[24] ICSID Arbitration Rule 37.

[25] UN doc A/CN.4/556, 46–65. See also J Crawford, 'Holding International Organisations and Their Members to Account', 5th Steinkraus-Cohen International Law Lecture (2007).

[26] Contained in UN doc A/CN.4/637.

ceedings before the Court of Justice. Proceedings could be brought against the EU before several dispute settlement bodies and also in national courts of EU Member States, where immunity would not be invoked.

Commenting on draft Article 63 (64 following adoption by the ILC on second reading in 2011)—which provides for non-application of the draft articles where responsibility is governed by special rules of international law which may be contained in the rules of the organisation applicable to the relation between the organisation and its members, the Commission explained a number of the special features of EU law affecting its action in the international sphere. It noted that in areas of EU competence only the EU may be able to undo breaches of international law rooted in EU rules or practice, while Member States may be powerless to do so. It criticised the draft article for implying that internal EU rules were to be qualified as international law, arguing that they were rather, in the interpretation of the Court of Justice, 'more of a constitutional nature'. It did not, however, suggest that the complexities of the evolving rules of EU external competence gave rise to practical difficulties for non-Member States for which a special practice should be applied by the EU—consistent with its own desire to accept accountability. Such provision, based on external agreements concluded by the EC or EU, could with advantage be added to the draft article on *Lex specialis*.

IV. THE TREATY OF LISBON

The entry into force in 2009 of the Treaty of Lisbon—while it undoubtedly simplified responsibility of Europe and its Member States in some areas by establishing the European Union as an entity with clear international legal personality,[27] clearer legal obligations and ability to make restitution or provide compensation—has, however, thrown up new uncertainties in the area of investment. Article 207 of the Treaty on the Functioning of the European Union, replacing old Article 133 in the European Community Treaty has extended the scope of the common commercial policy to include 'foreign direct investment'. Exclusive competence for foreign direct investment has thus passed to the Union, but leaving competence in regard to other forms of investment such as portfolio investment under shared competence as before. The EU has followed the definition of foreign direct investment developed by the IMF and the OECD specifying that 'Foreign direct investment is the category of international investment that reflects the objective of a resident entity in one economy('direct investor') obtaining a lasting interest in an enterprise resident in another economy

[27] Art 1 of the Treaty on European Union provides that 'The Union shall replace and succeed the European Community'. Art 47 of the TEU provides that 'The Union shall have legal personality'.

('direct investment enterprise'). The concept of 'lasting interest' comprises the existence of a long-term relationship and significant influence on the management of the enterprise.[28]

Most BITs of Member States contain a wide definition of the investments covered which includes all forms of investment—portfolio as well as direct investment. While increased competence may well give the Union more effective negotiating power in negotiating new and comprehensive agreements with, for example, Canada, China, Russia and India, it does give rise to new uncertainties for third countries anxious to know how to proceed in order to establish effective responsibility in the context of an investment dispute with one or more European Member States.

The continued effectiveness of the protection of European outward investment as well as of inward investment by non-Member States and their investors required certainty as to the status of the network of BITs—about 1200—concluded by almost all EU Member States and also clarity on how the Union will make use of its new powers in the investment field. The Commission began the discussion in July 2010 by publishing two documents—a Communication entitled 'Towards a comprehensive European international investment policy'[29] and a proposal for a regulation of the European Parliament and the Council establishing transitional arrangements for bilateral agreements between Member States and third countries.[30] The Commission made clear that its objective 'is to provide legal certainty to both EU and foreign investors operating under the terms of these agreements'[31] and that the two documents were only the first steps in the development of a European investment policy.

Article 3 of the draft regulation should ensure that there will be little question as to the continued validity of the existing BITs with non-Member States. It provides

Notwithstanding the Union's competence relating to investment and without prejudice to other obligations of member states under the law of the Union, member states are authorised in accordance with Article 2(1) of

[28] Communication from the EC and its Member States to the WTO Working Group on the Relationship between Trade and Investment, 16 April 2002, WT/WGTI/W/115. For EU practice on the definition of 'direct investment, see Bennion (2010) n13 above, 9–10 and 81–82, and ECJ Judgment in Case C-446/04 *Test Claimants in the FII Group Litigation v Commissioners of Inland Revenue* [2006] ECR-11573, para 181.

[29] COM(2010) 343 final, 7 July 2010.

[30] COM(2010) 344 final, 7 July 2010. For a general explanation of how the Commission envisages the development of European investment policy and practice, see interview with Tomas Baert, DG for Trade, Services and Investment, in *Investment Treaty News*, 23 September 2010. For an analytical account of the draft regulation, responses to it and its implications, see G De Baere and P Koutrakos, 'The interactions between the European Court of Justice and the legislature in the European Union's external relations' in P Syrpis (ed), *The Relationship between the Judiciary and the Legislature in the Internal Market* (Cambridge, Cambridge University Press, 2012).

[31] Communication, para 2.

the Treaty to maintain in force bilateral agreements relating to investment that have been notified in accordance with Article 2 of this Regulation.

So presumably a non-Member State can continue to rely on the existing dispute settlement provisions in these BITs and if—as is increasingly likely—there is a European dimension to the issue, the Commission will be entitled to intervene or make representations as at present within the framework of arbitration under the procedures of ICSID or those of the UN Commission on International Trade Law (UNCITRAL).[32] So far there have been few claims against European Member States under their BITs, and those that have been made have not been successful—though this is changing, and some investment claims have been made against, for example, the Czech Republic and Poland.[33]

More difficult, however, will be the position if a BIT is—with appropriate authorisation as envisaged—amended. The Commission envisages in particular amendments for the purpose of making the BITs EU-compatible, and some of these (such as amending the provisions on free movement of capital to give the Member States rights to impose restrictions on free movement which Europe has never found necessary to impose in the past and may never wish to impose in the future) do not seem to take account of the probable desire of non-Member States to have reciprocal rights to impose restrictions.[34] It has not expressly covered the possibility of updating a BIT for other reasons such as new investment laws in the non-Member State or a wider acceptance of jurisdiction for settlement of potential disputes with investors. Most of the existing BITs comprise both direct and indirect investment within their terms. In the context of a negotiation to amend a BIT, or an authorised negotiation with a new non-Member State, the non-Member State may reasonably seek clarification of the future position regarding responsibility and dispute settlement.

The draft Regulation also envisages in Article 6 that existing BITs may be disallowed by the Commission as incompatible with EU law and so placed in a kind of limbo—with continued validity under international law in accordance with their terms, but with the EU Member State under

[32] On third party intervention under UNCITRAL procedures, see J Bischoff, 'Just a Little Bit of "Mixity"? The EU's Role in the Field of International Investment Protection Law' (2011) 48 *Common Market Law Review* 1527, 1557.

[33] For precise statistics, see the Study made for the Directorate-General for External Policies of the European Parliament by S Woolcock and J Kleinheisterkamp 'The EU Approach to International Investment Policy after the Lisbon Treaty', EXPO/B/INTA/FWC/2009-01/Lot (London, London School of Economics, 2009).

[34] In Cases C-205/06 *Commission v Austria* [2009] 2 *Common Market Law Reports* 50 and C-249/06 *Commission v Sweden* [2009] 2 *Common Market Law Review* 49 and in Case C-118/07 *Commission v Finland*, the ECJ held that provisions on free movement of capital in BITs concluded before accession to the EU by Austria, Sweden and Finland were inconsistent with powers of the EU in certain circumstances to impose restrictions on free movement of capital. For comment on the implications of seeking to revise these provisions, and similar provisions in almost all of the other BITs of Member States, see Comment on these cases by E Denza (2010) 35 *European Law Review* 263.

obligation to amend or seek to terminate them. If, however, the Member State disputes the withdrawal of authorisation by the Commission, the question would ultimately have to be resolved by the ECJ. Such a position is hardly conducive to a continuing stable investment framework with the relevant non-Member State.

V. RESPONSIBILITY AND DISPUTE SETTLEMENT POST-LISBON

The Commission's Communication 'Towards a comprehensive European International Investment Policy' in its final section says that the issue of international responsibility between the EU and the Member States in EU investment agreements needs to be addressed. It says

The European Union, represented by the Commission, will defend all actions of EU institutions. Given the exclusive external competence, the Commission takes the view that the European Union will also be the sole defendant regarding any measure taken by a Member State which affects investment by third countries, nationals or companies falling within the scope of the agreement concerned.[35]

This admittedly cryptic provision suggests either that future agreements will relate only to FDI and be concluded by the EU alone or else that the Commission is claiming exclusive competence not only for FDI as granted by the Lisbon Treaty but for other forms of investment as well. The Commission has, however, made clear that it expects future Europe wide agreements with investment provisions to be mixed,[36] and there is no realistic prospect that the Member States would accept Union only agreements on investment protection unless of a very limited kind. Indeed, some Member States argue that mandates for future agreements should make it explicit that investment is now a matter under shared competence. The section on responsibility, however, says nothing about the likely possibility that future agreements are likely to continue to be mixed, containing provisions on portfolio investment or other terms covered by shared competence, and it says nothing about the position regarding the numerous BITs which from the point of view of non-EU investors will for a considerable time form the main guarantee of security when they invest in the Union. The Commission does, however, say that it will address the issue in developing its new investment policy, and work by and for the EP shows great awareness of the impending complexities.[37]

[35] Communication, 10.

[36] See interview with Tomas Baert of the European Commission, cited in n 30 above, where he refers to the likelihood that investment protection will be dealt with by Europe in the context of free trade agreements which normally contain other provisions outside the investment context requiring an agreement to be mixed.

[37] See, eg the study referred to n 33 above.

The previous section of the Commission's Communication does, however, correctly identify as a major obstacle to the inclusion of effective investor–state dispute settlement provisions the fact that the EU is not a party to the International Convention on the Settlement of Investment Disputes (since Article 67 limits participation to states) and says that it will explore the possibility of EU accession—which would require amendment of the Convention but does not appear an unattainable objective in the medium term. The international community now has no objection to the Union as participant in any new multilateral régime or international organisation, but is obviously reluctant to embark on the prolonged process of treaty amendment for the sole benefit of the Union. In consequence the EC and now the Union has been able to accede to existing organisations or multilateral treaties only when they are revised or replaced for wider reasons.[38] Non-Member States are likely if properly advised to demand effective dispute settlement provisions—which are increasingly understood to imply the possibility of recourse to ICSID—before they agree to the replacement of their BITs with Member States by a more comprehensive investment agreement with the EU and its Member States. The EU has not so far been a party to UNCITRAL dispute settlement procedures, but as pointed out by Bischoff, there is no bar to its participation, since its facilities are not limited to members of UNCITRAL.[39]

In the meanwhile, Article 13.3 of the draft Regulation provides that:

For all agreements falling within the scope of this Regulation, the Member State concerned shall seek the agreement of the Commission before activating any relevant mechanisms for dispute settlement included in the agreement and shall, where requested by the Commission, activate such mechanisms. Such mechanisms shall include consultations with the other party to the agreement and dispute settlement where provided for in the agreement. The Member State and the Commission shall fully cooperate in the conduct of procedures within the relevant mechanisms, which may include, where appropriate, that the Commission participates in the relevant procedures.

This provision does not, however, expressly deal with the possibility of proceedings against a Member State by the other party to the agreement—in which context it would also be highly desirable for the Commission to become involved and to participate where it has an interest in the issue and where the 'relevant procedures' and practice permit this.

The European Parliament as co-legislator for the draft Regulation has now published its position which includes a number of amendments with relevance to the question of responsibility. The transitional protection for BITs duly notified to the Commission would last for 10 years instead of

[38] See, eg the various commodity organisations, the Food and Agricultural Organization, the World Trade Organization and the World Customs Organisation.

[39] Bischoff, n 32 above, 1567.

5, and the Commission would have a discretionary rather than a mandatory power to review these BITs for compatibility with EU law, or if they 'constitute a serious obstacle to the conclusion of future Union agreements on investment with non-member countries'. The power to withdraw authorisation of a BIT would also be limited to cases of conflict with EU law or where the BIT constitutes a 'serious obstacle' to future agreements on investment with the relevant country. The provisions on withdrawal of authorisation are generally more flexible and would include the possibility of renegotiation of the relevant BIT by the Member State party, or a recommendation to the Council that it should authorise a new Union agreement with the country concerned.[40] Taken together, these amendments would enhance the security to be enjoyed for investors currently covered under existing BITs during a 'transitional period' which will inevitably be very prolonged.

VI. NEW UNION AGREEMENTS

It is clear that the Union will not seek to negotiate any 'Model EU Agreement', given the time likely to be wasted in arriving at agreement between at least 27 Member States on its precise terms and the disparity of circumstances in likely negotiations. The objective will rather be to include provisions which reflect the new Union powers in agreements already under negotiation. The states with which there are ongoing negotiations are Canada, India and Singapore, and the Commission is seeking to amend the negotiating mandates in regard to these countries accordingly. Precision in regard to dispute settlement terms is already a live issue in Council discussions, and this is the context in which future policy is likely to be formulated. Member States are insisting before approving any fresh negotiating mandate that it must be made clear how responsibility for implementing any final agreement will be allocated between the Union and its Member States.[41]

Beyond the question of dispute settlement, it will be important that the EU acknowledges as a general principle that the Member States of an international organisation operating in the areas of finance or investment should ultimately be responsible for the obligations of that organisation. The reasons of policy which from the middle of the nineteenth century led at the national level to the establishment of limited liability companies so as to encourage traders to assume large commercial risks without the accompanying risk of personal bankruptcy do not seem to apply to the case of states setting up an international organisation to perform functions

[40] EP Press Release of 11 May 2011, 'Bilateral Investment Treaties: Limiting the Commission's Authority'.

[41] M Maes in *Investment Treaty News*, 1 July 2011.

more effectively than they could themselves.[42] There is no obvious need for there to be a 'corporate veil' shielding states from liability if their organisation defaults, and it is highly unlikely that a general acceptance that joint and several responsibility should be the presumption at least in the case of organisations operating in commercial, financial or investment areas will deter states from setting up future international organisations. Other states will more readily do business with an international organisation whose Member States accept ultimate responsibility for its debts and errors, and the EU in entering more extensively into the field of investment is well placed to set a constructive example in this regard.[43] A similar approach has consistently been taken in regard to the granting of immunities to international organisations operating in financial or commercial fields, such as the International Monetary Fund, the International Bank for Reconstruction and Development, and commodity organisations such as the International Sugar Council and the International Tin Council.[44] Immunities have been limited on the basis that this will make the organisations in question more acceptable as commercial operators.

VII. CONCLUSION

There are a number of practical steps which the EU could take in order to ensure that its development of a comprehensive investment policy remains consistent with standards of international responsibility which it has generally upheld in its own earlier practice:

1. Clarify that Member States may with authorisation amend their BITs for reasons of improving investor protection and not only to ensure compatibility with EU law and policies, and that when this happens non-Member States and their investors will not be deprived of their existing dispute settlement entitlements;
2. Offer a clearer indication as to the circumstances in which the Commission might withdraw authorisation of an existing BIT on the ground

[42] A Digman, in his entry on 'limited liability' in P Cane and J Conaghan (eds), *New Oxford Companion to Law* (Oxford, Oxford University Press, 2008), states that 'The impact of the registered company with limited liability is said to have facilitated the second industrial revolution in late nineteenth-century Britain. Limited liability obviously encourages investment as the shareholder's risk is minimized'.

[43] To similar effect, see K P Sauvant and LE Sachs (eds), *The Effect of Treaties on Foreign Direct Investment: Bilateral Investment Treaties, Double Taxation Treaties and Investment Flows* (Oxford, Oxford University Press, 2009) Preface, lxii: 'As international investment rule-making involves the great majority of countries, is a dynamic process and proceeds at a rapid pace, all countries have the opportunity to participate actively in designing the international investment law system and to seek to influence it in a manner that ensures that their interests are taken into account'. See also Bischoff (2011), n 32 above, 1564–66.

[44] See I Roberts (ed), *Satow's Diplomatic Practice*, 6th edn (Oxford, Oxford University Press, 2009) ch 21, paras 22–23.

that it 'undermines the Union's policies relating to investment'. Such a withdrawal would not affect the validity of the agreement in international law and would probably be challenged by the Member State party before the ECJ, but would be likely to result in a prolonged period of uncertainty not conducive to the stability of investments in or by the relevant non-Member State. The proposal by the Parliament to narrow the grounds on which the Commission might withdraw authorisation would be helpful, but still lacks clarity as to what might constitute a 'serious obstacle' to a future agreement with the relevant country;

3. Seek to include in future multilateral agreements covering investment to be negotiated by the EU together with its Member States provisions similar to those in the Energy Charter Treaty under which the other party or one of its investors may on application be informed within 30 days of the appropriate respondent to any claim—and add to any such model provision a fall-back sanction of joint and several liability of the Union and its Member States in the event of non-compliance with this requirement;
4. Actively pursue the objective of amendment of the ICSID Convention to permit EU accession;
5. Seek to ensure that the ILC Draft Articles on Responsibility of International Organisations—in particular Article 64 on Lex specialis—enable the EU to include in its future mixed agreements provisions which entitle it to name the appropriate respondent to a claim or action at the time when it arises—having regard to the fact that this is from the standpoint of non-Member States and their investors the procedure which best reconciles their rights with the evolving and complex nature of EU external competence.

Taken together, these steps would respond to the suggestion made by Pieter Jan Kuijper that the Union should:

> put its own house in order in respect of responsibility for mixed agreements . . [T]his may have positive influence on the general law of the responsibility of international organizations, since it can be recognized as *lex specialis* under the new rules on the responsibility of international organizations being discussed by the ILC.[45]

[45] PJ Kuijper, 'International Responsibility for EU Mixed Agreements' in C Hillion and P Koutrakos (eds), *Mixed Agreements Revisited: The EU and its Member States in the World* (Oxford, Hart Publishing, 2010) 227.

9

The 'Odd Couple': The Responsibility of the EU at the WTO

ANDRÉS DELGADO CASTELEIRO AND JORIS LARIK

I. INTRODUCTION: THE 'ODD COUPLE' OF THE EU AND THE WTO, A CASE APART FOR INTERNATIONAL RESPONSIBILITY?

WHEN ASSESSING THE issue of the responsibility of the European Union (EU) under international law, the area of trade, and in particular the framework of the World Trade Organisation (WTO), provides a highly interesting as well as a highly peculiar case study. As one of the world's leading trade powers,[1] incurring responsibility for its behaviour in light of the obligations under WTO law is evidently an issue of great practical importance. In contrast to, at times, rather theoretical debates among scholars of international law, this is something which affects European citizens quite tangibly when European products and consequently companies and jobholders become the targets of countermeasures by the trading partners of the EU as a result of a lost dispute and lacking compliance in the eyes of the WTO Dispute Settlement Body (DSB).[2]

Beyond this practical relevance, in legal terms, the WTO and the EU could well be described as an 'odd couple' in international law. Both

[1] See, eg S Meunier and K Nicolaïdis, 'The European Union as a Trade Power' in C Hill and M Smith (eds), *International Relations and the European Union* (Oxford, Oxford University Press, 2011).

[2] A prominent example for this are so-called 'carousel sanctions' implemented (or threatened) by the United States against the EU. See, eg R Ford, 'Beef Hormone Dispute and Carousel Sanctions: A Roundabout Way of Forcing Compliance with World Trade Organization Decisions' (2002) 27 *Brooklyn Journal of International Law* 543; W Kerr and J Hobbs, 'Consumers, Cows and Carousels: Why the Dispute over Beef Hormones is Far More Important than its Commercial Value' in N Perdikis and R Read (eds), *The WTO and the Regulation of International Trade: Recent Trade Disputes Between the European Union and the United States* (Cheltenham, Edward Elgar, 2005).

are rather the exception than the rule, above all due to their respective internal compulsory dispute settlement mechanisms. Albeit to varying degrees, both have been discussed in 'constitutional' terms.[3] Certainly, neither could be considered as just an 'average' international organisation (IO). Furthermore, with regard to the EU, the question of its responsibility within the WTO dispute settlement mechanism could be seen as a mirror of the debate on the international legal nature of the EU itself. Is the EU indeed an actor in its own right, albeit of a sui generis kind? Or is it in reality 'just' the 'most developed form of international organization',[4] of which the Member States remain the true masters? This raises questions also for the general evolution of the international system, as the EU is often seen as a model for other IOs.[5] For instance, the Andean Community[6] and the African Union[7] were designed following the template of the EU. In addition, it is argued that the constitutional features of the EU offer answers for dealing with legitimacy issues of IOs, including the WTO.[8] Against this backdrop, the way in which the Union and its Member States, which all remain full members of the WTO as well as participants in WTO dispute settlement, bear responsibility within the WTO could be seen either as a case apart, an exception, or the most advanced way of managing the international responsibility of a non-state entity such as the Union.

Consequently, the international responsibility of the EU in the WTO constitutes a good example for appraising the specificities which make the EU an international actor like no other. In fact, the interrelation of the

[3] See, eg from among the vast literature, respectively, on the WTO, E-U Petersmann, 'Multilevel Trade Governance in the WTO Requires Multilevel Constitutionalism' in C Joerges and E-U Petersmann (eds), *Constitutionalism, Multilevel Trade Governance and International Economic Law* (Oxford, Hart Publishing, 2011); R Howse and K Nicolaïdis, 'Legitimacy and Global Governance: Why Constitutionalizing the WTO Is a Step Too Far' in R Porter, P Sauvé, A Subramanian and A Beviglia Zampetti (eds), *Efficiency, Equity, and Legitimacy: The Multilateral Trading System the Millennium* (Washington, DC, Brookings Institution Press, 2001); and on the EU, N Walker and S Tierney, 'Introduction: A Constitutional Mosaic? Exploring the New Frontiers of Europe's Constitutionalism' in N Walker, J Shaw and S Tierney (eds), *Europe's Constitutional Mosaic* (Oxford, Hart Publishing, 2011); N Walker, 'The Place of European Law' in G De Búrca and JHH Weiler (eds), *The Worlds of European Constitutionalism* (Cambridge, Cambridge University Press, 2011).

[4] J Klabbers, 'Contending Approaches to International Organizations: Between Functionalism and Constitutionalism' in J Klabbers and A Wallendahl (eds), *Research Handbook on the Law of International Organizations* (Cheltenham, Edward Elgar, 2011) 24 (fn 16). In this regard, Weiler and Trachtman speak of the EU as either sui generis or nirvana. JHH Weiler, and JP Trachtman, 'European Constitutionalism and Its Discontents' (1996–97) 17 *Northwestern Journal of International Law & Business* 355.

[5] M Cremona, 'The EU as a Global Actor. Roles, Models, and Identities' (2004) 41 *Common Market Law Review* 554.

[6] KJ Alter et al, 'Transplanting the European Court of Justice: the Experience of the Andean Tribunal of Justice' (2011) 1 *Oñati Socio-Legal Series* 12.

[7] K Nicolaïdis and R Howse, '"This is my EUtopia…": Narrative as Power' (2002) 40 *Journal of Common Market Studies* 768.

[8] Cremona, above n 5.

Union and its Member States in the WTO dispute settlement system highlights not only the special features of the EU, but also of its Member States as 'strange subjects' of international law,[9] ie subjects, which, while nominally sovereign, are significantly conditioned in their behaviour through their being members of the European Union. The relations between the EU and its Member States in the WTO dispute settlement system illustrate neatly how the ability of the Member States to bear responsibility is constrained in the international sphere by this very membership in the EU.

With this in mind, the present contribution shows how the special way in which the EU handles its responsibility at the WTO has a significant impact on its relations with its Member States and their role in the WTO dispute settlement system. More specifically, it argues that the institutional design of the WTO dispute settlement system as well as the special features of the relations between the EU and its Member States in the field of trade render the latter almost invisible, hiding them behind the veil of the EU, which constitutes both an exception to the general rule of joint responsibility as well as an example for a more advanced way of dealing with international responsibility. Moreover, this contribution shows that the other WTO contracting parties have come to accept, by and large, the invisibility of the EU Member States in the WTO dispute settlement system.

In order to elaborate these points, the contribution is structured as follows. First, after recalling the main issues surrounding the responsibility of the EU in international law in a more general way, we present the main aspects of the practice of the EU and its Member States as a target of trade disputes at the WTO. In the second part, we focus on the factors that shape the pragmatic approach to responsibility of the Union. These are, on the one hand, the specificities of the WTO framework, and on the other the position of the EU and its Member States within the WTO.

II. BEYOND THE VEIL: THE EU, ITS MEMBER STATES AND INTERNATIONAL RESPONSIBILITY

Before turning to the 'odd couple' of the WTO and EU as such, the general debate in international law on the responsibility of international organisations will be recalled. This is the backdrop against which the actual practice within the WTO will be assessed, and which serves to highlight the particularity of this case study.

[9] B De Witte, 'The Emergence of European System of Public International Law: The EU and its Member States as Strange Subjects' in J Wouters, A Nollkaemper and E de Wet (eds), *The Europeanisation of International Law: The Status of International Law in the EU and its Member States* (The Hague, TMC Asser Press, 2009) 252.

A. Attribution, the Veil of the Organisation and Secondary Responsibility

As a starting point, it should be borne in mind that rather than providing for reparations for injury, the rules on the responsibility of international organisations concern the allocation of powers, and subsequently the allocation of responsibilities for any possible damage caused.[10] Logically, the main discussions focus on how the rules of attribution allocate the responsibilities between the IO and its members. In other words, the debate revolves around the question of who has committed the wrongful act and consequently who has to remedy it: the IO or its member states? Analysing the complexities of the internal structure of the IO (a structure in which its members assume a predominant position)[11] thus raises many legal questions concerning the allocation of responsibilities pertaining to, inter alia, the porosity of the institutional veil of the IO,[12] its 'volonté distincte'[13] or the dichotomy between autonomy and accountability of the organisation and its members.[14]

Accordingly, the analysis of the responsibility of the EU and its Member States is going to revolve around these issues in one way or another. The multi-layered nature of the EU, in which the Member States implement the *acquis communnautaire*, including international agreements concluded by the Union, logically poses the question of who bears responsibility as well. Should we understand that EU Member States are to be considered as EU 'organs' when they are implementing EU law? Or, instead, should we refuse the possibility of a *dédoublement fonctionnel* on the side of the Member States, and accept that regardless of the fact that organs of the Member States are implementing EU law, they continue to be organs of these Member States? Many scholars have answered this question arguing in favour of the joint and several responsibility of the Union and its Member States, especially in mixed agreement settings.[15] One of the main

[10] A Nollkaemper, 'Constitutionalization and the Unity of the Law of International Responsibility' (2009) 16 *Indiana Journal of Global Studies* 538.

[11] N Blokker, 'Preparing Articles on Responsibility of International Organizations: Does the International Law Commission Take International Organizations Seriously?' in J Klabbers and A Wallendahl (eds), *Research Handbook on the Law of International Organizations* (Cheltenham, Edward Elgar, 2011) 321.

[12] See, eg PJ Kuijper, 'Introduction to the Symposium on Responsbility of International Organizations and of (Member) States: Attributed or Direct Responsbility or Both?' (2010) 7 *International Organizations Law Review* 9; C Brölmann, *The Institutional Veil in Public International Law: International Organisations and the Law of Treaties* (Oxford, Hart Publishing, 2007) 255.

[13] Klabbers, above n 4, 11.

[14] R Collins and N White, 'Moving Beyond the Autonomy–Accountability Dichotomy: Reflections on Institutional Independence in the International Legal Order' (2010) 7 *International Organizations Law Review* 1.

[15] See, eg International Law Commission, Second Report on Responsibility of International Organizations by Mr. Giorgio Gaja, Special Rapporteur, Fifty-fifth session, 2 April

arguments supporting the joint and several responsibility of the EU and its Member States is to be found in the case law of the Court of Justice of the EU (CJEU). In a case concerning the European Development Fund (*Parliament v Council*),[16] according to the Court of Justice:

> in the absence of derogations expressly laid down in the [Lomé] Convention, the Community and its Member States as partners of the ACP States are jointly liable to those latter States for the fulfilment of every obligation arising from the commitments undertaken, including those relating to financial assistance.[17]

However, even though certainly not an erroneous ruling,[18] the CJEU's statement is nonetheless to be qualified. First, as Kuijper rightly stressed, this concerned a bilateral mixed agreement.[19] This factor was acknowledged by the Court in the same judgment by stating that 'in accordance with the essentially bilateral character of the cooperation, the obligation to grant 'the Community's financial assistance' falls on the Community and on its Member States, considered together.[20]

Therefore, the joint and several responsibility of the EU and its Member States should be constrained to international agreements of a bilateral nature, and should not be extended automatically to multilateral ones like the WTO agreements. Moreover, when viewed within the larger context of the case law of the Court of Justice on mixed agreements, it can be inferred that, even though the Court speaks about liability, it is perhaps focusing on the binding character of the agreement. In other words, it is concerned rather with a general responsibility to comply with the obligations flowing from the agreement than with a specific responsibility arising from the commission of a wrongful act. The Court would be confirming that the EU is bound by the totality of the international agreements it has concluded, regardless of the competence involved, unless it is expressly provided otherwise.

The Court recognized that fact in *Hermes*, where it ruled 'that the

2004, A/CN.4/541, para 65; E Neframi, 'International Responsibility of the European Community and of Member States under Mixed Agreements' in E Cannizzaro (ed), *The European Union as an Actor in International Relations* (The Hague, Kluwer Law International, 2002); M Cremona, 'External Relations of the EU and the Member States: Competence, Mixed Agreements, International Responsibility, and Effects of International Law' (2006) *FIDE National Reports*; M Björklund 'Responsibility in the EC for Mixed Agreements' (2001) 70 *Nordic Journal of International Law* 373.

16 CJEU, Case C-316/91 *Parliament v Council* [1994] ECR 661.

17 Ibid, para 29.

18 See the comment of the European Commission to Art 9 of the Draft Articles on the Responsibility of International Organizations (DARIO), International Law Commission, Responsibility of International Organizations: Comments and Observations Received from International Organizations, Sixty-third Session, 14 February 2011, A/CN.4/637, 25.

19 PJ Kuijper, 'International Responsibility for EU Mixed Agreements' in C Hillion and P Koutrakos (eds), *Mixed Agreements Revisited: The EU and Its Member States in the World* (Oxford, Hart Publishing, 2010) 210.

20 Case C-316/91 *Parliament v Council* [1994] ECR 661, para 33.

WTO Agreement was concluded by the Community and ratified by its Member States without any allocation between them of their respective obligations towards the other contracting parties'.[21] Consequently, when no instrument apportioning the obligations between the EU as its Member States has been provided, the EU and its Members States are bound and, in principle, responsible for the agreement in its entirety.

However, the fact that the international obligations contained in an international agreement have not been apportioned between the EU and its Member States does not mean that, in the event that one of them commits an internationally wrongful act, both will be jointly liable. While the EU and its Member States are bound by all the obligations enshrined in the agreement, their responsibility will vary depending on the kind of internationally wrongful act committed and the rules of attribution and responsibility which apply to that wrongful act. Thus, there will be situations in which the responsibility would be borne jointly by the EU and its Member States (for instance if they aid or assist each other in the commission of the wrongful act).[22] But there are also other scenarios in which the EU will be the only one responsible (for instance if an action of the Commission breached an obligation enshrined in a Union agreement).[23] Depending on how the internationally wrongful act was committed, the responsibility will vary accordingly.

B. Pragmatic Approach to Responsibility

The WTO constitutes a very interesting example for assessing the question of the international responsibility of the EU. Despite their nominal full membership and despite having been targeted as defendants by other WTO Members, the Member States of the EU remain passive and let themselves be defended by the Union, which in turn is accepted by the third parties and the WTO organs. In fact the whole discussion on the joint and several liability of the EU and its Member States in the WTO is put aside in favour of sole responsibility of the Union in the WTO dispute settlement system.

In terms of numbers, the EU is not only one of the major players in international trade, it is also a very active player in trade dispute litigation.[24] Out of the 438 disputes that have been submitted to WTO

[21] Case C-53/96 *Hermès* [1998] ECR I-3603, para 24; see also P Eeckhout, 'The EU and its Member States in the WTO—Issues of Responsibility' in L Bartels and F Ortino (eds), *Regional Trade Agreements and the WTO Legal System* (Oxford, Oxford University Press, 2006) 453.

[22] See DARIO, Art 14, read jointly with Art 19.

[23] Ibid, Art 6.

[24] S Billiet, 'The EC and the WTO Dispute Settlement: The Initiation of Trade Disputes by the EC' (2005) 10 *European Foreign Affairs Review* 197.

Table 1. The EU and its Member States in the WTO Dispute Settlement System

	Complainant	Third party	Respondent	Total
European Union[a]	87	118	70	275
Member States[b]	0	0	13	13

[a] The data also includes disputes brought against the EU and any number of its Member States.
[b] The data also includes joint disputes with the EU. However, those brought against two or more Member States over the same-subject matter are counted as one dispute.

dispute settlement,[25] the EU has participated either as claimant, respondent or third party in 266 of them.[26] Of these 266 disputes, 70 were defensive cases, 111 as a third party, and 85 as claimant.[27] In contrast, EU Member States have only participated in 13 disputes in one way or another.

Table 1[28] shows that the mixed character of WTO agreements[29] is not really reflected in the practice of WTO dispute settlement. None of the EU Member States has initiated any kind of dispute or intervened as third party in any area.[30] This includes cases concerning the Agreement on Trade-Related Aspects of Intellectual Property Rights (TRIPS), where Member States had retained competences as explicitly confirmed by the CJEU.[31] Furthermore, a closer look at the disputes involving Member States reveals that not all Member States have been subject to complaints, and most of the time they are not the only respondents. As Table 2 shows, first, not all Member States have been involved in dispute settlement procedures. In fact, only 11 Member States have ever participated in WTO disputes. Secondly, Table 2 also reveals that in most of these disputes the EU ended up intervening, either because it was targeted alongside

[25] See the WTO website under: www.wto.org/english/tratop_e/dispu_e/dispu_status_e.htm (accessed on 1 June 2012).

[26] To compare, the US has been involved in 310 disputes, Japan in 152, Canada in 125, China in 124, India in 116, and Brazil in 106. The figures are as of 1 June 2012 and can be found at: www.wto.org/english/tratop_e/dispu_e/dispu_by_country_e.htm.

[27] Ibid.

[28] The data is taken from www.wto.int/english/tratop_e/dispu_e/dispu_by_country_e.htm (accessed on 1 June 2012).

[29] See CJEU, Opinion 1/94 [1994] ECR I-05267.

[30] There are cases in which current EU Member States brought complaints to the WTO prior to their accession to the EU. These concerned the Czech Republic, Hungary and Poland.

[31] CJEU, Case C-431/05 *Merck Genéricos* [2007] ECR I-7001, para 47; see also already CJEU, Joined Cases C-300/98 and C-392/98 *Dior and others* [2000] ECR I-11307, para 48.

its Member States,[32] or because the EU was the party that agreed on a solution to the dispute.[33]

Table 2[34] shows that since the creation of the WTO, Member States have been targeted individually on three occasions. These three disputes concerned TRIPS-related issues.[35] Furthermore, it should be noted that in those disputes in which the Member States were alone, as well as in those in which they were targeted jointly but without the EU, the proceedings either resulted in a mutually agreed solution reached by the parties, or have been formally pending for years.[36] Consequently, in these disputes no panel has pronounced itself on the substance or the responsibility of the Member States for breaching a WTO obligation.

This rather modest role played by EU Member States in WTO dispute settlement is the result of two factors inherent in the WTO and the position of the EU in the latter. First, by favouring negotiation at all stages,

[32] This was the case in the following disputes: WTO, Panel Report, 'European Communities—Customs Classification Of Certain Computer Equipment', WT/DS62/R, WT/DS67/R And WT/DS68/R, 22 June 1998, Modified By The Appellate Body WT/DS62/AB/R, WT/DS67/AB/R, WT/DS68/AB/R; WTO, Request for Consultations, 'France—Measures Relating to the Development of a Flight Management System', WT/DS173/1, 31 May 1999; WTO, Request for Consultations, 'European Communities—Measures Relating to the Development of a Flight Management System', WT/DS172/1, 31 May 1999; WTO, Notification of Mutually Agreed Solution, 'European Communities—Enforcement of Intellectual Property Rights for Motion Pictures and Television Programs', WT/DS124/2, 26 March 2001; WTO, Notification of Mutually Agreed Solution, 'Greece—Enforcement of Intellectual Property Rights for Motion Pictures and Television Programs', WT/DS125/2, 26 March 2001; WTO, Request for Consultations, 'European Union and a Member State—Seizure of Generic Drugs in Transit', WT/DS408/1, WT/DS409/1, 19 May 2010; WTO, Panel Report, 'European Communities and Certain Member States—Measures Affecting Trade in Large Civil Aircraft', WT/DS316/R, WT/DS347/1, 30 June 2010; WTO, Notification of Mutually Agreed Solution, 'Ireland—Measures Affecting the Grant of Copyright and (WT/DS82) European Communities—Measures Affecting the Grant of Copyright and Neighbouring Rights', WT/DS115/3, 13 September 2002.

[33] This occurred in the following disputes: WTO, Notification of Mutually Agreed Solution, 'Belgium—Administration of Measures Establishing Customs Duties for Rice', WT/DS210/6, 20 January 2002; WTO, Request for Consultations, 'Belgium—Measures affecting Commercial Telephone Directory Services', WT/DS80/1, 13 May 1997.

[34] The data is taken from www.wto.int/english/tratop_e/dispu_e/dispu_by_country_e.htm (accessed on 1 June 2012).

[35] WTO, Notification of Mutually Agreed Solution, 'Denmark—Measures Affecting the Enforcement of Intellectual Property Rights', WT/DS83/2, 13 June 2001; WTO, Notification of Mutually Agreed Solution, 'Portugal—Patent Protection under the Industrial Property Act', WT/DS37/2, 8 October 2010; WTO, Notification of Mutually Agreed Solution, 'Sweden—Measures Affecting the Enforcement of Intellectual Property Rights', WT/DS86/2, 11 December 1998.

[36] WTO, Request for Consultations, 'Belgium—Certain Income Tax Measures Constituting Subsidies', WT/DS127/1, 11 May 1998; WTO, Request for Consultations, 'France—Certain Income Tax Measures Constituting Subsidies', WT/DS131/1, 11 May 1998; WTO, Request for Consultations, 'Greece—Certain Income Tax Measures Constituting Subsidies', WT/DS129/1, 11 May 1998; WTO, Request for Consultations, 'Ireland—Certain Income Tax Measures Constituting Subsidies', WT/DS130/1, 11 May 1998; WTO, Request for Consultations, 'Netherlands—Certain Income Tax Measures Constituting Subsidies', WT/DS128/1, 11 May 1998.

Table 2. Cases Brought against EU Member States in the WTO Dispute Settlement System

	Single respondent	Respondent with other MS	Respondent with the EU and other MS	Total
Belgium		1	2	3
Denmark	1			1
France		1	3	4
Germany			2	2
Greece		1	1	2
Ireland		1	2	3
Netherlands		1	1	2
Portugal	1			1
Spain			2	2
Sweden	1			1
UK			3	3

WTO dispute settlement procedures allow the EU to intervene at any given moment. A good illustration of this practice is the dispute *Belgium—Administration of Measures Establishing Customs Duties for Rice*, in which the US brought a claim against Belgium regarding the application of customs duties for rice. It appeared that the Belgian customs authorities were not correctly implementing the 'Schedule of Specific Commitments of the European Communities and their Member States LXXX, a part of the GATT 1994'.[37] In the end, a mutually agreed solution was adopted. At first sight it would seem logical that the solution would be agreed between Belgium and the US, since Belgium was the respondent party. However, the parties that reached an agreement were the US and the EU.[38] This single example shows how the dispute settlement system allows for parties not involved in the dispute not only to intervene but also negotiate on behalf of their Member States and eventually resolve the dispute.

Moreover, the intervention by the EU at any stage of the dispute takes place not only in controversies over a matter which clearly falls under the exclusive competence of the Union—such as the custom duties for rice—

[37] WTO, Request for Consultations, 'Belgium—Administration of Measures Establishing Customs Duties for Rice', WT/DS210/1, 19 October 2000.

[38] WTO, Notification of Mutually Agreed Solution, 'Belgium—Administration of Measures Establishing Customs Duties for Rice', WT/DS210/6, 2 January 2002.

but also in areas where its competence may be less clear, eg in disputes concerning the application of the TRIPS agreement before the entry into force of the Lisbon Treaty. For instance, in *Ireland—Measures Affecting the Grant of Copyright and Neighbouring Rights*,[39] it was also the EU that ultimately responded and reached a solution.

The second factor that favours EU participation in disputes brought against its Member States has to do with the rules governing the relationship between the EU and its Member States. First, most cases brought against EU Member States concern issues falling within the scope of EU competence (either exclusive or shared). This has been the case in all the disputes concerning the GATT or GATS in the pre-Lisbon setting. Continuing with the example of *Belgium—Administration of Measures Establishing Customs Duties for Rice,* the mutually agreed solution 'recognised that the Belgian authorities were acting under EU law'.[40] Consequently, the solution to the dispute was reached by the EU. It can be easily sustained that in the WTO, the EU intervenes in any dispute which touches upon the scope of EU law. Second, if a Member State objected to intervention by the Union in a dispute that concerned issues falling under the scope of EU law, the Commission could easily open infringement proceedings against this Member State for breaching its duty of cooperation. Therefore, especially in the post-Lisbon setting, the scope of EU competence in relation to the WTO and the duty of cooperation favour participation of the EU in disputes brought against its Member States.

In any case, one has to distinguish the fact that the EU partakes in any dispute which touches upon an element of EU law, the nature of the competence of the Union which is involved, and the acceptance by third parties and the panels of the sole liability under international law on the part of the EU in those cases. In this context, it should be highlighted that in most cases where a Member State has been brought to consultations it has been done alongside the EU. In fact, out of the 13 consultations brought against Member States, seven were also brought against the EU.

Against this backdrop, it could be argued that it is foremost the 'unity in the international representation'[41] of the Union in a dispute that is enforced by the EU and its Member States by allowing the EU to speak on behalf of its Member States, but which does not imply that the EU

[39] WTO, Notification of Mutually Agreed Solution, 'Ireland—Measures Affecting the Grant of Copyright', WT/DS82/3 and 'European Communities—Measures Affecting the Grant of Copyright and Neighbouring Rights', WT/DS115/3, 13 September 2002.

[40] WTO, Request for Consultations, 'Belgium—Administration of Measures Establishing Customs Duties for Rice', WT/DS210/1, 19 October 2000.

[41] The importance of maintaining this unity within the WTO (and the mixed agreements it comprises for the EU) was already stressed by the Court of Justice in CJEU Opinion 1/94 [1995] ECR I-05267, para 108.

should be exclusively responsible.[42] However, all these cases revolve in one way or another around issues concerning the implementation of EU law by the organs of the Member States, ie they entail situations which could be described as EU 'executive federalism'.[43] Therefore, the EU takes responsibility at the WTO based on its own understanding that Member States, when implementing EU law, are acting functionally as EU organs.[44] Otherwise put, the EU considers that it should be exclusively responsible for any breach that falls within the scope of EU Law. As the practice shows, the WTO dispute settlement organs and third parties, by having ultimately always accepted the responsibility of the EU in these cases, have acquiesced to this modus operandi.

The *LAN* dispute is a good example in this respect.[45] The US brought separate panels against EU, Ireland and the UK regarding the tariff treatment of Local Area Network (LAN) equipment and personal computers with multimedia capability ('PCs with multimedia capability').[46] In the end, a procedural agreement was reached between the US, the EU and its two Member States. The complaints lodged against the latter were merged into a single claim against the EU. Furthermore, the EU during the LAN case declared that it was 'ready to assume the entire international responsibility for all measures in the area of tariff concessions, whether the measure complained about has been taken at the [EU] level or at the level of Member States'.[47]

With this statement, contrary to what the International Law Commission (ILC) argues,[48] the EU was not acknowledging its responsibility as a way of attributing the conduct to itself. The EU was not arguing that it wanted to be held responsible regardless of what the rules of attribution stated; indeed it argued that the rule of attribution in those cases

[42] G Luengo Hernández de Madrid, *Regulation of Subsidies and State Aids and EC Law: Conflicts in International Trade Law* (The Hague, Kluwer Law International, 2007) 511.

[43] On the concept of executive federalism see R Schütze, 'From Rome to Lisbon: "Executive Federalism" in the (new) European Union' (2010) 47 *Common Market Law Review* 1385.

[44] Kuijper, above n 19, 214.

[45] WTO, Panel Report, 'European Communities—Customs Classification of Certain Computer Equipment', WT/DS62/R, WT/DS67/R And WT/DS68/R, 22 June 1998, Modified By The Appellate Body WT/DS62/AB/R, WT/DS67/AB/R, WT/DS68/AB/R.

[46] WTO, Request for the Establishment of a Panel by the United States, 'Ireland—Customs Classification Of Certain Computer Equipment', WT/DS68/2, 10 March 1997; WTO, Request for the Establishment of a Panel by the United States, 'United Kingdom—Customs Classification Of Certain Computer Equipment', WT/DS68/3, 10 March 1997; WTO, Request for the Establishment of a Panel by the United States, 'European Communities—Customs Classification Of Certain Computer Equipment', WT/DS68/4, 13 February 1997.

[47] WTO, Oral pleading of the European Commission to the Panel 'European Communities—Customs Classification Of Certain Computer Equipment', 12 June 1997, para 6; which can also be found in ILC, Second Report on Responsibility of International Organizations, above n 15, para 61.

[48] ILC, *Draft Articles on the Responsibility of International Organizations, with Commentaries* (Geneva, UN, 2011) 29.

involving organs of its Member States functionally acting as EU organs means that their conduct should be attributed to the EU and not to the Member States.[49] The fact that none of the Member States, panels or third parties in the relevant disputes ventured into such discussion, as well as the fact the EU in each case stepped up to the dispute and was accepted as the legitimate representative, confirm this more pragmatic approach.

III. EXPLORING THE 'ODD COUPLE': THE SPECIAL FEATURES OF THE WTO AND OF THE EU AS ITS MEMBER

The previous section highlighted the pragmatic approach of the EU and the WTO bodies as regards the responsibility of the former and identified two factors which favoured this approach to responsibility: The systemic design of the WTO and the constitutional principles governing the relations between the EU and its Member States. This section will analyse these factors in a more detailed manner.

A. The Special Features of the WTO Dispute Settlement Mechanism

It should be recalled that international responsibility is inextricably linked to the rules and design of dispute settlement mechanisms, which are entrusted with determining the existence of that very responsibility. WTO dispute settlement is no exception to that rule.[50] Thus, the principles and rules governing the resolution of disputes between the WTO contracting parties are of considerable influence for ascertaining which party bears responsibility for breaches of WTO obligations.

What is rather exceptional though is the compulsory, quasi-judicial dispute settlement mechanism introduced with the conclusion of the Uruguay Round and codified in the Dispute Settlement Understanding (DSU), with an appellate system and reverse consensus in the Dispute Settlement Body.[51] As a result we find a sizeable body of practice and case law here that can be utilized for the study of international responsibility in the

[49] ILC, Responsibility of International Organizations: Comments and Observations Received from International Organizations, above n 18, 24.

[50] X Fernández Pons, *La Organización Mundial del Comercio y el Derecho Internacional: Un Estudio sobre el Sistema de Solución de Diferencias de la OMC y las Normas Secundarias de Derecho Internacional General* (Madrid, Marcial Pons, 2006) 265.

[51] See, eg T Cottier, 'Dispute Settlement in the World Trade Organization: Characteristics and Structural Implications for the European Union' (1998) 35 *Common Market Law Review* 325; J Jackson, 'The WTO Dispute Settlement System after Ten Years: The First Decade's Promises and Challenges' in Y Tanigushi, A Yanovich and J Bohanes (eds), *The WTO in the Twenty-first Century: Dispute Settlement Negotiations, and Regionalism in Asia* (Cambridge, Cambridge University Press, 2007).

area of international trade; a feature which is less present in other areas of international law.

With specific regard to the EU, an examination of its practice at the WTO yields the opposite picture to the one portrayed by the CJEU in *Parliament v Council*. As was shown earlier, generally the EU and its Member States do not appear side by side as bearers of joint and several responsibility under the WTO dispute settlement system. Instead, the EU Member States play a rather residual role in WTO dispute settlement,[52] while the EU bears virtually exclusive responsibility. Practice also revealed that the rules of attribution and responsibility are applied in such a way that the vast majority of the wrongful acts committed within the territory of the EU are attributed to the EU and not to its Member States. That is due on one hand to the systemic design of the WTO and its rules on responsibility and dispute settlement and, on the other, to the special features of the EU as an actor within the WTO (especially Union competence in the area, and the traditional role that the EU has played in the WTO). As far as the former is concerned, four salient features stand out: The emphasis on, and prioritisation of, mutually agreed solutions, the inclusiveness of the rules of standing, the interlinkages between the different WTO Agreements, and finally the enforcement mechanism through suspension of concessions (and the way it is used against the EU).

As to the first feature, according to Article 3.2 DSU, the WTO dispute settlement mechanism has as its prime objective to preserve the rights and obligations of its Members under the WTO agreements. To this end, the DSU favours the solution of disputes through diplomatic means, more precisely through negotiations ('consultations' in WTO jargon). This is clearly established in Article 3.7 DSU, which provides that 'a solution mutually acceptable to the parties to a dispute and consistent with the covered agreements is clearly to be preferred'.[53] Only when consultations fail, a WTO Member may resort to solving the dispute through adjudicative means (ie a panel).[54] However, even if the adjudicative phase has already started, the parties to the dispute can continue to negotiate with a view to finding a mutually agreed solution. It should also be underlined that the panels have an obligation of giving the parties the adequate opportunity to develop such a mutually satisfactory solution.[55] A WTO Member thus can continue to negotiate a mutually agreed solution with the other party after a panel has been established. This was the case, for instance, in *EC—Scallops*. A panel was requested and established following a complaint brought by Chile and Peru against the EU (at the time the

[52] See also Billiet, above n 24, 197; and generally Eeckhout, above n 21.

[53] P Van Den Bossche, *The Law and Policy of the World Trade Organization: Text, Cases and Materials* (Cambridge, Cambridge University Press, 2008) 173.

[54] Art 4.7 DSU.

[55] Ibid Art 11.

European Communities) concerning a French Government Order laying down the official name and trade description of scallops.[56] Eventually, however, the parties reached a mutually agreed solution.[57] In this regard, the possibility provided for in Article 12.12 DSU for suspending the panel proceedings for 12 months is often used to continue with the consultations after the panel has been established. The EU and New Zealand, for instance, availed themselves of this option in the *EC—Butter* dispute.[58]

Hence, the DSU provides enough procedural mechanisms that allow WTO Members to resort to negotiations and consultations at any stage of the proceedings, which gives a high degree of flexibility to the parties to the dispute. As we have seen earlier, EU Member States have consistently preferred to let the Union reach mutually agreed solutions than to leave the dispute to be resolved through adjudication.

The second feature, the rules on standing in WTO dispute settlement proceedings, can also be seen as a means of granting manoeuvring space and room for negotiation. The DSU is marked by flexibility as regards the set of parties involved in disputes. As the Appellate Body established in *EC—Bananas III*, there is broad discretion on whether to bring a case against another WTO Member.[59] It does not matter whether the WTO Member has a legal interest worth protecting under the WTO Agreements. As long as there is a potential interest, or a future opportunity to compete, the WTO Member has the right to start consultations under the DSU.[60] This broad understanding of the active responsibility to bring claims has not only helped the US to lodge claims against the EU in the *EC—Bananas III* dispute, even though the US did not export any bananas to the EU,[61] but has also allowed the EU to bring disputes on issues in which its competence on the issue was not altogether clear.[62]

[56] WTO, Request for the Establishment of a Panel by Peru, 'EC–Trade Description of Scallops', WT/DS12/7, 22 September 1995; WTO, Request by Chile for the Establishment of a Panel, 'EC–Trade Description of Scallops', WT/DS12/6, 27 September 1995.

[57] WTO, Notification of Mutually Agreed Solution, 'EC–Trade Description of Scallops', G/L/94, G/TBT/D/9 WT/DS12/12, WT/DS14/11, 19 July 1996. The timeline of this dispute can be found at: wto.org/english/tratop_e/dispu_e/cases_e/ds12_e.htm (accessed on 1 June 1 2012).

[58] WTO, Panel Report, 'European Communities—Measures Affecting Butter Products', WT/DS72/R, 24 November 1999, para 12.

[59] WTO, Appellate Body Report, 'EC–Bananas III', WT/DS27/AB/R, 9 September 1997, para 132.

[60] See C López-Jurado Romero de la Cruz, 'La Solución de Diferencias en la OMC' in LM Hinojosa Martínez and J Roldán Barbero (eds), *Derecho Internacional Económico* (Madrid, Marcial Pons, 2010) 192; Van Den Bossche, above n 53, 185.

[61] WTO, Panel Report, 'EC–Bananas III', WT/DS27/R/USA, 22 May 1997, 8.

[62] See, eg WTO, Request for Consultations, 'China—Measures Affecting Financial Information Services and Foreign Financial Information Supplier', WT/DS372/1, 5 March 2008; WTO, Request for Consultations, 'United States—Measure Affecting Government Procurement', WT/DS88/1, 26 June 1997. Both disputes concerned issues falling within shared competence of the Union (the General Agreement on Trade in Services (GATS) and the Agreement on Government Procurement (GPA)). Nevertheless, it is the EU which requested

Furthermore, Article 4.11 of the DSU allows third party interventions during consultations in similarly broad terms as the ones envisaged in Article 4.2 of the DSU as interpreted in *EC—Bananas III*.[63] Importantly, the broad construction of third party intervention is not restricted to the consultations phase. Accordingly, the EU can act as third party in any dispute brought against any of its Member States, and consequently influence the course of the ensuing proceedings.

Turning to the third feature, the WTO system is structured in such a way that most of the times an internationally wrongful act may constitute a breach of multiple WTO Agreements. For instance, the obligations enshrined in the GATT are so similar to those enshrined in GATS[64] that a breach of a provision of the former could lead to the breach of the same provision in the latter. Moreover, there are also sectoral agreements such as the Agreement on Agriculture, which develop in more detail the rules contained in GATT. The *EC—Bananas III* dispute is a good example of the interaction between this web of agreements. In this dispute, the US alleged that the bananas import regime established by the EU breached the GATT, the Agreement on Agriculture, as well as the GATS. The report of the Panel did not exclude this possibility. It acknowledged that a single measure can fall under the scope of both the GATT and the GATS.[65] These intersections between different WTO agreements make a strict application of the ensuing legal obligations by the EU and its Member States, according to the division of competences in Union law, virtually impossible (as it is almost impossible to disentangle the different EU competences involved in a dispute concerning those agreements).

Lastly, should negotiations fail and a panel report conclude that WTO obligations have been breached by a Member, which are subsequently not removed within a so-called 'reasonable period of time' (Article 22.1 DSU) the DSU provides for decentralized but supervised enforcement. This operates through compensation and the suspension of concessions equivalent to the nullification and impairment of benefits guaranteed by WTO law caused by the inconsistent measures (Article 22.4 DSU). According to Article 22.2 DSU, in case the parties fail to agree on compensation, 'any party having invoked the dispute settlement procedures may request authorization from the DSB to suspend the application to

consultations. See also Billiet, above n 24, 209; also J Heliskoski, 'Joint Competence of the European Community and its Member States and the Dispute Settlement Practice of the World Trade Organization' (1999–2000) 2 *Cambridge Yearbook of European Legal Studies* 80.

[63] WTO, Appellate Body Report, 'EC–Bananas III', WT/DS27/AB/R, 9 September 1997, para 132.

[64] Van Den Bossche, above n 53, 336.

[65] WTO, Panel Report, 'European Communities—Regime for the Importation, Sale and Distribution of Bananas'. WT/DS27/R/USA, 22 May 1997, para 7.283.

the Member concerned of concessions or other obligations under the covered agreements'. These suspensions do not have to concern the same sector in which the violation took place only, but can also be applied to other sectors or even other agreements if this is deemed 'practicable or effective' (Article 22.3 DSU). Should a dispute arise about the level or nature of the suspension, this will be solved through arbitration (Article 22.6 DSU).

From the examples provided earlier, we can see that the issue of responsibility for breaches of obligations under the WTO, also on the part of the EU, is far from a theoretical matter. In comparison to other international organisations and dispute settlement mechanisms, it is indeed rather highly regulated and judicialised. Cases of violations can be brought to adjudication without the consent of the party against which a complaint has been brought. Moreover, via the suspension of concessions scheme, the level of the damage (in terms of impairment of benefits) is determined and can be used against the culprit to induce compliance. When recourse was made to such measures by WTO Members against the EU, it has always been targeted as a whole. This is possible given the particular position that the EU assumes within the EU framework (a point to which we shall return in the next section).

It should be stressed though that these suspensions differ from reparations as known in traditional international responsibility. The former do not constitute a means of redress, but merely serve as a temporary means to induce actual compliance. As the DSU puts it, 'neither compensation nor the suspension of concessions or other obligations is preferred to full implementation of a recommendation to bring a measure into conformity with the covered agreements' (Article 21.1 DSU). In this way, they are more akin to, and represent a further development and sophistication of, termination or suspension of the operation of a treaty following a material breach under the Law of Treaties (Article 60 VCLT and Article 60 VCLTIO).

B. The Special Features of the EU within the WTO Structure

In order to grasp the operation of international responsibility of the EU in the area of trade, one has also to consider, next to the specific setup of the WTO, the special position of the EU therein. This position is characterised both by the historically grown succession of the EU into most of the competences of its Member States, as well as by the continuing dual existence of the Union and its Members as full WTO Members and the ensuing necessity of cooperation and coordination.

At the outset, the European Economic Community (EEC) of 1957 was founded in the shadow of the pre-existing 1948 GATT. In many ways, the

Rome Treaty resembled a mini-GATT at the regional level in Europe.[66] This raised first of all the question of compatibility of the envisaged customs union with GATT rules. This, however, has remained a rather theoretical issue, as compatibility of the EU with Article XXIV GATT on customs unions was never ascertained either through dispute settlement or by the Committee on Regional Trade Agreements.[67] More important in practical terms and for present purposes is the development by which the Community succeeded the Member States within GATT due to its competence in the area of trade. This was acknowledged by the CJEU in the famous *International Fruit* decision.[68]

Henceforth, a modus operandi has developed between the Community (and later the EU) and its Member States by which the Commission represents the Community in trade negotiations, while the Member States remain in the background, acting first and foremost within the Council and the Trade Committee (the former 'Article 133 Committee') to grant mandates to the Commission and oversee its actions.

It should be underlined that from the beginning, Community competence in trade, as it concerned only goods at the time before the WTO agreements, was of an exclusive nature.[69] This means the Member States did not retain any competence of their own, but as founding members of the GATT they continued to be, at least formally, contracting parties in their own right.[70] This way of working, with the Commission as the protagonist and the Member States in the background, already fostered the impression of the EU as a fairly unified and singular entity.

However, the advent of the WTO and the expansion of the areas covered beyond goods to include services (GATS) and intellectual property (TRIPS) raised the question of whether the scope of the Common Commercial Policy (CCP) then also went beyond trade in goods. In Opinion 1/94, the Court acknowledged that now there existed areas of the WTO that fell outside of the scope of the 'classic' CCP and represented a competence shared between the Union and the Member States.[71] The

[66] G de Búrca and J Scott, 'The Impact of the WTO on EU Decision-making' in G de Búrca and J Scott (eds), *The EU and the WTO: Legal and Constitutional Issues* (Oxford, Hart Publishing, 2001) 2; P Eeckhout, *EU External Relations Law* (Oxford, Oxford University Press, 2011) 11.

[67] P Mavroidis, 'Do not Ask Too Many Questions: The Institutional Arrangements for Accommodating Regional Integration within the WTO' in E Kwan Choi and JC Hartigan (eds), *Handbook of International Trade* (Oxford, Blackwell, 2005).

[68] CJEU, Joined Cases 21–24/72 *International Fruit Company v Produktschap voor Groenten en Fruit* [1972] ECR 1219, para 18; in detail on CCP competence see Eeckhout, above n 66, 11–69.

[69] See in particular CJEU, Opinion 1/75 [1975] ECR 1355.

[70] *International Fruit*, above n 68, para 18; see also R Holdgard, *External Relations Law of the European Community: Legal Reasoning and Legal Discourses* (Alphen aan den Rijn, Wolters Kluwer, 2008) 198; J Klabbers, *The European Union in International Law* (Paris, Pedone, 2012) 74.

[71] CJEU, Opinion 1/94 [1994] ECR I-05267.

border between exclusive EU competence and competence shared with the Member States remained a moving and elusive target, despite attempts to codify the state of affairs in the Amsterdam and Nice Treaties.[72] In any event, the emergence of areas in the WTO framework that were not of exclusive EU competence brought the Member States closer to the fore again, also as visible bearers of responsibility, at least until the entry into force of the Lisbon Treaty.[73]

By virtue of the Lisbon Treaty, in force since 1 December 2009, the entire area of the WTO framework has come under CCP's exclusive competence, including trade in goods, services, intellectual property and even investment aspects.[74] According to the competence catalogue now contained in the Treaties, in areas of exclusive competence such as the CCP, 'only the Union may legislate and adopt legally binding acts, the Member States being able to do so themselves only if so empowered by the Union or for the implementation of Union acts'.[75] Thus, EU Member States no longer retain competences in this field, but only exert influence through the internal mechanisms of the EU institutional structure. The Council still maintains oversight over the Commission as the Union's trade negotiator through a special committee, now called the 'Trade Policy Committee' (known pre-Lisbon as the 'Article 133 Committee').[76] Additionally, the Lisbon reform brought an important institutional innovation, ie the requirement of consent by the European Parliament also for trade agreements, which was previously lacking.[77] Still, the Member States continue to be contracting parties of the WTO, even though the EU has taken over comprehensive competence in the area of trade.[78] Using the terminology introduced by Schermers, the WTO agreements come very close to being 'false' mixed agreements from the point of view of the EU.[79]

[72] *Cf* Art 133 TEC in the Amsterdam and Nice versions.

[73] See in particular CJEU, Opinion 1/08 [2009] ECR I-11129, paras 117–74; see also A Alemanno, 'Opinion 1/08, Community Competence to Conclude with Certain Members of the World Trade Organization Agreements Modifying the Schedules of Specific Commitments of the Community and Its Member States Under the General Agreement on Trade in Services' (2010) 104 *American Journal of International Law* 467.

[74] Arts 3(1)(e) TFEU and 201(1) TFEU; see also F Hoffmeister, 'The European Union's Common Commercial Policy a year after Lisbon—Sea Change or Business as Usual?' in P Koutrakos (ed), 'The European Union's External Relations a Year after Lisbon', CLEER Working Paper 2011/3, 83–87; Eeckhout, above n 66, 59.

[75] Art 2(1) TFEU.

[76] Art 207(3) third indent TFEU.

[77] Ibid and 218 TFEU; see also D Kleimann, 'Taking Stock: EU Common Commercial Policy in the Lisbon Era' (2011) 66 *Aussenwirtschaft* 216.

[78] But note Art 207(6) TFEU, which essentially imposes a safeguard against the use of CCP powers for harmonisation where this is excluded otherwise by the Treaties. *Cf* further A Dashwood, 'Mixity in the Era of the Lisbon Treaty' in C Hillion and P Koutrakos (eds), *Mixed Agreements Revisited* (Oxford, Hart Publishing, 2010) 357; and Hoffmeister, above n 74, 86–87.

[79] HG Schermers, 'A Typology of Mixed Agreements' in D O'Keeffe and HG Schermers (eds), *Mixed Agreements* (Deventer, Kluwer Law and Taxation, 1983) 27.

This coexistence between Union (and its predecessors) and the Member States has from the beginning necessitated coordination and cooperation. This was clearly stated by the CJEU in Opinion 1/94 which highlighted the importance for the EU and its Member States of speaking with a single voice at the WTO.[80] There is no doubt, as the Court acknowledged, that the duty of cooperation[81] plays a very important role in the relations between the EU and its Member States in the daily management of the WTO framework, both in trade negotiations and dispute settlement.

The duty of cooperation between the EU and its Member States seems to work smoothly in negotiations within the WTO framework.[82] For instance, during the negotiations of GATS schedules of specific commitments, EU Member States had no problem in letting the Commission act as the sole negotiator and voice, even though, in theory, there was room for independent Member State action in that area.[83] However, the fact that Member States cooperate with the Commission and allow it to be the sole negotiator does not mean that they are giving up part of their competences in favour of the EU. As Opinion 1/08 shows, while Member States are willing to accept the Commission as the sole negotiator on issues not covered by exclusive Union competence, they still want to sign the outcome of those negotiations.[84]

In dispute settlement proceedings, cooperation and coordination between the EU and its Member States also play a crucial role. As has been shown earlier, EU Member States play a minimal role in dispute settlement proceedings in the WTO. They have never lodged a complaint, but still this does not mean that Member States do not have a say in the disputes brought by the Commission. The Trade Policy Committee oversees the actions of the Commission also in that regard.[85] A good example of how such cooperation takes place is the *PolyGram* dispute.[86] The EU brought a complaint against Canada on the refusal of the latter to allow the distribution of films by PolyGram (a Dutch company). The EU argued through the Commission that the refusal amounted to a breach of the GATS. At the time of the dispute, GATS fell within shared competence

[80] CJEU, Opinion 1/94 [1994] ECR I-05267, paras 106–09.

[81] Art 4 (3) TEU (formerly Art 10 TEC).

[82] Council Conclusions of July 26, 2006, Council doc. 12019/06.

[83] P Eeckhout, 'External Relations of the EU and the Member States Competence, Mixed Agreements, International Responsibility, and Effects of International Law' in *FIDE 2006* (2006) 9.

[84] CJEU, Opinion 1/08 [2009] ECR I-11129; see also M Cremona, 'Balancing Union and Member State interests: Opinion 1/2008, Choice of Legal Base and the Common Commercial Policy under the Treaty of Lisbon' (2010) 35 *European Law Review* 679.

[85] R Torrent, *Derecho y Práctica de las Relaciones Económicas Exteriores en la Unión Europea* (Barcelona, Cedecs, 1998) 166.

[86] WTO, Request for Consultations, 'Canada—Measures Affecting Film Distribution Services', WT/DS117/1, 22 January 1998.

under EU law, and PolyGram was a Dutch Company. Thus, in theory the Netherlands could have brought the dispute on its own motion. However, the Trade Policy Committee (at that time still called the '133 Committee') decided that the Commission should bring the claim and not the Member State in question.[87] There were two reasons for allowing the Commission to lodge the complaint. First, the Committee followed the Commission's view that if the Netherlands were to lodge the complaint individually, that would amount to a breach of the duty of cooperation.[88] Secondly, the Netherlands lacked the expertise in WTO issues so it preferred to let the Commission take the lead.[89]

Similarly, in defensive cases the significance of cooperation and coordination should not be underestimated, especially in cases brought against the EU and its Member States. For instance, in the *Airbus* dispute,[90] when the US targeted not only the EU but also the four Member States involved in the Airbus venture, the EU and its Member States were represented by the Commission. Nevertheless, France, Germany, Spain and the United Kingdom closely collaborated with the Commission in the preparation of the defence.[91] Moreover, the Commission argued that the EU was exclusively responsible for those actions for which the US argued a breach of WTO law.[92]

Overall the practice in the WTO shows how the duty of cooperation has allowed the EU to speak with one voice rather unproblematically, with that voice being the Commission. Furthermore, given the new competences involved in the WTO agreements as well as the recent case law on the duty of cooperation established by the CJEU,[93] it is difficult to envisage

[87] Heliskoski, above n 62, 81.

[88] Ibid.

[89] Torrent, above n 85, 163.

[90] WTO, Request for Consultations, 'European Communities and Certain Member States—Measures affecting Trade in Large Civil Aircrafts', WT/DS316/1, 12 October 2004.

[91] Ibid. See also European Communities—Measures Affecting Trade in Large Civil Aircraft (DS316), Oral Statement of the European Communities to the First Meeting of the Panel, para 4, available at: trade.ec.europa.eu/doclib/docs/2007/march/tradoc_133827.pdf (accessed on 1 June 2012).

[92] See European Communities—Measures Affecting Trade in Large Civil Aircraft (DS316), First Written Submission by the European Communities, para 155, available at: trade.ec.europa.eu/doclib/docs/2007/april/tradoc_134551.pdf (accessed on June 1, 2012).

[93] These cases concern various policy fields, such as environmental policy, CJEU, Case C-246/07 *Commission v Sweden (PFOS)* [2010] ECR I-03317; maritime safety, CJEU, Case C-45/07 *Commission v Greece (IMO)* [2009] ECR I-00701; or inland waterway transport, CJEU, Case C-433/03 *Commission v Germany (Inland Waterways)* [2005] ECR I-06985; CJEU, Case C-266/03 *Commission v Luxembourg (Inland Waterways)* [2005] ECR I-04805. In all these cases, the Court concluded that the Member States should have refrained from committing certain acts. See also A Delgado Casteleiro and J Larik, 'The Duty to Remain Silent: Limitless Loyalty in EU External Relations?' (2011) 36 *European Law Review* 524. Note also the controversy over acts of certain Member States in the framework of the Convention on Trade and Endangered Species (CITES), which were at odds with a common position agreed at EU level. The acts were withdrawn following the threat by the Commission

situations in which EU Member States could deviate from a concerted Union strategy in the WTO, or even act without consulting the European Commission in advance.

Lastly, we should return to the enforcement mechanism provided by the DSU through which suspensions of concessions can be authorised against WTO Members found to have violated their obligations under the WTO agreements. The combined result of this particular enforcement mechanism and the position the EU has assumed in the WTO is that the Union can be targeted as a whole, and not the individual Member States in which the violation was committed. This makes sense, since the Union is the bigger target providing a wider selection of vulnerable sectors and companies to single out in the quest for inducing compliance. This is confirmed by practice, as there is no instance thus far in which a WTO Member has requested suspension of concessions against a single EU Member State.

As shown earlier, in the cases where Member States have been targeted either individually or alongside the EU for complaints, in most cases a mutually agreed solution was reached by the EU. At the same time, suspensions have been applied against the EU in its entirety. Prominent examples include suspensions by the US in the course of the bananas and hormones disputes. These targeted a range of products from various Member States, with specific targets such as Italian pecorino cheese in the former case,[94] and French Roquefort cheese in the latter.[95]

The EU is thus treated as a single unit when it comes to the application of suspension of concessions in the WTO framework. This is confirmed further when we consider their legal fallout within the EU. As we have seen, companies from Member States, even if these states have not contributed to the violations apart from the fact of being members of the EU, can suffer adverse consequences for their business if such suspensions target them. Some of the targeted companies subsequently lodged claims for damages with the EU courts, culminating in the famous *FIAMM & Fedon* decision, in which the CJEU refused to grant such damages.[96] This illustrates that this united stand of the Union has indeed significant repercussions 'behind the veil', which may effectively amount to intra-EU

to commence an infringement procedure for breach of the duty of cooperation. See Hoffmeister, above n 74, 94–95.

[94] See WTO, Recourse by the United States to Article 22.2 of the DSU, 'European Communities—Regime for the Importation, Sale and Distribution of Bananas', WT/DS27/43, 14 January 1999, 3.

[95] WTO, Recourse by the United States to Article 22.2 of the DSU, 'EC—Measures Concerning Meat and Meat Products (Hormones)', WT/DS26/19, 18 May 1999, 3 (on so-called 'carousel sanctions' see above n 2).

[96] CJEU, Joined Cases C-120/06 P and C-121/06 P *FIAMM & Fedon* [2008] ECR I-06513.

redistribution.[97] In this particular case, upholding the controversial—and WTO law inconsistent—banana trade regime of the EU came at the price of harming others, such as the FIAMM and Fedon companies and their employees.

IV. CONCLUSION: A 'RESPONSIBLE' POWER

The aim of this contribution was to show that the special features of the WTO, as well as those of the position of the EU therein, reveal a particular approach to international responsibility which is marked by both pragmatism and assertiveness of the EU.

Generally, both the EU and the WTO are amongst the most sophisticated international organisations to be found (to the extent that the EU can still be considered as an IO, that is). They remain an 'odd couple' until the present day, due to their emphasis on being 'rules-based', including compulsory dispute settlement. Nevertheless, the WTO remains also to a large extent 'member-driven'. Among these members, we continue to find, nominally, both the EU and its Member States. However, the competences to act in the WTO have shifted over time towards the EU, culminating in the Lisbon Treaty, which both expanded the CCP and made it an entirely exclusive competence. Moreover, while WTO dispute settlement is entirely geared towards finding negotiated outcomes and adjudication is only seen as a last resort, in the EU strict and enforceable loyalty obligations apply.

The combination of these factors frames the way in which the Union and its Member States assume responsibility for their acts in dispute settlement concerning trade matters. We have seen that in practice, other WTO Members have at times tried to target individual Member States for consultations and panel requests, on their own or alongside the Union. However, the EU consistently came forward while the Member States stepped back, either to negotiate a mutually agreed solution or to plead the case and face, if necessary, the consequences en bloc. This was so in instances where a matter may be considered coming within the widely defined scope of EU law, but where the competence of the Union was not a self-evident issue. Despite these attempts, third parties always accepted the Union taking over, and also WTO panels and the Appellate Body refrained from questioning this approach.

This acceptance stems from pragmatic and strategic approaches fostered by the design of the WTO dispute settlement system. Undoubtedly, the possibility of adopting countermeasures against the EU in its entirety is more attractive than applying those same countermeasures to Ireland or

[97] See P Mavroidis, 'It's Alright Ma, I'm Only Bleeding' in A Epiney, M Haag and A Heinemann (eds), *Challenging Boundaries: Essays in Honour of Roland Bieber* (Baden-Baden, Nomos, 2007).

Luxembourg, or any single Member State for that matter. While we may continue to argue about whether the EU is still a 'political dwarf', it is obvious that third countries prefer to take aim at the 'economic giant'[98] as the easier target.

This leads us to conclude that in the particular area of trade within the framework of WTO dispute settlement, the question is less about the veil of the organisation and other rather abstract debates that preoccupy international law scholars. Rather, the model we find in the EU of 'executive federalism' and consistent representation of the Union and its Member States on the international scene necessitates different notions to deal with responsibility. Here, the EU is clearly more than a veil draped over the Member States. It exercises visible and tangible control over and on behalf of its Member States. Nowhere does that become more evident than at the WTO in Geneva.

Overall, the responsibility of the EU in the WTO can be seen as an example of international actorness of the Union. First, the concerns on the lack of responsibility of international organisations[99] are nowhere to be seen in the case of the EU at the WTO. The Member States are not hiding behind the EU so as to avoid their responsibilities. Neither does the EU use its internal division of competences to evade its responsibility. Instead, in the WTO we witness an eagerness of the EU to be held responsible in lieu of its Member States.[100] Indeed, it could be argued that the responsibility of the EU at the WTO is a success story. On the one hand, third countries can avail themselves fully of the remedies offered by the WTO to urge the EU to stay faithful to 'free and fair trade' and the 'strict compliance' with its international obligations.[101] On the other, despite the adverse consequences that may follow from accepting responsibility, it nonetheless serves as a way for the Union to assert itself on the global stage. While not always compliant with WTO law, at the very least it is a 'responsible' power in international trade.

Nonetheless, in closing, it should be underlined once more that this is possible above all by the also rather unique framework of the WTO, which allows for the emergence of dispute settlement practice diverging from the norm. The extent to which this approach to responsibility could be transferred to other policy areas in which the EU is also active is a different question. It may, eventually, remain a feature reserved only to this 'odd couple'.

[98] To use the famous expression by Belgian Foreign Minister Mark Eyskens in 1991, quoted in S Marsh and H Mackenstein, *The International Relations of the European Union* (New York, Pearson/Longman, 2005) 248.

[99] See HG Schermers and N Blokker, *International Institutional Law. Unity within Diversity* (Leiden, Martinus Nijhooff, 2011) 1009–20.

[100] See also Eeckhout, above n 21, 543.

[101] To use the aims the Union has set itself in the post-Lisbon EU Treaties, Art 3(5) TEU.

10

The Wrong Trousers:[1] *State Responsibility and International Environmental Law*

CATHERINE REDGWELL

I. I INTRODUCTION

QUITE APART FROM the many issues arising in the application of responsibility to international organisations (IOs) considered elsewhere in this volume, there are many problems in applying the traditional system of state responsibility to address breach of international environmental obligations.[2] Recent literature has focussed in particular on the 'super wicked problem'[3] of climate change as highly illustrative of the problems of applying traditional state responsibility in the context of a multilateral, transboundary, intergenerational environ-

[1] Inspired by G Prins and S Rayner's critique of international governance of climate change entitled *The Wrong Trousers: Radically Rethinking Climate Policy* (2007), available at http://www2.lse.ac.uk/researchAndExpertise/units/mackinder/pdf/mackinder_Wrong%20 Trousers.pdf, the title of which refers to an episode in the exploits of the animated characters of Wallace and his faithful hound Gromit ('The Wrong Trousers', 1993) where automated trousers take Wallace where he does not wish to go.

[2] The literature on this subject is vast. For a concise overview, see: M Fitzmaurice, 'International Responsibility and Liability' in D Bodansky, J Brunnee and E Hey (eds), *The Oxford Handbook of International Law* (Oxford, Oxford University Press, 2007) 1010; P Birnie, A Boyle and C Redgwell, *International Law and the Environment*, 3rd edn (Oxford, Oxford University Press, 2009) ch 4 (hereinafter 'BBR'); P Sands and J Peel, with A Fabra and R MacKenzie, *Principles of International Environmental Law*, 3rd edn (Cambridge, Cambridge University Press, 2012) ch 17.

[3] RJ Lazarus, 'Super Wicked Problems and Climate Change: Restraining the Present to Liberate the Future' (2009) 94 *Cornell Law Review* 1153, 1159, drawing on public policy literature which characterises a 'public-policy problem with the kinds of features presented by climate change as a "wicked problem" that defies resolution because of the enormous interdependencies, uncertainties, circularities, and conflicting stakeholders implicated by any effort to develop a solution'.

mental problem.[4] Why this is so has been ascribed variously to the nature of international environmental law more broadly; to the nature of climate change in particular; and/or to inherent deficiencies in seeking recourse to the law of state responsibility. Thus, for example, Nollkaemper posits 'the idea that the nature of international environmental law opposes a quest for hard compliance'[5] such as that found through recourse to rules on material breach of treaty and state responsibility. Fitzmaurice suggests that it is 'the very nature of [the problems posed by] climate change itself, such as the multitude of parties involved, and issues of causation and proof' which poses difficulties in the application of state responsibility.[6] Others, such as Tomuschat, argue that climate change cannot be addressed properly on the basis of state responsibility, which he calls 'a lawyer's trick and a shortcut to the desired goal', and that the solution lies elsewhere, such as in the development of a bespoke liability regime.[7]

This chapter examines the difficulties of the application of the traditional system of state responsibility in the international environmental context, with illustrations drawn from a range of environmental problems including climate change.[8] It concludes that, while there are some faint glimmerings of acceptance of the novel approach first suggested by the ILC its draft Articles on State Responsibility (ASR) in terms of enforcement of

[4] See, eg R Verheyen, *Climate Change Damage and International Law: Prevention Duties and State Responsibility* (The Netherlands, Brill Academic Publishers, 2005); C Voigt, 'State Responsibility for Climate Change Damages' (2008) 77 *Nordic Journal of International Law* 1; M Fitzmaurice, 'Responsibility and Climate Change' (2010) 53 *German Yearbook of International Law* 89; DM Ong, 'International Legal Efforts to Address Human-induced Global Climate Change' in M Fitzmaurice, D Ong and P Merkouris (eds), *Research Handbook on International Environmental Law* (London, Edward Elgar, 2010) 454; C Tomuschat, 'Global Warming and State Responsibility' in H Hestermeyer et al (eds), *Law of the Sea in Dialogue* (Berlin, Springer-Verlag, 2011) 3.

[5] A Nollkaemper, 'Compliance Control in International Environmental Law: Traversing the Limits of the National Legal Order' (2002) 13 *Yearbook of International Environmental Law* 186.

[6] Fitzmaurice, above n 4, 137.

[7] Tomuschat, above n 4, 29. There are a number of examples of bespoke liability regimes, most notably in the oil pollution (eg the 1992 Convention on Civil Liability for Oil Pollution Damage) and nuclear (eg 1997 Protocol to the Vienna Convention on Civil Liability for Nuclear Damage) contexts. Attempts generally to codify strict liability rules for dangerous activities or substances have been less successful, with the Council of Europe's 1993 Lugano Convention on Civil Liability for Damage Resulting from Activities Dangerous to the Environment still not in force. Unlike the bespoke arrangements noted above, it does not provide for compensation funds to be established. In 2006 the ILC adopted draft principles on liability and compensation for environmental damage which provides for states to make polluters liable to transboundary 'victims' in their national law: ILC Report (2006) GAOR A/61/10, paras 51–67.

[8] Indeed, during negotiation of the UNFCCC some states supported the inclusion of a provision to the effect that the Convention would not prejudice the rules of international law regarding state responsibility and liability: see the declarations at the time of signature by Kiribati, Tuvalu and Nauru. Sands et al argue that the definition of 'adverse effects of climate change' and the Art 4(4) obligation of assistance (see also KP Art 2(3)), while 'not a formal expression of liability under the principles of state responsibility', 'reflects an admission of responsibility with financial consequences', above n 2, 734.

erga omnes partes obligations, it remains the case that state responsibility is ill-suited effectively to address the major environmental problems of the twenty-first century. Instead, the past 20 years or so have seen the development of alternatives to state responsibility and traditional dispute settlement mechanisms in an attempt to fill 'the responsibility gap' with treaty-based compliance mechanisms[9] which, inter alia, can be applied to all parties including for example the EU.[10] These are not a substitute for responsibility, neither in the sense of replacing or duplicating the function of responsibility,[11] nor in the legal relationship of compliance mechanisms with traditional methods of dispute settlement through which responsibility may be invoked, and to which such mechanisms are invariably expressed to be subordinate.[12]While their complementarity leaves room for the possibility for progressive development of state responsibility rules to fill the 'responsibility gap', neither development addresses the 'wrong trousers' question of the suitability of developing state responsibility rules to address climate change damage.

[9] M Fitzmaurice and C Redgwell, 'Environmental Non-Compliance Procedures and International Law' (2000) XXXI *Netherlands Yearbook of International Law* 35, 65. But a liability gap remains: see Tomuschat, above n 4, and below.

[10] The 1998 Aarhus Convention on Access to Information, Public Participation and Access to Justice in Environmental Matters is the most well-developed example of non-state actor participation, including the possibility for NGOs to bring non-compliance complaints before the Compliance Committee and (for NGOs with observer status under the Convention) to nominate members of the Compliance Committee. There are 46 parties to the Convention, including the EU, which has been the subject of compliance cases before the Commmittee: for a summary see A Andrusevych, T Alge, C Konrad (eds), *Case Law of the Aarhus Convention Compliance Committee (2004–11)*, 2nd edn (Lviv, Resource and Analysis Centre Society & the Environment, 2011).

[11] As discussed further below, the primary objective of compliance mechanisms is to ensure a return to compliance with treaty obligations rather than to require reparation by the defaulting state for the harm caused to another state or states for breach of an international obligation.

[12] This follows the pattern of the first non-compliance procedure (NCP) to be established, under the 1987 Montreal Protocol to the 1985 Vienna Convention for the Protection of the Ozone Layer, which clearly seeks to give priority to the traditional dispute settlement mechanism, providing in the opening paragraph establishing the NCP under the Protocol that '[t]he following procedure has been formulated pursuant to Article 8 of the Montreal Protocol. It shall apply without prejudice to the operation of the settlement of dispute procedure laid down in Article 11 of the Vienna Convention [on the Protection of the Ozone Layer]'. Under the 1992 Climate Change Convention the NCP provisions of the 1997 Kyoto Protocol co-exist with the dispute settlement provisions (and with the Multilateral Consultative Process) of the Convention. For analysis of the 'specialized non-compliance systems' under Art 13 UNFCCC (the Multilateral Consultative Process) and Art 18 of the Kyoto Protocol (NCP), see J Werksman, 'Compliance and the Kyoto Protocol: Building a Backbone into a "Flexible" Regime' (1998) 9 *Yearbook of International Environmental Law* 48.

II. ONE SIZE DOESN'T FIT ALL: THE DEFICIENCIES OF STATE RESPONSIBILITY IN AN ENVIRONMENTAL CONTEXT

A. Establishing the Existence and the Contours of a Primary Obligation

It is axiomatic that state responsibility attaches where there is breach of an international obligation. Yet the existence of an obligation against which breach may be measured is not always very easy to establish in the environmental context.[13] Breach of an obligation may be derived from international treaty or customary international law, with international environmental law very heavily dominated by the former.[14]

The distinctive character of multilateral environmental treaty obligations arises from a number of factors: the pace, magnitude and irreversibility of environmental problems which renders enforcement inter partes ineffective; the failure to operationalise traditional rules on liability and responsibility; the ability accurately to measure compliance against quantifiable targets; and the necessity for national implementation to render international environmental obligations effective. Moreover, in the climate change context the effects of non-compliance may be subtle and cumulative, with the full effects manifest only over a considerable time period. In common with other transfrontier environmental problems, it may also be difficult to attribute particular harm to the actions or omissions of one state or states.

To be sure, these distinctive features and the problems to which they give rise in a state responsibility context are not characteristic of all environmental treaties. Some areas of international environmental law embody detailed technical standards set forth in binding treaty instruments the breach of which may be fairly readily established. An example is the discharge limits found in many pollution treaties.[15] Others, however, are progressively to be achieved or differentiated,[16] or use open-textured

[13] As Fitzmaurice notes, 'answering the central background questions of the law of state responsibility, pertaining to the status or content of the primary rule that was breached, is particularly taxing within international environmental law', above n 4, 1013.

[14] C Redgwell, 'International Environmental Law' in M Evans (ed), *International Law*, 3rd edn (Oxford, Oxford University Press, 2010). Very few environmental treaty obligations are self-executing or directly effective in character, a rare example in the EU context being recognition by the ECJ of Art 6(3) of the 1980 Athens Protocol for the Protection of the Mediterranean Sea against Pollution from Land-based Source as directly effective in Case C-213/03 *Syndicat professionnel coordination des pecheurs de l'Etang de Berre de la region v Electricite de France*, 15 July 2004, C228/15 (Second Chamber), para 47.

[15] Examples are the 1979 LRTAP and 1973/78 MARPOL Conventions and Protocols.

[16] The principle of 'common but differentiated responsibilities' has been a keystone concept in the climate regime; for further discussion see Hilson in this volume. However, Rajamani argues that 'symmetry' rather than differentiation will become the central organising concept of the future climate regime as the post-2020 climate regime negotiations proceed post Durban: L Rajamani, 'The Durban Platform for Enhanced Action and

language, such that the precise contours or content of the obligation becomes difficult to establish and thus compliance difficult to measure. Matters are further complicated where a different measuring stick is provided according to the circumstances of each state. Examples are the 'according to their capabilities' language of the 1992 Convention on Biological Diversity and the identification under the Kyoto Protocol (KP) of a category of states for which a collective exception has been made ex ante (eg non Annex I developing countries under the KP do not have specific GHG emission targets).[17] Many environmental treaties also rely on vaguely worded principles which do not apply in an all or nothing fashion and where divergent views may exist on their legal status (eg the precautionary principle (or approach), the polluter pays principle and the principle of sustainable development).[18]

An illustration of these problems of establishing both the legal status and content of primary obligations in the environment context is responsibility for climate change damage. There is no general prohibition on activities which produce greenhouse gas (GHG) emissions which arise from a wide-range of human activities.[19] Nor is the mere existence of GHG emissions[20] a breach per se of the KP, though clearly non-compliance with emissions limits for Annex I parties and with other KP obligations would be. The KP is binding on 192 parties, including the EU which has agreed to an internal legally-binding burden-sharing system (the 'EU

the Future of the Climate Regime' (2012) 61 *International & Comparative Law Quarterly* 501.

[17] For critique of the fuzzy edges of the definition of 'developing state' in the climate regime, see L Rajamani, 'From Berlin to Bali and Beyond: Killing Kyoto Softly' (2008) 57 *International and Comparative Law Quarterly* 909 and 'The Making and Unmaking of the Copenhagen Accord' (2010) 59 *International and Comparative Law Quarterly* 824.

[18] For general discussion see n 2 for sources cited. Proposals to include reference to the polluter pays principle in the UNFCCC were rejected during negotiations.

[19] Though not addressed in detail in this chapter, it should be observed that this also gives rise to the problem of attribution in respect of the responsibility of the state for actions or omissions by private individuals that are not organs or agents of the state. In this instance the responsibility of the state is indirect in the sense of the failure to exercise due diligence over actors and activities under the jurisdiction and control of the state which give rise to the possibility of significant transboundary harm, discussed further below; see also Fitzmaurice, above n 4, 115 and 121. She also observes that since state responsibility rules do not embrace the liability of private actors, yet private actors are largely responsible for the emission of GHG contributing to global warming, then state responsibility for environmental damage will inevitably have a limited role to play, above n 4, 1011.

[20] The emission of the chief GHG, CO_2, is thus not per se unlawful and it is not clear that it constitutes 'pollution'. Concurring, see Tomuschat, above n 4, 17 ('it is highly doubtful whether one can speak of "pollution" through GHG'). This has implications for the application of other environmental principles such as the polluter pays principle, quite apart from its doubtful legal status. Lefeber nonetheless considers whether the principle could form the basis 'to hold developed countries liable for the financing of adaptation measures' and argues it can be extended to the state within whose control the 'polluting activity' is carried out and where it makes significant contribution to national GNP: R Lefeber, 'Climate Change and State Responsibility' in Rayfuse and Scott, above n 4, 326–27.

bubble'[21]), though its Member States remain responsible under the KP for failing to meet their individual GHG emissions targets and timetables. Whilst in such instance the identification of the wrongdoing state would be possible—eg the Annex I party failing to meet its GHG emission reduction targets within the stipulated timetable[22]—there remains the problem then of identification of the injured state (considered below). The problem is compounded by the use of vague and open-textured language in the UNFCCC and KP. There are, of course, customary law principles which might avail, in particular recognition that it is part of the primary obligation of the state to prevent significant transboundary harm and to exercise due diligence—eg through prior environmental impact assessment[23]—to prevent or minimise the risk of such harm.[24] This could provide a customary law basis for holding states responsible for failing to prevent significant transboundary harm caused by GHG emissions, eg through appropriate mitigation measures.[25]

Beyond the question of 'is there an obligation which has been breached and can the contours of the obligation be established', lies the related question of what constitutes harm (or damage) and at what point it crosses the threshold so that failure to prevent or reduce such harm constitutes

[21] Most recently, Council Decision 406/2009/EC of 23 April 2009 on the effort of Member States to reduce their greenhouse gas emissions to meet the Community's greenhouse gas emission reduction commitments up to 2020, [2009] OJ L140, 136–48. See generally L Kramer, 'European Union Law' in R Lord, S Goldberg, L Rajamani and J Brunnee (eds), *Climate Change Liability: Transnational Law and Practice* (Cambridge, Cambridge University Press, 2012) ch 14. As under the KP, the 'big question' of compliance with targets and timetables for Member States, in this instance with their 2020 reduction commitments, has yet to be confronted.

[22] However, as the recent example of Canada demonstrates, withdrawal from the KP (which it permits) means that any consequences of Canada's GHG emissions can only be addressed outside the climate regime, as a matter of other treaty obligations or customary international law (eg the obligation to exercise due diligence). See 'Canada to Withdraw from Kyoto Protocol' www.bbc.co.uk/news/world-us-canada-16151310 (accessed on 13 December 2011).

[23] See *Case Concerning Pulp Mills on the River Uruguay (Argentina v Uruguay), Judgment of 20 April 2010*, ICJ Reports 2010, para 197; see also the discussion of the obligation of due diligence in the Advisory Opinion of the Seabed Disputes Chamber of ITLOS in *Responsibilities and Obligations of States Sponsoring Persons and Entities with respect to Activities in the Area* (1 February 2011), paras 110–20 and 218.

[24] Recognition of the prevention of harm as an obligation of due diligence underlies the first part of the ILC's draft Convention on the Prevention of Transboundary Harm (Arts 3–7) with the duty to adopt preventive measures recognised in Art 3.

[25] Lefeber argues that due diligence 'requires states to take mitigation action to limit or reduce aggregate emissions through general measures, economy wide and/or sector specific, such as cap and trade, or carbon capture and storage, and/or specific conditions imposed on major emission sources, such as the use of the best available technology by coal-fired power stations', above n 19, 336–37. He further argues that there is a subjective element to an assessment of the degree of due diligence standard required, based on available means in the context, which could allow for the application of common but differentiated responsibilities, 335.

an internationally wrongful act.[26] While harm or damage per se is not a general requirement for state responsibility to attach for breach of an international obligation, in the environmental context there are a number of examples where the threshold of harm or damage caused is integral to the substantive content of the obligation and hence to a determination of whether breach has occurred. As we have already seen, in a customary law context the trigger for the application of the due diligence standard for the prevention of transboundary harm is that such harm, threatened or caused, must be significant. In a treaty context, an example is the negotiation of the 1997 UN Convention on the Non-Navigational Uses of International Watercourses, during which there was considerable discussion of what the threshold of harm in Article 7 should be (and discussion of how to translate the apparently subtle distinctions between 'appreciable' 'and 'significant' into the different official UN languages). In the end the threshold of 'significant' was adopted, with an (ultimately rather unhelpful) attempt to remove any further ambiguity by defining this in the commentary to mean 'not necessarily substantial but more than trivial'.[27]

B. To Whom Are Obligations Owed: To Other States or to the International Community as a Whole?

As noted above, the vast bulk of international environmental obligations are contained in treaties. This has no particular consequences for responsibility beyond the obvious necessity for the responsible and injured states to be parties to the treaty containing the international obligation[28] owed to the injured state and which is claimed to have been breached. While very few multilateral environmental agreements enjoy universal participation, many now enjoy widespread participation so in principle establishing such common ground should be relatively straightforward. In the climate context, however, non-participation in (the US) or withdrawal from (Canada) the KP of key GHG emitters has implications not only for the effectiveness of the climate regime but also for the identification of obligations breached. Here it is the nature of the international

[26] See, generally, M Bowman and A Boyle (eds), *Environmental Damage in International and Comparative Law; Problems of Definition and Valuation* (Oxford, Oxford University Press, 2002). On environmental harm generally, see P Wetterstein (ed), *Harm to the Environment: The Right to Compensation and the Assessment of Damages* (Oxford, Clarendon Press, 1997); F Francioni and T Scovazzi (eds), *International Responsibility for Environmental Harm* (London, Graham & Trotman, 1991).

[27] 'Significant harm' is also the threshold employed in the ILC draft Convention on the Prevention of Transboundary Harm; another example is the 1977 Convention on the Prohibition of Military or Any Other Hostile Use of Environmental Modification Techniques, Art I of which prohibits military or any other hostile uses of environmental modification having 'widespread, long-lasting or severe' effects.

[28] Unless, of course, the obligation has parallel existence at customary international law.

environmental obligations owed which gives rise to difficulties, added to those of content and legal status noted above.

Many international environmental obligations are of a multilateral or erga omnes character (owed to the community of states as a whole—erga omnes—or a group of states based on a multilateral environmental agreement (MEA)—erga omnes partes) and do not readily divide into the traditional dichotomy of wrongdoing and injured state. Obligations erga omnes partes are of particular relevance in the environmental context, instancing 'the case of the international regime . . . the maintenance and implementation of which all states parties have a common interest'.[29] This of course is recognised in the ASR[30] in Articles 42 and 48 and in the accompanying commentary and substantially reproduced in Articles 43 and 49 of the 2011 draft articles on the responsibility of international organizations. While these provisions remain de lege ferenda[31] the recent Advisory Opinion of the Seabed Disputes Chamber found obligations to protect the environment of the high seas and in the Area are of an erga omnes character, and provides some support for an actio popularis to enforce breach of such erga omnes obligations, relying inter alia on Article 48 of the ILC draft articles.[32]

Of particular novelty is the definition of 'injured state' in Article 48 which recognises the general interest of states in securing compliance with obligations owed to the international community as a whole. Obligations erga omnes in the environmental field are addressed under the heading of '"victimless" breaches of community obligations' where, 'if restitution is materially impossible, then other States may be limited to seeking cessation, satisfaction, and assurances against repetition . . . [A]ny State party to the relevant collective obligation should be entitled to invoke responsibility in these respects'.[33] Obligations erga omnes partes are also catered for in Article 48 which refers to groups of states, including the state invoking responsibility. The obligation not to omit excess CFCs into the atmosphere under the Ozone Convention and Montreal Protocol is

[29] ILC Third Report of the Special Rapporteur on State Responsibility, (2000) A/CN.4/507/Add 3, para 106(b), 49.

[30] In general terms, David Caron considers the Articles on State Responsibility may have been the 'last great codification exercise' undertaken by the ILC: 'The ILC Articles on State Responsibility: The Paradoxical Relationship Between Form and Authority' (2002) 96 *American Journal of International Law* 857. For an overview of more recent work of the ILC, including the new (2011) topic 'protection of the atmosphere' and concerns regarding its interconnectedness 'with the politically controversial issue of climate change' see D McRae, 'The Work of the International Law Commission, 2007–11: Progress and Prospects' (2012) 106 *American Journal of International Law* 322, 337.

[31] Redgwell, above n 13.

[32] Advisory Opinion, above n 23; D French, 'From the Depths: Rich Pickings of the Principles of Sustainable Development and General International Law on the Sea Floor—the Seabed Disputes Chamber's 2011 Advisory Opinion' (2011) 26 *International Journal of Marine and Coastal Law* 525, 545–46.

[33] A/CN.4/507/Add.4, 8, para 379.

a specifically cited example of a multilateral obligation without any particular obligee or beneficiary; '[t]his is a purely solidary obligation and there will never be a demonstrable connection with any particular State party'.[34] A similar point could be made regarding the reduction of GHG emissions under the KP. Nonetheless under the ASR, countermeasures may be applied for breach of such obligation not only by states acting in concert (collective countermeasures) but also where an individual state, which has not suffered individual injury in consequence of the breach of a multilateral obligation, nonetheless asserts a right to react to that breach in the public interest.[35] However, one limitation on the exercise of countermeasures by third states (viz, 'not directly affected' states) where there also exists an injured state is that the latter must request such measures which are then taken on its behalf.[36]

C. Remedies

The general rule in respect of reparation for a breach of an international obligation requires the state found to be in breach to provide restitution, or if this is not possible, to compensate for the losses.[37] In an environmental context, the possibility of restoring the status quo ante or restitution in kind is not always possible—species extinction or global warming make the point. Indeed, Boyle has observed 'the difficulty of reconciling doctrinal support for state responsibility for environmental damage with the realities of state practice'.[38]

There are a number of examples of treaty parties preferring to establish regulatory regimes based on principles such as the precautionary principle, common but differentiated responsibility, and equitable sharing of burdens and benefits, rather than addressing directly compensation for

[34] A/CN.4/507, 51, para 109.

[35] For the form such countermeasures might take for the failure of climate change mitigation obligations—eg trade related environmental measures such as border adjustment tax to offset emissions on imported products—see Lefeber, above n 19, 348

[36] Art 54 ASR, a restriction echoing the conditions on the lawful exercise of collective self-defence in the *Nicaragua* case. As Crawford et al. note, this is a tenable if not a compelling argument: J Crawford, P Bodeau and J Peel, 'The ILC's Draft Articles on State Responsibility: Towards Completion of Second Reading' (2000) 94 *American Journal of International Law* 660.

[37] *Case Concerning the Factory at Chorzów (Claim for Indemnity; Merits)*, PCIJ, Ser A, No 17 (1928), 47: 'The essential principle . . . is that reparation must, as far as possible, wipe out all the consequences of the illegal act and re-establish the situation which would, in all probability, have existed if the act had not been committed. Restitution in kind, or, if this is not possible, payment of a sum corresponding to the value which a restitution in kind would bear'.

[38] AE Boyle, 'Remedying Harm to International Common Spaces and Resources: Compensation and Other Approaches' in Wetterstein, above n 26, 89.

damage.[39] The climate change regime furnishes one such example. Such regulatory approaches are multilateral in character whilst compensation for damage is generally pursued on a bilateral basis.[40] This is likely to continue to be so notwithstanding the ILC's innovative approach to categories of obligations and to injured parties under the draft articles, not only because in the vast majority of cases regulation is preferable to ex ante remediation but also because increasing recourse to compliance mechanisms (discussed below) provides a multilateral forum with wider responses available than under state responsibility.

As noted above, apart from limiting the general remedies available when pursuing an erga omnes or erga omnes partes claims under Articles 42 and 48, there is no attempt in the ILC ASR, nor in those on the prevention of transboundary harm, to develop remedies specifically adapted to environmental damage. The sole codification attempt to do so generally for the environment, the Lugano Convention,[41] is regional in scope and has not enjoyed widespread support. The remedies available for breach of environmental obligations are thus determined by general international law. Where responsibility is established, an obligation arises first to discontinue the wrongful conduct, second to offer guarantees of non-repetition, and third to make 'full reparation' for the injury caused. 'Full reparation' is 'restitution, compensation, and satisfaction, either singly or in combination (art 34 ASR) assessed on a case-by-case basis. In the climate change context, restitution is impossible in the sense of restoring the status quo ante—even if the benchmark of for example pre-industrial levels or 1990 emissions levels could be agreed—and satisfaction is inadequate.

Compensation according to general state responsibility principles is also problematic in the climate change context, not least because of significant difficulties in establishing a causal connection between the wrongful act and the damage caused as the 'normal' consequences of

[39] Where the polluter pays principle is most rigorously applied under international environmental treaties, it is with respect to imposing liability on private actors—eg ship owners or nuclear operators—either exclusively or in conjunction with state responsibility; see above n 7.

[40] As Boyle, above n 38, notes, the responsibility of Iraq for environmental damage caused during its invasion and occupation of Kuwait, recognised in Security Council Resolution 687, is one of the few examples of exclusively state liability for environmental damage, albeit with claims presented via an international forum, the United Nations Compensation Commission. The *Wimbledon* case (1923) PCIJ Series A, No 1 is an interesting example of both bilateral and multilateral remedies being sought in the context of an obligation erga omnes partes: France sought reparation on its own part in respect of losses suffered, whilst the three other states were concerned to establish the principle in dispute, and thereby achieve cessation of the wrongful act. It is cited in the ILC Third Report, para 114 (fn 206) as an example of the question whether other states 'should be able to seek compensation or take countermeasures on their own account'.

[41] See n 7.

the wrongful act.[42] Particularly problematic is the 'backward looking' nature of state responsibility with respect to restitution and compensation. In the environmental context, there is a sliding scale of 'ideal remedies' ranging from prevention of future harm or risk of harm, securing better cooperation, to obtaining compensation for damage to people/property and natural resources, clean-up costs and restoration, where damage actually occurs. There are only limited examples of preventive remedies in the case law, including interim orders of protection and the requirement to cooperate in protecting the marine environment.[43] Moreover, in *Pulp Mills*, even though the application for provisional measures was unsuccessful, in resisting the application it was necessary for Uruguay to demonstrate to the Court that it had carried out an environmental impact assessment and that adequate measures to prevent or to minimize the risk of harm to the River Uruguay had been taken or were planned.[44]

Quantification of loss, especially 'non-financially assessable' damage, is a further difficulty especially in the environmental context. Article 36 of the ILC draft articles refers only to financially assessable damage being compensable,[45] yet many environmental components and values do not have an easily ascribed, or any, market value. While a small number of bespoke regimes can surmount some of these difficulties, these are largely concerned with civil liability rather than state responsibility.[46] Neither the UNFCCC nor the KP contain bespoke rules addressing the injurious consequences of climate change and proposals to confer on the KP Compliance Committee the power to require a state to pay for restoration of damage to the environment were rejected.[47]

Beyond these difficulties in the application of the traditional law of state responsibility in the environmental context, perhaps the most import objection is that it serves as an inadequate model for the enforcement of international standards of environmental protection, and cannot replace the need for a system of regulatory supervision at the international,

[42] Lefeber, above n 19, 343.

[43] Indeed, interim orders to cooperate in protecting the marine environment have been made by ITLOS even where there is no proof of imminent harm: see *MOX Plant (Provisional Measures)*, ITLOS No 10 (2001);, *Land Reclamation (Provisional Measures)*, ITLOS No 12 (2003) and, generally, S Rosenne, *Provisional Measures in International Law* (Oxford, Oxford University Press, 2005).

[44] See discussion, above n 22.

[45] Even here there are related questions of proportionality. The *Zoe Colocotroni* case is a domestic example of (dis)proportionate loss assessment despite the attempt to rely on market mechanisms—the commodification of components of the environment (loss of organisms in a mangrove swamp replaced based on market rates for laboratory specimens which could not reasonably be reinstated to the degraded mangrove environment). See discussion in C Redgwell, 'Compensation for Oil Pollution Damage' (1992) 16 *Marine Policy* 90.

[46] Eg for oil pollution liability, nuclear liability and liability for space objects.

[47] See discussion in R Lefeber, 'From The Hague to Bonn to Marrakech and Beyond: A Negotiating History of the Compliance Regime under the Kyoto Protocol' (2001) 14 *Hague Yearbook of International Law* 25, 31–39.

regional and national levels.[48] With protection of the global atmosphere recognised as the common concern of human kind,

> What gives such obligations a real *erga omnes* character is not that all states have standing before the ICJ in event of a breach, but that the international community can hold individual states accountable for compliance with their obligations through institutions such as the Conference of the Parties to the Climate Change Convention, or other comparable bodies endowed with . . . supervisory powers.[49]

To this observation might be added that non-state parties may equally be held to account to such bodies or institutions. It is to the development of treaty regimes of environmental protection 'enforced', inter alia, by multilateral compliance mechanisms, we now turn.

III. A SHIFT IN FOCUS: FROM RESPONSIBILITY TO COMPLIANCE

Treaty-based compliance mechanisms reflect the need to ensure both continuing participation in the treaty, and fulfilment of generally non-reciprocal obligations designed to ensure the achievement of common goals. This enhances the need for a mechanism which places emphasis upon prevention as well as upon cessation of the harmful activity and a return to compliance. The preventive element is reflected in a trend away from relying solely upon dispute settlement provisions, towards the addition of provisions addressing assessment,[50] monitoring,[51] verification,[52] verification of compliance,[53] and implementation.[54] This is a trend

[48] BBR, above n 2, 237.

[49] Ibid, 131–32 (footnote omitted). While compulsory third party dispute settlement is rarely provided for in environmental agreements, the UNFCCC and KP are an exception. However, to date only the Netherlands and the Solomon Islands have accepted it. See, generally, MMTA Brus, *Third Party Dispute Settlement in an Interdependent World* (Dordrecht, Boston, Martinus Nijhoff Publishers, 1995) 37.

[50] Eg Art 6, 1987 Montreal Protocol to the 1985 Ozone Layer Convention.

[51] Eg Art 9, 1979 Convention on Long-Range Transboundary Air Pollution Treaty.

[52] Eg Art 19, 1989 Basel Convention on the Control of Transboundary Movements of Hazardous Wastes and their Disposal.

[53] This is particularly relevant in arms control treaties, eg 1987 US/USSR Treaty on the Elimination of Intermediate Range and Shorter Range Missiles. This is carried out, inter alia, through compulsory inspections. See, generally, S Oeter, 'Inspection in International Law: Monitoring Compliance and the Problems of Implementation in International Law' (1997) *Netherlands Yearbook of International Law* 28. A further example is found in the fisheries context, for example the international observer scheme provided for in Art 21 of the 1995 Straddling Stocks Agreement. Art VII of the 1959 Antarctic Treaty and Art 14 of the 1991 Madrid Protocol provide further examples of compliance linked with inspection. On the latter see further R Wolfrum, 'Means of Ensuring Compliance with and Enforcement of International Environmental Law' (1999) 272 *Hague Academy of International Law Recueil des Cours* 9, 45.

[54] Art 13 FCCC.

observable not only in the environmental sphere, though of particular import within it, as recent developments under the UNFCCC and KP underscore.[55] Additionally, as already noted, such procedures are also able to accommodate a wider range of actors—IOs and even NGOs in the case of some NCPs—thus widening the range of participants beyond the traditional category of states.[56] Standard environmental texts tend to address the issue of compliance[57] exclusively as a question of enforcing or ensuring compliance with treaty obligations through formal and informal methods for settling disputes and monitoring compliance.[58] With a number of environmental treaties now providing for a compliance procedure,[59] increased attention on the role of international compliance in the effective implementation and enforcement of international environmental treaties is unsurprising.[60] As the burgeoning literature underscores, the

[55] See further C Redgwell, 'Non-Compliance Procedures and the Climate Change Convention' in W Bradnee Chambers (ed), *Global Climate Governance: Inter-linkages between the Kyoto Protocol and other Multilateral Regimes* (Tokyo, UNU/IAS, 1998) 13; J Brunnee, M Doelle and L Rajamani (eds), *Promoting Compliance in an Evolving Climate Regime* (Cambridge, Cambridge University Press, 2012); J Brunnee, 'Climate Change and Compliance and Enforcement Processes' in Rayfuse and Scott, above n 4.

[56] See further n 10.

[57] An interesting issue not considered here is what constitutes compliance. Kingsbury rightly critiques the literature as setting up a (false) dichotomy between compliance and non-compliance, when in practice it is, at best, a continuum: see further B Kingsbury, 'The Concept of Compliance as a Function of Competing Conceptions of International Law' (1998) 19 *Michigan Journal of International Law* 345. Nor should compliance be viewed as synonymous with effectiveness since the latter depends in part upon the strength of the obligations, their clarity, and their relationship with the overall objectives of the treaty in question. Low standards, and/or ambiguous ones, reduce effectiveness even where 'compliance' has been ensured. On effectiveness, see generally DG Victor, K Raustiala and E B Skolnikoff (eds), *The Implementation and Effectiveness of International Environmental Commitments* (Cambridge, MA, MIT Press, 1998). During debate of the Special Rapporteur's Second Report on State Responsibility (1999) the suggestion that 'non-compliance' be employed in the draft articles to refer to a failure to carry out an obligation not involving a breach of international law was rejected: ILC Report 1999, para 115, reproduced at www.un.org/law/ilc/reports/1999.

[58] This may be through traditional dispute settlement machinery, treaty supervisory bodies and mechanisms, or non-compliance procedures. See, eg BBR, above n 2, 237–50; Sands et al, above n 2, ch 5.

[59] While the KP makes explicit provision in Art 18 for the subsequent development of a compliance procedure, Churchill and Ulfstein argue that 'subsidiary bodies for operating non-compliance mechanisms could also be established without an explicit provision in the [multilateral environmental agreement] on the basis of "implied powers"'. RR Churchill and G Ulfstein, 'Autonomous Institutional Arrangements in Multilateral Environmental Agreements: A Little-Noticed Phenomenon in International Law' (2000) 94 *American Journal of International Law* 644. Or the COP may assume this role, as has been the case under CITES, for example: S Biniaz, 'Remarks about the CITES Compliance Regime' in U Beyerlin, PT Stoll and R Wolfrum (eds), *Ensuring Compliance with Multilateral Agreements: A Dialogue Between Practitioners and Academia* (The Hague, Martinus Nijhoff, 2006) 89.

[60] For a recent overview see T Treves et al (eds), *Non-Compliance Procedures and Mechanisms and the Effectiveness of International Environmental Agreements* (The Hague, TMC Asser Press, 2009); J Klabbers, 'Compliance Procedures' in Bodansky et al, above n 2, 995–1009; M Fitzmaurice, 'Compliance with Multilateral Environmental Agreements' (2007) *Hague Yearbook of International Law* 19. On compliance with soft law see D Shelton (ed),

primary objective in establishing compliance procedures is to provide, within a multilateral context, encouragement to treaty parties to comply with their treaty obligations and, in the event of non-compliance, to provide a 'softer' system to address non-compliance than that afforded by traditional dispute settlement procedures under general international law.[61] In the climate change context for example, these 'traditional procedures' comprise the multilateral consultative process and dispute settlement provisions of the UNFCCC,[62] which are extended to the KP with its additional, bespoke, compliance procedures.[63] Facilitating as well as enforcing compliance are clearly a part of this process, as the mandate of the Kyoto Protocol's bifurcated compliance body, with its facilitative and enforcement branches, underscores: '[t]he objective of the procedures and mechanisms on compliance is to facilitate, promote and enforce compliance with commitments under the Protocol'.[64] Practice under the first ever compliance mechanism, established under the Montreal Protocol, reveals a particular reliance on facilitative approaches even though the Implementation Committee thereunder is not bifurcated in the manner of the KP Compliance Committee.[65] Unlike the Montreal Protocol, the KP has not yet had to face the 'big compliance questions' arising from failure to meet GHG emission targets, since the end of the first commitment period, and thus the deadline for compliance, is 2012.[66]

Commitment and Compliance: The Role of Non-Binding Norms in the International Legal System (Oxford, Oxford University Press, 2000). In the climate change context see n 55.

[61] See, generally, Fitzmaurice and Redgwell, above n 9. However, as Nollkaemper, above n 5, 165 (fn 3), rightly points out, the similarities between traditional dispute settlement and non-compliance procedures are important too since '[b]oth types of procedures can seek to determine conformity with behaviour and changes that are required to promote compliance'.

[62] Art 13 UNFCCC; Art 16 KP. The MCP approved by COP4 (see Decision 10/CP.4) has the objective, inter alia, of providing advice to Parties with difficulties in implementing the Convention, and may be invoked by a Party or Parties experiencing difficulties with their own implementation. Members of the MCP are experts (scientific, socio-economic, environmental). Clearly envisaged as performing a facilitiative role, disagreement over representation on the Committee (Decision 10/CP.4 contains bracketed text on this issue) and the establishment of the compliance procedure of the Kyoto Protocol have impeded the full operationalisation of the MCP.

[63] For background see F Yamin and J Depledge, *The International Climate Change Regime: A Guide To The Rules, Institutions And Procedures* (Cambridge, Cambridge University Press, 2004) ch 12.

[64] 'Procedures and Mechanisms Relating to Compliance Under the Kyoto Protocol: Text proposed by the Co-Chairmen of the Joint Working Group on Compliance', FCCC/SB/2000/11, 24 October 2000, Section I, para 1 and Section II, para 2, respectively.

[65] Fitzmaurice and Redgwell, above n 9; on the early operation of the procedure see Werksman, above n 11.

[66] Nonetheless there have been a number of implementation issues addressed by the Enforcement Branch arising from reporting and inventory commitments regarding (chronologically) Greece, Canada (before withdrawal from the KP), Croatia and Bulgaria. See further www.unfccc.int/files/kyoto_protocol/compliance and, on the initial experiences of the Compliance Committee, S Oberthur and R Lefeber, 'Holding Countries to Account: The Kyoto Protocol's Compliance System Revisited after Four Years of Experience' (2010) 1 *Climate Law* 133.

The function of compliance facilitation is not merely to respond to threatened or actual non-compliance with treaty (or even soft law) obligations. Rather, compliance facilitation entails the complex and ongoing task of ensuring that treaty parties 'buy into', and are able to achieve, treaty and/or soft law objectives.[67] Soft law instruments require softer forms of compliance. It is thus not surprising that, in the context of the Copenhagen Accord and the Cancun Agreements, for example, reference is made to monitoring, reporting and verification (MRV) rather than 'compliance', which has a particular resonance with binding target and timetable mitigation commitments. Of course, this search for terminological differentiation between 'enforcement', 'compliance' and 'verification' is not unique to the climate change context. For example, recent scholarship on the role of legally non-binding norms in the international system speaks not of compliance but of 'conformance' with such legally non-binding norms.[68]

One of the functions of compliance facilitation is to address (potential or actual) problems of effective implementation. In general, there are six types of obstacles to effective implementation of, and compliance with, treaty obligations, which may operate individually or collectively: (i) financial; (ii) technical; (iii) scientific; (iv) legal and administrative; (v) political; and (vi) textual.[69] In recognition of these potential compliance obstacles, compliance facilitation is now a key feature of contemporary environmental treaty arrangements. Methods for encouraging compliance range from the facilitative to the coercive; or, as Werksman characterises compliance approaches, from a 'soft managerial approach' relying primarily upon 'cooperative problem solving' to an enforcement approach, 'which relies on stronger tactics to deter non-compliance or to coerce non-complying states into complying'.[70] Indeed, these approaches are not mutually exclusive. As Mitchell observes, most multilateral environmental agreements—the UNFCCC and KP included—exhibit elements of both the

[67] On 'managing compliance' see A Chayes and A Handler Chayes, *The New Sovereignty: Compliance with International Regulatory Agreements* (USA, Harvard University Press, 1995). On regime evolution and legitimacy, see also D Bodansky and E Diringer, *The Evolution of Multilateral Regimes: Implications for Climate Change* (Pew Centre on Global Climate Change, December 2010).

[68] The International Organization for Standardization distinguishes between 'conformance' and 'compliance': the former refers to environmental management system standards, whilst the latter refers to public regulatory standards. See N Roht-Arriaza, '"Soft Law" in a "Hybrid" Organization: The International Organization for Standardization' in Shelton, above n 58, fn 264. Shelton on the other hand clearly does refer to 'compliance' with soft law norms, as her title indicates.

[69] See further C Redgwell, 'National Implementation' in Bodansky et al, above n 2, 922.

[70] Werksman, above n 11. In these admittedly broad characterisations Werksman explicitly relies on the extensive literature on compliance with multilateral environmental agreements, in particular K Danish, 'Management v Enforcement: The New Debate on Promoting Treaty Compliance' (1997) 37 *Virginia Journal of International Law* 789 (enforcement) and *The New Sovereignty*, above n 64 ('managerialist').

enforcement and managerial approaches.[71] The insight from the managerial approach, which underscores a facilitative approach to compliance, is that states rely on a range of mechanisms to induce actors to behave in a manner consistent with treaty obligations and that failure to comply may be explained by incapacity, inadvertence, or normative differences. This differentiation between the managerial and enforcement approaches is also a reflection of the various reasons for non-compliance by states with their international obligations when, inter alia, confronted by the obstacles to implementation noted above. Such reasons may range from free riding to exploit the economic advantage derived from non-compliance,[72] to an inability to meet treaty obligations because of their high cost or a lack of capacity, for instance a lack of relevant technology or expertise.[73] Compliance mechanisms, both formal and informal, need to reduce or eliminate the economic benefits to be derived from non-compliance[74] and to facilitate compliance where obstacles relating to lack of capacity, particularly for developing states, are identifiable.

What makes the climate change context so interesting is 'because its approach to compliance and enforcement has gone considerably beyond the general trends in international environmental law' with respect to both facilitation and enforcement of compliance.[75] And it is in this latter regard, albeit remaining to be tested by 'the big compliance questions' under the KP, that compliance, enforcement and responsibility may more accurately be portrayed as part of a continuum in securing the observance of international obligations.

IV. CONCLUSION

A recent evaluation of the impact of climate change on the law of state responsibility reaches the modest conclusion that '[c]limate change and its injurious consequences are likely to become a testing ground for the law of state responsibility in this century'.[76] Yet

[71] RB Mitchell, 'Compliance Theory: Compliance, Effectiveness, and Behavioural Change in International Environmental Law' in Bodansky et al, above n 2, 911.

[72] See, generally, J Heister, E Mohr, F Stahler, PT Stoll and R Wolfrum, 'Strategies to Enforce Compliance with an International CO_2 Treaty' (1997) 9 *International Environmental Affairs* 23–24 ('reasons for non-compliance').

[73] See RB Mitchell, 'Compliance Theory: an Overview' in J Cameron, J Werksman and P Roderick (eds), *Improving Compliance with International Environmental Law* (London, Earthscan, 1996) 11–13.

[74] As Marauhn observes, 'compliance control is a device for generating confidence of states that the benefits of respecting and implementing the obligations of the treaty outweigh the costs'. T Marauhn, 'Towards a Procedural Law of Compliance, Control in International Relations' (1996) 56 *ZaöRV* 698; see also Redgwell, above n 54, 14.

[75] Brunnee, above n 55, 292 citing Oberthur and Lefeber, above n 66, 134.

[76] Lefeber, above n 19, 349.

> to date there have been few attempts to construct the legal bases and pathways for asserting the responsibility of any specific State for alleged climate change-induced damage due to the actions, or more likely the omissions, of that State in respect of its international obligations to prevent, mitigate and/or reduce greenhouse gas emissions that apparently cause such climate change-induced damage.[77]

There is, of course, nothing to prevent the parties to the UNFCCC and KP from developing primary rules on such injurious consequences, though unsuccessful attempts thus far to do so within the climate change regime, and without it in terms of the articulation of general rules on environmental damage, suggest that the obstacles to such approach remain large. At Cancun lip-service was paid to the need for a work programme to address it,[78] but the prospects for international agreement are slight.

Such failure may be an explanation for the rise in climate change litigation before domestic courts as litigants seek various avenues to challenge GHG emitting activity in the absence of applicable international regulation and its robust international enforcement.[79] However, such litigation may encounter obstacles similar to those identified above for the international level such as identifying the appropriate plaintiff and establishing a causal link between the damage suffered and the (in)actions of the plaintiff. For example, it is doubtful that the EU environmental liability Directive will play a significant role in climate change litigation owing to this difficulty, since the Directive applies to damage 'caused by pollution of a diffuse character, where it is possible to establish a causal link between the damage and the activities of individual operators'.[80]

Another fertile source of litigation has been challenge to climate change legislation;[81] for example, in the EU context the majority of the public law litigation[82] has been challenges between the EU institutions and the Member States over 'allocation of power, the validity of EU legislative

[77] Ong, above n 4, 454.

[78] *The Cancun Agreements: Outcome of the Work of the Ad Hoc Working Group on Long-term Cooperative Action under the Convention*, UNFCCC Decision 1/CP.16 (2010), paras 25–29.

[79] See, generally, R Lord, S Goldbert, L Rajamani and J Brunnee (eds), *Climate Change Liability: Transnational Law and Practice* (Cambridge, Cambridge University Press, 2012); WCG Burns and HM Osofsky (eds), *Adjudicating Climate Change: State, National and International Approaches* (Cambridge, Cambridge University Press, 2009). Such litigation also includes legal challenges to climate change regulatory measures. For a detailed list of US and non-US cases, see www.law.columbia.edu/centers/climatechange. For analysis of the value of litigation as more than mere gap filling in the treaty regime and national policies, see HM Osofsky, 'Climate Change and Dispute Resolution Processes' in Rayfuse and Scott, above n 4, 350, 362.

[80] Art 4(4) of Directive 2004/35 on environmental liability with regard to the prevention and remedying of environmental damage, [2004] OJ L143, 56; see Kramer, above n 21, 357.

[81] There is no comprehensive climate change legislation in the EU as such, which has adopted a range of measures ranging from establishing a scheme for GHG emissions allowance trading (the EU ETS) to energy efficiency measures: Kramer, above n 21, 353–57.

[82] Private litigation before EU courts is less likely owing to the Art 263(4) TFEU require-

provisions and the enforcement of EU legislation in the Member States'.[83] With the recent inclusion of aviation emissions within the EU ETS (and active discussion of adding maritime transport),[84] there is widened scope for challenge of EU measures supranationally, including under the WTO where the EU is a party to the covered agreements and subject to compulsory dispute settlement thereunder. Such EU unilateralism is, however, contingent in the sense that the 'externalization' of the ETS or geographic extension of such measures can be avoided if goods and services are subject to adequate climate change regulation in the flag state or state of origin.[85]

With these recent trends towards a bottom-up approach to addressing climate change commitments through national and regional measures, there is increased reliance at the international level on monitoring, reporting and verification rather than 'compliance', the latter having particular resonance with binding target and timetable mitigation commitments. The sophisticated compliance and enforcement system consonant with the 'managerial' approach to compliance which evolved under the KP has been anchored by such commitments. It thus remains to be seen whether this 'highly institutionalised approach to compliance and enforcement' which has evolved, in part to address the frailties of traditional state responsibility in the climate change context, will endure or whether 'a more decentralised system with elements of self-help'[86]—or more contingent unilateralism in the EU context—will emerge. In the event what we are left with is the potential application of an imperfect lex lata on state responsibility, a compliance regime increasingly cast adrift from concrete, top-down commitments, and no clear liability rules to address the injurious consequences of climate change: the wrong—or at least an extremely ill-fitting—pair of trousers indeed.

ment of the direct and individual effect of legislative acts/decisions: for recent discussion of the sparse climate change related case law see Kramer, ibid, 369–70.

[83] Kramer, ibid, 369.

[84] Directive 2008/101/EC amending Directive 2003/87, OJ (2008) L8/3, discussed in J Scott and L Rajamani, 'EU Climate Change Unilateralism' (2012) 23 *European Journal of International Law* 469.

[85] It is beyond the scope of this chapter to explore in detail these aspects of externalization of the EU as 'norm entrepreneur' and its forcing effect on multilateral negotiations, considered more fully by Scott and Rajamani, above n 84, and by J Scott, 'The Multi-Level Governance of Climate Change' (2011) 1 *Carbon and Climate Law Review* 25.

[86] Brunnee, above n 4, 319.

11

Common but Differentiated Responsibilities in EU Climate Change Law: A Case of Double Standards?

CHRIS HILSON*

I. INTRODUCTION

A CRITICISM WHICH is often levelled at EU external policy is one of double standards, with the field of human rights providing a good example. The sorts of human rights demands which the EU has imposed externally on third countries (including accession states), have often been much higher than those which the EU has lived up to itself, internally.[1] This issue is, of course, problematic now, not only morally and politically but potentially also legally because of Article 1(3) TEU, which requires the Union to 'ensure consistency between the different areas of its external action and between these and its other policies'.

The aim in this chapter is to investigate the issue of double-standards in relation to external and internal EU climate change law and policy. It does so by exploring, specifically, the potential for inconsistency in relation to the principle of Common But Differentiated Responsibilities (CBDR). Historically, as will be shown, this has formed a cornerstone not only of public international law on climate change, but also (as one might expect) of the EU's related external policy on the subject. The question then arises as to whether the EU has followed a similar approach in relation to its internal policy on climate change: are there echoes of the equitable principle of CBDR at work there, or has the EU held itself

* I am grateful to those present at the Bristol workshop for their comments and also to Ross Connell for his library assistance in connection with this chapter.

[1] See, eg A Williams, *EU Human Rights Policies: A Study In Irony* (Oxford, Oxford University Press, 2005).

to different standards (whether more, or less, favourable) in its relations with poorer Member States?

This chapter's principal claim is that arguments about double standards need to be examined in terms of their normative background assumptions. Arguments about double standards will often presuppose a cosmopolitan political theory;[2] if, in contrast, one adopts a more communitarian or statist approach,[3] then arguments about double standards are less likely to be regarded as persuasive. While Article 1(3) TEU may require 'consistency' between external and internal climate policy, that must similarly presuppose a debate on what type and degree of consistency is appropriate. There are echoes here of debates concerning formal versus substantive equality. It cannot be right for formal consistency to be imposed in all cases. Rather, what should be required is substantive consistency, whereby room is left for different treatment depending on the normative background that the EU wishes to bring to the policy field concerned. In some cases, the EU may lean more towards cosmopolitanism (with, say, fundamental rights), in which case a more formal reading of consistency may be appropriate; however, in other instances (for example climate justice), it may wish to argue for a more statist direction, with a corresponding, substantive approach to consistency which allows for unlike cases to be treated differently.

A focus on CBDR rather than the responsibility of an international organisation like the EU in terms of 'state responsibility' arguably requires some justification in a collection primarily addressed to the latter. The justification is a fairly straightforward one: the formal doctrine of state responsibility is ill-suited to tackling modern environmental problems such as climate change,[4] where one typically finds instead the principle of CBDR. State responsibility for climate change is likely to require suing states to establish, inter alia, a precise causal connection between EU greenhouse gas (GHG) emissions and harm suffered. This is bound to prove elusive given the contribution of many other states to the problem.[5] What CBDR offers instead is a way of holding states (or international organisations like the EU) responsible for harm—not via a reparation-based liability regime as one finds with state responsibility, but rather via a principle which shapes the obligations of states and

[2] See, eg P Harris and J Symons, 'Justice in Adaptation to Climate Change: Cosmopolitan Implications for International Institutions' (2010) 19 *Environmental Politics* 617, 627. These authors argue for a cosmopolitan conception of justice in relation to climate change adaptation based, inter alia, on the principle of universality which holds that 'principles that govern international obligation should be consistent with those implemented domestically'.

[3] On communitarian approaches to climate justice, see, eg J Paavola, N Adger and S Huq, 'Multifacted Justice in Adaptation to Climate Change' in N Adger et al (eds), *Fairness in Adaptation to Climate Change* (Boston, MA, MIT Press, 2006) 265.

[4] See, eg C Voigt, 'State Responsibility for Climate Change Damages' (2008) 77 *Nordic Journal of International Law* 1; see also ch 11 by Redgwell in this volume.

[5] Voigt, ibid.

others in multilateral environmental agreements. Given that developed countries or blocs like the EU bear the greatest share of responsibility for historical GHG emissions, many claim that they are therefore obliged, in international climate change agreements, to take on the greater burden of action to mitigate further harm and to assist in adaptation. While CBDR shares with state responsibility the idea of looking backwards,[6] unlike state responsibility, CBDR does so in order to inform future preventive regulatory action.

II. THE PRINCIPLE OF COMMON BUT DIFFERENTIATED RESPONSIBILITIES

It is beyond the scope of this chapter to explore the wider ramifications of the CBDR principle[7] in great depth. However, before examining how CBDR has featured in international climate change law, it is first necessary to briefly unpack what the principle involves. The 'common' aspect of CBDR is usually associated with notions in international law of 'common heritage' or 'common concern'.[8] However, while climate change is, in that sense, obviously a common problem and the atmosphere a common resource, it is not altogether obvious how that distinction helps specifically with the idea of common responsibilities. After all, as Stone has descriptively observed of the United Nations Framework Convention on Climate Change (UNFCCC, which will be examined further below), 'not every country that faces the *common problem* shares in a *common responsibility* to fix it'.[9] To take matters further, one needs to define 'common' more closely. What common can obviously not mean in the context of CBDR is 'uniform', because that runs flatly against the 'differentiated' element, which is also part of the principle. What it must mean therefore is that responsibilities are 'shared' or in common. Thus, under the UNFCCC, Annex I (developed) and non-Annex I (developing) countries have in common that they have some responsibilities or obligations under the Convention, but those responsibilities are not common in the sense of being uniform.

[6] Though not exclusively so with CBDR (see n 15).

[7] The term 'principle' is used loosely here: as will be seen later in the chapter, explicit legal reference to CBDR as a principle is not particularly common in many policy documents—no doubt because some powerful states have been keen to avoid its recognition as a formal principle of international environmental law.

[8] See, eg C Stone, 'Common But Differentiated Responsibilities in International Law' (2004) 98 *American Journal of International Law* 276; L Rajamani, 'The Principle of Common but Differentiated Responsibility and the Balance of Commitments under the Climate Regime' (2000) 9 *RECIEL* 120; L Rajamani, *Differential Treatment in International Environmental Law* (Oxford, Oxford University Press 2006).

[9] Stone, above n 8, 276, text in fn 2 (emphasis in original).

While the 'differentiated' part of CBDR appears relatively straightforward,[10] connoting non-uniformity, the difficulty arises in deciding on the basis for such differentiation. Here one has to resolve the nature and extent of the relevant responsibilities. A widespread assumption—in particular among developing countries (and resisted by many developed countries)[11]—is that responsibility within CBDR refers to historical responsibility for greenhouse gas emissions, which have caused anthropogenic climate change. Such responsibility is said to lie squarely with developed, Annex I, countries which would indicate that they should therefore take on the burden of action to tackle climate change. Reference is also commonly made by developing countries (and again resisted by many developed countries) to the equitable 'polluter pays principle',[12] with this associated with legal liability for past, historical emissions. To the extent that CBDR is a matter of equity or justice, it appears here as a matter more of corrective than distributive justice. However, one might equally argue that the polluter pays principle need not be restricted to liability for past pollution, but that it also involves the idea of responsibility for current or future pollution. In addition, because climate change gives rise to the allocation of burdens, it involves notions of distributive justice. It is beyond the scope of this chapter to delve too deeply into the growing literature on justice and climate change:[13] however, suffice to say that the idea that developing countries should be held responsible for historical emissions has been contested, inter alia, on the basis that the current generation would be paying for a problem which they did not cause.[14]

Finally, and again related to ideas of distributive justice, CBDR is closely associated with the notion of capability or capacity to pay. While responsibility is often seen as 'backward looking',[15] capability is more obviously forward looking.[16] In formal terms, as will be shown in the next section, the most recent official documents specifically discussing climate change, place capability and responsibility alongside each other but clearly as

[10] Though *cf* Stone, above n 8, 277.

[11] Rajamani (2006), above n 8, 76, 81, 137.

[12] The polluter pays principle is itself not formally expressed in the UNFCCC, the claim instead being that it is implicit in the CBDR principle.

[13] See, eg S Caney, 'Cosmopolitan Justice, Responsibility, and Global Climate Change' (2005) 18 *Leiden Journal of International Law* 747; H Shue, 'Global Environment and International Inequality' (1999) 75 *International Affairs* 531; E Page, 'Distributing the Burdens of Climate Change' (2008) 17 *Environmental Politics* 556; S Jagers and G Duus-Otterström, 'Dual Climate Change Responsibility: On Moral Divergences Between Mitigation and Adaptation' (2008) 17 *Environmental Politics* 576.

[14] See, eg Caney, above n 13. Note, however, that Caney adopts a somewhat rigid definition of CBDR.

[15] Though as Jagers and Duus-Otterström, for example, note, responsibility can also be forward looking, above n 13, 579–80.

[16] D Butt, '"The Polluter Pays": Backward-Looking Principles of Intergenerational Justice and the Environment' in L Foisneau, C Hiebaum and J Carlos Velasco (eds), *Global Justice: Open Democracies* (Dordrecht, Springer, 2012). Though *cf* Rajamani (2006), above n 8, 149.

separate elements of CBDR. Thus, common policy wording speaks of states acting 'in accordance with their common but differentiated responsibilities and respective capabilities'. However, for some commentators, CBDR itself encapsulates capabilities.[17] On this view in other words, rather than being separate, one embraces the other. There is some, albeit limited support for such a view in official, non-climate specific documents. Principle 7 of the Rio Declaration, which will be examined again in the next section, for example states that 'The developed countries acknowledge the responsibility that they bear in the international pursuit of sustainable development in view of the pressures their societies place on the global environment and of the technologies and financial resources they command'.[18]

Here technological and financial capability seems to inform, in part, the notion of responsibility in relation to sustainable development.[19] More generally though, one might also regard capabilities as reinforcing the idea of historical responsibility on the part of developed countries for climate change: they are responsible because they can afford to be made responsible. Again, whether an emphasis on financial capability in relation to tackling climate change is fair has been the subject of debate: as Butt notes for example, 'if someone smashes one of the windows of my house, I do not ask who in the village is best placed to pay for its repair. I rather insist that the person responsible for breaking it bears the cost'.[20]

III. APPLICATION IN INTERNATIONAL CLIMATE CHANGE LAW AND POLICY

Although practical examples of the CBDR principle at work can be traced back some way in international law, it only took formal shape as a principle with this name at Rio.[21] Principle 7 of the 1992 Rio Declaration on Environment and Development proclaims that:

> States shall cooperate in a spirit of global partnership to conserve, protect and restore the health and integrity of the Earth's ecosystem. In view of the different contributions to global environmental degradation, States have common but differentiated responsibilities. The developed countries acknowledge

[17] See, eg Rajamani (2000), above n 8, 123 and (2006), above n 8, 150 (though *cf* 137–38); Butt, above n 16.

[18] UNEP, 'Rio Declaration on Environment and Development' (Rio de Janeiro 3rd to 4th June 1992) www.unep.org/Documents.Multilingual/Default.Print.asp?DocumentID=78&ArticleID=1163&l=en, Principle 7.

[19] Similarly, see, eg V de Lucia, 'Common but Differentiated Responsibility' in CJ Cleveland (ed), *Encyclopedia of Earth* (Washington, DC, Environmental Information Coalition, National Council for Science and the Environment, 2007), available at www.eoearth.org/article/Common_but_differentiated_responsibility, cited by Butt, above n 16.

[20] Butt, above n 16.

[21] Rajamani (2000), above n 8, 120.

the responsibility that they bear in the international pursuit of sustainable development in view of the pressures their societies place on the global environment and of the technologies and financial resources they command.[22]

However, for present purposes, the most significant expression of the principle[23] is to be found in the 1992 United Nations Framework Convention on Climate Change (UNFCCC), Article 3(1) of which states that:

The parties should protect the climate system for the benefit of present and future generations of humankind, on the basis of equity and in accordance with their common but differentiated responsibilities and respective capabilities. Accordingly, the developed country parties should take the lead in combating climate change and the adverse effects thereof.[24]

The Convention process thereafter followed the usual course of regular Conferences of the Parties (COPs), a number of which stand out in the history of the Convention as critical junctures for deciding on the direction of travel. Mention of CBDR can be found in all of the key documents associated with these COPs. Thus for example the first COP in 1995—which set out what became known as the Berlin Mandate—confirms CBDR as expressed in Article 3(1) of the Convention and also expresses:

The fact that the global nature of climate change calls for the widest possible cooperation by all countries and their participation in an effective and appropriate international response, in accordance with their common but differentiated responsibilities and respective capabilities and their social and economic conditions.[25]

The Berlin Mandate essentially resolved to tighten the Convention and secure its future operation and led directly to the Kyoto Protocol with its binding commitments for Annex I countries. The Protocol was adopted in Kyoto on 11 December 1997 following the third COP of the UNFCCC, though it only entered into force on 16 February 2005.

CBDR makes an appearance in Article 10 of the Kyoto Protocol, although its wording is somewhat watered down: instead of (as in Article 3(1) of the UNFCCC) acting 'in accordance with' CBDR, Kyoto merely requires parties to 'take into account' their common but differentiated

[22] UNEP, above n 18.

[23] Though not expressed as a principle as such.

[24] UNFCCC (adopted, May 9 1992, entered into force March 21 1994) 1771 UNTS 107, Art 3(1), available at unfccc.int/resource/docs/convkp/conveng.pdf. See also Art 4(1) and the Convention's preamble. The latter states 'that the global nature of climate change calls for the widest possible cooperation by all countries and their participation in an effective and appropriate international response, in accordance with their common but differentiated responsibilities and respective capabilities and their social and economic conditions'.

[25] Report of the Conference of the Parties on its First Session, Held at Berlin from 28 March to 7 April 1995, FCCC/CP/1995/7/Add 1, para I, 1(e). This wording is largely repeated later in the document in the preamble to Decision 5/CP 1.

responsibilities, whilst noting that this does not introduce any new commitments for non-Annex I parties.

The next key milestone conference on climate change[26] took place at Bali, Indonesia in 2007, at which the so-called 'Bali Roadmap' was agreed. A core part of the roadmap was the 'Bali Action Plan', which consisted of a comprehensive process to tackle the post-Kyoto[27] framework—a process that culminated in the 15th COP at Copenhagen in 2009. The Bali Action Plan is perhaps most striking in its explicit referencing of CBDR as a 'principle'—something repeated in the similar mention of CBDR in the 2009 Copenhagen Accord.[28]

Interestingly, by the time of the 2010 Cancún agreements arising from COP 16 in Mexico, direct reference to CBDR as a formal 'principle' had virtually disappeared. However, for the first time we see explicit reference made to the historical responsibility of developed states—something that a number of such states had been keen to avoid including in earlier documents.[29] In discussing the need for enhanced action on mitigation, the COP Decision:

> *Emphasiz[es]* the need for deep cuts in global greenhouse gas emissions and early and urgent undertakings to accelerate and enhance the implementation of the Convention by all parties, on the basis of equity and in accordance with their common but differentiated responsibilities and respective capabilities, *Acknowledging* that the largest share of historical global emissions of greenhouse gases originated in developed countries and that, owing to this historical responsibility, developed country parties must take the lead in combating climate change and the adverse effects thereof.[30]

IV. EU SUPPORT FOR CBDR IN EXTERNAL CLIMATE CHANGE POLICY

The aim of this section is to examine some of the key EU policy documents, which largely track the milestone post-UNFCCC COPs, in order to see to what extent support for CBDR is expressed as a matter of EU external

[26] Which included but was wider than just the UNFCCC COP 13. My selection of 'milestones' here is inevitably subjective to a degree—selections by others might well differ.

[27] The Kyoto Protocol was originally due to end by 2012.

[28] The COP 'took note of' the Accord in Decision 2/CP.15 (Report of the Conference of the Parties on its Fifteenth Session, Held in Copenhagen from 7 to 19 December 2009, FCCC/CP/2009/11/Add.1, para 1).

[29] See, eg Rajamani, above n 8.

[30] Report of the Conference of the Parties on its Sixteenth Session, Held in Cancun from 29 November to 10 December 2010, FCCC/CP/2010/7/Add.1, Decision 1/CP.16, 'The Cancun Agreements: Outcome of the Work of the Ad Hoc Working Group on Long-term Cooperative Action under the Convention', preamble to Section III A. CBDR is also mentioned in paragraphs 1, 14 and 139(a). Only the latter of these directly mentions CBDR as a 'principle'.

policy. As we shall see, a number of such documents mention CBDR specifically by name. However, it is also necessary to be aware that the concepts underpinning CBDR may still be present in a document even though the phrase itself is absent.

Things do not start that promisingly insofar as the 1995 EU Environment Council Conclusions[31] around the time of the Berlin Mandate contain no mention of CBDR—formally or otherwise. Next, with Kyoto, although there was no formal mention of CBDR in the 1997 Commission Communication, *Climate Change—The EU Approach for Kyoto*,[32] the document does contain significant discussion of the key elements associated with the principle.

Thus, paragraph 2 highlights the lack of historical responsibility on the part of developing countries for climate change and also the issue of capacity: 'Moreover, much of the expected negative impact of climate change is likely to occur in countries that have only marginally contributed to causing the problem and without the financial resources to compensate for any possible damage'.

However, although observing the need for industrialised countries to take the lead in reducing greenhouse gas emissions on the basis of common commitments across such countries,[33] the Communication also argues for better-off developing countries to accept their share of responsibility:

> Both greenhouse gas emissions and the economic capability to limit or reduce greenhouse gas emissions vary enormously among developing countries. It is important, therefore, that the more developed among the developing countries gradually assume bigger responsibilities when their level of development justifies it. There is no room for free riders on this issue.[34]

Moving forward to the preparations for Bali, the EU Environment Council Conclusions of 30 October 2007[35] contain similar references to the need for common commitments by industrialised nations and responsibility of the more economically advanced developing countries to play their part. The language of capabilities—arguably implicit above in the Kyoto Commission Communication—is also linked to the latter:

> RECALLS that the EU agreed an objective of a 30% reduction in greenhouse gas emissions by 2020 compared to 1990 as its contribution to a global and comprehensive agreement for the period beyond 2012, provided that other

[31] 18 December 1995, available at www.consilium.europa.eu/uedocs/cms_data/docs/pressdata/en/envir/011a0006.htm.

[32] Commission, 'Climate Change—The EU Approach for Kyoto' (Communication) COM(1997) 481 final.

[33] Ibid, paras 7–8.

[34] Ibid, para 8.

[35] Council of the European Union Press Release, 2826th Council Meeting (Luxemburg, 30 October 2007), available at www.consilium.europa.eu/uedocs/cms_data/docs/pressdata/en/envir/96961.pdf.

developed countries commit themselves to comparable emission reductions and economically more advanced developing countries to contributing adequately according to their responsibilities and respective capabilities.[36]

The Council Conclusions then also explicitly refer to CBDR: 'commitments by all Parties should take into account the principle of common but differentiated responsibilities and respective capabilities and their specific national and regional development priorities, objectives and circumstances, including changes in these'.[37]

The Copenhagen Council Conclusions echo much of what had come previously, but with a more explicit drawing of CBDR in terms of the responsibilities of developing countries other than Least Developed Countries (LDCs):

in accordance with the principle of common but differentiated responsibilities and respective capabilities, all countries, except LDCs, should commit themselves to preparing ambitious, credible and country-owned low-carbon development strategies/growth plans (LCDS/LCGP); UNDERLINES that the EC and its Member States will develop such strategies / plans, building on the energy and climate package.[38]

Finally, the Cancún Environment Council Conclusions adopt a somewhat more muted approach, perhaps reflecting the need for a less aggressive stance in order to place climate change negotiations on a more secure footing after the relative failure of Copenhagen. Explicit reference to developing country responsibilities, other than what is already implicit within the formal CBDR principle, is absent:

While recognising that developed Parties' commitments and developing Parties' actions will be different in nature, in line with the principle of common but differentiated responsibilities and respective capabilities, STRESSES the need to anchor all countries' pledges in Cancún, whether made pursuant to the Copenhagen Accord or otherwise, in the context of the United Nations Framework Convention on Climate Change (UNFCCC), with a view to facilitating the clarification of those pledges, mobilising support for their implementation and supporting discussions on options to strengthen the collective level of ambition with a view to meeting the 2°C objective.[39]

[36] Ibid, para 11.

[37] Ibid, para 13.

[38] Council 'Council Conclusions on EU position for the Copenhagen Climate Conference (7–18 December 2009)', 21 October 2009, available at www.consilium.europa.eu/uedocs/cms_data/docs/pressdata/en/envir/110634.pdf.

[39] Para 11, Council of the European Union, 'Preparations for the 16th session of the Conference of the Parties (COP 16) to the United Nations Framework Convention on Climate Change (UNFCCC) and the 6th session of the Meeting of the Parties to the Kyoto Protocol (CMP 6) (Cancún, 29 November to 10 December 2010)', 14 October 2010, 14957/10, ENV 693—the Environment Council conclusions are annexed to this document. Available at: www.register.consilium.europa.eu/pdf/en/10/st14/st14957.en10.pdf.

V. INTERNAL EU CLIMATE CHANGE POLICY: CBDR BY OTHER MEANS?

The first thing to note is that the formal, explicit language of CBDR is missing from EU internal policy on climate change; rather, one sees the language framed in terms of cohesion and solidarity.[40] Why might that be so? On the one hand, CBDR might be thought to have a persuasive international legitimacy and a pedigree which would appeal to poorer accession/cohesion Member States in making claims for differential treatment. However, on the other hand, such Member States may not have been keen to associate themselves with a concept that is intimately linked to developing countries—in other words it is not part of their self-identity as developed, industrialised countries.

The EU institutions themselves may also want to avoid use of the term in relation to internal policy so as not too invite direct comparisons and potential claims of inconsistency with its external policy on CBDR. In addition, cohesion and solidarity are more established EU concepts. EU cohesion or regional policy involves the use of 'structural funds', the vast majority of which are targeted at the poorest regions.[41] Solidarity is similarly concerned with the provision of support to those in need and finds expression across a number of EU policy fields including, for example, disaster relief, energy policy and (as will be seen below) climate adaptation.[42] That is not to say that the ideas behind CBDR have not been present in EU internal policy on climate change. CBDR is clearly a principle that informs burden sharing in international law, and, as will be seen below, internal 'burden sharing' in the EU is an approach which reflects CBDR. Ideas underlying CBDR are also, as we shall see, visible in other strands of EU internal policy such as emissions trading and renewable energy.

A. Burden and Effort Sharing

Although the EU has a relatively long history of attempts at 'burden sharing', which is essentially concerned with how the burden of commitments to tackle climate change mitigation[43] is shared out

[40] A Jordan et al, 'Governing the European Union: Policy Choices and Governance Dilemmas' in A Jordan and others (eds), *Climate Change Policy in the European Union: Confronting the Dilemmas of Mitigation and Adaptation* (Cambridge, Cambridge University Press, 2010) 42; A Jordan and T Rayner, 'The Evolution of Climate Policy in the European Union. An Historical Overview' in Jordan et al, ibid, 76.

[41] On cohesion policy, see further www.ec.europa.eu/regional_policy/what/cohesion/index_en.cfm, and J Bachtler and C Mendez, 'Who Governs EU Cohesion Policy? Deconstructing the Reforms of the Structural Funds' (2007) 45 *Journal of Common Market Studies* 535.

[42] See further M Ross and Y Borgmann-Prebil, *Promoting Solidarity in the European Union* (Oxford, Oxford University Press, 2010).

[43] Burden sharing has largely been absent from EU policy on adaptation, though as

(unequally) among disparate Member States, formal progress was only really made in the run up to the Kyoto Protocol. In its Conclusions of March 1997, the Environment Council stated that the EU's international climate change commitments would be fulfilled by the EU as a whole, through what has become known as the 'bubble approach'.[44] This idea, that the EU as a regional economic integration organisation, would be legally responsible for the EU's international climate change obligations via 'joint fulfilment',[45] was very much pushed for by the EU's poorer cohesion states, who were also pressing for internal EU differentiation via an equitable 'burden sharing' agreement.[46] The two elements go very much hand-in-hand: without joint fulfilment, cohesion states would be left with individual legally binding international obligations; and without burden sharing, these targets would be uniform with other, more highly developed EU Member States. Joint fulfilment (or the 'bubble approach'), left the EU free to set an overall reduction target and then to allow its economically weaker Member States the benefit of rising GHG emissions, with the greater mitigation burden taken on by the richer states.

The basis for the 1997 burden sharing agreement is also worth exploring. Although in the end, the differentiated targets agreed for individual Member States were the result of political horse-trading,[47] the initial basis for the agreement lay in the so-called 'Triptych approach' devised by Dutch academics commissioned by the Dutch EU Presidency.[48] This approach arrived at national targets by separating out three sectors (heavy

noted in C Haug and A Jordan, 'Burden Sharing: Distributing Burdens or Sharing Efforts?' in Jordan et al, above n 40, 100, this may change as the effects of climate change are felt unequally across the EU. See also J de Cendra de Larragán, 'Liability of Member States and the EU in View of the International Climate Change Framework: Between Solidarity and Responsibility' in M Faure and M Peeters (eds), *Climate Change Liability* (Cheltenham, Edward Elgar, 2011) 55, 78–79.

[44] 'A key provision of the Protocol for the EU is Art 4, usually referred to as the EC bubble, which allows the EC and the Member States to fulfil their commitments jointly, through a differentiated commitment between Members States (burden sharing)'—Commission, 'Climate Change: Towards an EU Post-Kyoto Strategy' (Communication) COM(98) 353 final.

[45] M Montini, 'EC External Relations on Environmental Law' in J Scott (ed), *Environmental Protection: European Law and Governance* (Oxford, Oxford University Press, 2009) 164.

[46] Such countries had also pressed for the EU to ratify the earlier UNFCCC as a block (eg on Spain, see X Labandeira Villot, 'Spain: Fast Growth in CO_2 Emissions' in U Collier and R Lofstedt, *Cases in Climate Change Policy: Political Reality in the European Union* (London, Earthscan, 1997) 152, who states that 'The Spanish position takes for granted that the EU target is designed to balance out the expected growth in emissions from some of its Member States by the reduction in emissions from other Member States', although in the end, a lack of binding commitments in the UNFCCC made this less of an issue.

[47] See N Lacasta et al, 'From Sharing the Burden to Sharing the Effort: Decision 406/2009/EC on Member State Emission Targets for non-ETS Sectors' in S Oberthür and M Pallemaerts (eds), *The New Climate Policies of the European Union: Internal Legislation and Climate Diplomacy* (Brussels, Brussels University Press, 2010) 95.

[48] Haug and Jordan, above n 43, 85.

industry, electricity generation sector and domestic sector) and devising different allocation rules for each.[49] Heavy (energy intensive) industries had common targets so as to create a level playing field across the EU.[50] However, most notable for present purposes, the domestic sector rules were based on per capita emissions and provided for poorer cohesion states to increase their emissions over time.[51]

As things turned out, the negotiating target which the EU set itself in the March 1997 Council Conclusions was stricter than that eventually agreed at Kyoto,[52] and thus the burden sharing agreement set out in those conclusions came to be revisited in the Council conclusions of 16 June 1998,[53] with the final version set out in Council Decision 2002/358/EC, which approved the Kyoto Protocol and paved the way for its simultaneous ratification by the EU and its Member States on 31 May 2002.[54]

Two principal views have been expressed regarding the EU's bubble and burden-sharing approach. The first is a negative one, to the effect that the EU's stance was a hypocritical attempt at double standards because it was pushing, externally, for a uniform approach among Annex I, developed countries, while proposing to implement a differentiated approach internally within the EU.[55]

The second, more positive view sees the EU recognition of its own North-South differences as a necessary prefiguring of international leadership, acknowledging the need for international North-South differentiation.[56] As Nigel Haigh puts it, 'If the EC as a whole accepts that joint implementation can entail the cohesion countries having unrestrained or only moderately restrained increases in CO_2 emissions, it is difficult not to follow the same argument for developing countries'.[57]

The above analysis makes it clear that the case against the EU in terms

[49] Lacasta, above n 47, 95.

[50] Haug and Jordan, above n 43, 85.

[51] Lacasta, above n 47, 95.

[52] In particular, while the EU had gone into the Kyoto negotiations proposing a 15 per cent cut in emissions, it came away signed up only to an 8 per cent reduction (albeit across a wider basket of gases).

[53] Doc 9702/98 of 19 June 1998 of the Council of the European Union reflecting the outcome of proceedings of the Environment Council of 16–17 June 1998, Annex I, available at http://europa.eu/rapid/pressReleasesAction.do?reference=PRES/98/205&format=HTML&aged=0&lg=lt&guiLanguage=en.

[54] Concerning the approval, on behalf of the European Community, of the Kyoto Protocol to the United Nations Framework Convention on Climate Change and the joint fulfilment of commitments thereunder [2002] OJ L130/1.

[55] S Oberthür and H Ott, *The Kyoto Protocol: International Climate Policy for the 21st Century* (Heidelberg, Springer-Verlag, 1999); Haug and Jordan, above n 43, 85. In the end of course, the EU failed to secure a uniform set of targets for Annex I countries, see Jordan and Rayner, above n 40, 65.

[56] K von Moltke and A Rahman, 'External Perspectives on Climate Change: A View from the United States and the Third World' in T O'Riordan and J Jäger (eds), *Politics of Climate Change: A European Perspective* (London, Routledge, 1996) 344.

[57] N Haigh 'Climate Change Policies and Politics in the European Community' in O'Riordan and Jäger, above n 56, 172–73.

of double standards only really stacks up as far as industrialised emissions are concerned: while advocating uniformity externally on these for industrialised Annex I countries, it supported differentiation internally within the industrialised EU. Had it not been prepared to recognise the principle of CBDR externally, the EU would—as Haigh's quote alerts us—have been in danger of engaging in double standards as between its own poorer states internally (for whom it was willing to allow lower commitments) and poor states externally. However, it did not succumb to this particular danger in the end. That said, whether one regards the EU as completely 'off the hook' on this basis depends on one's acceptance of EU cohesion states and developing countries as relevant comparators. This has of course been contested. As Haigh states, 'Relative to the richer EC Member States the cohesion counties have low per capita CO_2 emissions, but in a world context the cohesion countries are developed countries with relatively high per capita CO_2 emissions'.[58] Gupta similarly observes that some (in global terms) rich EU states get to increase their emissions instead of contracting (in the contract and converge sense); whereas only the truly poor need room to grow—and no states in the EU fit that bill.[59]

The EU's retort could, with some justification, be that unfairness is only apparent here if one adopts per capita CO_2 emissions as the relevant measure. If, instead, one relies on total CO_2 emissions across countries, then developing countries, with the majority of the world's population, would have less scope for growth in their CO_2 emissions and cohesion states in the EU would be seen in more benign terms given their overall, relatively insignificant contribution to global emissions.[60]

This retort is, however, difficult in terms of double standards due to the fact that the EU's internal Triptych basis for its burden sharing agreement included, as we saw above, a per capita emissions element in relation to the domestic sector. Furthermore, the rescuing of the EU's case has arguably been made even more difficult by the 2009 'Effort' Sharing Decision,[61] which maintains internal differentiation within the EU on the basis of 'solidarity' between Member States, but now principally calculates such

[58] Ibid 172.

[59] J Gupta, 'Good Governance and Climate Change: Recommendations from a North-South Perspective' in M Peeters and K Deketalaere, *EU Climate Change Policy: The Challenges of New Regulatory Initiatives* (Cheltenham, Edward Elgar, 2006) 303.

[60] See, eg Haigh, above n 57, 173, who states, similarly, that a difference between cohesion states and developing countries 'is that the cohesion counties represent a small proportion of the total EC population whereas the developing countries are a larger proportion of the world population'.

[61] Decision No 406/2009/EC of the European Parliament and of the Council of 23 April 2009 on the effort of Member States to reduce their greenhouse gas emissions to meet the Community's greenhouse gas emission reduction commitments up to 2020 [2009] OJ L140/136. The reframing as 'effort' rather than 'burden' sharing obviously carries more positive overtones and can be linked with an ecological modernisation view of climate change mitigation, which sees it as providing opportunities and not just cost burdens, see Lacasta, above n 47, 103.

differentiation via GDP per capita rather than the more complex Triptych approach outlined earlier.[62] This move to base its equitable allocation on this measure of capacity to pay (with capacity associated, it will be recalled, with the CBDR principle) poses some awkward questions for the EU. As Haug and Jordan put it:

> One might . . . question whether a wealth-based approach to allocation sends out the signal to international partners that the EU desires. If GDP per capita was to form the basis for burden sharing in any post-2012 international agreement, the large emerging economies like China or India would probably be exempt from emissions reduction targets for many years to come.[63]

However, the Effort Sharing Decision should not be seen in isolation, because it formed part of the EU's overall package on climate change and energy. Thus burden sharing and equity in a more general sense should be judged in view of the package as a whole.[64] In this regard, the European Council Presidency conclusions of March 2007, which were a key driver behind the new 2008 Climate Change and Energy Package, recognised the need to adopt a fair or equitable approach as between the Member States:

> The European Council decides that a differentiated approach to the contributions of the Member States is needed reflecting fairness and transparency as well as taking into account national circumstances.[65]

The key elements to the package are the revised EU Emission Trading Scheme (ETS), the revised Directive on Renewable Energy, the Effort Sharing Decision (covering non-ETS sectors) and the Directive on Carbon Capture and Storage (CCS). The latter Directive need not detain us here because it has little in the way of inter-state distributional impact.

B. ETS

Although the Commission had, in its original Green Paper,[66] proposed an auction-based emissions trading scheme based on a centralised cap, the

[62] Decision No 406/2009/EC, ibid, preamble 8.

[63] Haug and Jordan, above n 43, 94.

[64] Lacasta, above n 47, 100.

[65] Brussels European Council, 8–9 March 2007: Presidency Conclusions, para 33. See also the Commission's Impact Assessment for its 2008 Climate Change package, which cites these conclusions in a section on 'Fairness' SEC/2008/0085 final, stating that 'The European Council in March 2007 recognised that it is necessary to take into account Member States' different circumstances and the reality that differing levels of prosperity have an impact on Member States' capacity to invest'.

[66] European Commission, 'Greenhouse Gas Emissions Trading within the European Union' (Green Paper) COM(2000) 87 final; JB Skoerseth and J Wettestad, 'The EU Emissions Trading System Revised (Directive 2009/29/EC)' in Oberthür and Pallemaerts, above n 47, 67.

first ETS Directive[67] involved a decentralised system of 'national allocation plans' (NAPs)[68] and one based primarily on free rather than auctioned allowances.[69] NAPs allowed Member States a degree of flexibility and differentiation—however, many claimed too much. The Commission's attempts at reining in some of this discretion led to significant EU level climate change litigation challenges before the Court of Justice, particularly by poorer Central and Eastern European (CEE) accession states.[70]

The revised ETS regime, under Directive 2009/29/EC,[71] has moved to a single, centralised EU-level cap, thus abandoning the NAPs. It has also moved, for the most part, to an auction based system. While the NAPs in the previous regime offered poorer accession states some room for manoeuvre, the new ETS system makes some allowance for equity considerations via arrangements for auctioning of allowances by Member States. Thus, Article 10c provides for transitional arrangements allowing a generous (but thereafter declining) proportion of non-auctioned, free allocation for certain installations in the power sector. With one of the relevant criteria based on GDP per capita, these provisions are very much designed with the power sector of CEE states in mind.[72] In addition, recital 17 of the preamble states:

> The objectives of eliminating distortions to intra-Community competition and of ensuring the highest degree of economic efficiency in the transformation of the Community economy towards a safe and sustainable low-carbon economy make it inappropriate to treat economic sectors differently under the Community scheme in individual Member States. It is therefore necessary to develop other mechanisms to support the efforts of those Member States with relatively lower income per capita and higher growth prospects.[73]

Reflecting this, Article 10(2)(a) provides that 88 per cent of the total EU quantity of allowances should be divided up among Member States based on historical emission levels during 2005-07 and then auctioned by those

[67] Directive 2003/87/EC of the European Parliament and of the Council establishing a scheme for greenhouse gas emission allowance trading within the Community [2003] OJ L275/32.

[68] Ibid, Art 9 states: 'each Member State shall develop a national plan stating the total quantity of allowances that it intends to allocate for that period and how it proposes to allocate them. The plan shall be based on objective and transparent criteria, including those listed in Annex III'.

[69] Ibid, Art 10 states: 'For the three-year period beginning 1 January 2005 Member States shall allocate at least 95% of the allowances free of charge. For the five-year period beginning 1 January 2008, Member States shall allocate at least 90% of the allowances free of charge'.

[70] On which see N Singh Ghaleigh, 'Emissions Trading before the European Court of Justice: Market Making in Luxemburg' in D Freestone and C Streck (eds), *Legal Aspects of Carbon Trading: Kyoto, Copenhagen and Beyond* (Oxford, Oxford University Press, 2009).

[71] Directive 2009/29/EC of the European Parliament and of the Council amending Directive 2003/87/EC so as to improve and extend the greenhouse gas emission allowance trading scheme of the Community [2009] OJ L140/63.

[72] See Lacasta, above n 47, 76, 80.

[73] Directive 2009/29/EC, above n 71, preamble, recital 17.

Member States in those proportions. However, for present purposes, what is noteworthy is the additional 10 per cent of the total quantity which is allocated, under Article 10(2)(b) to Member States in need of solidarity and additional space to grow:

> 10% of the total quantity of allowances to be auctioned being distributed amongst certain Member States for the purpose of solidarity and growth within the Community, thereby increasing the amount of allowances that those Member States auction under [10(2)(a)].[74]

C. Renewable Energy

Distributional issues do not appear to have been a central concern with the first Renewable Energy Directive 2001/77,[75] perhaps because of the indicative rather than mandatory nature of the targets set for each Member State. However, with the new Directive 2009/28/EC,[76] equity issues were a concern, partly because of the presence of the new Central and Eastern European states and partly because of the now mandatory nature of the targets.

The new Directive sets a goal of a 20 per cent share of energy from renewable sources and a 10 per cent share of energy from renewable sources in transport. These EU level targets are then translated into individual Member State targets. The 10 per cent target is a uniform one for all Member States due principally to concerns about fuel specification and availability. The 20 per cent target is shared out on a differentiated basis, with regard being had to Member States' different starting points and potential. Recital 15 states that:

> It is appropriate to do this by sharing the required total increase in the use of energy from renewable sources between Member States on the basis of an equal increase in each Member State's share weighted by their GDP, modulated to reflect their starting points, and by accounting in terms of gross final consumption of energy, with account being taken of Member States' past efforts with regard to the use of energy from renewable sources.[77]

[74] The remaining 2 per cent of the total quantity to be auctioned are 'distributed amongst Member States the greenhouse gas emissions of which were, in 2005, at least 20 per cent below their emissions in the base year applicable to them under the Kyoto Protocol' (Art 10(2)(c)).

[75] Directive 2001/77 of the European Parliament and of the Council of 27 September 2001 on the promotion of energy produced from renewable energy sources in the internal energy market [2001] OJ L283/33.

[76] Directive 2009/28/EC of the European Parliament and of the Council of 23 April 2009 on the promotion of the use of energy from renewable sources and amending and subsequently repealing Directives 2001/77/EC and 2003/30/EC [2009] OJ L140/16.

[77] Ibid, preamble, recital 15.

D. Analysis of Internal Policies

Looking across the raft of measures that make up the EU climate and energy package, one can see that, although there is no mention of CBDR in formal terms, issues key to CBDR—such as capacity to pay—play a central role, with consideration of GDP or GDP per capita a feature of the Effort Sharing Decision, the revised ETS and the new Renewables Directive. In addition, solidarity—which involves an equitable duty towards weaker states—also finds expression in the ETS Directive.

The question which then arises is whether, as Haug and Jordan intimated above,[78] this amounts to hypocrisy on the part of the EU because it is adopting, in a number of key areas, a GDP per capita approach internally but is unlikely to want to advocate such an approach for developing countries in its external policy. Here it is necessary to return to the argument introduced towards the start of the chapter: the answer is that the case of double standards depends on the background normative assumptions upon which one is relying. A cosmopolitan may see a potential case of double standards here: it is true that there is, in a very formalistic sense, no inconsistency, because the EU does not use CBDR internally; nevertheless, if the EU is differentiating between states internally based on GDP per capita but is not willing to countenance this externally, then this is problematic in cosmopolitan terms. However, if one adopts a more statist approach to climate justice, then one might plausibly argue that the EU is perfectly entitled to draw its solidarity community narrowly to include only its own Member States—to whom it is therefore allowed to grant favourable treatment which it would not extend to others internationally.

VI. ADAPTATION

Although the main focus of this chapter has been on mitigation, it is worth considering briefly the role which CBDR plays in relation to international and EU policy on adaptation to climate change. Despite the fact that adaptation has featured, to a greater or lesser extent in international UNFCCC COP documentation over the years, it is only relatively recently that we find mention of CBDR within sections dealing with adaptation. In the 2009 Copenhagen Accord, adaptation is mentioned in the same paragraph as CBDR, but comes much later and thus seems somewhat distanced from it.[79]

At Cancun in 2010, in contrast, we see a much closer nexus between the two, with the parties invited 'to enhance action on adaptation under

[78] Haug and Jordan, above n 63.

[79] See n 28, para 1.

the Cancun Adaptation Framework, taking into account their common but differentiated responsibilities and respective capabilities, and specific national and regional development priorities, objectives and circumstances'.[80] That said, there is little in the way of a strong sense of developed country responsibility for adaptation in developing countries: instead, developed country parties are merely 'requested' to provide developing countries 'with long-term, scaled-up, predictable, new and additional finance, technology and capacity-building' to implement adaptation.[81]

Turning to the EU, there is little or no mention of CBDR, or anything resembling it, in the various EU Environment Council conclusions related to particular UNFCCC COP meetings. There is a passing reference in the Bali Council conclusions to adaptation and then, in the same paragraph, 'the need to address the inequalities exacerbated by climate change'.[82] However, that is more or less it. Things are a little more positive when it comes to Commission policy documents, where internal and external aspects of adaptation policy have tended to sit side-by-side within the same document. The 2007 EU Green Paper on adaptation does not use the precise term CBDR. Nevertheless, it does use the language of responsibility to justify developed country support for adaptation in developing counties: 'Being responsible for most of the historic accumulation of anthropogenic greenhouse gas emissions in the atmosphere, developed countries will need to support adaptation actions in developing countries'.[83]

However, by the time of the 2009 Adaptation White Paper,[84] this reference had been deleted. Nevertheless, the White Paper does include some discussion of external EU action on adaptation. It mentions, for example, the need to work with, in particular, neighbouring countries and the most vulnerable developing countries to improve their resilience and adaptation capacity. It also talks of the need for adaptation to be 'mainstreamed' into all of the EU's external policies. However, CBDR specifically receives merely a passing reference in the White Paper in a footnote.[85] What it does mention is solidarity—but only internally: 'Adaptation will require solidarity among EU Member States to ensure that disadvantaged regions and regions most affected by climate change will be capable of taking the measures needed to adapt'.[86]

It will be interesting to see how EU policy on adaptation develops. However, a strong case can be made that CBDR should have a much

[80] See n 30, para 14.
[81] Ibid, para 18.
[82] See n 35, para 19.
[83] Commission, 'Adapting to Climate Change in Europe—Options For EU Action' (Green Paper) COM(2007) 354 final, 22.
[84] Commission, 'Adapting to Climate Change: Towards a European Framework for Action' (White Paper) COM(2009) 147 final.
[85] Ibid, fn 14.
[86] COM(2009) 147 final, above n 84, para 2.3.

more explicit presence in relation to external adaptation policy than it has at present. As things stand, there is an uneasy tension in the White Paper between emphasising solidarity internally and making little mention of CBDR in relation to external action on adaptation.

VII. CONCLUSION

This chapter has attempted to add to the existing literature by providing a fuller account, than can be found there, of the formal usage of CBDR in both international law and policy on climate change and EU external policy in the area. The latter, in particular, has never been examined systematically, and even the former has not been explored historically through the various COPs associated with the UNFCCC.

The chapter then analysed EU internal policy on climate change where, though the formal language of CBDR is absent, many of the underlying ideas associated with it are also to be found. The key question posed was whether EU climate policy can be accused of double standards, with a different approach being adopted to the basis for differentiation externally than the one adopted in relation to the EU's own Member States internally. The suggested answer was that a case of hypocrisy was only made out if one's underlying normative assumptions are cosmopolitan in nature. However, the EU does need to address the issue of CBDR much more explicitly in relation to its external policy on adaptation. As things stand, there is clearly a risk of inconsistency between considering solidarity internally on adaptation and yet not considering the functionally equivalent CBDR in relation to external policy. There is also the risk of an inconsistency in terms of consideration of CBDR as between EU policies on mitigation and those on adaptation.

12

*Beyond the Either/Or: Dual Attribution to the European Union and to the Member State for Breach of the ECHR**

ENZO CANNIZZARO

I. INTRODUCTION

THE ACCESSION OF the EU (European Union) to the European Convention of Human Rights (ECHR) constitutes an important yardstick for appraising, and possibly for developing, the law governing the responsibility of international organisations.

It is common knowledge that an attempt to codify this law was undertaken by the ILC, which approved the draft Articles on the Responsibility of International Organisations, at its 63rd session in 2011 and which were noted by the General Assembly later that year.[1] In the course of its work, one of the most controversial issues was the question of attribution to, and responsibility of, international organisations for conduct carried out by organs of their Member States. The difficulties encountered by the ILC in this regard mirror the uncertainties in scholarly opinions and the inconsistencies in international practice.[2]

One context in which issues of attribution are likely to be of relevance is litigation before the European Court of Human Rights (ECtHR) involving the alleged breach of the Convention by EU Member States when acting

* An account of the provisional outcome of further negotiations on the Accession Treaty which resumed in the autumn of 2012, and which are still in progress at the time of writing, is given in a postscript at page 359.

[1] With resolution 66/100 of 9 December 2011, the General Assembly took note of the draft articles and decided to include the item in the agenda of its sixty-ninth session, to be held in 2014.

[2] See the cases discussed in the Second Report of the Special Rapporteur, Giorgio Gaja, UN Doc A/CN 4/541 of 2 April 2004, and the Seventh Report of the Special Rapporteur, Giorgio Gaja, UN Doc A/CN 4/610 of 27 March 2009.

within the framework of EU law. The consideration of the case law of the ECtHR was widely considered in the works of codification of the ILC and might have inspired some solutions adopted in the draft Articles.

Hitherto, the consideration of such issues was governed by the fact that the Member States are parties to the Convention but the EU is not. Attribution of conduct to the EU would therefore have the effect of removing such actions from the scope of the Convention *rationes personae*. Yet, following the indication of Art 6, para 1, of the TEU, on 4 June 2010, the Council of the Union decided to commence negotiations on the accession of the EU, nominated the European Commission as Union negotiator and adopted negotiating Directives. Given the prospect of the EU's accession to the ECHR, one might expect that the issue of attribution will become increasingly significant in its future case law.

The negotiating Directives do not set out any particular positions regarding the question of attribution, but they do deal with the issue indirectly. In the part concerning issues of procedure before the ECtHR, they point out that proceedings must involve Member States and/or the Union, as appropriate. By using the and/or dyad, the Council seems to recognise that applications for alleged breaches of the Convention could be brought against multiple defendants: one or more of the Member States and/or the EU itself. The Directives further establish a principle which must be included in the accession agreement. According to that principle, either entity, the EU or one or more of its Member States, has the right to join the proceedings commenced against the other when there is an intrinsic link between the alleged violation of the Convention and its law. Thus, without expressly addressing the issue of attribution, the negotiating Directives made it clear that this is an issue which the Accession Treaty has to address and, more broadly, that this issue needs to be clarified in order to determine the future relationship between the EU and the Member States as parties to the ECHR, within the scope of their respective competence.

Resolving these questions is proving to be a lengthy and complex task. It is well known that an informal group was set up by the Steering Committee for Human Rights (CDDH) of the Committee of Ministers of the Council of Europe, to negotiate with the Commission. The negotiations commenced with great enthusiasm but soon became considerably more problematic than had been expected. At the time of writing, there is no final outcome; indeed, there is growing anxiety as to the capacity of the negotiators to agree on all the controversial points at stake.

Among these points, one of the most controversial remains the identification of the appropriate entity, the EU and/or one or more of its Member States, against which proceedings are to be commenced before the ECtHR in a given case, since it entails the need to determine a test for attributing the wrongful conduct. There are a number of reasons why this issue is so particularly difficult. First, the relations between the Union and its

Member States are particularly complex and unlikely to be captured by a pre-determined univocal scheme. Secondly, the obligations deriving from the ECHR are themselves multifarious in nature: some can be breached through executive action only, others can be breached by normative action, whilst others require a combination of the two.

For all these reasons, there is good reason to explore this issue in greater detail. Section II will consider, broadly and briefly, the rules on attribution laid down in the draft Articles on the Responsibility of International Organisations, and assess the adequacy of their approach to the future relationship between the EU and its Member States in the context of the ECHR. Section III will look at the case law of the ECtHR in order to search for general trends which might provide guidance when seeking to identify a workable test for attribution. Section IV, critically considers the solutions which are being worked out in the course of the negotiation of the Accession Treaty. It will be argued that the accession agreement should avoid the 'either/or' dichotomy inherent in the classical rules on attribution and adopt a dual attribution rule.[3] Finally, the virtues and the inevitable drawbacks of such an approach will be considered.

II. ATTRIBUTION: AN INSIDIOUS NOTION IN THE LAW OF INTERNATIONAL RESPONSIBILITY

A. Committing Wrongful Conduct through the Exercise of EU Competences?

In the classical conceptualisation of the law of international responsibility, it is widely accepted that the same wrongful act may entail a number of secondary consequences of both a substantive and instrumental procedural nature. In contrast, international law has traditionally taken a very cautious approach when considering the possibility of attributing the same conduct to more than one subject. Thus, whereas there might be a plurality of actors responsible for the same conduct, dual or multiple attribution, although not expressly excluded, seems to be confined to exceptional situations.[4]

[3] Terminology in this regard varies considerably. In this chapter I will use the term 'dual attribution' as meaning something different from 'dual responsibility'. Dual responsibility means that two, or possibly more, entities are distinctly responsible for the same wrongful event brought about by individual conduct in breach of different obligations. This is well epitomised by the decision of the ECtHR in *Ilaşcu and others v Moldova and Russia*, no 48787/99, judgment of 8 July 2004. Dual responsibility is thus to be kept well distinct from forms of joint or collective responsibility. Dual attribution, a term only recently popularised, has a broader and less precise scope and should mean that the same conduct can be attributed to two or, possibly, more entities, which have concurred in bringing about the same event.

[4] See *ILC's Commentary of the Articles on the Responsibility of IOs*, UN doc A/66/10, 81: 'Although it may not frequently occur in practice, dual or even multiple attribution

This is logical enough when the wrongful act consists of a single instance of conduct, whether it be an action or an omission, and which is necessarily to be attributed to one entity. However, a similar approach is also taken in cases where the wrongful act constitutes the final result of a chain of actions and omissions, each of which has been performed by different actors. Whilst it is perfectly possible for each action or omission to produce legal consequences for the separate actors or entities engaged in its commission, the wrongful act tends to be conceived of as the final product of the chain, and is generally attributed to a single entity.

The need to identify the author of a breach which consists of a sequence of actions performed by different actors makes the issue of attribution a crucial one in the law of Responsibility of International Organisations. Particular difficulties arise where the international organisation is the EU, an entity which exercises a wide normative competence but whose normative acts are mainly brought into being through the actions of organs of the Member States.

The attribution of wrongful conduct to the EU is relatively straightforward where there is a direct and immediate correspondence between the obligation breached and the exercise of EU competence. It is considerably more difficult where the obligation breached requires material conduct by Member States, with the exercise of EU competence constituting the legal pre-condition for the action taken by them. This is certainly the situation as regards most human rights obligations, which typically are not breached through the enactment of legal rules by the EU, but rather by implementing action on the part of the Member States.

In those cases where the conduct of a Member State is intended to implement EU rules, the alleged breach has a composite origin: rather than being univocally linked to a single international actor, it is the culmination of a series of linked, though segmented, actions. Both of the two entities, the EU and the Member States, have contributed to it, though neither can be considered as its sole author. The question which arises

of conduct cannot be excluded. Thus, attribution of a certain conduct to an international organisation does not imply that the same conduct cannot be attributed to a State; nor does attribution of conduct to a State rule out attribution of the same conduct to an international organisation'. In its recent decision of 5 July 2011, *Nuhanovic v Netherlands*, para 5.9, the Court of Appeal of The Hague seems to have admitted, albeit only theoretically, the possibility to attribute conduct performed by a national contingent in the context of a UN peacekeeping operation to both the sending state and the UN (text in *Oxford Reports on International Law in Domestic Courts*, ILDC 1742 (NL 2011)). Noteworthy, the existence of a dual attribution was pointed out in the context of the 'effective control' test; this should entail that if two entities have individually the duty to prevent a certain event from occurring, and if they have the effective power to do so, their failure to act must be simultaneously attributed to either one. On the decision of the Court of Appeals, see A Nollkaemper, 'Dual Attribution. Liability of the Netherlands for Conduct in Dutchbat in Srebrenica' (2012) 9 *Journal of International Criminal Justice* 1143. On dual attribution, in general terms, see L Condorelli, 'Le statut des forces de l'ONU et le droit international humanitaire' (1995) 78 *Rivista di diritto internazionale* 881, 893ff.

is to which of the actors is the breach to be attributed, alternatively or cumulatively, and which must assume responsibility for it?

B. The Effective Control Test in the Works of Codification of the Law of Responsibility of International Organisations

The ILC draft Articles adopt a rigid distinction between attribution and responsibility, and take a strict approach to attribution. Wrongful acts are attributed to an international organisation only if such acts are performed by its organs or, if they are performed by the organs of a Member State or another international organisation, if they do so under its strict and operative control.

The general rule on attribution of conduct performed by state organs placed at the disposal of an international organisation is set out in Draft Article 7, which provides:

> The conduct of an organ of a State or an organ or agent of an international organisation that is placed at the disposal of another international organiszation shall be considered under international law an act of the latter organisation if the organisation exercises effective control over that conduct.

Thus the test for attribution is whether the organ is acting under the effective control of the international organisation. The commentary to the Articles makes clear that it has the effect of attributing to the organisation single actions performed under its direct operational control.[5] It does not result in acts which are in fact performed by organs of Member States being attributed to the international organisation, even though they are performed at its behest and under its 'ultimate' control.

The strictness of this approach based on effective control is mitigated to a degree by the adoption of a more flexible approach to the distribution of responsibility. The draft Articles contain provisions dealing specifically with the responsibility of international organisations as regards the conduct of states and other international organisations. In particular, Article 17(1) indicates that the use of normative power by an international organisation might engage its international responsibility if it imposes, or even authorises, conduct inconsistent with its international obligations. This provision, however, does not go as far as attributing responsibility to the international organisation for their role in relation to wrongful conduct of the Member State. It only relates to situations in which an international

[5] Official Records of the General Assembly, Sixty-sixth session, Supplement No 10 (A/66/10), 23. For a recent assessment of the notion of "effective" control" under Art 7, see T Dannenbaum, 'Translating the Standard of Effective Control into a System of Effective Accountability: How Liability Should Be Apportioned for Violations of Human Rights by Member State Troops Contingents as United Nations Peacekeepers' (2010) 51 *Harvard International Law Review* 113.

organisation uses its normative power to bring about a course of conduct by a Member State rather than undertake that course of conduct itself, and which would have been unlawful had it done so. It therefore attributes direct responsibility to the international organisation for inducing Member States to perform conduct in lieu of the organisation itself. Consistently with this idea, Article 17(3) makes it clear that international organisations would incur responsibility for imposing or authorising conduct by states in such circumstances even if that conduct did not in and of itself amount to a breach of the state's own international obligations.

This makes it clear that the two kinds of responsibility—the responsibility of an international organisation for its own normative activity under Article 17(1), and responsibility arising out of wrongful conduct of states acting under the effective control of an international organisation under Article 7—are different in nature. Whereas under Article 7 an international organisation incurs responsibility for wrongful conduct, under Article 17 its conduct is not unlawful as such. The differing nature of responsibility in these two situations also entails different legal consequences, reflecting the different content of the international organisations' responsibility in each of them.

Be that as it may, neither of these two legal approaches to attribution of responsibility seems to apply neatly to the various situations created by actions taken jointly by the EU and by its Member States which seems to straddle the boundaries between them and thus require a combination, in different degrees, of the normative elements of both in order to capture the essence of the situation. As things stand, situations in which the EU exerts normative influence over conduct of Member States which results in those states acting in breach of their international legal obligations tends to fall outside of the classical framework established to address the international responsibility of international organisations.

III. THE CASE LAW OF THE EUROPEAN COURT OF HUMAN RIGHTS

In judicial practice, issues of attribution to the EU of conduct amounting to a breach of human rights obligations have been considered almost exclusively by the ECtHR. A common feature of these cases is the tendency of the Court to attribute to the Member State conduct allegedly in breach of the Convention, regardless of the fact that the conduct in question was taken in pursuance of normative measures enacted by the EU. The most obvious explanation for this is that, for the time being, it is only the Member States and not the Union itself which are parties to the ECHR. Thus attributing conduct to the EU would have resulted in the conduct falling outside the scope of the Convention, resulting in a gap in its system of protection.[6]

If one looks more closely at these cases, however, there are useful insights to be had since they shed light on the most common situations in which the action of the EU interfaces with that of the Member States as regards questions of human rights and do offer some guidance on how the resulting problems might be resolved. In particular, the case law seems to suggest that it may be possible to develop a number of possible tests for the purpose of attribution. The first tends to give importance to the degree of discretion left to national authorities when implementing EU obligations. The second tends to focus on the nature of the legal act which gives rise to the alleged violation of the Convention. The third focuses on the degree of normative control exerted by one entity upon the other.

A. Cantoni and the Degree of Discretion to National Authorities

A first approach, conceptually very simple, is to consider the binding effect of the measures taken by the EU and the degree of discretion which the Member State has as regards its implementation. In a number of cases in which it has been alleged that Member States have been in breach of the Convention, the Member States have argued that their conduct ought to be attributed to the EU since it is the implementation of EU rules which require them to act in breach of their obligations under the Convention.

The possibility of attributing responsibility to the EU in situations where conduct allegedly inconsistent with the ECHR was imposed on Member States by a binding EU measure has been considered and rejected by the Court in a number of cases. In *M v Federal Republic of Germany*,[7] the applicant complained that a writ issued by German authorities for giving effect to a fine decided by the European Commission (at that time the 'Commission of the European Communities'), and upheld by the ECJ, was in violation of Art 6 of the European Convention. Germany asked that the

[6] This was the practical effect of the decision of the Court in *Behrani v France; Saramati v France, Germany and Norway*, no 71412/01 and 78166/01, decision of 2 May 2007 where responsibility was attributed to the United Nations rather than to its Member States. A different course was taken in *Al-Jedda v the United Kingdom*, no 27021/08, judgment of 7 July 2011. In this case, the ECtHR, applied two different test: the 'effective control' test envisaged by the draft Arts on the Law of Responsibility of International Organisation and the 'ultimate authority and control' test. The Court concluded that the internment of the applicant within a military detention facility run by British troops in Iraq, whose deployment was authorised by the UN Security Council, could not be attributed to the UN, since the UN had neither effective control nor ultimate authority and control over the acts and omissions of troops within the Multi-National Force. Consequently, the conduct was to be attributed solely to the UK. *Cf* paras 83–84.

[7] *M & Co v Federal Republic of Germany*, no 13258/87, decision of 9 January 1990. This was in fact decided by the European Commission on Human Rights, prior to its being abolished in 1998 by Protocol No 11 to the European Convention.

European Commission of Human Rights dismiss the case, claiming that it could not be 'responsible under the Convention for acts and decisions of the European Communities'.[8] The European Commission of Human Rights did not take a position on the issue of attribution, observing that 'a transfer of powers does not necessarily exclude a state's responsibility under the Convention with regard to the exercise of the transferred powers' and that states are thus required to ensure that the guarantees of the Convention remain 'practical and effective'. However, whilst a state party remained liable for any 'resulting breach' of the Convention, the Commission took the view that 'the transfer of powers to an international organisation is not incompatible with the Convention provided that within that organisation fundamental rights will receive an equivalent protection'.

In *Cantoni*[9] the ECtHR had to face similar objections raised by the defendant state. The Court was asked to decide whether a French national statutory provision which made it a criminal offence to sell medical products outside a pharmacy was in breach of Article 7 of the European Convention due to a lack of precision in the definition of the prohibited conduct. France claimed that it ought not to be held responsible under the Convention since the statutory provisions were introduced in order to implement a Directive which, in spite of its nature, did not leave the Member State with any margin for discretion as to the manner of implementation. In a rather terse passage, the Court found that 'the fact, pointed to by the Government, that Article L. 511 of the Public Health Code is based almost word for word on Community Directive 65/65 (did) not remove it from the ambit of Article 7'. Although very concise, this passage conveys the idea that state action performed in order to fulfil an obligation under EU law still remains an act attributable to the state for the purposes of the European Convention, and must be subject the same degree of scrutiny under the Convention system, as any other act of that state.

B. Matthews and the Legal Nature of the Act

A different situation, conceptually the opposite from that in *Cantoni*, was considered by the ECtHR in *Matthews*.[10] The applicant in *Matthews* claimed that the exclusion of residents of Gibraltar from being able to

[8] Germany argued that 'the Federal Minister of Justice, in granting a writ of execution for a judgment of the European Court of Justice, did not have to examine whether the judgment in question had been reached in proceedings compatible with fundamental rights guaranteed by the European Convention on Human Rights or the German Basic Law. He only had to examine whether the judgment was authentic. Therefore he neither had to determine a civil right, nor a criminal charge within the meaning of Art 6 of the Convention'.

[9] *Cantoni v France*, no 17862/91, judgment of 15 November 1996.

[10] *Matthews v the United Kingdom*, no 24833/94, judgment of 18 February 1999.

vote in elections to the European Parliament (a situation resulting from Annex II of the Act concerning the election of the representatives of the European Parliament by direct universal suffrage of 20 September 1976) amounted to a breach of Protocol I, which provides for the right to free elections.

In the proceedings before the Court the parties expressed different views regarding the nature of the Act which laid at the heart of the alleged breach and, consequently, on the attribution of the allegedly wrongful conduct. In the UK's view, this Act, having the status of a treaty, was to be assimilated to an Act of the EU Institutions. It was 'adopted in the Community framework and could not be revoked or varied unilaterally by the United Kingdom'. In the UK's opinion, this meant that the Court should dismiss the claim since it could not be held responsible for possible violations which were the result of an Act of the EU. The applicant drew the opposite conclusion, maintaining that since the 1976 Act was an international treaty entered into by the UK, the breach of the European Convention which the Act brought into being was to be attributed to the UK and it was the UK which was to be held responsible.

The Court endorsed the views of the applicant. It did not enter into a discussion of the nature and effect of the 1976 Act under EU law, but limited its analysis to the process of formation of the Act under international law. Proceeding on this basis, the Court could easily conclude that, whereas

> acts of the EC as such cannot be challenged before the Court because the EC is not a Contracting Party . . . in the present case, the alleged violation of the Convention flows from an annex to the 1976 Act, entered into by the United Kingdom, together with the extension to the European Parliament's competences brought about by the Maastricht Treaty. The Council Decision and the 1976 Act, and the Maastricht Treaty, with its changes to the EEC Treaty, all constituted international instruments which were freely entered into by the United Kingdom.[11]

As a result, the Court found that depriving British citizens residing in Gibraltar the right to vote in elections to the European Parliament amounted to a violation by the United Kingdom of its obligations under Article 3 of the First Protocol to the ECHR.

Unlike the cases mentioned in the previous paragraph, in the *Matthews* case the Court engaged in a close analysis of the process underlying the action alleged to form the basis of the breach of the Convention; it gave considerable importance to the role of state consent in that process, and downplayed the nature of the act within the EU legal system. Arguably, the fact that the legal nature of acts of this type is highly disputed within the EU legal system, meaning that it could not easily be equated to an

[11] Ibid, para 33.

act of the EU, might be a reason not to make any generalisations on the basis of this decision. *Matthews* also highlights the ambiguous nature of some such acts and suggests that it may be necessary to look beyond the formal nature of EU acts in order to understand the real role of Member States in their process of formation.

C. Bosphorus and the 'Ultimate Normative Control' Test

In *Bosphorus*, the Court was called to decide whether Ireland should be considered responsible under the European Convention for actions which it performed under the normative influence of EU law. The applicant, the Turkish company *Bosphorus*, claimed that by impounding an aircraft, which it was leasing from a Yugoslavia company, Ireland was breaching the right to property protected by Article 1 of the First Protocol. The Irish measure was taken in order to implement EU Regulation 990/93/EC, which was in turn giving effect to the sanctions regime adopted by the UN Security Council against Yugoslavia, and in particular UN Resolution 820 (1993). The EU Regulation was preceded by a decision taken by the Member States in the framework of political cooperation and, in the words of the ECJ, through this act, the Member States decided 'to have recourse to a Community instrument to implement in the Community certain aspects of the sanctions taken against the Federal Republic of Yugoslavia by the Security Council of the United Nations'.[12]

The reasoning of the European Court is well known. First, the Court engaged in a lengthy and complex demonstration that the Irish measures were 'not the result of an exercise of discretion by the Irish authorities, but rather amounted to compliance by the Irish State with its legal obligations flowing from Community law'.[13] This conclusion was not exclusively based on the binding effect of Regulation 990/93/EC but also on the basis of the decision of the ECJ which had binding force upon the Irish judges who had referred the question to it (C-84/95).[14] As a result, the legality of the impounding of the aircraft within the EU legal order was firmly established. Second, the Court found that the EU 'is not itself held responsible under the Convention for proceedings before, or decisions of, its organs as long as it is not a Contracting Party'.[15] The consequence of this finding was that Ireland was held responsible for conduct of its organs, albeit its conduct was dictated by acts of the EU.

[12] See ECJ, Case C-84/95 *Bosphorus Hava Yollari Turizm ve Ticaret AS v Minister for Transport, Energy and Communications and others*, judgment of 30 July 1996, [1996] ECR I-03953.

[13] See n 10, para 148.

[14] See n 10.

[15] Ibid, para 152.

Finally, the Court devised a means of attenuating the responsibility of the EU Member States when they act in compliance with EU law, stating that

> State action taken in compliance with such legal obligations is justified as long as the relevant organisation is considered to protect fundamental rights, as regards both the substantive guarantees offered and the mechanisms controlling their observance, in a manner which can be considered at least equivalent to that for which the Convention provides.[16]

At the same time, the Court in *Bosphorus* reaffirmed that states are unconditionally responsible under the Convention when they are giving effect to obligations 'freely entered into' by them.[17] Therefore, in order to determine in which situations states will be held responsible under the Convention, *Bosphorus* seems to call for a comprehensive evaluation, seeking to identify, in each case, whether it is the EU or the Member State which has ultimate normative control effective enough to direct the action of the other.

The application of this test, however, might give rise to considerable difficulty. The *Bosphorus* case itself[18] shows that the search for the entity which exercises ultimate control might prove almost impossible in the context of the multifaceted political and constitutional setting of the EU. The content of the Irish measure was entirely predetermined by the EU Regulation which in turn was enacted to give effect to a decision of the Member States in the framework of political cooperation, the process of adoption of which indisputably relied on the unanimous consent of the Member States themselves.[19] From both a factual and a legal point of view, the identification of the entity which directed, through its normative activity, the action of the other remains highly controversial.

[16] Ibid, para 155. For a recent case in which the ECtHR exercised effective scrutiny in order to assess the respondent states' compliance with the principle of equivalent protection, see *Gasparini v Italy and Belgium*, no 10750703, judgment of 12 May 2009. The Court concluded that 'the protection afforded to the applicant in the present case by NATO's internal dispute resolution mechanism was not "manifestly deficient" within the meaning given to that expression by the *Bosphorus* judgment, particularly in the specific context of an organisation such as NATO'.

[17] Ibid, para 157.

[18] For an examination of the issues of attribution raised in *Bosphorus*, see G Gaja, 'The Review by the European Court of Human Rights of Member States' Acts Implementing European Union Law: "Solange" Yet Again?' in P-M Dupuy, B Fassbaender, MN Shaw and KP Sommermann (eds), *Völkerrecht als Wertordnung. Festschrift für Christian Tomuschat* (Kehl, NP Angel Verlag, 2006) 518.

[19] In its judgment of 30 July 1996, Case C-84/95 *Bosphorus Hava Yollari Turizm ve Ticaret AS v Minister for Transport, Energy and Communications and others*, above n 11, the ECJ said: 'it should be noted that by Regulation No 990/93 the Council gave effect to the decision of the Community and its Member States, meeting within the framework of political cooperation, to have recourse to a Community instrument to implement in the Community certain aspects of the sanctions taken against the Federal Republic of Yugoslavia by the Security Council of the United Nations . . .' (para 13).

Although not expressly dealing with attribution, the *Bosphorus* case illustrates difficulties surrounding this process in the intricate context of EU-Member State relationships. It highlights the need to consider the force of law whilst at the same time recognizing the weaknesses and ambiguities of this approach. Not surprisingly, in spite of the many different readings offered by international scholars, the case still defies clear explanation and remains somewhat impenetrable.

IV. TOWARDS A SPECIAL RULE ON ATTRIBUTION?

A. Implications from the Analysis: Effective Approach v Normative Approach

The analysis presented in Section III leads to a double-edged conclusion. On the one hand, it demonstrates the difficulty of applying a test of attribution which is based on the 'effective control' approach adopted in the Draft Articles on the Responsibility of International Organisations. On the other hand, it also illustrates the difficulties which flow from adopting tantalizing but insidious alternative tests and, in particular, the 'ultimate normative control' test.

The approach based on 'effective control' does not seem capable of capturing all the subtleties of the relationships between the EU and its Member States. In particular, it fails to work properly in situations where organs of one entity discharge functions on behalf of, or even under the direction of, organs of another. This is frequently the case as regards administrative organs of a state which are called to enact measures whose content is predetermined by the administration organs of the EU.

Significantly, however, the practice of co-administration also offers examples, albeit less frequent, which work in the opposite direction; that is, measures taken by EU organs which are predetermined by the national organs of Member States, as in the case of *Oleificio Borelli*.[20] In such situations, the degree of the normative control exercised by the organs of one entity upon the organs of the other seems to be an important factor for determining attribution. Similar examples of ad hoc hierarchical relations can be found in other areas, such as the binding effect of decisions of the ECJ upon national judges who have made referrals to the Court. It seems safe to conclude that it is difficult to determine attribution in situations where the combined action of both EU and Member State organs are at issue and both have contributed to the course of conduct in question.

On the other hand, it would be unwarranted to regard normative control as the only criterion for attribution. As the *Bosphorus* case shows,

[20] Judgment of 3 December 1992, Case C-97/91 [1992] ECR I-6313.

there is a fundamental tension between autonomy and dependence within the EU legal order. The adoption of the normative control approach inevitably raises the question of how to determine the degree of normative influence necessary to entail attribution in a given case, bearing in mind that there are many potentially applicable approaches, such as exclusive or shared competence; binding acts or soft law; direct or indirect effect, and so on, and not all need point to the same outcome even in relation to the same situation.

Finally, focussing on the normative dimension is difficult to combine with traditional understandings of attribution, and in particular with the idea that conduct may be attributed to an entity even when it is acting ultra vires, since this implies that an action may be attributed to an entity even if it is beyond the limits of its normative competence.[21] It is not coherent to assume that the conduct of state organs acting under EU law is to be attributed to the EU when it is in accordance with EU law, but must be attributed to the Member States when it is in breach of EU law. This is tantamount to saying that the normative approach determines attribution only when the law is effectively complied with. Yet the degree of effectiveness of legal obligations is an important, perhaps the most important, criteria when applying the normative approach.

These observations demonstrate the difficulties of determining attribution, in this particular context at least, through an either/or scheme. Attribution is, by nature, an all-or-nothing notion that does not mesh easily with the more nuanced and multi-coloured logic which inspires the legal relationship between the EU and its Member State, in particular in the field of the obligations deriving from a human rights treaty addressing both entities within their respective field of competence.

All this seems to point to the need for a special rule on attribution to be included in the EU accession agreement to the European Convention on Human Rights. The possibility of a *lex specialis* applicable to the EU was also envisaged by the ILC Draft Article 64, which provides that:

> These draft articles do not apply where and to the extent that the conditions for the existence of an internationally wrongful act or the content or implementation of the international responsibility of an international organisation, or of a State in connection with the conduct of an international organisation, are governed by special rules of international law. Such special rules of international law may be contained in the rules of the organisation applicable to the relations between an international organisation and its members.

[21] See Art 8 of the Draft Articles on the Responsibility of International Organisations, which provides that '[t]he conduct of an organ or agent of an international organisation shall be considered an act of that organisation under international law if the organ or agent acts in an official capacity and within the overall functions of that organisation, even if the conduct exceeds the authority of that organ or agent or contravenes instructions'.

Moreover, in its Commentary to Article 64 (*Lex Specialis*), the ILC refers to the approach taken by a number of WTO panels, noting that:

> [T]his approach implies admitting the existence of a special rule on attribution, to the effect that, in the case of a European Community act binding a Member State, state authorities would be considered as acting as organs of the Community.[22]

B. The Co-respondent Mechanism

This idea might have inspired the drafting of the rule including a co-respondent mechanism, allowing either entity, the EU or one of the Member States, to act as a co-respondent in proceedings brought against the other entity before the ECtHR.

This mechanism, broadly envisaged by the negotiating Directives adopted by the Council in 2010, was included in various versions in the draft accession agreement. The difference between these versions does not allow one to identify clearly the legal nature of this mechanism. The most immediate impression is that it aims at establishing, without making it obvious, a special rule on attribution. Alternatively, this mechanism could be seen as rendering superfluous the search for the sole author of the breach and replacing it with an approach which seeks to distribute responsibility among a plurality of entities which have contributed to the breach without the need to identify one entity as the sole author.

The draft accession treaty seems to consider that the co-respondent will be a full-fledged party to the proceedings before the ECtHR. The status of the co-respondent as a party to the proceedings arguably should mean that it will be considered as a co-author of the alleged violation.[23] As a party to the proceedings, the co-respondent would be under a legal obligation to abide by the judgments of the Court and to bear the responsibility flowing from that violation.[24]

The decision to include this mechanism in the Accession Treaty was probably inspired by a sense of expediency. The co-respondent mechanism offers significant advantages for the entities party to the Convention and for individual applicants. The EU and the Member States might claim the right to be party to the proceedings. This would allow the EU to present before the ECtHR arguments related to EU law without having to rely on the Member States. Applicants might also avoid the complicated operation

[22] UN doc A/66/10, 167.

[23] This conclusion emerges from the reading of Art 34 of the ECHR, which indicates that proceedings are started by applicants claiming 'to be the victim of a violation by one of the High Contracting Parties of the rights set forth in the Convention or the protocols thereto'.

[24] See Art 46, para 1, ECHR, which envisages that '(t)he High Contracting Parties undertake to abide by the final judgment of the Court in any case to which they are parties'.

of singling out which entity has committed the allegedly wrongful conduct: in most cases a *probatio diabolica*.

Beyond such practical or pragmatic motivations, however, the co-respondent mechanism also has sound theoretical underpinnings. It expresses the idea that, where the competence of the EU and of the Member State is closely interwoven and a breach is the result of composite conduct, either the breach must be collectively attributed or, without prejudice to the issues of attribution, the various entities involved must accept responsibility for their contribution to the breach. This does not, however, necessarily entail a collective allocation of responsibility: an issue which remains outside the scope of this Chapter.[25]

The co-respondent mechanism reflects the fact that there might be situations in which the application of the classical test on attribution will lead to inappropriate or untenable solutions. However, in the light of the difficulties in determining in the abstract what such situations may be, this special rule on attribution should be flexibly applied and have as wide a scope of application as possible.

These were the features of the co-respondent mechanism which emerged from the first draft of the Accession Treaty. Article 4 of that draft conceived this mechanism as a flexible tool to be used in proceedings brought against one entity, either the EU or one or more of the Member States, in situations where there was an apparent 'substantial link' between the alleged violation and other entity.

Clearly, this lacked precision and prompted the observation that the requirement of a substantial link does not clarify how substantial that link must be to justify the triggering of the mechanism. On the other hand, this was probably one of the test's main virtues. It would be incoherent to assume, on the one hand, that a special rule is needed to overcome the rigidity of the rules on attribution and, on the other hand, to rigidly pre-determine the situations in which such a special rule must apply. It is much more appropriate to have an expansive approach to such a special rule, without pre-determining the situations in which it might apply, leaving it to subsequent practice to identify the precise scope of its application.

In the course of the negotiations, however, the mechanism underwent significant changes. Without entering into details, and without investigating the reasons for the change, the final draft, made public in July 2011,[26] made the functioning of the mechanism dependent upon the degree of discretion enjoyed by the entity that performed the final act. If such conduct

[25] As pointed out above, dual attribution of the conduct does not necessarily entail that responsibility must be allocated according to a dual or to a collective scheme. Nor dual or collective responsibility is necessarily based on dual attribution of the wrongful conduct. An example of dual responsibility which does not entail dual attribution of the conduct comes from the above mentioned decision of the ECtHR *Ilascu and others v Russia and Moldova*, no 48878/99, judgment of 8 July 2004.

[26] Doc CDDH-UE (2011), fn 16.

is performed by a Member State, the EU is entitled to join the proceedings as a co-respondent only if it is proven that the violation could have been avoided by disregarding an EU law obligation incumbent upon the acting state. In other words, the EU cannot be a co-respondent if EU law does not impose upon the Member State obligations inconsistent with the ECHR, either because the Member State has a margin of discretion allowing them to implement binding EU law in accordance with the obligations flowing from the European Convention, or because the conduct inconsistent with the Convention is not required by EU law but simply recommended or authorised. Conversely, if the conduct in question is carried out by the EU, a Member State can be a co-respondent only if the violation could have been avoided only by disregarding an obligation incumbent upon the EU by virtue of an act which only the Member State can repeal. This provision is intended to prevent the Member State from being a co-respondent unless the EU action allegedly in breach of the Convention is not required by the founding treaties.

Thus, the scope of the mechanism of the co-respondent tends to interest with the two situations evoked in *Cantoni* and in *Matthews*. In *Cantoni*, the defendant state claimed to be exempted from responsibility under the Convention because it had acted under a binding EC act which left no margin for discretion. On the basis of the provision included in the draft accession treaty, the EU would have the right to join such proceedings as a co-respondent, since the national statute, whose application was at the origin of the alleged breach, was the simple reproduction of provisions of a EU Directive, which predetermined the action of the Member State organs. In *Matthews*, the applicant claimed that the attribution of the conduct to the UK was the result of the particular nature of the 1976 Act, an international treaty freely entered into by the Member State and binding on the EC. After the Accession Treaty, such a claim would be presumably brought against the EU, and, in such a case, the UK would have the right to join the proceedings as a co-respondent, since the EU's action was completely pre-determined by an act adopted by the Member State whose formation was based on the consent of the UK.

However, this approach also has its shortcomings. It is based on a facile paradigm according to which an entity can be a co-respondent only if it has compelled the other to commit the alleged breach. This solution is not a felicitous one, as it does not take sufficiently into account the effect of non-binding acts. For example, the EU could not join as co-respondent proceedings started by individuals against acts taken by national antitrust authorities following the guidance contained in non-binding notices of the Commission on antitrust law, in spite of the high degree of effectiveness of these instruments. Likewise, one of the entities, either the EU or the Member States, cannot join proceedings started before the European Court against the final act adopted by the other, that concludes a complex procedure of co-administration, composed of binding and non-binding measures and deliberations of administrative organs of either entities: since each act of the sequence exerts varying degrees of influence on the other, none can be deemed to predetermine the content of the final act.

As has been said, one of the aims of the co-respondent mechanism should be to facilitate the search for the author of the breach, which might prove a difficult task for individuals that have suffered harm. To achieve this, the accession agreement should include a provision to the effect that individual applications are admissible if they are brought either against the entity which performed the conduct allegedly in breach of the Convention, or against either entity whose law has an intrinsic link with the alleged breach.

The beneficial effect of such a provision is obvious, since it would allow individual claimants to rely on the presumption of multiple attribution and avoid imposing the burden of identifying the sole entity to which the wrongful conduct must be attributed. In cases where the wrongful conduct is the final result of a chain of binding and non-binding acts adopted by EU and by Member State Institutions, this appears inappropriate, particularly given the time limits on the submission of an application.

V. CONCLUSION

As a consequence of its accession to the ECHR, the EU will be the first international organisation to be party to a major human rights treaty.[27] Not surprisingly, therefore, accession is seen as an historical event which could serve as a model for future membership of other international organisations to human rights treaties.

Among other beneficial effects, accession is also expected to remedy the current situation whereby the Member State might be called on to bear the responsibility flowing from breach of the Convention even if the conduct amounting to a breach was carried out in order to comply with obligations deriving from EU law. This is a technical issue, but it has theoretical significance. It makes it necessary to mould and adapt the general law on attribution of wrongful conduct to international organisations to the idiosyncratic situations created by the accession of the EU to the ECHR. The solution of this issue thus requires great legal skill and, equally, great political sensitivity.

[27] In 2009 the EC became party to the UN Convention on the Rights of People with Disabilities. See the Council Decision of 26 November 2009 concerning conclusion of the Convention, 2010/48/EC, OJ 53 L23 of 27 January 2010. Absent a general competence of the EU to conclude international conventions on human rights, this decision is based, inter alia, on a provision of the founding Treaties which gives to the Union the power to 'take action to combat discrimination based on . . . disability' (Art 13 TEC, which corresponds to Art 19 TFEU).

In order to fulfil this task, the adoption of a special mechanism might be opportune; a mechanism that allows for either entity, the EU or the Member State, to be a co-respondent in proceedings against the other. This mechanism might be construed according to two alternative schemes. It can be seen as a special rule on collective responsibility. Alternatively, and without indulging in theoretical inquiries upon its precise nature, it can be seen as a mechanism rendering superfluous the process of attribution of the alleged wrongful conduct to a particular entity. In either case, its effect is to open the way to the logically subsequent step of allocating responsibility among the various actors, which contributed to the breach.

Due to the infinite variety of situations which might give rise to a breach of the Convention as a result of combined action by the EU and by its Member States, such a mechanism ought to be as flexible as possible. It should provide a general frame of reference, leaving the task of determining the detailed legal regime to subsequent judicial and diplomatic practice.

On the conceptual level, this mechanism can help to dispel some of the mysteries which still linger concerning the identification of the author of a human rights breach committed through a combination of normative acts and material conduct undertaken in varying degrees by the EU and its Member States. It can also serve as an icebreaker in the still treacherous waters of collective attribution and allocation of responsibility among a plurality of co-authors.

13

The International Responsibility of the Union in the Context of its CSDP Operations

FREDERIK NAERT*

I. INTRODUCTION

THIS CHAPTER AIMS to identify and analyse the elements of EU (European Union) practice relating to responsibility in the military and civilian crisis management operations[1] conducted by the EU in the framework of the Common Security and Defence Policy (CSDP[2]).

To this effect, I will examine the CSDP operations and their legal framework, focusing on aspects related to responsibility (II). In particular, first, I will provide a brief overview of the legal basis under EU law, Council decisions and the scope of CSDP operations (A). Then, I will look at the planning and decision-making (B), command and control and force generation (C) and international agreements (D), as well as specific aspects of responsibility under EU law (E). On the basis of this analysis, I will present some conclusions and reflections (III) as regards international responsibility, individual responsibility, civil responsibility as well as on EU and international law aspects of responsibility, and an overall assessment of the arrangements concerning responsibility.

* This chapter is based on a paper entitled 'Practice of the European Union' which the author presented at the expert seminar on 'The Responsibility in Multinational Military Operations: A Review of Recent Practice', organised by the University of Amsterdam's Centre for International Law and the International Law Centre of the Swedish National Defence College in Amsterdam on 16 December 2010. The views expressed are solely those of the author and do not bind the Council of the EU or its Legal Service.

[1] Sometimes the term 'operations' is used for military operations and 'missions' for civilian missions but I will use both interchangeably.

[2] Previously, this policy was named the 'European Security and Defence Policy' (ESDP).

By way of introduction, one has to keep in mind that different kinds of responsibility may be relevant in CSDP operation, in particular:

- International responsibility of states and international organisations, including the EU. A further distinction can be made between responsibility under (general) international law and under EU law.
- Individual disciplinary or criminal responsibility (under domestic, EU, and/or international law).
- Civil responsibility of natural or legal persons (under domestic or international law).

These forms of responsibility may overlap. For instance, a private person may be able to bring a civil action for damages for conduct which engages the international responsibility of a state, eg regarding a human rights violation.

This chapter focuses on international responsibility, under both EU law and general international law, but also touches upon other aspects of responsibility. It will not distinguish the kinds of responsibility in section II but will do so as much as possible in section III.

It must be stressed that international responsibility requires two elements. First, there is the question of attribution, which has been the subject of considerable attention in relation to peace/crisis management operations.[3] As attribution is addressed extensively in the chapter by Christian Tomuschat,[4] it is not dealt with in this chapter in any detail. Nevertheless, a number of elements in EU practice which are relevant for the purposes of attribution will be identified. Second, it is necessary to identify a breach of an international obligation.[5] The latter may be complicated for international organisations since they are often not a party to treaties governing substantive areas of international law. In this respect, the EU is in a different position than most other international organisations as it is a party to an increasing number of multilateral international agreements (in addition to numerous bilateral ones) and hence it has many

[3] See notably the International Law Commission's 2011 Draft Articles on the Responsibility of International Organisations (ILC, 'Report of the Sixty-third session', UN Doc A/66/10, 52–172), in particular Arts 6 and 7 and associated commentaries. For case law of the European Court of Human Rights, compare *Behrami and Behrami v France* and *Saramati v France, Germany and Norway* (31 May 2007, admissibility, Application Nos 71412/01 and 78166/01) with *Al-Jedda v UK* (7 July 2011, Application No 27021/08). For two recent domestic cases in the Netherlands, see *M M–M, DM and AM (Mustafić) and HN (Hasan Nuhanović) versus the State of the Netherlands*, Court of Appeals, The Hague, case no 200.020.173/01 and 200.020.174/01, judgments of 5 July 2011 (English translations available at http://jure.nl/br5386 and http://jure.nl/br5388). See also several annotations in (2011) 50 *Military Law and the Law of War Review* 315 and KM Larsen, *Human Rights Treaty Obligations of Peacekeepers* (Cambridge, Cambridge University Press, 2012).

[4] See ch 1 in this volume.

[5] See Art 2 of the ILC's 2001 Draft Articles on Responsibility of States for Internationally Wrongful Acts (ILC, 'Report of the Fifty-third Session', UN Doc A/56/10, 26–143) and Art 4 of its Draft Articles on the Responsibility of International Organisations, above n 3.

treaty law obligations. Nevertheless, it is not a party to any treaty in the field of international humanitarian law (IHL),[6] which is one of the areas of international law most relevant to military operations. Neither is it a party yet to any human rights treaty, with the exception of the Disabilities Convention.[7] However, it is negotiating its accession to the European Convention on Human Rights (ECHR).[8] Therefore it may well be necessary to look at other sources of obligations of international organisations under international law, including customary international law, especially as regards IHL. This is not addressed in the present chapter.[9]

Furthermore, once the principle of responsibility is established, it is a further step to determine how it is implemented and how redress can be obtained.

II. CSDP OPERATIONS AND THEIR LEGAL FRAMEWORK, WITH A FOCUS ON ASPECTS RELATED TO RESPONSIBILITY[10]

Provisions relating to responsibility and claims are primarily contained in international agreements concluded in the area of the CSDP, which occupy a central place in this section (D). However, in order to fully

[6] I use the term IHL interchangeably with the *ius in bello* or the law of armed conflict.

[7] The EU has concluded the Convention on the Rights of Persons with Disabilities (New York, 13 December 2006): see Council Decision 2010/48/EC of 26 November 2009, [2010] OJ L23/35. It ratified the Convention on December 23, 2010.

[8] See Art 6(2) TEU and Protocol No 5 to the Treaty of Lisbon as well as Art 17 of Protocol No 14 ECHR (Strasbourg, 13 May 2004, CETS No 194, entered into force on 1 June 2010), which inserted a new paragraph in Art 59 ECHR stating that '[t]he European Union may accede to this Convention'. The negotiations on this accession started in July 2010 and are ongoing. See generally www.coe.int/lportal/web/coe-portal/what-we-do/human-rights/eu-accession-to-the-convention. See also ch 13 in this volume by Enzo Cannizzaro.

[9] See extensively F Naert, *International Law Aspects of the EU's Security and Defence Policy, with a Particular Focus on the Law of Armed Conflict and Human Rights* (Antwerp, Intersentia, 2010), chs 7–9.

[10] See more extensively, F Naert, 'Legal Aspects of EU Military Operations' (2011) 15 *Journal of International Peacekeeping* 218. For a legal analysis of the CSDP more generally, see Naert, above n 9; S Blockmans (ed), *The European Union and International Crisis Management: Legal and Policy Aspects* (The Hague, TMC Asser Press, 2008); M Trybus and N White (eds), *European Security Law* (Oxford, Oxford University Press, 2007). For a broader analysis, see G Grevi, D Helly and D Keohane (eds), *European Security and Defence Policy: the First Ten Years (1999–2009)* (Paris, EU ISS, 2009), www.iss.europa.eu/uploads/media/ESDP_10-web.pdf. On the legal framework for military/peace operations more generally, see T Gill and D Fleck (eds), *The Handbook of the International Law of Military Operations* (Oxford, Oxford University Press, 2010); U Häußler, *Ensuring and Enforcing Human Security: The Practice of International Peace Missions* (Nijmegen, Wolf Legal Publishers, 2007) and R Arnold and G-J Knoops (eds), *Practice and Policies of Modern Peace Support Operations under International Law* (Ardsley, Transnational, 2006). Many of the documents relating to CSDP operations are accessible to the public: nearly all the legal instruments are published in the Official Journal and several other documents are available through the public register of Council documents (www.consilium.europa.eu/documents/access-to-council-documents-public-register?lang=en). The CSDP pages on the EU's website

understand these provisions, first a brief overview of the legal basis for CSDP operations under EU law, and of Council decisions establishing these operations, is necessary (A). In addition, a succinct analysis of the planning and decision-making (B) and command and control and force generation (C) for CSDP operations is required to identify the respective responsibilities of the different actors in a complex institutional setting, and to be able to assess the question of attribution. Finally, a number of specific aspects of responsibility under EU law should also be examined (E).

A. Legal Basis under EU Law, Council Decisions and Scope of CSDP Operations

Pursuant to Article 42(1) TEU, the CSDP 'shall provide the Union with an operational capacity drawing on civil and military assets. The Union may use them on missions outside the Union for peace-keeping, conflict prevention and strengthening international security in accordance with the principles of the United Nations Charter'. Article 43 TEU adds that these missions 'shall include joint disarmament operations, humanitarian and rescue tasks, military advice and assistance tasks, conflict prevention and peace-keeping tasks, tasks of combat forces in crisis management, including peace-making and post-conflict stabilisation' and may all 'contribute to the fight against terrorism, including by supporting third countries in combating terrorism in their territories'.

CSDP operations can therefore be tailored to the specific situation and may vary greatly, ranging from consensual rule of law, police, security sector reform, border assistance or monitoring missions, to peacekeeping and potentially even peace enforcement. The 'tasks of combat forces in crisis management, including peacemaking' cover peace enforcement (ie imposing peace against the will of a state) and hence potentially high intensity combat operations.

The basic legal instrument governing each CSDP operation is a Council decision, based on Articles 43 and 28 TEU, in accordance with the voting rules laid down in Articles 31 and 42(4) TEU. This legal instrument—which is an act of the Council and not of the Member States jointly[11]—is the successor to the joint actions adopted pursuant to Article 14 pre-Lisbon TEU. These decisions 'shall lay down their objectives, scope, the means to be made available to the Union, if necessary their duration, and the conditions for their implementation' and 'shall commit

(www.consilium.europa.eu/eeas/security-defence?lang=en) are also a useful tool, especially the section on 'EU Operations' and the heading 'legal basis' under each operation.

[11] In the framework of the EU the latter decisions exist in the form of decisions 'of the representatives of the Governments of the Member States meeting in the Council'.

the Member States in the positions they adopt and in the conduct of their activity' (Art 28 TEU).

These acts generally set out, inter alia, the mission and mandate, the structure/organisation of the operation, including the designation of the commanders/head of mission and headquarters, as well as the command and control relations, and contain provisions on the status of forces/mission, financial arrangements, participation of third states (ie non-EU Member States), relations with other actors, handling of EU classified information and on the launching and termination/duration of the operation. In military operations, there is usually a further Council decision launching the operation, together with the approval of the Operation Plan and the rules of engagement.

B. Planning and Decision-Making[12]

The key decision-making body in the CSDP is the Council, with the European Council providing strategic guidance.

The Council's work is prepared by several preparatory bodies and by the High Representative of the Union for Foreign Affairs and Security Policy (High Representative), who is assisted by the European External Action Service (EEAS) (Article 27 TEU).[13] The latter includes various structures originating in the General Secretariat of the Council, including the EU Military Staff,[14] the Civilian Planning and Conduct Capability (CPCC) and the Crisis Management and Planning Directorate.[15] The relevant Council preparatory bodies include the Political and Security Committee (PSC),[16]

[12] See also F Naert, 'The Application of Human Rights and International Humanitarian Law in Drafting EU Missions' Mandates and Rules of Engagement' in M Aznar and M Costas (eds), *The Integration of the Human Rights Component and International Humanitarian Law in Peacekeeping Missions Led by the European Union* (Valencia, CEDRI/ATLAS, 2011) 61–71 (available as KU Leuven Institute for International Law Working Paper No 151 at www.law.kuleuven.be/iir/eng/research/wp.html); G Grevi, 'ESDP Institutions' in Grevi et al (eds), above n 10, 53–59.

[13] See also Council Decision 2010/427/EU of 26 July 2010 establishing the organisation and functioning of the European External Action Service, [2010] OJ L201/30 (corrig [2010] OJ L217/12), especially Art 2(1), first hyphen.

[14] See Council Decision 2001/80/CFSP of 22 January 2001, [2001] OJ L27/7, as amended by Council Decision 2005/395/CFSP of 10 May 2005, [2005] OJ L132/17 and Council Decision 2008/298/CFSP of 7 April 2008, [2008] OJ L102/25, and www.consilium.europa.eu/eeas/security-defence/csdp-structures-and-instruments/eu-military-staff?lang=en. This now has to be read together with the EEAS decision, above n 13.

[15] See Council Decision 2010/427/EU, above n 13, especially Art 4(3)(a), third hyphen; Art 7(1) and the Annex.

[16] See Council Decision 2001/78/CFSP of 22 January 2001, [2001] OJ L27/1.

the EU Military Committee (EUMC),[17] the Political-Military Group and the Committee for Civilian Aspects of Crisis Management.[18]

The PSC plays a crucial role and exercises, under the responsibility of the Council and of the High Representative, 'political control and strategic direction'[19] of CSDP operations, and the Council may authorize the PSC to take the relevant decisions concerning the political control and strategic direction of the operation (Article 38 TEU).

In practice, the PSC is invariably authorised to take certain decisions, including to amend the planning documents, the Chain of Command and the rules of engagement, and on the appointment of the Operation/Force Commander or Head of Mission, while the powers of decision with respect to the objectives and termination of the operation remain vested in the Council.

Examples of how this is reflected in specific legal acts are provided by Articles 5-7 of Council Joint Action 2008/851/CFSP of 10 November 2008 on a European Union military operation to contribute to the deterrence, prevention and repression of acts of piracy and armed robbery off the Somali coast,[20] Articles 4-6 of Council Decision 2011/210/CFSP of 1 April 2011 on a European Union military operation in support of humanitarian assistance operations in response to the crisis situation in Libya (EUFOR Libya) (for a post-Lisbon example),[21] as well as Articles 4, 11 and 12 of Council Joint Action 2008/124/CFSP of 4 February 2008 on the European Union Rule of Law Mission in Kosovo, EULEX KOSOVO.[22]

In the planning and decision-making process, documents are developed and approved through close interaction between the planners/experts and the politicians/diplomats. Key decisions are taken by the Council itself (ie Ministers). Furthermore, once an Operation Commander (for military operations) or Head of Mission (for civilian missions) has been appointed, he/she also plays an important role in the planning process. The 'crisis management procedures' describing this process are set out in a document entitled 'Suggestions for procedures for coherent, comprehensive EU crisis management'.[23] While these procedures are in practice generally quite closely adhered to,[24] they are flexible and only provide guidelines.[25]

[17] See Council Decision 2001/79/CFSP of 22 January 2001, [2001] OJ L27/4 and www.consilium.europa.eu/eeas/security-defence/csdp-structures-and-instruments/eu-military-committee-(eumc)?lang=en.

[18] See Council Decision 2000/354/CFSP of 22 May 2000, [2000] OJ L127/1.

[19] Council Doc 11096/03 EXT 1 (26 July 2006) defines both notions.

[20] [2008] OJ L301/33.

[21] [2011] OJ L89/17.

[22] [2008] OJ L42/92.

[23] Council Doc 11127/03 of 3 of July 2003. See also the EU Concept for Military Planning at the Political and Strategic Level, Council Doc 10687/08 of 16 June 2008.

[24] For coordination or supporting actions, the planning documents may be different.

[25] Doc 11127/03, iii.

In essence,[26] these procedures provide for the development of four planning documents, each to be submitted to PSC and then to the Council,[27] after having been examined by the relevant preparatory bodies (see above), which issue advice or recommendations or may amend the documents. These documents become increasingly detailed and are the Crisis Management Concept, (Military, Police or Civilian) Strategic Options, a Concept of Operation (CONOPS) and Operation Plan (OPLAN). The OPLAN contains the specifics of the operation and is often rather long, in part due to many annexes, which normally address, inter alia, legal issues and the use of force. In military operations in which the use of force is authorized (beyond self-defence), there are also Rules of Engagement (ROE) requested by the Operation Commander and authorized by the Council. ROE may be described as instructions concerning the use of force.[28] Member States may issue caveats applicable to their contingents but these may only impose further restrictions on the use of force or on certain tasks.

These operation-specific planning documents take into account generic CSDP documents, including a series of concepts.[29] They are not legal instruments, are normally classified, and are developed in parallel with the legal instruments mentioned above (II.A) and below (II.D). The OPLAN is implemented by further documents such as standard operating procedures or instructions.

C. Command and Control and Force Generation

The highest level of military command in EU military operations rests with the Operation Commander. The Operational Headquarters (OHQ) may be made available by a Member State (eg in operation Atalanta), by NATO under the Berlin plus arrangements (eg in operation Althea), or may consist of the EU Operations Centre, which then has to be activated (in its conclusions of 1 December 2011 (§ 32), the Council agreed to accelerate planning for the activation of the Operations Centre for the Horn of Africa operations; it was subsequently activated for the first time

[26] See also Council Doc 10687/08, above n 23, 11. Some phases/documents are omitted here. In its Conclusions of 1 December 2011 on CSDP (§ 31), the Council invited the High Representative to propose a review of these procedures, which date from 2003. At the time of writing, this review in ongoing.

[27] Via the Committee of Permanent Representatives, unless a written procedure is used.

[28] On ROE in general, see the International Institute of Humanitarian Law's *Rules of Engagement Handbook* published in 2009 (see www.iihl.org/iihl/Documents/rule%20engagement%20definitive.pdf).

[29] See, eg EU Concept for the Use of Force in EU-led Military Operations, EU Council Doc 17168/09 of 4 December 2009, declassified to a limited extent in EU Council Doc 17168/09 EXT 1 of 2 February 2010, and the EU Concept for Logistic Support for EU-led Military Operations (EU Council Doc 10963/08 of 19 June 2008).

for an operation, albeit in a supporting role and without prejudice to the respective chains of command of these missions[30]).

The Operation Commander will normally receive operational control over forces put at his disposal by the participating states via a transfer of authority.[31] When forces deployed in an EU operation revert to national command, there is a 'reverse transfer of authority' (this has eg occurred in the context of the EU's counter-piracy operation Atalanta). The next command level, the highest one in the field, is the Force Commander.

The EUMC is not in the chain of command of military CSDP operations, but it monitors the execution of such operations and receives reports from the Operation Commander and the Chairman of the EUMC is the primary point of contact for the Operation Commander.[32]

On the civilian side, there is a permanent Civilian Operation Commander, who, as a rule, commands all civilian operations and is supported by the Civilian Planning and Conduct Capability.[33] The command and control relationships in civilian missions and the respective responsibilities are usually defined in the Joint Action/Council decision in greater detail than for military operations.[34]

Operation personnel are put at the disposal of/seconded to the operation by Member States and, where applicable, by third states participating in an operation. In addition, staff may sometimes be contracted.[35] For military operations, a force generation process takes place.[36] For civilian operations, the manning/recruitment process involves a 'call for contributions'.

Not every Member State necessarily participates (significantly) with personnel in each operation.[37] Furthermore, the Treaty of Lisbon has introduced the possibility to entrust the execution of a task, within the

[30] See Council Decision 2012/173/CFSP of 23 March 2012 on the activation of the EU Operations Centre for the Common Security and Defence Policy missions and operation in the Horn of Africa, [2012] OJ L89/66, especially Arts 1 and 2.

[31] For the command and control arrangements in military CSDP operations, see Council Doc 11096/03 EXT 1 (26 July 2006; this is a partially declassified version), especially 14–15. At 6–7, this document defines Operational Control (OPCON) as 'the authority granted to a commander to direct forces assigned, so that the commander may accomplish specific missions or tasks which are usually limited by function, time or location; to deploy units concerned and to retain or assign tactical control of those units. It does not include authority to assign separate employment of components of the units concerned. Neither does it of itself, include administrative or logistic responsibility'. The current EU Concept for Military Command and Control is now in the public domain: see EU Council Doc 01688/3/08 of 13 September 2012.

[32] See, eg Arts 7 and 6(3) of Council Joint Action 2008/851/CFSP, above n 20.

[33] For the command and control arrangements in civilian CSDP operations, see Council Doc 9919/07 EXT 2 (1 February 2008; this is a partially declassified version).

[34] See, eg Council Joint Action 2008/124/CFSP, above n 22, Arts 7, 8 and 11.

[35] Ibid Arts 9(2)–(4) and 10(3).

[36] See EU Concept for Force Generation, EU Council Doc 10690/08 of 16 June 2008, especially §§ 5–6, 10, 22 and 32.

[37] Non-participation has not been limited to Denmark (which does not participate in the elaboration and implementation of EU decisions and actions with defence implications; Art 5 Protocol on the Position of Denmark) and qualified abstention (Art 31(1) TEU).

Union framework, to a group of Member States which are willing and have the necessary capability for such a task (Articles 42(5) and 44 TEU). This goes beyond existing practice by allowing those states to agree among them on how to manage the operation, within certain limits and while keeping the Council informed. It is not addressed here and has not yet been used in practice.

D. International Agreements

Under Article 24 pre-Lisbon TEU, the EU concluded many international agreements relating to CSDP operations, including on the participation of third states and on the status of forces/missions.[38] Such agreements are now governed by Articles 37 TEU and 218 TFEU.

(i) SOFA/SOMAs with Host States

The EU will normally conclude a Status of Forces Agreement (SOFA) or Status of Mission Agreement (SOMA) with the host state to regulate the status of an operation in the host state.[39] There are models for these agreements, which serve as the basis for negotiating SOFA/SOMAs for a given operation.[40] There may also be SOFA-like transit agreements with states through which an operation has to transit; such agreements differ somewhat from SOFAs.[41]

Pending the conclusion or entry into force of status agreements, host states may grant privileges and immunities through unilateral declarations. Alternative arrangements may also exist, including the extension of a status agreement for a non-EU operation to an EU operation by a UN Security Council resolution (as for operation Althea in Bosnia and

[38] See A Sari, 'The Conclusion of International Agreements by the European Union in the Context of the ESDP' (2007) 56 *International & Comparative Law Quarterly* 53–86 and P Koutrakos, 'International Agreements in the Area of the EU's Common Security and Defence Policy' in E Cannizzaro, P Palchetti and R Wessel (eds), *International Law as Law of the European Union* (Leiden, Martinus Nijhoff, 2011) 157–87.

[39] See more extensively A Sari, 'Status of Forces and Status of Mission Agreements under the ESDP: the EU's Evolving Practice' (2008) 19 *European Journal of International Law* 67.

[40] See EU Council Documents 12616/07 (6 September 2007) and 11894/07 (20 July 2007) and COR 1 (5 September 2007) on the one hand and 17141/08 (15 December 2008) on the other hand. For an example of a specific SOFA, see Agreement between the European Union and the Republic of Chad on the status of the European Union-led forces in the Republic of Chad, [2008] OJ L83/40.

[41] See, eg the transit agreement with Cameroon for EUFOR Tchad/RCA ([2008] OJ L57/31). For instance, its Art 15 on claims differs considerably from the model SOFA.

Herzegovina[42] and EUFOR RD Congo in the Democratic Republic of the Congo[43]) or by agreement.

The model SOFA (I will not cover the model SOMA here) provides, inter alia, that 'EUFOR and EUFOR personnel shall respect the laws and regulations of the Host State and shall refrain from any action or activity incompatible with the objectives of the operation' (Art 2(1))[44] and lays down the privileges and immunities of the EU-led Force (EUFOR) and of its personnel in the host state.

More specifically, EUFOR's facilities shall be inviolable, its facilities, their furnishings and other assets therein as well as its means of transport shall be immune from search, requisition, attachment or execution, its archives, documents and official correspondence shall be inviolable, and EUFOR, its property and assets, wherever located and by whomsoever held, shall enjoy immunity from every form of legal process (Article 5).

Article 6 of the model SOFA details the privileges and immunities of EUFOR personnel. The main relevant aspects are the following:

- EUFOR personnel shall not be liable to any form of arrest or detention and shall enjoy immunity from the criminal jurisdiction of the Host State under all circumstances, unless it is expressly waived by the Sending State or EU institution concerned.
- EUFOR personnel shall enjoy immunity from the civil and administrative jurisdiction of the Host State in respect of words spoken or written and all acts performed by them in the exercise of their official functions. If any civil proceeding is instituted against EUFOR personnel before any Host State court, the EU Force Commander and the competent authority of the Sending State or EU institution shall be notified immediately and shall certify to the court whether the act in question was committed in the exercise of their official functions prior to initiation of the proceeding before the court. This certification is binding upon the jurisdiction of the Host State. If the act was committed in the exercise of official functions, the proceeding shall not be initiated and the claims provisions (see below) shall apply. If the act was not committed in the exercise of official functions, the proceeding may continue. However, EUFOR personnel shall not be subject to any restrictions on their personal liberty or to any other measures of constraint.
- No measures of execution may be taken in respect of EUFOR personnel, except in the case where a civil proceeding not related to their official functions is instituted against them (see above) and papers, correspondence and property of EUFOR personnel shall enjoy inviolability,

[42] See UN Security Council Resolutions 1551 (9 July 2004), § 20 and 1575 (22 November 2004), § 12.

[43] See UN Security Council Resolution 1671 (25 April 2006), § 12.

[44] In this context, 'respect' is usually interpreted as less binding than 'comply with'.

except in case of measures of execution which are permitted as set out above. However, property of EUFOR personnel, which is certified by the EU Force Commander to be necessary for the fulfilment of their official functions, shall be free from seizure for the satisfaction of a judgment, decision or order.

- The immunity from the jurisdiction of the host state does not exempt EUFOR personnel from the jurisdictions of the respective sending states. For example, a French soldier in EUFOR Tchad/RCA who killed two fellow French soldiers, a UN peacekeeper and a local peasant was prosecuted in France[45] in what is one of the few cases of alleged (serious) criminal conduct in an EU operation.[46] Moreover, Article 8 of the model SOFA, provides that the

> competent authorities of a Sending State shall have the right to exercise on the territory of the Host State all the criminal jurisdiction and disciplinary powers conferred on them by the law of the Sending State with regard to all EUFOR personnel subject to the relevant law of the Sending State.

Personnel employed locally shall enjoy privileges and immunities only to the extent admitted by the host state, which, however, shall exercise its jurisdiction in such a manner as not to interfere unduly with the operation (Article 7).

Furthermore, SOFAs usually contain a provision on claims for death, injury, damage and loss. Hence Article 15 of the model SOFA reads as follows:

[45] See, eg www.lci.tf1.fr/france/justice/2009–04/le-legionnaire-meurtrier-ne-supportait-plus-les-brimades-4868436.html and www.lefigaro.fr/actualite-france/2009/04/09/01016–20090409ARTFIG00527-tchad-le-legionnaire-francais-meurtrier-arrete-.php.

[46] T Hadden (ed), *A Responsibility to Assist. Human Rights Policy and Practice in European Union Crisis Management Operations. A COST Report* (Oxford, Hart, 2009), lists 12 cases concerning sending state criminal jurisdiction (112) but none of these concern EU operations. A study specifically on the EU police and military operations in Bosnia and Herzegovina in the framework of an ATLAS project concluded that 'It is very evident that there is a legitimate culture of zero tolerance in both EUFOR and EUPM. From the interviews conducted it is apparent that personnel understand that the Codes of Conduct in the respective missions will be fully applied in the case of wrongdoing. There appears to be no record and interviewees reported no cases of human rights violations by the personnel of either EUFOR or EUPM': F Donlon, 'EUPM and EUNAVFOR [sic] Missions in Bosnia-Herzegovina: Analytical Report' (July 2010), available at projetatlas.univ-paris.fr/IMG/pdf/ATLAS_BiH_Mission_Report_2010.pdf, 63. The ATLAS report on EULEX Kosovo (the only other mission specifically covered by the project) does not mention any allegations of human rights violations either: C Navarro Susino, 'Success or Failures in the Integration of a Human Rights Component in the EU Civilian European Union Rule of Law Mission in Kosovo (EULEX)' (May 2010), available at projetatlas.univ-paris.fr/IMG/pdf/Kosovo_Report_FINAL-2.pdf. There was one case in which allegations of abuse were made in respected of operation Artemis (see, eg www.dw.de/dw/article/03223692,00.html) but an investigation in the Member State concerned appears to have concluded that the allegations were unfounded (see www.fr.wikipedia.org/wiki/Op%C3%A9ration_Art%C3%A9mis under 'Affaire "Joseph"').

1. EUFOR and EUFOR personnel shall not be liable for any damage to or loss of civilian or government property which are related to operational necessities or caused by activities in connection with civil disturbances or protection of EUFOR.

2. With a view to reaching an amicable settlement, claims for damage to or loss of civilian or government property not covered by paragraph 1, as well as claims for death of or injury to persons and for damage to or loss of EUFOR property, shall be forwarded to EUFOR via the competent authorities of the Host State, as far as claims brought by legal or natural persons from the Host State are concerned, or to the competent authorities of the Host State, as far claims brought by EUFOR are concerned.

3. Where no amicable settlement can be found, the claim shall be submitted to a claims commission composed on an equal basis of representatives of EUFOR and representatives of the Host State. Settlement of claims shall be reached by common agreement.

4. Where no settlement can be reached within the claims commission, the dispute shall:
a) for claims up to and including 40 000 EUR, be settled by diplomatic means between the Host State and EU representatives.
b) for claims above the amount referred to in point a), be submitted to an arbitration tribunal, the decisions of which shall be binding.

. . .

6. An administrative arrangement shall be concluded between EUFOR and the administrative authorities of the Host State in order to determine the terms of reference of the claims commission and the tribunal, the procedure applicable within these bodies and the conditions under which claims are to be lodged'.

A few points merit specific mention. First, the claims that are exempted under paragraph 1 only relate to property and not death or injury to persons. Second, EUFOR and its representative are not further defined in the claims provision so one has to apply the general definitions given in Article 1(3)a, d and e of the model SOFA, ie:

"European Union-led Forces (EUFOR)" shall mean EU military headquarters and national contingents contributing to the operation, their equipment and their means of transport;

"EU military headquarters" shall mean the military headquarters and elements thereof, whatever their location, under the authority of EU military commanders exercising the military command or control of the operation;

"national contingents" shall mean units and elements belonging to the [EU] Member States . . . and to other States participating in the operation.

Third, whereas the claims commission functions at the operational/theatre level of EUFOR, the next step (diplomatic means or arbitration) involves the political/Brussels level of the EU. Similarly, Article 16 provides for a two levels of process in relation to disputes between the parties about the SOFA generally:

> 1. All issues arising in connection with the application of this Agreement shall be examined jointly by representatives of EUFOR and the Host State's competent authorities.
>
> 2. Failing any prior settlement, disputes concerning the interpretation or application of this Agreement shall be settled exclusively by diplomatic means between the Host State and EU representatives.

I am aware of one case in which a dispute over the scope of tax exemptions required negotiations, which led to an agreed solution.

An analysis of the issues raised by the funding of CSDP operations and who pays any damages awarded is provided below (II.E).

Fourth, in practice, with the possible exception of operation Althea,[47] to my knowledge in none of the operations has a claims commission or arbitral tribunal actually been set up. There also appear to be very few cases in which claims have been brought in courts.[48] It would therefore appear that most of the claims brought have been settled amicably. Furthermore, rather few claims seem to have been brought at all.

Finally, Article 10(4)–(5) of the model SOFA states that the law applicable to contracts concluded by EUFOR in the host state shall be determined by the contract, which may stipulate that the above claims dispute settlement procedure (Article 15(3)–(4)) shall be applicable to disputes arising from the application of the contract.

(ii) SOFA and Claims Agreements between Member States

In addition, there is an agreement between the Member States of the EU to regulate the status of their forces and personnel within each other's territory (EU SOFA),[49] which has not yet entered into force. Pending its entry into force, other existing agreements are applied (eg the NATO

[47] This EU operation applies the SOFA that applied to NATO's IFOR and SFOR operations. Under the latter operations, a claims commission was actually established and used in practice. Furthermore, Althea is (or at least was when it was launched) the EU's biggest military operation and it is the longest running one too. I have not verified whether this claims commission has also been used in relation to Althea.

[48] I am aware of one case in which victims hit by a crashed Unmanned Arial Vehicle (unarmed and used only for surveillance), or their relatives, brought a case before a domestic court in a Member State, or at least intended to do so, as they were not satisfied with the compensation offered in a proposal for an amicable settlement. I do not have any information on whether/how the case proceeded.

[49] 16 November 2003, [2003] OJ C321/6. See extensively A Sari, 'The EU Status of Forces Agreement: Continuity and Change in the Law of Visiting Forces' (2007) 46(1–2) *Military Law and the Law of War Review* 9. This agreement includes a long article 18 on claims in relation to activities in the territory of Member States.

SOFA[50]) and/or specific arrangements can be made (eg between an EU Operational Headquarters and its host state). This is complemented by an agreement between the Member States of the EU concerning claims introduced between them in the context of an EU crisis management operation,[51] which has not yet entered into force either. However, there is a declaration in relation to this agreement, which states that:

> In signing this Agreement, all Member States will endeavour, insofar as their internal legal system enables them, to limit as far as possible their claims against any other Member State for injury, death of military or civilian personnel, or damage to any assets owned, used or operated by themselves, except in cases of gross negligence or wilful misconduct.

These agreements and arrangements differ significantly from SOFAs with host states of EU operations and are not discussed here. While some questions have arisen when specific OHQs were designated and set up, I am not aware of any difficulties which would have arisen in practice in this respect.

(iii) Participation Agreements

The modalities of the participation of third states in a CSDP operation are laid down in a participation agreement concluded between that state and the EU either ad hoc for a given operation or in the form of a framework agreement for CSDP operations generally.

By way of example, I will briefly examine the relevant provisions of the Agreement between the Union and Ukraine establishing a framework for the participation of Ukraine in the European Union crisis management operations.[52]

> Ukraine shall associate itself with any EU Council Joint Action/Decision on a CSDP operation in which it participates, in accordance with the provisions of this Agreement and any required implementing arrangements and without prejudice to the Union's decision-making autonomy (Article 2).
>
> Ukraine shall ensure that its forces and personnel participating in the EU operation undertake their mission in conformity with the Joint Action and subsequent amendments, the Operation Plan and implementing measures and personnel seconded by Ukraine shall carry out their duties and conduct themselves solely with the interest of the EU military crisis management operation in mind (Articles 5, 6(1) and 9).

[50] Agreement on the Status of the North Atlantic Treaty Organisation, National Representatives and International Staff, Ottawa, 20 September 1951, 200 *United Nations Treaty Series* 3.

[51] 28 April 2004, [2004] OJ C116/1. Under this agreement, several categories of claims are waived between the Member States.

[52] [2005] OJ L182/9.

The chain of command reflects that within the EU: full command rests with the national authorities, which shall transfer the Operational and Tactical command and/or control of their forces and personnel to the EU Operation Commander or Head of Mission; Ukraine shall have the same rights and obligations in terms of the day-to-day management, of the operation as participating EU Member States; and it shall appoint a National Contingent Point of Contact or Senior Military Representative to represent its contingent and be responsible for day-to-day contingent discipline (Articles 6 and 10). In military operations, the EU Operation Commander may, following consultations with Ukraine, at any time request the withdrawal of Ukraine's contribution (Article 10(4)).

Article 3 addresses the status of personnel and forces. It provides for the applicability of any SOFA/SOMA with the host state and refers to status arrangements between Ukraine and the headquarters or command elements located outside the state(s) in which the EU crisis management operation takes place and to which Ukraine contributes personnel (paragraphs 1-2). It adds that:

3. Without prejudice to the [SOFA/SOMA] . . ., Ukraine shall exercise jurisdiction over its personnel participating in the EU . . . operation.

4. Ukraine shall be responsible for answering any claims linked to participation in an EU . . . operation, from or concerning any of its personnel. Ukraine shall be responsible for bringing any action, in particular legal or disciplinary, against any of its personnel in accordance with its laws and regulations.

5. Ukraine undertakes to make a declaration as regards the waiver of claims against any State participating in an EU . . . operation in which Ukraine participates, and to do so when signing this Agreement. A model for such a declaration is annexed . . . .

6. [EU] Member States undertake to make a declaration as regards the waiver of claims, for any future participation of Ukraine in an EU . . . operation, and to do so when signing this Agreement. A model for such a declaration is annexed . . . .

These annexed declarations provide that Ukraine on the one and the EU Member States on the other hand will endeavour, insofar as their internal legal systems so permit, to waive as far as possible claims against each other for injury, death of their personnel, or damage to, or loss of, any assets owned by themselves and used by the EU crisis management operation if such injury, death, damage or loss arose in connection with the EU crisis management operation, except in case of gross negligence or willful misconduct.

In the Framework Participation Agreement with Montenegro, concluded after the entry into force of the Lisbon Treaty, the corresponding provision is no longer unilateral by the third state in combination with a waiver between the Member States and this third state, but rather a mutual waiver between '[t]he Parties', ie the EU and the third state, as well as between the Member States and this third state.[53] This is also the case in the framework participation agreements with the US and with the former Yugoslav Republic of Macedonia.[54]

Furthermore, Article 11(2) states that 'In case of death, injury, loss or damage to natural or legal persons from the State(s) in which the operation is conducted, Ukraine shall, when its liability has been established, pay compensation under the conditions foreseen in the [SOFA], if available . . .' (similarly, Article 7(2)).

Finally, disputes concerning the interpretation or application of this Agreement shall be settled by diplomatic means between the Parties (Article 15).

The provisions of the recent framework participation agreement with the US[55] contain several significant variations compared to those in the standard framework participation agreements.

I am not aware of any difficulties in the application of these arrangements.

(iv) Other Agreements/Arrangements

There are usually additional arrangements, often memoranda of understanding and technical arrangements, between participating states on their cooperation within a CSDP operation.

There may also be other types of agreements specific to a given operation. For instance, in the framework of the EU's counter-piracy operation Atalanta/EUNAVFOR Somalia, pursuant to Article 12 of Council Joint Action 2008/851/CFSP,[56] the EU has concluded 'transfer agreements' with Kenya,[57] the Seychelles[58] and Mauritius.[59]

In addition, there may be agreements and/or arrangements with other international organisations regarding a specific operation. This could

[53] See Art 3(5)–(7), [2011] OJ L57/2.

[54] Respectively [2011] OJ L143/2 and Council doc 6653/12 of 2 March 2012, both Art 3(5)–(7). Here, in addition to its own waiver, the EU undertakes to ensure that its Member States make a waiver declaration.

[55] [2011] OJ L143/2.

[56] Above n 20. This Article provides that suspected pirates or armed robbers at sea captured by Atalanta may not be transferred to a third state 'unless the conditions for the transfer have been agreed with that third state in a manner consistent with relevant international law'.

[57] [2009] OJ L79/49 (no longer in force).

[58] [2009] OJ L315/37.

[59] [2011] OJ L254/3. Incidentally, the European Parliament has brought an action for annulment before the ECJ against the Council decision on the conclusion and signature of this agreement, claiming that the Parliament's consent was required pursuant to Art 218(6) TFEU because, in its view, the Agreement does not exclusively relate to the CFSP, and that it was not adequately informed at all stages of the negotiation and conclusion of this agreement. See Case C-658/11 *Parliament v Council* (pending).

and third paragraphs of Article 340'. However, the latter is qualified by Article 275 TFEU, which provides that, subject to two exceptions that are not relevant here,[69] the ECJ 'shall not have jurisdiction with respect to the provisions relating to the [CFSP] nor with respect to acts adopted on the basis of those provisions'. Therefore the ECJ is not competent for actions for damages relating to the conduct of CSDP operations.

This does not mean that there is no competent jurisdiction to judge such cases. First, as mentioned above, there are claims settlement procedures in the host state provided for under SOFAs/SOMAs. In addition, once they have entered into force, the provisions of the EU SOFA and EU Claims Agreement[70] will also be relevant. Second, pursuant to Article 19(1), second subparagraph TFEU, 'Member States shall provide remedies sufficient to ensure effective legal protection in the fields covered by Union law'. This is a horizontal provision that also covers the CSDP. In this context, pursuant to Article 274 TFEU, 'Save where jurisdiction is conferred on the [ECJ] by the Treaties, disputes to which the Union is a party shall not on that ground be excluded from the jurisdiction of the courts or tribunals of the Member States'. While the Union shall enjoy in the territories of the Member States such privileges and immunities as are necessary for the performance of its tasks, under the conditions laid down in the Protocol of 8 April 1965 on the privileges and immunities of the European Union[71] (Article 343 TFEU), this Protocol does not (unlike for most other international organisations) grant the EU immunity from jurisdiction before the courts of its Member States, but merely provides that the Union's premises and buildings are inviolable and exempt from search, requisition, confiscation or expropriation and that its property and assets shall not be the subject of any administrative or legal measure of constraint without the authorisation of the ECJ (Art 1).[72]

Consequently, when the ECJ has no jurisdiction, as in the case of CSDP operations, the Union does not enjoy immunity from the jurisdiction of the Member States' courts. This gives rise to a number of questions and challenges. For instance, while a national court may find that there is responsibility, it probably has no competence to rule on the validity of an EU legal instrument. Therefore it would be up to the Council to draw the consequences from any such judgment and amend or repeal a legal instrument where necessary. Presumably, the authorities of the Member State concerned would raise this matter in the competent Council instances. Complications may arise if there would be several judgments

[69] Namely adjudicating the delimitation between CFSP and other Union competences and reviewing the legality of restrictive measures against natural or legal persons.

[70] See nn 49, 51.

[71] Now Protocol (No 7) on the Privileges and Immunities of the European Union, as amended by the Treaty of Lisbon.

[72] In addition to a number of other privileges and immunities.

coming to different conclusions. Hopefully, Member States' courts will take into account relevant judgments in other Member States and divergent outcomes will not occur too often.

There may also be a question whether, in case the EU would not comply with a ruling awarding damages, the ECJ could authorise enforcement as required under the Protocol on the EU's Privileges and Immunities (see above) given its lack of jurisdiction in CSDP matters. Ideally, this question will remain a purely theoretical one. Furthermore, the question may arise whether a SOFA/SOMA with a host state could also have effects in a Member State court, notably through private international law. Taking into account these issues, the present situation may not be perfect. Nevertheless, this is the solution imposed by the Treaties as they stand and the challenges should not be exaggerated. Indeed, so far most of these questions do not seem to have arisen in practice. Furthermore, if necessary, the EU could establish specific mechanisms to handle actions for damages, as it does in host states through SOFA/SOMAs.

A further question is the meaning of 'institutions' in this context. The Council obviously falls within this term. There is also case law from the ECJ ruling that this is not limited to institutions in the strict sense[73] but it is questionable whether this can be stretched to include operations and it remains to be seen whether it would cover the EEAS.

It should be added that some of these issues may possibly be clarified in the framework of the EU's accession to the ECHR. I will not elaborate on this here as the negotiations on this accession are still ongoing and are addressed elsewhere in this volume.[74] It may suffice to mention two particular aspects. First, in the light of the ECJ's very limited jurisdiction in the area of the CFSP, this policy raises specific challenges: eg, probably, remedies before Member State courts will therefore have to be taken into account. Second, it will be interesting to see how responsibility in relation to CSDP missions will be apportioned. One option could be to refer to international law criteria for attribution, Another could be a more generic solution apportioning responsibility to either the Union or the Member States. Other solutions might also be possible.

[73] See CFI, Case T-209/00 *Frank Lamberts v European Ombudsman*, judgment of 10 April 2002, §§ 48–50 and the appeal in that case, ECJ, Case C-234/02 P *European Ombudsman v Frank Lamberts*, judgment of 23 March 2004, §§ 34–35 and 49 and Case C-370/89 *Société Générale d'Entreprises Electro-Mécaniques and Roland Etroy v European Investment Bank*, judgment of 25 May 1993, §§ 12–16.

[74] See ch 13 by Cannizzaro in this volume. See also very briefly, above n 8.

(ii) Particular Provisions in Council Joint Actions/Decisions and in Practice

Some Council joint actions or decisions contain specific provisions relevant to responsibility which have not been addressed above. For instance: Article 13 of Council Joint Action 2008/851/CFSP[75] provides that 'The conditions governing the presence on board merchant ships, particularly those chartered by the WFP, of units belonging to Atalanta, including privileges, immunities and other guarantees relating to the proper conduct of the operation, shall be agreed with the flag States of those vessels'.

In Article 1(1) of Council Joint Action 2007/192/CFSP of 27 March 2007 concerning EUSEC RD Congo, it is stated that 'Under no circumstances may the [EU] or the Secretary-General/High Representative for the [CFSP] be held liable by contributing Member States as a result of acts or omissions by the Head of Mission in the use of funds from those States [providing financial contributions for specific projects]'.[76]

In relation to EULEX Kosovo, the EU established a Human Rights Review Panel for complaints from any person claiming to be the victim of human rights violations by EULEX Kosovo in the conduct of its executive mandate.[77] The panel received 44 complaints in the period 2010-11. Of these complaints, 28 were inadmissible, one was struck out and eight were carried over into 2012. In the seven admissible claims (in whole or in part), the panel found human rights violations in only two cases.[78]

(iii) Other Specific Issues

There may be issues of duty of care towards mission staff, including in relation to the (physical) security of this staff. In civilian missions, the Council Joint Action/Decision usually sets out at least some of the responsibilities in this respect.[79]

In civilian missions, the budget is normally funded by the EU budget[80] and the Head of Mission signs a contract (as special advisor in the CFSP[81])

[75] See above n 20.

[76] [2007] OJ L87/22. Similarly, Art 5(4) Council Decision 2010/565/CFSP of 21 September 2010 on this operation, [2010] OJ L248/59.

[77] See www.hrrp.eu and the fact-sheet on 'EULEX Accountability' at http://www.eulex-kosovo.eu/docs/Accountability/EULEX-Accountability-05.01.2010.pdf. See also Marhic, above n 61, 117–18,

[78] 2010 and 2011 *Annual Reports*, both 15, both available at www.hrrp.eu/annual-report.php.

[79] See, eg Council Joint Action 2008/124/CFSP, above n 22, Arts 7(5) and 14(1)–(2).

[80] Pursuant to Art 41(2) TEU, operating expenditure to which the implementation of the Common Foreign and Security Policy gives rise 'shall also be charged to the Union budget, except for such expenditure arising from operations having military or defence implications and cases where the Council acting unanimously decides otherwise'.

[81] See also Commission Communication on Specific Rules of Special Advisors entrusted

with the Commission in relation to the implementation of the mission budget.[82]

Responsibility for the implementation of the budget is therefore a specific issue and the Head of Mission is responsible to the Commission only in this respect. This may also be relevant in the context of procurement for missions.[83] It may moreover be relevant for contracted staff because, as a rule, the conditions of employment and the rights and obligations of international and local civilian staff shall be laid down in the contracts between the Head of Mission and the members of staff.[84] In relation to all other aspects of the conduct of the mission, the Head of Mission is responsible to the Civilian Operations Commander and the PSC/HR/Council (see above).

In military operations, costs are carried by each participating state, except for defined common costs, which are charged to the Member States (not the EU budget[85]) and administered by a mechanism called Athena.[86] Article 43 of the Athena decision provides that:

> 1. The conditions governing the disciplinary or criminal liability of the operation commander, the administrator and other staff made available in particular by the Community institutions or Member States in the event of misconduct or negligence in the implementation of the budget shall be governed by the Staff Regulations or the arrangements applicable to them. In addition, ATHENA may at its own initiative or at the request of a contributing State bring a civil action against the abovementioned staff.
>
> 2. In no case may the European Communities or the Secretary-General of the Council be held liable by a contributing State as a result of the performance of their duties by the administrator, the accounting officer or the staff assigned to them.
>
> 3. The contractual liability which may arise from contracts concluded in the context of implementation of the budget shall be covered through ATHENA by the contributing States. It shall be governed by the law applicable to the contracts in question.

with the implementation of operational CFSP actions and contracted international staff, C(2009) 9502 of 30 November 2009.

[82] Eg Council Joint Action 2008/124/CFSP, above n 22, recital 12, Arts 8(5) and 16(2)–(4).

[83] For an action brought in this context, see CFI, Case T-511/08 *Unity OSG FZE/Council and EUPOL Afghanistan*. However, the case was removed from the register and is therefore not very instructive.

[84] See, eg Council Joint Action 2008/124/CFSP, above n 22, Art 10(3).

[85] See Art 41(2) TEU, above n 80. The Treaty of Lisbon has introduced Art 41(3) TEU, which states that the Council is to adopt a decision establishing a start-up fund. That decision has not yet been adopted.

[86] See Council Decision 2011/871/CFSP of 19 December 2011 establishing a mechanism to administer the financing of the common costs of European Union operations having military or defence implications (Athena), [2011] OJ L343/35.

4. In the case of non-contractual liability, any damage caused by the operation headquarters, force headquarters and component headquarters of the crisis structure, the composition of which shall be approved by the operation commander, or by their staff in the course of their duties shall be covered through ATHENA by the contributing States, in accordance with the general principles common to the laws of the Member States and the Staff Regulations of the forces, applicable in the theatre of operations.

5. In no case may the European Communities or the Member States be held liable by a contributing State for contracts concluded in the framework of budget implementation or for damage caused by the units and departments of the crisis structure, the composition of which shall be approved by the operation commander, or by their staff in the course of their duties'.

In addition, pursuant to its Article 15(1), 'The common costs listed in Annex I shall be at the expense of ATHENA whenever they are incurred' and its Annex I, point 2 covers 'Indemnities for damages and costs resulting from claims and actions to be paid through ATHENA'.

III. SOME CONCLUSIONS AND REFLECTIONS

I will now summarise the main elements of EU practice in relation to responsibility in CSDP operations and will add some reflections.

A. International Responsibility

CSDP operations are established by the Council of the EU, governed by EU legal instruments, including international agreements, and EU-approved operational planning documents and rules of engagement, and are conducted by Headquarters and forces/personnel put under the command and control of the EU/Civilian Operation(s) Commander, who acts under the political control and strategic direction of the Political and Security Committee.

Under international law, it is likely that these combined elements amount to a degree of (effective) control by the Union entailing,[87] at least in principle, attribution of the acts of an operation and its personnel (not of a private nature) to the Union. For the Union's responsibility to arise in

[87] I will not enter into the required degree of control here, as this is addressed in ch 1 in this volume by Tomuschat. See also, above n 3, and Naert, above n 9, 355–57, 435–49, 506–26, 641–46. Compare more extensively A Sari and R A Wessel, 'International Responsibility for EU Military Operations: Finding the EU's Place in the Global Accountability Regime' in B Van Vooren, S Blockmans and J Wouters (eds), *The Legal Dimension of Global Governance: What Role for the EU?* (Oxford, Oxford University Press, 2012 forthcoming), draft available at www.utwente.nl/mb/pa/research/wessel/wessel88.pdf.

such cases, it is also necessary that there is a breach of an international obligation of the Union.

This does not necessarily preclude any responsibility of the Member States, e.g. for their actions in relation to decision making and implementation in the framework of CSDP operations.[88] In this context, one may recall the obligation under Article 1 common to the 1949 Geneva Conventions to 'respect and to ensure respect for the present Convention in all circumstances', which is also reaffirmed in Article 1(1) of the 1977 Additional Protocol I to these Conventions, as well as to the obligation of EU Member States to respect the human rights laid down in the EU's Charter of Fundamental Rights 'when they are implementing Union law' (Art 51(5) of this Charter[89]).

EU practice prior to the Treaty of Lisbon clearly focused on the responsibility of Member States rather than that of the Union. Now that the Treaty of Lisbon has definitively settled the issue of the Union's international legal personality, it seems that in addition, the responsibility of the Union is to some extent being addressed, as reflected in the waiver of claims provisions in recent agreements.

However, apart from the mentioning of the Union's responsibility in the latter context, there are virtually no provisions dealing with the question of attribution. Therefore the above considerations rely primarily on the application of general international law rules (in an area in which these rules are not necessarily entirely clear) to EU operations on the basis of responsibilities in relation to the planning and conduct thereof. As very few cases, if any, have arisen in which the international responsibility of the Union and/or one or more Member States was actually at stake, it remains to be seen what point of view the Union and the Member States would take in such a case. The arrangements on the EU's accession to the ECHR, once agreed, may provide an important indication in this respect.

In agreements concerning CSDP missions, the EU usually provides that disputes between the parties are to be settled by negotiation or diplomatic means. This has rarely given rise to problems.

B. Individual Responsibility

The provisions relating to jurisdiction over EU-led forces/personnel, including extensive immunities from the jurisdiction of host state courts under status agreements, do not seem to have given rise to difficulties.

[88] See F Naert, 'Binding International Organisations to Member State Treaties or Responsibility of Member States for Their Own Actions in the Framework of International Organisations' in J Wouters, E Brems, S Smis and P Schmitt (eds), *Accountability for Human Rights Violations by International Organizations* (Antwerp, Intersentia, 2010) 129–68.

[89] [2010] OJ C83/389.

Furthermore, specifically as regards criminal jurisdiction, there seem to be very few cases in which allegations of (serious) criminal offences have been made.

C. Civil Responsibility

In the host state, under status agreements, a CSDP operation and its personnel are usually exempted from claims for damage to property linked to operational necessity, while for other claims brought by legal or natural persons from the host state or by the operation, a specific mechanism is provided. Overall, relatively few cases of claims seem to have been brought, and nearly all of these have been handled though the first stage of the standard claims settlement process, ie amicable settlement.

Similarly, very few, if any, cases have been brought before courts within the EU. This means that it has not yet been clarified in jurisprudence how and before what courts non-contractual liability of the Union or the Member States would be assessed. It is submitted that this would have to before domestic courts of the Member States given the lack of jurisdiction of the ECJ.

Claims between Member States, third states participating in an operation, and/or the Union also do not seem to have arisen, or, if they have, do not seem to have posed any difficulties. There have not been calls for changing the arrangements that have been developed.

D. EU and International Law Aspects

The above analysis shows that, at least in some respects, one has to distinguish (general) international and EU law aspects. In particular, in cases where the EU is responsible under international law, EU law may nonetheless require the involvement of Member State courts and may provide that a Member State will ultimately pay compensation or be responsible for answering a claim.

E. Overall Assessment of the Legal Framework in Relation to Responsibility

Many of the issues pertaining to the different kinds of responsibilities that may arise in CSDP operations, have been addressed at least to some extent in the legal and operational framework for CSDP operations as developed over time and applied in practice. Yet it would seem that very few issues of responsibility have actually arisen in practice. After nearly ten years of operations that is rather remarkable, including as regards conduct within the EU given that the EU SOFA has still not yet entered into force.

This means it is somewhat difficult to provide an overall assessment of these arrangements. On the one hand, this situation may indicate that the law is generally well respected in the conduct of these operations and/or that the arrangements put in place work quite well. On the other hand, as a consequence, these arrangements have perhaps not yet really been tested, neither in court nor in more conflictual cases. Also, a number of issues may not yet have come to the fore.

As long as that is the case, the current system is not likely to change significantly and such changes do not seem to be necessary at present.

POSTSCRIPT

An interesting judgment was delivered by the Cologne administrative court of 11 November 2011 (available in German at http://www.justiz.nrwe/ovgs/vg_koeln/j2011/25_K_4280_09urteil20111111.html). The court ruled that Germany was responsible for the transfer of suspected pirates held on board a German ship participating in the EU's operation Atalanta to Kenya on the basis of Germany's role in the transfer and found that the prison conditions in the period immediately following the transfer violated human rights. The reasoning of the court is very narrow and the judgment is under appeal.

14

EU Foreign, Security and Defence Policy: A Competence-Responsibility Gap?

RAMSES A WESSEL AND LEONHARD DEN HERTOG*

'Europe should be ready to share in the responsibility for global security . . .'[1]

I. INTRODUCTION

EVEN AFTER 20 years existence of a Common Foreign and Security Policy of the EU (European Union), the division of competences between the Union and its Member States in this area remains unclear.

Insight in this division has become more important in view of the increasing role of the EU in global security governance.[2] Due to its complex and to some extent sui generis nature, the question to which extent the EU would in general be covered by the rules on international legal responsibility has led to some debate. However, most contributions focused exclusively on the European Community, or, later, on the Union's competences on the basis of the TFEU.[3] The relevance of more clarity

* The authors wish to thank Christiane Ahlborn (Amsterdam Center for International Law) for her useful comments on an earlier draft of this paper.

[1] European Council, *European Security Strategy—A Secure Europe in a Better World*, 2003. See also: European Council, *Report on the Implementation of the ESS—Providing Security in a Changing World*, 2008, 1.

[2] See also M Emerson et al, *Upgrading the EU's Role as Global Actor: Institutions, Law and the Restructuring of European Diplomacy* (Brussels, Centre for European Policy Studies, 2011).

[3] See E Paasivirta and PJ Kuijper, 'Does One Size Fit All?: The European Community and the Responsibility of International Organisations' (2007) 36 *Netherlands Yearbook of International Law 2005* 169; S Talmon, 'Responsibility of International Organizations: Does The European Community Require Special Treatment?' in M Ragazzi (ed), *International*

regarding the different roles an international organisation and its Member States play on the global scene was recently underlined, when the Court of Appeal in The Hague ruled that the Netherlands was responsible for some actions of its Dutch batallion (Dutchbat) as part of the UN military mission during the Srebrenica crisis in 1995.[4]

The Treaty of Lisbon clarified the international legal status of the EU by codifying its international legal personality (Article 47 TEU). At the same time it refrained from categorising the nature of the competence under both the Common Foreign and Security Policy (CFSP) and the Common Security and Defence Policy (CSDP) under one of the headings in Title I TFEU: exclusive competences (Article 3), shared competences (Article 4), and competences to support, coordinate, or supplement the actions of the Member States (Articles 5 and 6). Article 2(4) TFEU merely states that a competence exists:[5] 'The Union shall have competence, in accordance with the provisions of the Treaty on European Union, to define and implement a common foreign and security policy, including the progressive framing of a common defence policy'. One may argue that CFSP and CSDP are not categorised in the TFEU because these policy areas (in contrast to all other policy areas of the Union) do not find their basis in the TFEU, but in the TEU. Yet, even there, no express indications can be found as to the type or division of competence we are dealing with in this area. While it may be tempting to argue that we are most probably dealing with a combination of supportive, coordinating, supplementing, or at best shared competences,[6] the exclusion of mixed agreements calls for international agreements in the area of CFSP and CSDP to be exclusively concluded by the EU.[7]

The purpose of the present contribution is to investigate some questions emerging from the new and ambitious global role of the EU, in combination with the unclear division of international responsibility between the

Responsibility Today (Leiden, Martinus Nijhoff Publishers, 2005) 405; F Hoffmeister, 'Litigating Against the European Union and its Member States' [2010] *European Journal of International Law* 723.

[4] Court of Appeal The Hague, *Mustafic* and *Nuhanovic* [2011] LJN BR0132.

[5] Yet, compare the (we would argue, somewhat absurd) view that a CFSP competence as such is lacking as Member States merely use the Union to exercise their own competences. C Hermann, 'Much Ado About Pluto? The Unity of the Legal Order of the European Union Revisited' in M Cremona and B de Witte, *EU Foreign Relations Law, Constitutional Fundamentals* (Oxford, Hart Publishing, 2008) 20.

[6] *Cf* M Cremona, 'Defining Competence in EU External Relations' in A Dashwood and M Maresceau (eds), *Law and Practice of EU External Relations: Salient Features of a Changing Landscape* (Cambridge, Cambridge University Press, 2008) 34, fn 65: 'the CFSP appears to be a type of sui generis competence that shares characteristics of both shared and complementary competences'.

[7] *Cf* RA Wessel, 'The EU as a Party to International Agreements: Shared Competences, Mixed Responsibilities' in A Dashwood and M Maresceau (eds), *Law and Practice of EU External Relations: Salient Features of a Changing Landscape* (Cambridge, Cambridge University Press, 2008) 152, 156–57.

EU and its Member States in the area of foreign, security and defence policy. In that sense this chapter aims to contribute to the on-going debate on the relationship between international law and EU law,[8] albeit with a strict focus on the perhaps still different position of CFSP and CSDP. As the EU has become increasingly active in global governance, the questions of who takes responsibility (internally) and who can be held responsible (externally) become more important.

The following section will re-assess the division of competences within the post-Lisbon EU in the area of CFSP and CSDP. The main question here is who may act under CFSP and CSDP. Furthermore, the analysis will present the international legal framework regarding international responsibility of the EU and its Member States in the area of CFSP and CDSP. In the concluding section we aim to see to which extent there is a fit between internal competences and external responsibility.

II. WHO ACTS UNDER CFSP AND CSDP?

A. The Nature of the European Union

The legal nature of the EU remains important in order to be able to say something on its possible international responsibility. The Lisbon Treaty not only integrated the European Community into the EU, but the current Treaty on European Union also explicitly provides that 'The Union shall have legal personality' (Article 47), thus making an end to the academic discussion on the legal status of the Union.[9] That there is still some uneasiness on the part of some Member States is reflected in Declaration no 24, attached to the Lisbon Final Act: 'The Conference confirms that the fact that the European Union has a legal personality will not in any way authorise the Union to legislate or to act beyond the competences conferred upon it by the Member States in the Treaties'.

Like many Declarations, this one is also stating the obvious. After all, the principle of attributed (or conferred) powers forms a starting point in international institutional law and is even explicitly referred to in the new TEU, this time with no exception for the (CFSP):

> Under the principle of conferral, the Union shall act only within the limits of the competences conferred upon it by the Member States in the Treaties to

[8] See, generally E Cannizzaro, P Palchetti and RA Wessel (eds), *International Law as Law of the European Union* (Leiden, Martinus Nijhoff Publishers, 2011).

[9] See on this discussion the many references in RA Wessel, 'The International Legal Status of the European Union' (1997) *European Foreign Affairs Review* 109; as well as RA Wessel, 'Revisiting the International Legal Status of the EU' (2000) *European Foreign Affairs Review*, 507.

attain the objectives set out therein. Competences not conferred upon the Union in the Treaties remain with the Member States (Article 5).[10]

Similar careful considerations can be found in Declarations no 13 and 14, which underline that the changes 'do not affect the *responsibilities* of the Member States, as they currently exist'[11] and do not 'prejudice the specific character of the security and defence policy of the Member States'.

Hence, since the entry into force of the Lisbon Treaty we are left with one international legal entity: the EU. And, it is difficult not to regard this entity as an international organisation and hence within the scope of the Draft Articles on the International Responsibility of International Organizations (DARIO) as adopted by the International Law Commission (ILC) of the UN in August 2011 and endorsed by the UN General Assembly in December 2011.[12] This latest version of the Draft Articles is the latest stage in a development that started in 2002, when the ILC took up this project. The convergence of the 'bits and pieces' that were originally said to make up the Union's structure[13] has created a new institutional and normative situation. Indeed, the past years revealed that the nature of the Union can best be understood when the complex relation between the different policy areas and between the Union and its Member States is taken into account.[14] This complex nature has not prevented the Union from becoming an international 'independent actor'.[15]

Indeed, by now it has become widely accepted that the EU as such may bear international responsibility for an internationally wrongful act.[16] It seems to fit the definition of an international organisation used in the DARIO:

[10] On the basis of Art 5 TEU the principles of proportionality and subsidiarity also apply to all Union policy areas, although the Protocol on the Application of the Principles of Subsidiarity and Proportionality seems to focus on 'legislative acts' only and these acts cannot be used for CFSP matters.

[11] Emphasis added.

[12] ILC 'Draft Articles on the responsibility of international organisations, with commentaries 2011', adopted by the ILC at its sixty-third session, in 2011, and submitted to the General Assembly as part of the Commission's report covering the work of that session (A/66/10) (2011) *Yearbook of the International Law Commission*, vol II, part two, 5; see in particular pt 6, where the Commentary refers to Art 57 of the Articles on Responsibility of States for Internationally Wrongful Acts.

[13] *Cf* D Curtin, 'The Constitutional Structure of the Union: A Europe of Bits and Pieces' [1993] *Common Market Law Review* 17.

[14] RA Wessel, 'The Dynamics of the European Union Legal Order: An Increasingly Coherent Framework of Action and Interpretation' [2009] *European Constitutional Law Review* 117. Compare for a political science perspective also S Stetter, *EU Foreign and Interior Policies: Cross-Pillar Politics and the Social Construction of Sovereignty* (Oxford, Taylor & Francis, 2007).

[15] Paasivirta and Kuijper, above n 3, 181, use the term to differentiate the European Community from more 'classical' international organisations, which are in their view predominantly a forum for their members.

[16] *Cf* Hoffmeister, above n 3, 724.

> For the purposes of the present draft articles, the term 'international organization' refers to an organization established by a treaty or other instrument governed by international law and possessing its own legal personality. International organizations may include as members, in addition to States, other entities.

Obviously, the act must be attributable to the EU under international law.[17] It has been observed that the ILC Draft Articles make no mention of the notion of 'regional economic integration organization' (REIO).[18] This notion was invented to permit an organisation like the EU to participate in multilateral treaties and conventions as a contracting party alongside states.[19] In the absence of special rules for the EU, we will follow the general rules on responsibility of international organisations in our assessment of the responsibility of the EU and its Member States in the area of foreign, security and defence policy.

B. The Legal Nature of the External Competence: CFSP

Although 'the nature of the Union's external competence is an important factor in the allocation of international responsibility',[20] this nature is not so easy to establish in the area of foreign, security and defence policy. As indicated above, both CFSP and CSDP are not mentioned in the categorisation of competences in Article 3 TFEU. There are indeed good reasons to argue in favour of a 'shared competence' external action in this area.

A shared competence allows both the Union and its Member States to take the necessary decisions, but Member States' competences may be exercised only to the extent that the Union has not exercised its competence (Article 2, paragraph 2 TFEU). In fact, it could be argued that this is the case in CFSP. Although there are good reasons to presume that pre-emption does not apply to CFSP,[21] it is equally difficult to maintain that established CFSP decisions and international agreements do not at all restrict Member States' freedom to act externally. As argued elsewhere, possible internal restraints on Member States' freedom to conclude international agreements in CFSP fields can stem from both CFSP treaty norms and CFSP secondary measures. The degree of restraining effect of those

[17] ILC Draft Arts, Ch II deals with the question of attribution.

[18] The 2004 Energy Charter Treaty, art 2 defines a REIO as 'an organization constituted by states to which they have transferred competence over certain matters a number of which are governed by this Treaty, including the authority to take decisions binding on them in respect of those matters'.

[19] Paasivirta and Kuijper, above n 3, 205.

[20] Hoffmeister, above n 3, 743.

[21] See Cremona, above n 6, fn 65 as well as D Thym, 'The Intergovernmental Constitution of the EU's Foreign, Security & Defence Executive' [2011] *European Constitutional Law Review* 453.

CFSP norms is also determined by the potential role that the judiciary may play in ensuring that those norms are enforced, as well as the interpretation given to the specific CFSP principle of loyal cooperation.[22] As 'rules of the organization' (see section II below) these restraints may play a role in establishing responsibilities.

In that sense, the effect of CFSP norms on Member States' powers could be envisaged in the light of the Court's pronouncements on the effects of Community powers in the fields of development cooperation or humanitarian aid. This case law suggests that since the Community competence in these fields is not exclusive but 'parallel', the Member States are accordingly entitled to enter into commitments themselves vis-à-vis non-Member States, either individually or collectively, in the Council or outside it, or even jointly with the Community.[23] If we would accept the idea of 'shared' competences under CFSP, Member States would have less room for manoeuvre. Could this even lead to 'exclusivity' in relation to CFSP? Article 3, paragraph 2 TFEU reads:

> The Union shall also have exclusive competence for the conclusion of an international agreement when its conclusion is provided for in a legislative act of the Union or is necessary to enable the Union to exercise its internal competence, or insofar as its conclusion may affect common rules or alter their scope.

Indeed, CFSP rules will not find their basis in a 'legislative act'.[24] That being said, when this provision is read in conjunction with the loyalty principle enshrined in Article 24, paragraph 3 TEU, it seems too early to rule out exclusivity in the field of CFSP completely. The Union's external activities in the form of the conclusion of international agreements are booming, and Member States' actions increasingly risk affecting common rules or altering their scope. While the creation of CFSP norms depends on the political will of the Member States, once these norms have been established, their very purpose is to restrict the freedom Member States traditionally enjoy in their external relations. Allowing Member States to affect—or even act contrary to—common norms established by EU international agreements would amount to rendering most of the CFSP and CSDP provisions in the EU Treaty nugatory.

Also in relation to possible international responsibility, the emerging question is whether a hierarchy of competences can be established: to

[22] C Hillion and RA Wessel, 'Restraining External Competences of EU Member States under CFSP' in M Cremona and B De Witte (eds.), *EU Foreign Relations Law: Constitutional Fundamentals* (Oxford, Hart Publishing, 2008) 79.

[23] Joined Cases C-181/91 and C-248/91 *European Parliament v Council of the European Communities and Commission of the European Communities* [1993] ECR I-3685 (Bangladesh case); Case C-316/91 *European Parliament v Council of the European Union* [1994] ECR I-625 (EDF case).

[24] See Arts 24(1) TEU and 289(3) TFEU.

what extent are Member States bound by agreements concluded by the Union, and do these agreements restrict their individual freedom in external relations? In this respect, there appears to be no reason not to apply the so-called *Haegeman* doctrine to CFSP agreements and to regard them as forming 'an integral part of Union law'.[25] Article 216(2) TFEU indeed states that Member States are automatically bound by the agreements as a matter of EU law and vis-à-vis the EU. The question remains whether perhaps a 'direct effect' of the agreements could even be construed.[26] This would place the Member States in a different position towards the agreements than in other international organisations. Yet, no a priori external effects result from this.[27]

C. To What Extent are Member States Bound by EU External Action?

Indeed, apart from the question on the nature of the competence, the question who is bound (internally, inside the EU) by international agreements (and perhaps decisions) concluded in the area of CFSP and CSDP seems important to be able to assess the division of possible international responsibility.

In the area of CFSP and CSDP, international agreements are concluded by the Union. The Union has made full use of its competence in this area.[28] By using the pre-Lisbon Article 24 TEU competence (in conjunction with Article 38 TEU in the case of agreements in the area of police and judicial cooperation in criminal matters), the European Union has entered the international stage as a legal actor with obligations and responsibili-

[25] As provided by the ECJ in relation to international agreements concluded by the European Community: Cases C-181/73 *Haegeman* [1974] ECR 449 and C-104/81 *Kupferberg* [1982] ECR 3641. See in the same line D Thym, 'Die völkerrechtlichen Verträge der Europäischen Union' (2006) 66 *Zeitschrift für ausländisches öffentliches Recht und Völkerrecht* 900.

[26] See for a negative answer to this question Thym, above n 21.

[27] *Cf* also the Drafting history of the infamous Art 36 bis of the 1986 Vienna Convention on the Law of Treaties. C Bröllmann, *The Institutional Veil in Public International Law: International Organisations and the Law of Treaties* (Oxford, Hart Publishing, 2007).

[28] *Cf* A Sari, 'The Conclusion of International Agreements by the European Union in the Context of the ESDP' [2008] *International and Comparative Law Quarterly* 53; P Koutrakos, 'International Agreements in the Area of the EU's Common Security and Defence Policy' in Cannizzaro et al, above n 8, 157–87; and RA Wessel, 'The EU as a Party to International Agreements: Shared Competences, Mixed Responsibilities' in A Dashwood and M Maresceau (eds), *Law and Practice of EU External Relations* (Cambridge, Cambridge University Press, 2008) 152. Indeed, these 'agreements' can be considered treaties in the sense of Art 2(1)(a) of the 1969 and 1986 Vienna Conventions on the Law of Treaties as they fulfil all generally accepted criteria. See, in general, A Aust, *Modern Treaty Law and Practice* (Cambridge, Cambridge University Press, 2007); and J Klabbers, *The Concept of Treaty in International Law* (The Hague, Kluwer Law International, 1996). Most agreements can be found in the international agreements database of the Commission at www.ec.europa.eu/world/agreements/.

ties. This turned the provision into the general legal basis for the Union's treaty making whenever agreements could not be based on the Community Treaty. These days, the competence to conclude international agreements can be found in one single legal basis for the entire Union: Article 216 TFEU, which provides:

> The Union may conclude an agreement with one or more third countries or international organisations where the Treaties so provide or where the conclusion of an agreement is necessary in order to achieve, within the framework of the Union's policies, one of the objectives referred to in the Treaties, or is provided for in a legally binding act of the Union or is likely to affect common rules or alter their scope.

That this competence stretches beyond the TFEU itself, and includes the domain of CFSP, is underlined by Article 37 TEU which provides that 'the Union may conclude agreements with one or more States or international organisations in areas covered by this Chapter' (named 'Specific provisions on the Common Foreign and Security Policy').[29]

All international agreements are, in the end, concluded by the Council.[30] In contrast to other Union areas, no mixed agreements are concluded in the area of CFSP and CSDP. In fact, the entire decision-making process as well as the conclusion of the agreement does not reveal a separate role for the Member States. Apart from the references to the EU in both the texts and the preamble of the agreements, and the fact that adoption and ratification is done 'on behalf of the Union', this is confirmed by the central role of the Union's institutions and organs, and the final publication in the L-series of the Official Journal (decision on inter se agreements of the Member States are published in the C-series). Indeed, 'fairly strange operations would be needed to demonstrate that a treaty concluded under such circumstances has instead created legal bonds between the third party concerned and each one of the Member States of the European Union'.[31]

Nevertheless and in line with our observations in the previous section,

[29] This ch 2 also includes s 2: Provisions on the Common Security and Defence Policy.

[30] The debate on whether these agreements are concluded by the Council on behalf of the Union or on behalf of the Member States seems not only to be superseded by practice but also accepted by most experts in EU external relations law. *Cf* R Gosalbo Bono 'Some Reflections on the CFSP Legal Order' [2006] *Common Market Law Review* 354; Thym, above n 25, 863; C Tomuschat, 'The International Responsibility of the European Union' in E Cannizzaro (ed), *The European Union As an Actor in International Relations* (The Hague, Kluwer Law International, 2000) 181; RA Wessel, 'The EU As a Party to International Agreements: Shared Competences? Mixed Responsibilities?' in A Dashwood and M Maresceau (eds), *The Law and Practice of EU External Relations—Salient Features of a Changing Landscape* (Cambridge, Cambridge University Press, 2008) 145; RA Wessel and G Fernandez Arribas, 'EU Agreements with Third Countries: Constitutional Reservations by Member States' in S Blockmans (ed), *The European Union and International Crisis Management: Legal and Policy Aspects* (The Hague, TMC Asser Press, 2008) 291.

[31] Tomuschat, above n 30, 181–82. *cf* also P Eeckhout, *External Relations of the European Union* (Oxford, Oxford University Press, 2004) 159; P Koutrakos, *EU International Relations Law* (Oxford, Hart Publishing, 2006) 406–09 and Gosalbo Bono, ibid, 354–56.

internally both the Union and its Member States seem to be bound by the agreements. This is underlined by Article 216, para 2, which simply states: 'Agreements concluded by the Union are binding upon the institutions of the Union and on its Member States'. Prima facie, for third parties this does not change anything: only obligations for the EU arise from these international agreements, and Member States obligations subsequently follow on the basis of Union law. At the same time, the question emerges whether this provision would play a role in the light of the special position of 'the rules of the organization' in the law on the responsibility of international organisations (below).[32]

EU external action, however, not only takes shape in the form of international agreements: international responsibility may be triggered on the basis of a number of other actions and situations, including the external effects of CFSP decisions, CSDP actions and missions and the participation of the EU in international organisations.[33] Within the limited scope of the present chapter we will only be able to touch upon some of these issues.

III. EU EXTERNAL ACTION AND INTERNATIONAL RESPONSIBILITY

In our assessment of the applicable rules we will follow the DARIO, adopted on second reading in 2011. On the basis of Article 1, the Draft Articles 'apply to the international responsibility of an international organisation for an internationally wrongful act'; as well as 'to the international responsibility of a State for an internationally wrongful act in connection with the conduct of an international organisation'.[34]

Not being dealt with in the Articles on the responsibility of states for internationally wrongful acts, the latter paragraph is meant to incorporate inter alia those cases of state responsibility for internationally wrongful

[32] See extensively on these rules: C Ahlborn, 'The Rules of International Organizations and the Law of International Responsibility', Amsterdam Law School Legal Studies Research Paper No 2011-04.

[33] See on the latter KE Jørgensen and RA Wessel, 'The Position of the European Union in (other) International Organizations: Confronting Legal and Political Approaches' in P Koutrakos (ed), *European Foreign Policy: Legal and Political Perspectives* (Cheltenham, Edward Elgar Publishers, 2011) 261.

[34] The wording of this second paragraph used to read (in the 2009 version): 'The present draft articles also apply to the international responsibility of a State for the internationally wrongful act *of* an international organisation' (emphasis added). One may assume that the wording was changed since the conduct of the international organisation need not necessarily be wrongful, for example in the case of coercion. The authors thank C Ahlborn (PhD Researcher, University of Amsterdam) for this valuable comment. See for the previous version of the Draft Arts: ILC, 'Draft Articles on the Responsibility of International Organisations' Report of the International Law Commission on the Work of its 61st session (2009), UN Doc A/C 6/64/10, 39.

acts by an international organisation where a state is a member of that organisation, such as the Member States of the Union.[35]

The DARIO suggest as a point of departure that the EU is responsible for its own internationally wrongful acts. Draft Article 3 states: 'Every internationally wrongful act of an international organization entails the international responsibility of that organization'. Article 4 lists the conditions for an internationally wrongful act by an international organisation that entails the international responsibility of that organisation: 'There is an internationally wrongful act of an international organization when conduct consisting of an action or omission: (a) Is attributable to the international organization under international law; and (b) Constitutes a breach of an international obligation of that organization'. The next question is what conduct can be attributed to the Union.

According to Draft Article 6(1):

> The conduct of an organ or agent of an international organization in the performance of functions of that organ or agent shall be considered an act of that organization under international law, whatever position the organ or agent holds in respect of the organization.

This somewhat obvious rule indicates that conduct by organs and agents can establish the international responsibility of the Union. According to Draft Article 6(2), the 'rules of the organisation' shall be applied when determining the 'organs and agents'.[36] In view of the Union rules on 'internal' responsibility, there are good reasons to interpret the term 'organs and agents' as 'institutions, bodies, offices and agencies and their servants' as used is in the TFEU.[37] In any case, as is suggested by the broad definitions of 'organs and agents' in Draft Articles 2(c) and (d), the Draft Articles do not envisage the attribution of conduct to 'depend on the use of particular terminology in the internal law' of the Union.[38]

In the area of CFSP/CSDP this would thus cover not only conduct of the Council, but also of the High Representative of the Union for Foreign and Security Policy, the Political and Security Committee (PSC), the EU External Action Service (EEAS), agencies such as the European Defence

[35] See in particular pt 6 of the DARIO Commentaries where the Commentary refers to Art 57 of the Articles on responsibility of States for internationally wrongful acts.

[36] This is not the only criterion however, as 'in exceptional circumstances, functions may be considered as given to an organ or agent even if this could not be said to be based on the rules of the organisation': Draft Arts with commentaries, above n 34, 19.

[37] *Cf* Hoffmeister, above n 3, 740, who refers to Arts 340(2) and 263 TFEU as well as to Art 51(1) of the EU Charter of Fundamental Rights. Art 10(2) confirms that also 'the breach of any international obligation that may arise for an international organisation towards its members under the rules of the organisation' is included in the Draft Arts. Ahlborn, above n 32, argues that this second paragraph could have been deleted.

[38] Draft Arts with commentaries, above n 12, 17. The commentary invokes also some case law on the point such as the ICJ Advisory Opinion, *Reparation for Injuries Suffered in the Service of the United Nations*, ICJ Reports 1949, 177, where the Court held that an agent is 'any person through whom it [the international organisation] acts'.

Agency or the EU Institute for Security Studies and of individual representatives in the framework of EU's CFSP. It would also include the EU delegations (transformed from 'Commission delegations' as they existed in the pre-Lisbon era) and civilian and military missions. However, these missions are probably better covered by Article 7, as discussed below.

At the same time, however, Article 6 also raises the question of whether Member States could, in certain cases, be seen as organs or agents of the Union.[39] It is here that some argue, although it is not expressly acknowledged by the ILC,[40] that the 'organic link' between an international organisation and Member States is relevant.[41] For example, as even the ILC Rapporteur acknowledges,[42] WTO case law accepted Member States as 'organs' and 'agents' of the Union in several instances.[43] Moreover, from inter alia EU case law it can be deduced that the notion of 'normative control' by the EU over its Member States is relevant to establish an 'organ' or 'agent' situation, even if the Member State action merely 'falls in the scope of Union law' (as opposed to situations of Member States implementing Union law). Hoffmeister describes these situations as those in which 'the Member States are under a duty not to overstep certain boundaries set by Union law' and concludes from EU case law that 'when it is established that Union law governs both the substantive legality of and the available remedies for a measure, then the Union exercises normative control over it'.[44] This EU case law is relevant, especially in light of the increased importance of 'rules of the organisation' in the 2011 Draft Articles.[45] In the area of CFSP these cases would arguably be rare, but cannot be fully ruled out. An example could be Member State conduct

[39] Although 'the distinction between organs and agents does not appear to be relevant for the purpose of attribution of conduct to an international organisation', the 'agent' definition 'only covers persons or entities which do not come within the definition under subparagraph (c) [that of 'organ']: Draft Arts with commentaries, ibid, 18 and 12 respectively.

[40] Even more, the ILC stated in 2005 that 'it seems preferable at the current stage of judicial developments not to assume that a special rule has come into existence to the effect that, when implementing a binding act of the European Community, State authorities would act as organs of the European Community'; ILC, *Report of the Fifty-seventh Session, Responsibility of International Organisations* (2005) UN Doc. A/60/10, Commentary on pt 1, ch IV, 95, para 7. However, since then the ILC has become 'less categorical', see Hoffmeister, above n 3, 729.

[41] See Ahlborn, above n 32, 40.

[42] Draft Arts with commentaries, above n 12, 101.

[43] See, eg WTO Panel, 'Protection of Trademarks and Geographical Indications for Agricultural Products and Foodstuffs (adopted 20 April 2005)', WT/DS174/R, para 7.725. For a more WTO case law see Hoffmeister, above n 3, 371–74.

[44] Hoffmeister, ibid, 741–42.

[45] The 'rules of the organisation' are mentioned in Art 6(2) itself. The 'lex specialis' of Art 64 also acknowledges them. The Commentary to Art 64 states that they are of 'particular importance . . . as special rules concerning international responsibility in the relations between an international organization and its members'. Draft Arts with commentaries, above n 34, 102.

vis-à-vis a third state falling in the scope of a CFSP agreement concerning the exchange and protection of classified information.[46]

Moreover, Draft Article 7 makes clear that:

> The conduct of an organ of a State or an organ or agent of an international organization that is placed at the disposal of another international organization shall be considered under international law an act of the latter organization if the organization exercises effective control over that conduct.

The question, however, is whether the term 'placed at the disposal of' an international organisation is applicable at all to the general relationship between the EU and its Member States. Only then would the question whether the EU exercises effective control over the conduct of its Member States in the area of CFSP and CSDP be relevant.[47] The question has been addressed in relation to the European Community, and there seems to be a consensus that the idea of 'effective control' was not relevant when authorities of Member States merely carry out Community law.[48] Much more importantly however, as the commentaries to Article 7 reveal, this provision is most relevant in relation to civilian and military operations.[49] This Article deals with the 'situation in which the seconded organ or agent still acts to a certain extent as organ of the seconding State' which 'occurs for instance in the case of military contingents that a State places at the disposal of the United Nations for a peacekeeping operation, since the State retains disciplinary powers and criminal jurisdiction over the members of the national contingent'.[50] In contrast to 'normative control' as discussed above, the de facto effective operational control of the missions is the deciding factor here.[51]

The commentaries, by thoroughly analysing case law and UN legal opinions, reveal that for UN peacekeeping missions (in contrast to UN Security Council authorised military action) the UN will in principle bear

[46] See, eg the EU-Russia agreement on this matter: Agreement between the Government of the Russian Federation and the European Union on the protection of classified information, [2010] OJ L155/57.

[47] See ch 1 by Tomuschat in this volume.

[48] See Paasivirta and Kuijper, above n 3; PJ Kuijper, 'Introduction to the Symposium on Responsibility of International Organizations and of (Member) States: Attributed or Direct Responsibility or Both?' (2010) *International Organizations Law Review* 9.

[49] The commentaries to Art 7 deal extensively with those missions, in the context of UN missions. See: Draft Arts with commentaries, above n 34, 19–26. Hoffmeister also concludes that Art 7 'was mainly written to codify the rule relating to the international responsibility of the United Nations (or regional organisations) for a military operation using the forces of its Member States': Hoffmeister, above n 3, 726.

[50] See Draft Arts with commentaries, above n 12, 20.

[51] Ibid: 'The criterion for attribution of conduct either to the contributing State of organisation or to the receiving organisation is based according to Art 7 on the factual control that is exercised over the specific conduct taken by the organ or agent placed at the receiving organisation's disposal'.

responsibility, as it exercises effective control.[52] It is tempting to apply this argument *mutatis mutandis* to CSDP missions. After all, these missions may be under operational control of the EU, through CSDP bodies of the PSC, EUMC (Military Committee), EUMS (Military Staff) and the CPCC (Civilian Planning and Conduct Committee). However, attribution to the international organisation is no rigid rule, as the above-mentioned Srebrenica judgments revealed. A case-by-case analysis and application of the 'effective control' concept is crucial.[53]

Of possible relevance to the situation in CFSP and CSDP is Article 9 of the Draft Articles. On the basis of this Article conduct can also be considered as act of an international organisation 'if and to the extent that the organization acknowledges and adopts the conduct is question as its own'. This article applies only in cases where 'Conduct . . . is not attributable to an international organizations under articles 6 to 8' and could therefore be seen as an addendum to the general rules of attribution. The situation is mirrored by Article 62, which states that a Member State of an international organisation is responsible for an internationally wrongful act of that organisation if: '(a) It has accepted responsibility for that act towards the injured party; or (b) It has led the injured party to rely on its responsibility'. The subsidiary nature of this Article 62 responsibility allows for a shared responsibility of the organisation and its Member States (as do the other Articles on responsibility), in contrast to the attribution of conduct under Article 9 (as the other Articles on conduct).[54] Although it would be rare for a Member State to expressly accept responsibility for a wrongful act of the EU, the commentaries (rather vaguely) suggest that 'acceptance' should be widely interpreted. Hence, acceptance may also be 'implied' or could result 'from the constituent instrument of the international organisation or from other *rules of the organisation*'.[55] Interestingly enough, the commentaries briefly discuss the example of Article 216 TFEU, which states inter alia that the Member States are bound by EU international agreements, as an example of how this would not amount to 'acceptance'. This is only binding 'towards the organisation'

[52] Ibid, 19–26. See also on this point: Blokker 47. In the commentaries, the ILC also critiques, as do many academics, the ECtHR position on 'effective' and 'ultimate' control in the *Behrami and Behrami, and Saramati* cases, see: Draft Arts with commentaries, above n 34, 23 and fn 115 for a long list of critical academic contributions.

[53] See further on this issue: A Sari and R A Wessel, 'International Responsibility for EU Military Operations: Finding the EU's Place in the Global Accountability Regime' in B Van Vooren, S Blockmans and J Wouters (eds), *The Legal Dimension of Global Governance: What Role for the EU?* (Oxford, Oxford University Press, 2013, forthcoming).

[54] See also Kuijper, above n 48, 19 and Hoffmeister, above n 3, 727. See also Draft Arts 19, 63 which stipulate the additional nature of the Responsibility Articles Part Two, Ch IV and Part Five, respectively.

[55] Draft Arts with commentaries, above n 12, 97, emphasis added.

and does not 'produce legal effects in relation to third parties', as the ECJ also held before.[56]

In the area of CFSP it would be difficult to find 'valid' cases of acceptance. With regard to the second 'option' of Article 62—namely that a Member State 'has led the injured party to rely on its responsibility'—the commentaries take an identical wide interpretation of 'reliance'. It puts forward a scenario which is not wholly illusory in CFSP, namely when a third party has been led to 'reasonably assume that they [the Member States] would stand in if the responsible organisation did not have the necessary funds for making reparation'.[57] As CSDP missions are in principle Member State funded, a third party could reasonably assume that the Member States will also stand in if a wrongful act is committed in the course of the mission and reparation has to be paid. Moreover, Draft Article 40(2) stipulates that 'the members of a responsible international organisation shall take all the appropriate measures that may be required by the rules of the organisation in order to enable the organisation to fulfil its obligations under this Chapter [dealing with reparation]'. Thus, the Member States may also be 'drawn into' the reparation for Union responsibility even if they bear no responsibility for it.

The responsibility of the Union in relation to the role of the Member States is indeed at the core of our topic and is most prominently dealt with in Draft Article 17.[58] What happens if the Union adopts a CFSP or CSDP decision which would force (or authorize) the Member States to commit an internationally wrongful act? Article 17 foresees a number of situations:

> 1. An international organization incurs international responsibility if it circumvents one of its international obligations by adopting a decision binding member States or international organizations to commit an act that would be internationally wrongful if committed by the former organization.
>
> 2. An international organization incurs international responsibility if it circumvents one of its international obligations by authorizing member States or international organizations to commit an act that would be internationally wrongful if committed by the former organization and the act in question is committed because of that authorization.

[56] Ibid, 97, fn 356. See also: ECJ, *France v Commission* [1994] ECR I-3641, I-3574, para 25.

[57] Draft Arts with commentaries, above n 12, 98.

[58] See NM Blokker, 'Abuse of the Members: Questions concerning Draft Article 16 of the Draft Articles on Responsibility of International Organizations' [2010] *International Organizations Law Review* 35; as well as J d'Aspremont, 'Abuse of the Legal Personality of International Organizations and the Responsibility of Member States' [2007] *International Organizations Law Review* 91.

> 3. Paragraphs 1 and 2 apply whether or not the act in question is internationally wrongful for the member State or international organizations to which the decision or authorization is directed.

Hence, the European Union itself could incur international responsibility both in the case of binding decisions addressed to the Member States and when the latter act because of an authorisation by the Union. It is important to realise that this Article applies to 'circumvention' by the Union and that hence the conduct of the 'implementing' Member State itself need not necessarily be unlawful; it is the binding or 'authorising act' of the Union that, if it were to implement that itself, should qualify as unlawful.[59]

At the same time, Member States may be responsible once they hide behind an international organisation. Article 61 provides:

> 1. A State member of an international organization incurs international responsibility if, by taking advantage of the fact that the organization has competence in relation to the subject-matter of one of the State's international obligations, it circumvents that obligation by causing the organization to commit an act that, if committed by the State, would have constituted a breach of the obligation.
>
> 2. Paragraph 1 applies whether or not the act in question is internationally wrongful for the international organization.

As Kuijper rightfully argues:

> This article sets out a series of events that virtually no State could bring about all on its own, since it would need at least several other States as 'partners in crime' in order to incite the organization from the inside to commit an act contrary to the Member States' international obligations to which the organization would not be bound.[60]

Moreover, the EU would have to act not in its 'rule-making capacity' in the Article 17 situation, which is well imaginable, but in an 'operational capacity' in the Article 61 situation, something which is less common.[61] Nevertheless, also in the relationship between the EU and its Member States in the area of CFSP/CSDP these types of 'abuse' are not to be ignored completely. For example, in contrast with the Member States, the EU is not Party to the Geneva Refugee Convention. Hypothetically, the Member States could then attempt to circumvent their obligations under that treaty, namely 'using' a CSDP mission to act in contravention of the principle of *non-refoulement* in order to stop migration flows, for example

[59] Draft Arts with commentaries, above n 34, 40–42.

[60] Kuijper, above n 48, 28. See more extensively on Art 60: E Paasivirta, 'Responsibility of a Member States of an International Organization: Where Will it End? Comments on Article 60 of the ILC Draft on the Responsibility of International Organizations' [2010] *International Organizations Law Review* 49.

[61] Ibid.

in a maritime CSDP mission.[62]

It is in particular in this area where the debate on the Union's separate international legal status finally led to an acceptance of the legal personality of the European Union, including all its policy areas. It is in fact the existence of this international legal personality alongside the legal personalities of the Member States that potentially allow both to play 'hide and seek'.

A number of other, general, situations may be relevant in establishing the division of responsibilities between the EU and its Member States in the area of foreign, security and defence policy. These situations do not concern the specific relation between the organisation and its Member States, but relate more generally to relationships between international organisations and states. Nevertheless, we briefly address them here as 'Member States' are not excluded from the definition of a 'state'.[63]

First, Article 14 of the Draft Articles states that:

> An international organization which aids or assists a State or another international organization in the commission of an internationally wrongful act by the State or the latter organization is internationally responsible for doing so if: (a) the former organization does so with knowledge of the circumstances of the internationally wrongful act; and (b) the act would be internationally wrongful if committed by that organization.[64]

The mirror image is provided by Article 58, paragraph 1, which establishes under the same conditions the international responsibility of 'a State which aids or assists an international organization in the commission of an internationally wrongful act'. Given the close cooperation between the Union and its Member States in the formulation and implementation of CFSP and CSDP these provisions are relevant. It has been suggested elsewhere that this 'aiding or assisting' may also well take financial forms.[65] Due to the peculiar funding structure of CSDP missions—the Member States fund in principle the EU Missions—this may be a possible area of attention under Article 58.

A similar situation concerns the responsibility of an international organisation that directs and controls a state (or another international

[62] In the Mediterranean context it is not wholly unimaginable that a CSDP mission would come to deal with migrant boats on the move to the EU, as NATO did in 2011. One such incident, under which NATO did allegedly not live up to international search and rescue obligations leading to the death of 61 migrants, is currently being investigated by the Migration Committee of the Parliamentary Assembly of the Council of Europe. See www.assembly.coe.int/ASP/NewsManager/EMB_NewsManagerView.asp?ID=6789&L=2.

[63] In fact, 'states' are not defined at all and are not referred to in Draft Art 2, which defines 'international organization', 'rules of the organization', and 'agents'.

[64] Emphasis added.

[65] A Reinisch, 'Aid or Assistance and Direction and Control between States and International Organizations in the Commission of Internationally Wrongful Acts' [2010] *International Organizations Law Review* 70.

organisation) in the commission of an internationally wrongful act.[66] This is dealt with in Article 15 of the Draft Articles. Again a mirror image can be found, which provides that:

> A State which directs and controls an international organization in the commission of an internationally wrongful act by the latter is internationally responsible for that act if: (a) the State does so with knowledge of the circumstances of the internationally wrongful act; and (b) the act would be internationally wrongful if committed by that State. (Article 59, paragraph 1).

A situation in which Member States direct or control the EU in the execution of CFSP/CSDP may be difficult to find, but it is has been suggested that excessive control over the decision-making process of an organisation could lead to (joint) international responsibility.[67] Obviously, this would be difficult to reconcile with the idea of Member States as 'seat holders' in an organ of an international organisation, in which view the decision-making procedure as such is irrelevant as in the end it is the organisation that takes the decision.[68] Situations in which Member States are directed or controlled by the Union form the foundation of the CFSP. International wrongful acts by states on the basis of binding CFSP/CSDP decisions are thus not excluded.

To the above-mentioned Articles dealing with state responsibility for aiding, assisting, directing and controlling the conduct of international organisations (Articles 58 and 59), the ILC has added a second paragraph in the 2011 version of the Draft Articles which reads: 'An act by a State member of an international organisation done in accordance with *the rules of the organisation* does not as such engage the international responsibility of that State under the terms of this draft Article'.[69] This addition raises the importance of the 'rules of the organisation' as it suggests that it could prevent the international state responsibility from arising if the Member States acts in accordance with them. However, it seems to the authors that it could also potentially undermine the authority of the Draft Articles, as it seems to allow for a 'way out'. Could it possibly mean that, if Member States act on the basis of a CFSP decision, in accordance with EU law, they would not be held responsible under Articles 58 and 59? The commentary indicates that 'These criteria could entail some difficulties in ascertaining whether aid or assistance has taken place in borderline cases' and that this 'does not imply that the State would then be free to ignore its international obligations'. This is akin to statements

[66] Ibid, see more extensively.

[67] J d'Aspremont, above n 58, 92: 'member states exerting an excessive control over the decision-making process of the organization must be held, together with the organization, responsible for violations of international law committed by the organization'.

[68] RA Wessel, 'Revisiting the International Legal Status of the EU' [2000] *European Foreign Affairs Review* 507, 516.

[69] Emphasis added.

in ECtHR judgments, such as in the *Bosphorus* where the Court held that Member States cannot escape scrutiny by 'hiding' behind the EU to which competences were transferred.[70] The commentaries go on to state that such international obligations 'may well encompass the conduct of a state when it acts within an international organisation', thus leaving the boundaries between international and 'internal' EU law nebulous for the present purposes. Clearly, there is a dilemma here for the ILC or at least a paradox for the reader. The commentaries then finish by saying that if such a situation would occur, the Member States would still be liable, but under the Articles on the responsibility of states for internationally wrongful acts.[71] To the authors it is rather unclear how this latest addition to the DARIO contributes to a clearer delimitation of responsibility.

The Draft Articles foresee situations in which either the organisation or the state is subject to coercion by the other. The applicable rules can be found in Draft Articles 16 and 60. In view of the theoretical nature of these provisions with regard to the relationship between the EU and its Member States, we leave this possibility out of our discussion.

Finally it should be pointed out that a '*lex specialis*' has been added in Article 64 of the Draft Articles which stipulates that the Articles will not apply if 'special rules of international law' such as 'rules of the organisation applicable to the relations between an international organisation and its members' cover the responsibility questions. The Commentaries discusses a specific example under which these 'rules of the organisation' may come into play: the European Union and its Member States.[72] It is thus here that—as we have seen before—the internal rules of the Union, including those on competences, may make their way into questions of international responsibility.

III CONCLUSION: A COMPETENCE-RESPONSIBILITY GAP?

A first glance at the division of international responsibility between the EU and its Member States suggests that the EU itself would be primarily responsible for any international wrongful act in the area of foreign, security and defence policy. What kind of internationally wrongful act could this be? Obviously, not living up to international agreements concluded with third states or other international organisations could result in such international responsibility.

Also acts by any agent of the Union (eg the Institutions, but also the High Representative, Special Envoys and CSDP missions) which would

[70] See 30 June 2005, Application No. 45036/98, *Bosphorus v Ireland*.
[71] Draft Arts with commentaries, above n 12, 91.
[72] Ibid, 100–01.

be in violation of international obligations would be attributable to the Union. Given the upgraded role for the EU in global governance, more rules have become applicable to its actions.

While one could perhaps argue that there once was a difference between Community law and CFSP law, at least post-Lisbon it has become difficult to maintain that the constitutional relationship between the Union and its Member States differs on the basis of a policy area.[73] So far, however, this special relationship between the EU and its Member States is not reflected in the Draft Articles. As we have seen, the 'effective (factual) control' argument may be decisive in establishing the division of responsibility between the EU and its Member States in very concrete situations in the framework of EU military missions; but the complex nature of CSDP decision-making and implementation calls for a case-by-case analysis which is to take account of the special position Member States have in conducting EU military missions. With its focus on the agency paradigm of attribution, the DARIO's relevance may be limited in relation to CSDP missions.[74]

Indeed, the complex nature of the cooperation between the EU and its Member States in external situations is not only related to the division of competences, but also to the actual use of these competences in concrete situations. This allegedly makes the assessment of international responsibility even more difficult. Even after almost twenty years of CFSP, we have not been able to fully grasp the complexity of the relationship between the EU and its Member States relationship in this area. Yet, with the increasing external activity of the Union, there is a need to become more precise.

In general, the rules in the TEU provide no indications for a conclusion that in CFSP/CSDP the Member States would by definition be the first ones to incur international responsibility. This would be confirmed by the specific rules on the conclusion of EU international agreements, which uniformly cover both CFSP and non-CSFP agreements. As most EU external action is based on international agreements, this would not amount to a competence-responsibility gap. Yet, as we have seen, in the area of CSDP in particular, it may not always be easy to establish the actual responsibilities as they depend on more than just competences.

[73] See Wessel, above n 68. But see also, for instance, Kuijper, above n 48, 21, who argues that 'the divide on this point runs right across the EU, separating its traditionally supranational EC part from the intergovernmental CFSP-side'. In his view, 'the foreign policy powers of Member States are unaffected by the fact that certain aspects of foreign- and defense policy are run on a common basis' (20, fn 36). *cf* also Thym, above n 21, 454, who accepts the 'horizontal constitutionalisation' (the same constitutional control standards apply to all areas of Union action), but maintains that Union law is of a different nature in CFSP and CSDP, where it is 'a manifestation of intergovernmental executive power', rather than 'law-making'.

[74] See more extensively Sari and Wessel, above n 28.

From our analysis, the contours of how internal CFSP competences influence the external responsibility under the DARIO emerge. Although we have seen that the Union incurs responsibility, as a point of departure, the specific CFSP/CSDP 'rules of the organisation'[75] allow for more complex situations. The internal division of competences therefore 'pierces' the institutional veil of the Union, inter alia via the acknowledgement of the 'rules of the organisation'. For example, the 'rules of the organisation' are important in determining whether Member States could be seen as agents or organs of the Union (*cf* Article 6(2)). However, the inverse situation is also envisaged, under which the Member States may 'hide' behind the institutional veil of the Union. For example, if they implement binding decisions or authorisations they could be freed of international responsibility (*cf* Article 17). Hence, the internal division of competences is certainly relevant for the allocation of responsibility, albeit perhaps more as an exception than as the standard rule. Of course, in the implementation of the responsibility, there is a limit; the DARIO also stipulates that 'the responsible international organisation may not rely on its rules as justification for failure to comply with its obligations' (Article 32(1)).

Another set of questions relate to the development of the European External Action Service and to the emerging diplomatic service in third countries and the changing status of the EU in some international organisations. The applicability of 'state rules' in this area to the EU has hardly been touched upon in academic writings.

These are just some first thoughts that come to mind when we consider the (planned) increasing activities of the Union at the global level. Given the particularities of CFSP/CSDP these issues deserve special attention in the study of the international responsibility of international organisations.[76]

[75] Defined in Draft Art 2 as 'in particular, the constituent instruments, decisions, resolutions and other acts of the organization adopted in accordance with those instruments, and established practice of the organization'.

[76] See ch 14 by Naert in this volume.

Postscript to Chapter 12

ENZO CANNIZZARO

IN THE AUTUMN of 2012, after the completion of Chapter 12, negotiations resumed with a view to amending the draft Accession Treaty. The EU negotiators proposed that an attribution provision should be included in Article 59(2) of the ECHR, providing that the conduct of a Member State would be attributed to that State even if such conduct was undertaken in order to implement binding rules of the European Union. This proposal has been favourably considered and will probably be part of the final agreement (see doc 47+1(2012)R03, App III, of 9 November 2012). However, a similar provision, providing that conduct performed in order to implement EU acts in the field of the Common Foreign and Security Policy (CFSP) should also be attributed to Member States, was not agreed on (see doc 47+1(2013)001, of 14 January 2013).

Thus, paradoxically, the new attribution provision could apply to the whole spectrum of the competences assigned to the EU except for the CFSP, in spite of the strict control exerted in this field by the Member States in respect of the Union's process of decision making. A compromise solution is being worked on, according to which the conduct of Member States will be attributed to them even if performed in order to implement Council decisions taken under the TEU (see doc 47+1(2013) R04, of 23 January 2013).

The most likely outcome is that the ECHR will include a rule on attribution which is intended to have the effect of making it clear that there is no special rule on attribution applicable to the relationship between the EU and its Member States for the purposes of the Convention. Not only is the logic of such an outcome questionable, but it also seems inconsistent with the view—tenaciously defended by the EU with regard to the ILC's Articles on the Responsibility of International Organisations—that the conduct of Member States' organs should be attributed to the EU if such acts were performed under the 'normative control' of the EU.

All in all, the history of the Accession Treaty can be seen as a missed opportunity to recognise the 'special' position of the EU as an International Organisation, and to promote the development of international law in this complex area.

Index